DISRUPTION

DISRUPTION

THE GLOBAL ECONOMIC SHOCKS OF THE 1970s AND THE END OF THE COLD WAR

MICHAEL DE GROOT

CORNELL UNIVERSITY PRESS

Ithaca and London

Publication of this book was made possible by a generous grant from Indiana University Bloomington.

Visit our website at cornellpress.cornell.edu.

First published 2024 by Cornell University Press

Library of Congress Cataloging-in-Publication Data

Names: De Groot, Michael, 1988– author.
Title: Disruption : the global economic shocks of the 1970s and the end of the Cold War / Michael De Groot.
Other titles: Global economic shocks of the 1970s and the end of the Cold War
Description: Ithaca [New York] : Cornell University Press, 2024. | Includes bibliographical references and index.
Identifiers: LCCN 2023023865 (print) | LCCN 2023023866 (ebook) | ISBN 9781501774119 (hardcover) | ISBN 9781501774133 (ebook) | ISBN 9781501774126 (pdf)
Subjects: LCSH: World politics—1945–1989. | International economic relations—History—20th century. | Cold War—Economic aspects. | Cold War—Influence.
Classification: LCC D843 .D338 2024 (print) | LCC D843 (ebook) | DDC 909.82/5—dc23/eng/20230624
LC record available at https://lccn.loc.gov/2023023865
LC ebook record available at https://lccn.loc.gov/2023023866

For my parents

Contents

ACKNOWLEDGMENTS

It is a great pleasure to acknowledge the people and institutions that made this book possible. I have been fortunate indeed to have had advisers who taught me what it means to be a historian through their mentorship and the standards that they set in their research. My advisers at Stanford University, Barton Bernstein and David Holloway, first kindled my interest in international history. At the University of Virginia, William Hitchcock provided sage advice and inspired me to tackle big questions. Melvyn Leffler and Stephen Schuker stimulated my interest in the relationship between international security and political economy, and Philip Zelikow, Brian Balogh, and Dale Copeland shaped this project in significant ways as well. I learned a great deal from Mary Barton, Vivien Chang, Benji Cohen, Erik Erlandson, Alexandra Evans, Jack Furniss, Stephanie Freeman, and Evan McCormick, and I thank them for making my time in Charlottesville so enjoyable.

A Henry A. Kissinger predoctoral fellowship allowed me to spend a very productive year at the Jackson Institute for Global Affairs at Yale University. I thank Ted Wittenstein, Nuno Monteiro, and Paul Kennedy for the opportunity to join this rich intellectual community. My time in New Haven was so rewarding in no small part because of conversations with Fritz Bartel, Mike Brenes, Tim Choi, Eliza Gheorghe, Mariya Grinberg, Ian Johnson, John Maurer, Veysel Simsek, Jan Stöckmann, and Evan Wilson. I am particularly indebted to Fritz Bartel for commenting on drafts of multiple chapters and pointing me to new sources.

A National Fellowship at the University of Virginia's Jefferson Scholars Foundation also supported my training, and I thank Brian Balogh for believing in the project. I was thrilled when Daniel Sargent agreed to serve as my "dream mentor" for this fellowship. His research had originally piqued my interest in the international political economy of the 1970s, and I am most grateful for his encouragement and expert advice at various stages of the project.

A fellowship with Perry World House at the University of Pennsylvania afforded me the opportunity to begin revising the manuscript for this book. I thank Bill Burke-White, Mike Horowitz, John Gans, and LaShawn Jefferson for a rewarding year. I had the great fortune of being part of an exceptionally collegial fellow cohort, and I thank Jonathan Chu, Michael Kenwick, Benjamin Laughlin, Ariadna Reyes Sanchez, Stephanie Schwartz, and Robert Shaffer for their camaraderie and for teaching me to think like a social scientist.

I had the tremendous pleasure of completing the book revisions as a faculty member at the Hamilton Lugar School of Global and International Studies at Indiana University Bloomington. My new colleagues made me feel at home as soon as I stepped onto campus, particularly the chair of the International Studies Department Purnima Bose and former HLS dean Lee Feinstein. HLS has provided an ideal interdisciplinary environment for me to think about global affairs in the past and present, and I appreciate my welcoming colleagues and thoughtful students for making my time in Bloomington so enjoyable and productive. Sarah Bauerle Danzman, Purnima Bose, Hal Brands, Nick Cullather, Emma Gilligan, Marianne Kamp, Padraic Kenney, Stephen Macekura, Norman Naimark, Serhii Plokhy, Mary Sarotte, Regina Smyth, Jessica Steinberg, and Adam Tooze generously participated in a manuscript workshop that the International Studies Department held for me in the summer of 2021, and their insights and suggestions significantly improved the manuscript and sharpened its arguments. I thank Barbara Breitung for helping me with the logistics of making research trips and attending conferences amid the ongoing pandemic.

For sharing their expertise and time, I thank Shigeru Akita, Valentin Bolotnyy, Brent Cebul, Tom Cinq-Mars, Gaetano di Tommaso, Monique Dolak, Michael Franczak, Marina Freidina, William Glenn Gray, Stephan Kieninger, Maximilian Krahé, Irina Kuznetsova, Andro Mathewson, Simon Miles, Kazushi Minami, Anna Pan, Angela Romano, Oscar Sanchez-Sibony, Timothy Sayle, James Mace Ward, and Odd Arne Westad. I owe special thanks to David Painter, who generously provided feedback on this project at various points and encouraged me to think deeply about the relationship between oil and power.

The book benefited from discussions with other scholars at conferences, workshops, and seminars at George Washington University's Elliott School of International Affairs; the RAND Corporation's Arroyo Center; the Hoover Institution's Applied History Workshop; the University of Vienna's Institute of East European History; the Leibniz Institute for Contemporary History Potsdam; the University of Toronto's Bill Graham Centre for Contemporary International History; Yale University's Brady-Johnson Colloquium in International Security and Grand Strategy and Brady-Johnson International Security Studies Research Workshop; the University of Pennsylvania's Perry World House; the University of Virginia's Jefferson Scholars Foundation; the IU-Sorbonne University Workshop; Indiana University's European History Workshop; the International Studies Association; the Association for Slavic, East European, and Eurasian Studies; the Society for Historians of American Foreign Relations; and the Southern Conference on Slavic Studies.

Archival research for this book was only possible because of the generous financial support from the Gerald R. Ford Presidential Foundation; the Society for Historians of American Foreign Relations; the Lynde and Harry Bradley Foundation; the Jefferson Scholars Foundation, Thomas Jefferson Memorial Foundation, Institute of the Humanities and Global Cultures, Society of Fellows, Graduate School of Arts & Sciences, and Corcoran Department of History at the University of Virginia; the Jackson Institute at Yale University; Perry World House at the University of Pennsylvania; and the Hamilton Lugar School at Indiana University Bloomington. Archival material from the United States, Europe, and Russia serves as the foundation of this book, and I appreciate the assistance of the many archivists from Simi Valley to Moscow who helped me track down crucial documents.

Working with Cornell University Press has been a pleasure. I am most grateful to Sarah Grossman for her support and editorial guidance, and to Karen Laun and the production team for preparing the manuscript for publication. I also appreciate the thoughtful feedback of an anonymous reviewer. Any errors of fact or interpretation are mine alone.

Portions of this book first appeared in "The Soviet Union, CMEA, and the Energy Crisis of the 1970s," *Journal of Cold War Studies* 22, no. 4: (2020): 4–30; and "Global Reaganomics: Budget Deficits, Capital Flows, and the International Economy," in *The Reagan Moment: America and the World in the 1980s*, ed. Jonathan R. Hunt and Simon Miles (Ithaca, NY: Cornell University Press, 2021), 84–102.

My greatest thanks go to my family. Stephanie De Groot, Josephine Maurice, Peter Maurice, Curtis Dikes, Jo Anne Yanagisawa, and Curtis Ogilvie have been constant sources of encouragement. Jennie Carrillo has powered me through the highs and lows at every stage of my academic journey from Palo Alto to Bloomington. My parents, Anthony and Wendy De Groot, have provided unconditional love and support, and this book is dedicated to them.

NOTE ON TRANSLITERATION

I have used a simplified form of the American Language Association–Library of Congress transliteration system for Bulgarian and Russian. I have not used it for names that have a popularly accepted spelling in English such as Yuri (rather than "Iurii") Andropov.

DISRUPTION

Introduction

"We who were going to balance the budget face the biggest budget deficits ever," US president Ronald Reagan grumbled to his diary in December 1981.[1] The Gipper grasped the irony. He had declared war against big government and muscled huge tax cuts through Congress, but his administration also poured hundreds of billions of dollars into defense and maintained social safety nets. The federal government then borrowed to finance the record budget shortfalls, tripling the national debt during Reagan's two terms. The trade deficit ballooned to record-breaking heights as well, surpassing the $100 billion mark for the first time in 1984.[2] The numbers were staggering.

Such devastating economic data would have spelled disaster for most countries. "If any other country had run its economy the way the United States have run theirs," the British ambassador Oliver Wright remarked in December 1985, "it would have had the IMF [International Monetary Fund] broker's men in long ago." Yet the United States was exceptional. Even as the US budget and trade deficits reached historic levels, foreign investors poured their savings into the United States, Wright explained, because of the size and resilience of its economy, its entrepreneurial energy, and its reputation as a safe haven for capital.[3] The foreign investment helped the United States finance a military buildup, fund social welfare programs, and sustain noninflationary growth.

The influx of capital and goods to the United States during the Reagan years reversed the imbalances that had previously undergirded America's Cold War. Boasting unmatched strength after World War II, the United States had been a net creditor with a trade surplus during the postwar period. In the 1980s, however, it became a net debtor with a large trade deficit. The foreign investment allowed the United States to live beyond its means, and US partners benefited from access to the booming US market, the relocation of manufacturing to the developing world, and the continued protection of the strengthened US military umbrella. While US hegemony endured, its material foundation had transformed.

On the other side of the Iron Curtain, the Soviet budget deficit grew rapidly in the second half of the 1980s under General Secretary Mikhail Gorbachev. The similarities with the United States ended there. Whereas Washington utilized debt as an asset, Moscow used credits to import food and could not reinvigorate its stagnating economy, stabilize its faltering allies, and combat the US offensive in the Cold War. The demands on the Soviet Union grew even larger as its Eastern European allies drowned in debt.[4] The Kremlin had provided emergency assistance and had subsidized trade to its Warsaw Pact partners throughout the Cold War but could no longer afford to throw a financial lifeline or deploy the Red Army to restore order. Instead, the Eastern European socialist regimes faced an inexorable assault on two flanks as they confronted their restless populations who clamored for political change and their foreign creditors who demanded structural adjustment.

Although the United States and the Soviet Union both sank deep into debt, the former had risen to the zenith of its power while the latter dropped to its nadir. Beyond nuclear parity, Washington outmatched Moscow in virtually every area that mattered. The Cold War became even more unbalanced when accounting for allies. Symbiotic relationships between the United States and Western Europe, Japan, and partners in the developing world such as South Korea and Saudi Arabia augmented US power. In contrast, the atrophy of Eastern Europe weighed on the Kremlin, and a debt crisis forced socialist regimes in Latin America and sub-Saharan Africa to embrace market reforms and look to the West. The Red Army, meanwhile, became bogged down in a disastrous war in Afghanistan, and Soviet influence waned in the developing world.

The shift in the global balance of power was profound, and the new link between East and West was even more so. The Cold War had erupted in the late 1940s as an ideological and geopolitical competition between two independent blocs that promoted antagonistic structures of political economy, social organization, and visions of world order. By the 1980s, the Cold War had evolved into a contest between a resurgent United States that unlocked the resources of a globalizing economy and an anachronistic Soviet petro-empire whose members could not survive without products, technology, and credits from the capitalist world. In other words, the socialist countries did not just confront an ascendant West; worse, they had become dependent on the industrial democracies for their very survival.

This outcome reflected improvisation rather than intelligent design. Drawing on archival evidence from both sides of the Iron Curtain, *Disruption* charts the emergence of this new order and illuminates how it prefigured the end of the Cold War. It shows how the global economic shocks of the 1970s created an international political economy that magnified US power in unexpected ways and fractured the Soviet bloc.

Neither the United States nor the Soviet Union believed that it could survive as an island in a world that the other dominated during the post-1945 period, so they sought allies in their quest to create a favorable balance of power. This book uses the concept of the *welfare empire* to describe how their blocs functioned. "Welfare" refers to the superpowers' distribution of resources to promote the physical safety, economic and social well-being, and political stability of their allies. "Empire" provides an analytical tool that describes the bloc hierarchy in which Washington and Moscow assumed singular responsibility for order and anchored their respective blocs' security architectures.[5] In the overseas European empires, the imperial powers had extracted resources from their colonies, but in the Cold War welfare empires, resources moved from the superpowers to their allies.

The superpowers maintained this distributive framework because they believed that it enhanced their own national security. National security meant more than physical survival. It entailed protecting a way of life at home as well. American policymakers feared that democratic capitalism—a modernity that promoted free elections, privileged the free market, protected private property, and guaranteed individual liberties—would not survive in the United States if it did not also prosper in key industrial regions overseas. Similarly, Moscow worried that Soviet socialism, whose brand of modernity consisted of a proletarian dictatorship, class-based rights, and command economy, would be threatened in the Soviet Union itself if the country became encircled by capitalist powers. Thus, the United States and the Soviet Union adopted "mental maps" of national security during the Cold War that expanded far beyond their own borders.[6]

The US welfare empire formed in the mid- and late 1940s because the Truman administration believed that American national security depended on binding Western Europe and Japan to the United States.[7] Washington dispersed

financial aid and military assistance to them to accelerate their postwar reconstruction, build local support for democratic capitalism, combat Soviet encroachment, and restore overseas markets for US exports. US firms established
overseas subsidiaries, exported technologies, and increased foreign direct investment. In addition to accepting responsibility for the Bretton Woods international monetary system, which precluded a dollar devaluation and depended
on dollars circulating overseas to lubricate international trade, the United
States provided an open market for Western European and Japanese products
and tolerated a degree of protectionism in return. Even so, the United States
still ran a trade surplus during the postwar period because of the strength of
American industry.[8]

For its part, the Soviet welfare empire crystallized in the mid- and late 1950s.
After confronting the threats to Soviet national security arising from the East
Berlin turmoil of June 1953 and the Polish and Hungarian uprisings in the fall
of 1956, Soviet leaders shifted from a policy of extraction to subsidization in
Eastern Europe.[9] By tolerating a pricing formula that undervalued raw materials and overvalued finished goods, the Soviet Union underwrote industrialization across its bloc and served as a reliable buyer of products that could not
sell on the world market. Quantifying the implicit Soviet subsidy is difficult,
but Soviet analysts estimated it in the billions of rubles annually after the 1973
oil shock, and a Western study placed it at $75.5 billion during the 1970s.[10] Mos-
cow also served as the bloc's lender of last resort and deployed the Red Army
to defend Soviet socialism in Eastern Europe.

The argument that the US and Soviet welfare empires had parallel structures requires the qualification that Western policymaking entailed negotiation and compromise while the Soviet Union often dictated terms to Eastern
Europe.[11] The Kremlin's Eastern European allies should not be dismissed as
mere puppets, but their fortunes depended on Moscow's favor and preferences.
The Kremlin used coercion to get its way, though Eastern European officials
could also exploit their positions to influence Moscow.[12] Indeed, dependence
was a double-edged sword.

The welfare empires functioned effectively during the first quarter century of
the Cold War in large part because they had strong economic foundations.
While their developmental models were based on ideologies that contradicted
each other, the Cold War protagonists shared a fixation on economic growth
as a means of promoting social cohesion, legitimizing their ideological systems, and implementing their blueprints for world order.[13] They enjoyed an
unprecedented era of prosperity between 1950 and 1973, an era known as the
"Golden Age." During this period, annual gross domestic product (GDP) per

capita grew an average of 4.1 percent in Western Europe, 2.5 percent in the United States, 8 percent in Japan, 3.8 percent in Eastern Europe, and 3.4 percent in the Soviet Union.[14] With the need to rebuild after World War II and ubiquitous drive to industrialize, opportunities abounded for extensive growth, defined as gains from additional inputs of manpower and materials. Inexpensive raw materials and labor powered the factories, technological breakthroughs in the United States circulated abroad, and productivity surged. The Bretton Woods international monetary system's fixed-exchange rate regime and the Soviet bloc's central planning encouraged price stability.

The economic growth provided the margins in both blocs to invest in the military-industrial complexes as well as raised living standards, minimized social tensions, and underwrote bloc cohesion. It created jobs, maintained low levels of inequality, increased the quality of life, and funded social programs. While the consumer abundance in Western societies remained out of reach for the Soviet bloc, which started at a much lower level than the richer industrial democracies, the socialists trumpeted their growth rates that rivaled those in the West, boasted about their social egalitarianism, and claimed that consumer luxuries were just around the corner.

Growth appeared limitless in the Golden Age, but stagflation in the West and its socialist cousin *zastoi* (stagnation) during the 1970s shattered the illusion. Whereas inflation (GDP deflator) ran 4.4 percent across the Organisation for Economic Co-operation and Development (OECD) area in the 1960s, it spiked to 11.5 percent in the 1970s.[15] Unemployment figures swelled to postwar highs in the West, and economic growth and productivity slowed everywhere. The Keynesian and Soviet socialist prescriptions on which the blocs had relied during the postwar period not only failed to solve the problems but aggravated them further. A wave of literature that included the Club of Rome's *The Limits to Growth* and E. F. Schumacher's *Small Is Beautiful* predicted a grim future of resource scarcity, competition, and hardship. Both blocs suffered from a "common crisis of industrial society," as Charles S. Maier describes.[16]

What had gone wrong? The unique constellation of factors that had made the Golden Age possible disappeared in the late 1960s and early 1970s. The exhaustion of the postwar growth models constituted the core problem. Societies finished reconstruction, mobilized their idle assets, applied the backlog of technological innovations, and completed industrialization. These developments had driven economic growth after the war, but states could pull each of these levers only a single time. Inflation crept upward as labor unions still demanded wage increases but productivity gains diminished. Cheap raw materials had fueled extensive growth during the Golden Age, but prices for energy, rubber, fibers, food, fertilizer, and metals began to rise on the world market. A major shock came in the fall of 1973 when oil prices quadrupled and pushed global capitalism into the sharpest recession of the postwar era. Another oil crisis followed in 1979. Price instability in global capitalism spread to the Soviet bloc because it used an average of world market prices to determine its own prices for intrabloc trade. Furthermore, while the Soviet Union provided its allies with the bulk of the raw materials that they needed, they still had to purchase the balance from suppliers outside the bloc at market prices. This book refers to these interrelated developments, which punished industrial states of all ideological stripes, as the global economic shocks of the 1970s.

With their postwar growth model struggling, the industrial democracies reoriented toward intensive development, which required utilizing existing resources more productively. The United States ceded manufacturing jobs to the developing world, but the country assumed a new position in the international division of labor as the US economy harnessed new technologies such as the microprocessor chip. Home to companies such as Apple, Fairchild, and Intel, the San Francisco Bay Area's Silicon Valley emerged as the global center of the information revolution. The paradigm of what constituted economic success in the ideological Cold War shifted from industry to computers.

The hub of global manufacturing moved to East and Southeast Asia. Japan led the pack and caught up with the transatlantic countries by the 1970s across a variety of sectors including automobiles and consumer electronics. It even surpassed the United States by the mid-1980s in GDP per capita.[17] Imitating the Japanese export-oriented industrialization model and utilizing their well-educated and inexpensive labor, South Korea, Hong Kong, Singapore, and Taiwan produced finished goods for global markets and displaced transatlantic manufacturing. Leveraging innovations in transportation and communications as well as trade liberalization, multinational corporations relocated operations to the developing world. Faced with cheaper competition, deindustrialization hastened in the transatlantic community.

The information revolution combined with changes in international trade and finance to thicken global ties. After the Bretton Woods system collapsed in the early 1970s, the gradual removal of controls reduced constraints on transnational capital flows, and the value of global financial markets exploded from $160 billion in 1973 to $3 trillion in 1985.[18] Transnational finance greased the wheels of international trade and transportation, and telecommunications breakthroughs shrank the globe. Global merchandise trade increased nearly sixfold in the 1970s.[19] The postwar order had kept economic globalization at bay, but now it resurged.

Soviet bloc officials recognized the supreme importance of adapting their economic growth model as well. "The economy had to be oriented from an extensive to an intensive type of development [*ot ekstenziven kum intenziven tip na razvitie*]," the Bulgarian premier Stanko Todorov reflected. "Labor productivity was significantly behind" and held back improvements in living standards.[20] Yet the political and economic inflexibility of Soviet socialism prevented the Soviet bloc from moving beyond its postwar focus on heavy industry. The ideological commitment to full employment and structural obstacles to innovation compelled central planners to keep inefficient factories in operation, and socialist manufacturing became increasingly uncompetitive on the world stage at both the high and low ends of the market. The regimes resorted to importing goods and technology from the West as a substitute for reforms.

Disruption maps the geopolitics of these interlocking economic vectors. It illuminates how Western and Soviet bloc officials navigated this era of transition and struggled to master structural developments that they did not fully understand and could not control. The strategic logic of sustaining the welfare empires remained compelling for US and Soviet policymakers, but their nations' capacity to shoulder the burden diminished. Archival documents reveal a common theme of frustration in both Washington and Moscow about having to sacrifice their own economic interests to promote the health of their most important allies, and they grappled with tradeoffs in the 1970s that they had not encountered before.

The Cold War anxieties of Western officials centered just as much, if not more, on internal vulnerabilities and intrabloc tensions as perceptions of Soviet strength during the 1970s. The memory of the Great Depression preoccupied them. Recalling the anxieties of the early Cold War, they feared that the economic and social upheaval would empower radical parties on the political far right and left, divide the West, and embolden the Soviet Union.[21] The major industrial democracies turned to economic summitry in the mid-1970s to coordinate responses to the interrelated political and economic crises. The meetings symbolized the commitment to international cooperation, even if officials disagreed on how to resolve common problems.

Democratic capitalism earned a new source of legitimacy when noninflationary growth returned in the mid-1980s. The OECD area never recaptured the figures of the 1950s and 1960s, but annual growth rates climbed to 4.7 percent by 1984 and did not slip below 3 percent until 1991. Inflation (GDP deflator) dropped from 13.2 percent in 1980 to 5.2 percent in 1985.[22]

The adaptation to the global economic shocks of the 1970s was improvised and messy. The harsh stance against inflation that the Federal Reserve under chairman Paul Volcker took in the late 1970s and 1980s catalyzed the recovery. In addition to restoring price stability, high interest rates attracted foreign

capital that funded Reagan's historic budget deficits and fueled the noninflationary recovery. Foreign capital powered the US economy, helped pay for social safety nets, and financed a military buildup as the Reagan administration
applied pressure against the Soviet Union. US allies in Western Europe and East
Asia, in turn, benefited from the stimulus that the US economy gave to the
global economy in the mid-1980s as well as the strengthening of the US military umbrella. It was not all good news, however. Inequality rose, the power of
organized labor diminished, and unemployment increased across most of the
OECD area during the 1980s.[23] Yet the resurgence of noninflationary growth
empowered liberal parties across the West.

The adjustment in the 1980s created a new international political economy
that sustained the West, an architecture that this book calls the *inverted* US welfare empire. This means that instead of disseminating resources to the rest of
the world, as it had during the first half of the Cold War, the United States became an importer and net debtor by the 1980s. The ratio of US manufactured to
raw material exports also declined as the economy became service oriented.

The US welfare empire inverted, but the Soviet counterpart collapsed. The
rigidities of the command economy and lack of institutional incentives to in-
novate meant that intensive growth stayed out of reach. Elites refused to make
structural changes that might endanger their careers or weaken the communist party's hold on power. Instead, Western imports temporarily masked
underlying problems. Some well-informed economic officials had reservations
about taking on debt to finance the goods and technology, but they generally
kept quiet. "Orders are not discussed, they are carried out" was the command
economy's motto.[24] Sovereign debt across Eastern Europe ballooned in the
1970s, and the Soviet Union sent much of its hard currency windfall from oil
exports back to the nonsocialist world to purchase food to compensate for its
escalating agricultural crisis.

Most socialist officials understood that the system had structural liabilities
and inefficiencies, but they could not see the full picture. Fearing that bad news
could jeopardize their careers, political elites withheld access to gloomy reports. "Only the positive part of development was reported," the chairman
of the East German State Planning Commission Gerhard Schürer recalled,
"while the negative part such as the large debt of the GDR [German Democratic Republic] was treated as 'secret' so that one could not have an exact picture of the economic situation."[25] Consequently, many socialist elites in the
1970s believed that they held the initiative in the Cold War and did not realize
that a financial sword of Damocles was rising over the bloc.

While Western Europe and Japan developed robust economies of their own
that enhanced the US-led security system and the West's ideological author-

ity to wage the Cold War, Eastern Europe increasingly became a burden on the Soviet Union. Subsidized Soviet oil and natural gas incentivized Eastern European planners to maintain energy-intensive industries and hardened their positions against systemic reforms. Combined with growing disillusionment across the bloc with Soviet socialism, the accumulation of Eastern European debt placed the Kremlin in a difficult position. The Soviet economy itself began to stagnate by the late 1970s and early 1980s, and Soviet officials faced agonizing questions about the extent to which they should divert scarce resources to ensure Eastern European stability. In the early 1980s, Moscow's refusal to intervene militarily in Poland's Solidarity crisis, during which Warsaw de facto defaulted on its debt and an independent trade union threatened the socialist regime, signaled that the Soviet Union had abdicated its role as the bloc's guarantor. Into the vacuum stepped Western international institutions and governments, which utilized their financial power to extract political concessions from the indebted regimes. Rather than an abrupt departure, the 1989 revolutions capped a long process in which the West used financial leverage to wrestle Eastern Europe away from the Soviet Union.

Economic historians have long seen the late twentieth century as a period of dramatic change, but economics plays a surprisingly small role in the literature on the end of the Cold War.[26] Instead, a loose consensus stresses the primary importance of Gorbachev for winding down the arms race, deescalating superpower tensions, encouraging political change behind the Iron Curtain, and withdrawing Soviet forces from Afghanistan.[27] Triumphalist accounts of the US contribution fell out of favor as archival evidence contradicted the contention that Reagan had a grand strategy that brought the Soviet bloc to its knees, and more recent interpretations based on the documentary record illustrate how Reagan's military buildup, economic statecraft, and diplomacy complemented Gorbachev's initiatives and changes in the international system.[28] Other scholars emphasize the social movements and changing international norms that created political change and halted the arms race.[29]

While these factors made meaningful contributions, *Disruption* contends that the global economic shocks of the 1970s were decisive and belong at the top of the causal hierarchy. It brings energy, debt, trade, finance, and monetary policy to the forefront, topics that are typically treated as "second-order" issues in Cold War scholarship. Yet the security architectures of the West and Soviet bloc cannot be understood without reference to the international political economy and ideological projects that supported them.[30]

Much of the literature characterizes the end of the Cold War as a contingent event whose proximate origins started with Gorbachev's rise to power in March 1985, but this book aligns with the minority that emphasizes structure over human agency.[31] This does not mean that the West's ability and East's inability to adapt to the economic shocks of the 1970s made the end of the Cold War inevitable or overdetermined. Rather, these economic transformations created opportunities to exploit structural advantages for the industrial democracies and increasingly narrowed options for the Soviet bloc in the 1980s. By associating US interests with a globalizing economy and safeguarding the dollar's centrality in global finance and international trade, US policymakers helped foster an international environment that allowed the United States to live beyond its means and continue to wage the Cold War. The accumulation of debt and atrophy of the Soviet bloc, in contrast, handcuffed socialist officials the following decade and circumscribed their flexibility.

Framed this way, Gorbachev's reforms played a reinforcing role in the disintegration of the Soviet bloc rather than the lead, as many scholars contend.[32] The Soviet bloc could work as a closed system, but the calculus changed as the bloc became dependent on Western goods and technology, more information became available about the disparities between East and West, and consumer expectations rose. The debt placed a financial noose around the necks of the regimes, and the Soviet leadership recognized already in the late 1970s and early 1980s that the Soviets did not have the ability to remove it. The situation had only worsened by the time Gorbachev became general secretary, and his refusal to intervene militarily in the 1989 revolutions completed the process that had been in motion for two decades.[33] The Cold War ended at the end of 1989 when the Soviet bloc ceased to exist as a community of socialist dictatorships dominated by Moscow.[34] Thereafter, the struggle to shape the post–Cold War international environment commenced.[35]

Victory and defeat depended on intrabloc cohesion as well as interbloc competition, and scholarship on the end of the Cold War should not only explain the collapse of the Soviet bloc but also account for why the West stabilized after an era of upheaval. The West's great achievement during the Cold War was mobilizing the combined power of the core capitalist countries and defying communist declarations that intracapitalist conflict would erupt. Memories of the 1930s and concern about Soviet power provided incentives for the industrial democracies to stay together, and the inverted US welfare empire provided a new structural framework that sustained the West. This process also suggests that the emergence of unipolarity in the early 1990s, usually described in terms of US preponderance, is as much a story about US dependence.[36]

Disruption takes a comparative approach that traces the divergent trajectories of the West and the Soviet bloc as they grappled with the global economic shocks of the 1970s. Chapters 1 and 2 chart the origins of the US and Soviet welfare empires and examine why their postwar developmental models and international economic architectures began to falter in the late 1960s and early 1970s. Chapters 3 and 4 focus on how the global oil crisis in 1973 aggravated those problems in the industrial democracies and Soviet bloc. Since the oil shock came on the heels of the collapse of the Bretton Woods system, it also contributed to the expansion of capital markets, which provided states on both sides of the Iron Curtain the means to cling to their postwar models. Chapter 5 highlights the late 1970s as a key juncture in which the Jimmy Carter administration reluctantly prioritized monetary stability over expansion, a policy that combined with the second oil shock to impose a corrective recession. Carter offered the nation a vision of the future that cohered around limits and living within US means, but he failed to win reelection in November 1980. His policies had a lasting and global impact, felt not least behind the Iron Curtain. Indeed, chapter 6 shows how the tight monetary policy of the Federal Reserve helped trigger a debt crisis in Eastern Europe and the Solidarity uprising in Poland. The Soviet Union's decision to allow events in Poland to run their course and cease serving as the bloc's lender of last resort in the early 1980s signaled a transfer of economic power that contradicted the logic of the Soviet welfare empire. Chapter 7 illustrates how the policies of the Reagan administration inadvertently completed the inversion of the US welfare empire, providing the United States with a second wind but also creating economic and social problems that continue to bedevil the country. Chapter 8 demonstrates how Gorbachev entered office with a grand vision of reinvigorating the Soviet Union and remaking international politics, but structural constraints overwhelmed his plans as he presided over the formal collapse of the Soviet welfare empire.

From the vantage point of the 1990s, the Western response to the malaise of the 1970s seemed successful. As the euphoria of the end of the Cold War grows more distant, however, the triumphalism appears misplaced. In developing solutions to the global economic shocks of the 1970s, the industrial democracies had sown the seeds of future problems. The deregulation of capital markets had helped fund the recovery during the 1980s but also made financial crises such as those that erupted in East Asia in 1997 and the transatlantic community in 2008 more explosive. While economic globalization has reduced global poverty and empowered the emerging middle class in developing countries, it has also caused the stagnation of wages for the lower and middle classes in the industrial democracies and, along with a low tax rate regime, increased inequality. One of the primary beneficiaries of economic globalization in the late twentieth and early twenty-first centuries, China has developed as a long-term rival to the United States, and an aggrieved Russia seeks to overturn the US-led international order and restore what it sees as its rightful place as a superpower. State capitalism and authoritarianism have gained momentum and provide an alternative to societies that have lost faith in the democratic capitalist model that had been so full of promise at the end of the Cold War.

The 1970s beckon as a historical analogy for the interlocking crises of the early 2020s. An energy shock, inflation, rising interest rates, and political polarization have taken hold, and the accumulation of debt from the world's fiscal response to the COVID-19 pandemic portends a financial crisis. The Russian Federation has invaded Ukraine in its effort to relitigate the end of the Cold War and the collapse of the Soviet Union, and China's designs on Taiwan raise the specter of war in East Asia. In today's backdrop of great power conflict and political economic disorder, understanding the 1970s has never been so urgent.

CHAPTER 1

American Power and the Collapse of the Bretton Woods System

"The time has come for a new economic policy for the United States," Nixon declared in a primetime address to the nation on August 15, 1971. With inflation exceeding 5 percent and unemployment approaching 6 percent, he announced a freeze on all prices and wages for a period of ninety days, slapped a 10 percent surcharge on imports, and temporarily suspended the convertibility of the dollar into gold. Nixon believed that a resurgence of noninflationary growth would carry him to reelection the following year and hoped that this so-called New Economic Policy would stabilize prices and put US citizens back to work.[1]

While his speech focused on technical monetary and economic issues, Nixon made clear the link between the New Economic Policy and strategic issues. During the postwar period, US economic supremacy had upheld the Bretton Woods system and undergirded the West's security architecture. With the "major industrial nations of Europe and Asia . . . shattered," Nixon noted, the United States extended nearly $150 billion in foreign assistance. Over the next quarter century, "largely with our help," the other industrial democracies recovered, and US economic dominance had eroded by the early 1970s. Nothing symbolized the US relative decline more than the emergence of a trade deficit in 1971, the first since the Grover Cleveland administration. "Now that other nations are economically strong, the time has come for them to bear their fair share of the burden of defending freedom around the world," Nixon declared. "The time has come for exchange rates to be set straight and for the major nations to compete as equals. There is no longer any need for the United States to compete with one hand tied behind her back."[2]

The New Economic Policy tried to redress the emerging contradictions in the US welfare empire. First, economic superiority had been the bedrock of US hegemony in the postwar period, but a new distribution of economic power within the West had emerged by the early 1970s. The New Economic Policy was Nixon's tactic to recapture US supremacy. By closing the gold window and imposing an import tax, he created leverage against US allies to force them into a general realignment of exchange rates against the dollar that he hoped would boost US exports. Nixon did not want to terminate the Bretton Woods system, which was an instrument that helped tie the industrial democracies together under US leadership; he intended to recalibrate it.

Second, Nixon's imposition of wage and price controls reflected the tensions emerging in the West's postwar growth model. Noninflationary growth during the first quarter century of the Cold War had built local support for different forms of democratic capitalism across the West, but the rise of inflation and unemployment portended social unrest and political instability. Friction grew among the industrial democracies as they competed to reshape the international economic architecture in a way that would minimize the negative effects on their own countries.

The Bretton Woods system became even more difficult to defend as offshore financial markets expanded. Created in the 1950s to hold the dollar-denominated funds of socialist countries, the London-based "Euromarkets" became a hub for trading assets in currencies denominated outside their country of issue, particularly dollars. As the Euromarkets surged in the late 1960s and early 1970s, investors speculated against currencies whose exchange rates did not align with their nation's economic fundamentals, creating a series of currency crises that dislodged fixed-exchange rates. Yielding to nascent financial globalization, the industrial democracies abandoned the Bretton Woods system in the spring of 1973. The Bretton Woods system had been an anchor of Western cohesion, but now the industrial democracies had been set adrift.

The primary lesson that US officials learned from the Great Depression and World War II was that the United States must never again allow a totalitarian power to seize control of Eurasia.[3] Vast oceans separated the United States from the other great powers, but the war had demonstrated that the "free security" that geography had given the United States no longer existed in the age of the aircraft carrier and long-range bomber.[4] Should Nazi Germany and Imperial Japan conquer the Eastern Hemisphere, President Franklin D. Roosevelt had warned the nation in a December 1940 fireside chat, "it is no exaggeration to say that . . . the Americas would be living at the point of a gun . . . loaded with explosive bullets, economic as well as military."[5] The Japanese attack on Pearl Harbor had demonstrated that adversaries thousands of miles away could utilize new technologies and weapons to strike the United States.

Truman and his team dwelled on this lesson as they contemplated how to deal with the Soviet Union after the war ended. They knew that defeating Nazi Germany had exhausted the Red Army and that the Soviets were in no position to launch an offensive against the Anglo-American powers, but the Kremlin could threaten the United States in other ways. Many people across Europe and Asia associated democracy and capitalism with the misery of the Great Depression, and US officials worried that a weak economic recovery would breed popular support for communism. Should communists seize power in war-torn areas and align with the Soviet Union, the Kremlin would gain control over Eurasia without resorting to violence. An autarkic Eurasia under Soviet domination would choke international commerce, shift the global balance of power against the Western Hemisphere, and force the United States to become a garrison state.[6]

Protecting democratic capitalism at home thus required preempting the Soviet threat abroad. Many US citizens "used to think that we could escape the troubles of the world by simply staying within our borders," Truman declared in a March 1947 address at Baylor University. "Two wars have shown how wrong they were. We know today that we cannot find security in isolation."[7] As Melvyn P. Leffler shows, the Truman administration believed that tying Western Europe and Northeast Asia to the United States was the key to ensuring that Eurasia did not fall under Soviet domination.[8]

The US welfare empire formed in the mid- and late 1940s because the Truman administration believed that the United States could not secure Western Europe and Northeast Asia without building local support for democracy and capitalism. Simply "locking" the Soviets out of these crucial regions would not keep the communist threat at bay, the Harvard historian Arthur Schlesinger Jr. contended in his 1949 book, *The Vital Center*. "If conditions inside the house are intolerable, if a few people live in luxury while the rest scramble for table leavings and sleep in the cellar, then eventually someone will admit the Communists by stealth."[9] As the harsh European winter of 1946–47 portended an economic disaster in Europe, the Truman administration initiated the European Recovery Program, more commonly known as the Marshall Plan, in the summer of 1947 to revive the European economies and prevent the communists from exploiting a depression. The United States also became a founding member of the North Atlantic Treaty Organization (NATO) in April 1949 not only to deter Soviet aggression but also as the price of gaining Western European—particularly French—acquiescence to rebuilding the industrial might of the western zone in occupied Germany and then to establishing the Federal Republic of Germany (West Germany). Washington additionally aided the Japanese recovery, which benefited from the material demands of the Korean War, and signed a security agreement with Tokyo.[10]

If references to World War II were "the coin of the realm in argument over NATO policy," as Timothy Sayle writes, then allusions to the Great Depression served the same role for international economics.[11] The rigidity of the gold standard, tariff wars, disruptive short-term capital flows ("hot money"), and the disintegration of international cooperation had plunged the global economy into depression during the 1930s. Unemployment soared, but adherence to the gold standard handcuffed the ability of governments to provide for the needy.[12] The Great Depression encouraged the formation of autarkic blocs, radicalized domestic politics, and revived militarism.

The postwar international economic architecture, a series of overlapping institutions known as the Bretton Woods system, was designed to ensure that the 1930s could never happen again. Anglo-American planners crafted a gold-dollar standard that fixed the US dollar to gold at $35 per ounce, and the other currencies had fixed but flexible rates against the dollar. Under the gold standard, countries with trade deficits had needed to deflate their economies, but placing the burden of adjustment on the working class was politically untenable in the postwar period. The Bretton Woods system, in contrast, allowed governments to construct welfare states regardless of external accounts. The International Monetary Fund (IMF) served as the lender of last resort and approved changes to fixed parities in the hope of avoiding a repeat of the competitive currency devaluations of the early 1930s after states had broken free of the gold standard. Hot money had paralyzed the European banking system in the spring of 1931, but the Bretton Woods system encouraged capital controls to restrict short-term capital. The Bretton Woods system promoted long-term investment, and the planners created the International Bank for Reconstruction and Development, more commonly known as the World Bank, to aid this effort. The General Agreement on Tariffs and Trade (GATT) of 1947 sought to liberalize markets and prevent a slide back to the closed international environment of the 1930s.[13]

The Bretton Woods system depended on US economic and monetary supremacy, and the United States accepted structural disadvantages to ensure that it functioned effectively. Because the fixed relationship between the dollar and gold served as the system's lynchpin, the United States could not devalue its currency to boost exports while others had the option. Washington also tolerated a degree of trade discrimination from its allies against US goods.[14] The United States accounted for 40 percent of the world's output in 1950, but the proportion fell to 30 percent by 1970.[15] The US share of world exports dropped from 22 percent in 1948 to 12 percent in 1971, whereas West Germany's portion jumped from 1 percent to 11 percent and Japan's take from less than 0.5 percent to 7 percent during the same period.[16] Some rebalancing was inevitable after reconstruction, but US policy encouraged rather than impeded the process.

As the United States implicitly subsidized the recovery of Western Europe and Japan, the Bretton Woods system facilitated the outward flow of US capital, goods, and resources. US multinational companies transmitted advanced technologies overseas through their foreign subsidiaries, and the United States was a net supplier of private and government long-term capital and grants to the rest of the world in every year after the war. The United States took advantage of the healthy overseas markets and continued to run trade surpluses with the rest of the world.[17] Washington assumed primary responsibility for the security of the Western world and maintained a sprawling system of overseas bases, and military spending overseas became a drain on the US balance of payments.

While Western Europe and Japan constituted the core of the US welfare empire, its reach extended into the developing world. Washington combatted revolutionary nationalism in the developing world to ensure that postcolonial states did not fall into the Soviet orbit and could provide badly needed markets and raw materials to bolster Western European and Japanese reconstruction.[18] As decolonization accelerated, the United States extended billions of dollars of aid to the developing countries, especially in the 1960s, expecting that democracy would accompany economic development and leave postcolonial states less vulnerable to communist subversion. Cold War geopolitics often trumped ideological purity, however, and Washington tended to support friendly authoritarian regimes rather than backing democratically elected leaders such as Iran's Mohammad Mosaddegh or Guatemala's Jacobo Árbenz Guzmán whom US officials could not control.[19]

Under the aegis of the US welfare empire, the industrial democracies enjoyed an unprecedented quarter century of prosperity. During the Golden Age between 1950 and 1973, Western European growth averaged 4.8 percent and labor productivity increased 4.8 percent annually. The establishment of the European Community (EC) in 1957 liberalized trade within Western Europe and created a large internal market. Japan's economic performance was even more impressive. During the Golden Age, Japan's economy grew on average more than 8 percent annually and per capita income increased sixfold.[20] The industrial democracies developed their own "varieties of capitalism" that shared a common commitment to making the market and the state work together but differed on issues such as industrial relations and corporate governance.[21]

Economic growth paid Cold War dividends. While providing the margins to maintain powerful militaries and invest in the development of new weapons, it also promoted social stability and bloc cohesion. The free market drove growth, and the state provided expansive social services, ameliorated external shocks, invested in education, and contributed to research and development projects. The footprint of the state in the economy grew rapidly, and government expenditure as a percentage of GDP jumped from 34.2 percent to 41.5 percent in Britain, 21.4 percent to 31.1 percent in the United States, and 30.4 percent to 42 percent in West Germany between 1950 and 1973.[22] Powerful unions commanded high wages for their workers and could rely on the state to assist in the push for a greater share of profits. Unemployment and inflation stayed low. Progressive tax policies redistributed wealth, and the state strengthened legal protections for workers.[23]

Strains in the international political economy that upheld US hegemony appeared in the 1960s, however. As Western Europe and Japan recovered from the war and earned more dollars, the dollar gap of the 1950s gave way to a dollar glut. By the mid-1960s, a "dollar overhang" emerged, which meant that the dollars circulating overseas exceeded US gold reserves. The dollar overhang cast doubt on the legitimacy of the dollar-gold exchange rate of $35 per ounce. Foreign investors and governments, particularly the French, exchanged their dollars for gold, and the US share of global reserves plummeted from nearly 50 percent to 10 percent between 1950 and 1970.[24] The doomsday scenario involved holders of dollars exchanging them at once when there was not enough gold to go around. A play on this possibility became the basis for the 1964 James Bond film, *Goldfinger*.[25]

The gold drain threatened the transatlantic security architecture. Since the second term of the Dwight D. Eisenhower administration, as Francis J. Gavin shows, Washington came under internal pressure to withdraw US troops from Western Europe to reduce the balance of payments deficits, but US officials feared that the redeployment of the US forces would undermine US strategy in Europe. Should the US forces withdraw, West Germany might feel compelled to seek its own nuclear deterrent, which could provoke Moscow into retaliating by trying to squeeze the West out of Berlin. In the early 1960s, the West German government agreed to "offset agreements" in which Bonn refrained from exchanging its dollars for gold and purchased US equipment to ease the US balance of payments problem in return for the US military presence.[26]

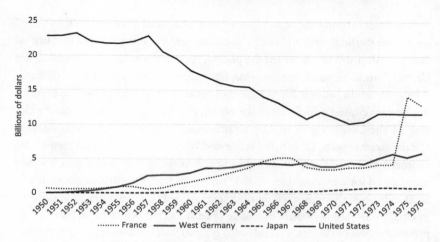

FIGURE 1.1.   The decline of US gold holdings, 1950–1976. Source: IMF, International Financial Statistics.

International confidence in the dollar also deteriorated as inflation rose in the second half of the 1960s. President Lyndon B. Johnson waged wars in Vietnam against communism and at home against poverty but did not raise taxes to finance them. The budget deficit jumped from $1.4 billion (0.2 percent of GDP) in 1965 to $25.2 billion (2.8 percent of GDP) in 1968.[27] Because the country approached full employment simultaneously, the fiscal stimulus aggravated a wage-price spiral. The consumer price index rose from under 2 percent in 1965 to more than 6 percent in 1969.[28] Rising prices forced US citizens to make lifestyle changes. "I used to like buying candy and cookies for the kids," a single mother in New Jersey lamented, "but the way prices are going up you just have to give up some things you like." Housewives reentered the work force to earn extra income, vacations were postponed, and housing prices jumped. "The only answer is price and wage controls," a Philadelphia doorman conceded. "Eventually they're going to have to institute them, because this can't go on."[29] By 1966, US citizens ranked inflation as the third most pressing problems facing the country, trailing only the Vietnam War and race relations.[30]

As confidence in the dollar fell, the resurgence of global finance placed pressure on the Bretton Woods system. The John F. Kennedy and Johnson administrations introduced capital controls to dampen the dollar outflow, so US corporations with Western European subsidiaries placed their profits into the Euromarkets. The value of these so-called Eurodollars, which constituted about three-quarters of the Euromarkets, spiked from $16.07 billion in 1966 to $98 billion in 1972.[31]

The international monetary crisis came to a head after a November 1967 assault on sterling, which US officials considered to be the dollar's first line of defense. After Britain devalued the pound, speculative attention turned to the United States. News of the growing US budget deficit and General William Westmoreland's request for yet another escalation of US military operations in Vietnam caused a flight from the dollar. Johnson's advisers proposed a closure of the London gold market to preempt a run on US reserves. To their foreign counterparts, US officials requested "that, just as the United States Government had acted responsibly during the years of the dollar gap, so they now hoped for a responsible attitude on the part of the surplus countries."[32] In March 1968, the industrial democracies agreed to a "two-tier gold system" in which Washington would exchange gold at $35 per ounce to official but not private holders of dollars. The IMF also created Special Drawing Rights (SDRs), which consisted of a basket of currencies, to supplement global reserves in the hope of taking pressure off the dollar.[33]

The reconstruction of Western Europe and Japan, the strengthening of their democratic institutions, and their geopolitical alignment with the United States vindicated US grand strategy during the early Cold War. But the Bretton Woods system was becoming a victim of its own success. The relative shift in economic power and outflow of dollars from the United States undermined confidence in the dollar-gold conversion rate, and the reemergence of global finance made it more difficult to maintain the fixed-exchange rate system.

In addition to the changing international balance of economic power, the crisis of the Bretton Woods system reflected stresses in the postwar growth model. Extensive growth yielded reduced returns. The backlog of mass-production technologies from the United States had already been utilized. Tight labor markets empowered unions to command wage increases that exceeded productivity gains, and inflation (gross national product [GNP] deflator) in the industrial democracies rose from an annual average of 2.6 percent during the first half of the 1960s to 4.2 percent during the second half.[34] By the time that Johnson left office, the international economic architecture and the developmental model that had sustained the West for a generation were straining.

Assuming the presidency in January 1969, Nixon inherited responsibility for managing a global order in transition. Along with his national security adviser Henry Kissinger, Nixon wanted to continue containing the Soviet Union and maintaining the US-led system of alliances. "If there should be a Eurasia, either controlled from Moscow or effectively dominated by Moscow, we would then find that all other parts of the world . . . would fall ideologically in that order,"

Kissinger explained. US society would undergo "an extreme radicalization" in response, and the United States could survive only "by a degree of regimentation that would leave dramatic transformations." The US "ability to influence events in the world would gradually vanish," he predicted. "Never could we survive as an island in a totally hostile environment."[35] Kissinger's logic echoed US grand strategic thinking since World War II.

Yet the United States no longer boasted the economic and military advantages that it had enjoyed at the beginning of the Cold War. Nixon and Kissinger resolved to uphold alliances and confront adversaries with different tactics. With the Soviet Union achieving strategic parity, they pursued détente with the Kremlin by dangling carrots such as nuclear arms agreements and increased access to US markets to entice Moscow to contain itself. The superpowers signed the Anti-Ballistic Missile Treaty and the Strategic Arms Limitation Treaty to reduce the threat of nuclear war and ease the strain of the arms race. The Nixon administration initiated a rapprochement with China, capitalizing on the Sino-Soviet split to place additional pressure on the Soviet Union. Washington hoped that triangular diplomacy would persuade Moscow and Beijing to lean on Hanoi to negotiate an end to the Vietnam War.[36]

While Nixon could boast some diplomatic success in dealing with Cold War adversaries, managing relations with Western Europe and Japan and the home front proved more elusive. Until the mid-1960s, US current account surpluses had generally offset military spending overseas and outflows of investment, but the trade surplus declined rapidly from $6.8 billion in 1964 to just $593 million in 1969. Because Johnson had encouraged higher interest rates in the spring of 1968 to combat rising inflation, $8.8 billion in short-term capital rushed to the United States in 1969. The hot money "sustained the US balance of payments," Daniel J. Sargent explains, but also made the stability of the Bretton Woods system dependent on the continued influx of capital to the United States. In the backdrop of a recession that began in late 1969, Nixon pressured the Federal Reserve chairman Arthur Burns in early 1970 to lower interest rates, hoping that engineering an economic boom would catapult him to reelection two years later. Easy money in the United States reversed the flow of capital across the Atlantic. The United States ran a nearly $6 billion deficit on short-term capital flows in 1970.[37]

The deterioration of the US balance of payments exposed relative economic decline. Nixon commented to a group of news executives in July 1971 that "the United States, as compared with the position we found ourselves in immediately after World War II, has a challenge such as we did not even dream of." The problem in the late 1940s was "that the United States had all the chips and we had to spread a few of the chips around so that others could play." Yet after the industrial nations rebuilt their economies, the United States no longer was "in the position of complete preeminence or predominance." Nixon identified "five great power centers in the world today": the United States, Western Europe, Japan, China, and the Soviet Union. Western Europe and Japan may be "friends" and "allies," but they were "competing and competing very hard with us throughout the world for economic leadership."[38]

Japan presented a growing commercial challenge. The United States ran its first postwar trade deficit with Japan in 1965, and the deficit surpassed $1 billion in 1968. By 1972, it had reached more than $4 billion.[39] The trendlines were "almost frightening," Secretary of the Treasury David Kennedy worried.[40] US policymakers griped that Japan took advantage of access to US consumers but refused to open the Japanese market to foreign competition. Japanese automobile exports became a particular source of consternation. With the United States levying only a modest tariff, Japanese automobile exports jumped from 69,000 in 1967 to 354,000 in 1970, even accounting for 20 percent of new car sales in Los Angeles during early 1971. General Motors was the largest US automobile exporter to Japan, but it captured only 0.1 percent of the Japanese market.[41]

With Japan's postwar reconstruction complete, Treasury officials believed that Tokyo should shoulder more responsibility for the functioning of the global economy, including opening its market to foreign competition as well as assisting East Asian regional development. Deputy Assistant Secretary of the Treasury for International Monetary Affairs F. Lisle Widman became "seriously concerned that we cannot maintain our partnership with Japan without a rather major allocation of the burden of defense and aid in the Far East."[42] Treasury and White House officials grew frustrated that their State Department counterparts downplayed economic tensions. "We have a serious problem at a number of key levels of State Department about their commonly held view that Japan is no 'economic threat,'" Assistant to the President for International Economic Affairs Peter G. Peterson wrote Nixon in July 1971.[43]

Others in the administration tried to prevent economic pressures from disrupting the political relationship. "It's possible that extreme nationalism could assert itself once again over real or imagined economic issues," a State Department official suggested. On a recent trip to several Asian capitals, Kissinger added, a US delegation asked its hosts which country posed the greatest threat to peace in the region. "To our absolute amazement," he said, "the majority said: 'Japan.'"[44] Washington needed to strike the delicate balance between asserting its economic interests while maintaining a strong political relationship to uphold the balance of power in East Asia.

COLLAPSE OF THE BRETTON WOODS SYSTEM

A similar dilemma between economics and security with regard to Western Europe preoccupied the administration.[45] On the one hand, "NATO was the blue chip" in the US-led system of alliances, as Nixon called it, organizing the transatlantic community against the Warsaw Pact as well as harnessing West German power.[46] "We can no more disengage from Europe than from Alaska," the president declared.[47] On the other hand, rumblings grew louder that Washington could no longer afford to prioritize security over trade to the extent that it had previously. "The Americans have suddenly woken up to the economic monster which is being created in Europe," noted Hugh Overton, the North American department head in the British Foreign and Commonwealth Office.[48]

The debate between two factions in the spring of 1970 over National Security Study Memoranda 79 and 91 illuminated concerns in the Nixon administration about the emerging disequilibrium between political ends and economic means. The studies contemplated the upcoming British entry into the European Community and the impact of Western European integration on US interests. The State Department drafted the reports and concluded that an enlarged and robust European Community comported with US national security objectives. As a collective, the European Community could "more effectively utilize the talents and resources of its member nations and thus be able to participate more fully in maintaining the security of the North Atlantic area and in promoting a more stable world order." The European Community also helped anchor West Germany in the West.[49]

The Departments of the Treasury, Commerce, and Agriculture and the Special Trade Representative had reservations about State's findings. Two extensive redrafts failed to close the gulf, and the dissenters instead submitted a joint rebuttal to the National Security Council in which they contended that a stronger European Community would "result in a fundamental change in the basic world balance of international economic and financial power" that would "profoundly affect the prospects for both the industrial and agricultural trade of the United States." Washington's priorities needed to change, they argued:

> Traditionally, the countries of Western Europe have given relatively high priority to economic self-interest. The United States, on the other hand, has for many years concentrated most of its attention on its political and military objectives, confident that its economic and financial interests would in large measure take care of themselves. In the enlarged EC, we will have a competitor large enough and strong enough to damage our interests seriously if we continue this practice. To ensure that the United States retains both the economic and financial ability and the domestic

political support needed to protect our longer range political and defense interest we will in the future need to give higher priority to the defense of our economic and financial interest vis-à-vis the enlarged Community.[50]

With Britain, Denmark, Ireland, and Norway scheduled to join in January 1973, the European Community was becoming a juggernaut. The Western European countries may have been US allies, but they had become economic rivals as well.

Congress seized on the link between the balance of payments deficits and the US military presence overseas. As he had since 1966, Democratic Senate majority leader Mike Mansfield proposed legislation in the spring of 1971 that would reduce the troop levels in Western Europe by half, which appealed to some in the Treasury. "There are two separate questions: our desire to stay in Europe and our ability to sustain that position," Under Secretary of the Treasury for International Monetary Affairs Paul Volcker commented.[51] Nixon and Kissinger campaigned against the amendment, even enlisting veteran Cold Warriors Dean Acheson, Dean Rusk, and Robert Lovett to lobby wavering senators.[52] A unilateral reduction of US troops was simply out of the question for the White House. C. Fred Bergsten, an international economist on the National Security Council (NSC) staff, stressed that Washington "should *never* reduce [troop levels] for balance of payments reasons." They would send a signal to Moscow that "the U.S. had become so pitifully weak on the economic and financial front that we could no longer make any pretense of maintaining our defense posture around the world."[53] The administration exhaled when the Senate rejected the legislation, but popular resentment continued to build. Critics charged that the United States ran balance of payments deficits in part because Western Europe refused to take responsibility for its own defense.

Isolationist sentiments surged as US exporters lost ground to foreign competitors. Trade unions pressed the White House to impose import quotas. Workers in the textile and clothing industries, which had long been protectionist-minded, were now joined by allies in fields such as steel, electrical manufacturing, and rubber. "If cars don't sell, everybody's out," the chairman of a Connecticut union workshop pointed out.[54] Illustrative of the zeitgeist, the American Federation of Labor and Congress of Industrial Organizations (AFL-CIO) itself, which had traditionally supported free trade, advocated for protectionist policies. Defending US jobs and lobbying against the relocation of factories abroad was "a problem for the entire trade union movement—not just the problem of some workers," argued AFL-CIO secretary-treasurer Lane Kirkland.[55] Agricultural policy became a key source of tension between the United States and the European Community, and US farmers protested that the latter's Common Agricultural Policy (CAP) imposed tariffs that priced them out of the

Western European market. With various stakeholders pushing for trade barriers, "neither the economic nor the foreign policy argument for liberal trade commands much support in the United States," Bergsten summarized in an article in *Foreign Affairs*.[56]

Social unrest reinforced the public's inward turn. No issue did more to challenge assumptions about the United States' place in the world than the Vietnam War. While the fighting took place in a small country thousands of miles away, television carried the horrors of the war directly into US living rooms. Sacrifice for the war fell to the young, disproportionally ethnic minorities and the underprivileged who did not have the means to evade conscription. Nearly sixty thousand US soldiers died, and many more suffered physical injuries and emotional scars—not to mention the millions of Vietnamese soldiers and civilians killed—for an unpopular war whose purpose few understood. During his 1968 presidential campaign, Nixon had claimed that he had a secret plan to end the war, but the carnage continued into his second term. The publication of the Pentagon Papers in the *New York Times* in the summer of 1971, on the heels of the expansion of the war into Laos, expanded the government's credibility gap. The war protests overlapped with other social currents such as the civil rights movement and the women's rights movement, forging a broad coalition that exposed stark socioeconomic, ethnic, gender, and generational divisions in the United States. Many US citizens thought that the nation needed to direct its attention toward solving the domestic problems and finding its own moral compass, not crusading to remake the world in its image.[57]

With the US welfare empire under fire, Western European officials wrestled with the consequences. They feared that congressional pressure would force Nixon to withdraw US troops from the Continent. The US public needed to understand that US forces "were not here simply for the sake of Europe, but in the common interest," West German chancellor Willy Brandt grumbled to the British prime minister Edward Heath. The US public "was unaware of the real facts," Heath added. Their countries provided ten soldiers on the continent for each US soldier.[58] They needed US troops on their soil because they believed that NATO's nuclear deterrent became credible only with US forces deployed to Western Europe.[59]

Although dependent on the US military umbrella, the Western Europeans disentangled security and economic issues in talks with US officials, opposing the "all one ball of wax" approach that the Nixon administration adopted.[60] Western European officials sharply criticized US economic policy. Claiming to speak on behalf of the entire European Community, French minister of finance Valéry Giscard d'Estaing "could not stress too strongly" to Kennedy his concern about the impact of "U.S. inflation on their own economies, on confidence in the dollar, on the world monetary system."[61] Washington needed to discipline itself so that others would not have to suffer the consequences.

While Western European officials criticized the United States, the Bretton Woods system suffered from a systemic problem.[62] Different national rates of inflation undermined the fixed-exchange rate regime. If exchange rates did not adjust to reflect changing fundamentals, then disequilibria in the balance of payments emerged.[63] Furthermore, as the Euromarkets grew, short-term capital moved across borders in search of a quick profit, which made it more difficult for monetary authorities to maintain fixed-exchange rates. More than any other currency, the Deutsche Mark stood at the center of a series of currency crises during the late 1960s and early 1970s because of its strength.

The noninflationary and export-driven West German growth placed pressure on the rest of the system. The divergence between West Germany and France in 1968 and 1969 illustrated the point. Social unrest gripped France in May 1968 as millions of workers went on strike and students protested the de Gaulle regime. Still jittery from the November 1967 sterling devaluation, investors fled the franc and sought refuge in the Deutsche Mark during the late summer and fall of 1968. In the first three weeks of November 1968 alone, $2.35 billion in foreign currencies flowed into the Bundesbank.[64] De Gaulle refused to devalue the franc as a matter of principle and insisted that Bonn bear the burden of adjustment. He knew that a West German revaluation would serve as a de facto devaluation of the franc, which would make French exports cheaper without sacrificing the franc's prestige.

The West Germans balked at the prospect of a Deutsche Mark revaluation. They did not want to bear the burden of the imbalances. They had to cope with a variety of domestic problems, as trade unions and students rallied against the government, and violent extremists such as the Red Army Faction launched an "anti-imperialist" struggle against Bonn. Both left- and right-wing parties made electoral gains in the late 1960s, and Bonn did not want a currency realignment to weaken public support for the Grand Coalition of the Christian Democratic Union (CDU) and Social Democratic Party (SPD).[65] At an emergency Group of Ten (G10) meeting in Bonn during November 1968, the minister of economics Karl Schiller resisted international pressure to revalue the Deutsche Mark. Schiller argued that West Germany, "which had achieved price stability with a growth rate of 6 per cent and a satisfactory labour situation through responsible Trade Union co-operation, should not be expected to take the full burden."[66] The West German public applauded Schiller's stance, and Chancellor Kurt Georg Kiesinger pledged that there would be no revaluation of the Deutsche Mark.[67]

The run on the franc resumed when de Gaulle resigned the French presidency in late April 1969 because speculators anticipated that a new French government might take a different stance on devaluation. More than $4 billion poured into West Germany over the next week.[68] The West German Cabinet debated how to respond. On one side, Schiller feared that maintaining the current parity would aggravate inflation, which had profound symbolism in West Germany given the memory of the 1923 hyperinflation. On the other side, the minister of finance Franz Josef Strauss argued that revaluation would hurt exporters, particularly farmers in his home state of Bavaria. Despite Bundesbank president Karl Blessing throwing his support behind Schiller, Kiesinger backed Strauss. The chancellor commented that a revaluation would disrupt trade with partners "whose price level is not distorted at all" and contemplated the "political ramifications" at home of reversing the decision of November 1968.[69] The speculation eased after Bonn announced that it would not revalue the Deutsche Mark.

Pressure on the franc subsided in August 1969 after the French government under new president Georges Pompidou announced an 11.1 percent devaluation of the franc but resumed on the Deutsche Mark as the West German federal elections approached at the end of September 1969.[70] In anticipation of an SPD victory in which Schiller would have an influential voice in policy, short-term capital amounting to $2.38 billion surged into West Germany during the third quarter of 1969, including nearly $1.25 billion in September alone. Kiesinger ordered that the foreign exchange market be closed, and the Cabinet finally agreed to float the Deutsche Mark to relieve the speculative pressure. In October 1969, Brandt won the chancellorship, the first time since 1930 that the SPD had held that position, and his government revalued the Deutsche Mark by 9.3 percent at the end of the month.[71]

The currency crises of the late 1960s provided an impetus for a renewed push for EC integration. Rather than face monetary instability as individual countries, the European Community elected to confront the challenge as a unit. Building on Brandt's initiative at the Hague Summit in December 1969, the members resolved to create a monetary and economic union. The European Council of Ministers tasked a committee under Luxembourgian prime minister Pierre Werner to plot a course.

Divergent national priorities complicated the scheme. France focused on keeping unemployment low, for example, while West Germany concentrated on managing inflation. These differences mapped onto the polarizing question of whether to prioritize monetary or economic integration. EC members such as France and Belgium with trade deficits, high inflation, and weaker currencies supported the former because monetary integration would reduce the bloc's exposure to dollar instability. Others such as West Germany and the Netherlands that had trade surpluses, lower inflation, and stronger currencies advocated the latter. They worried that monetary integration without economic synchronization would require the stronger countries to bail out their weaker neighbors. "Only when the instruments of economic policy are effective and used properly can we chart the course for close monetary cooperation," Dutch finance minister Johan Witteveen argued. His Belgian counterpart responded that if economic coordination were a precondition for monetary integration, the European Community would "never get there."[72]

Submitted in October 1970, the Werner Report outlined a compromise that satisfied nobody: the monetary and economic integrative processes would proceed simultaneously. A British official called the Werner Report an "ambitious Cartesian statement of ultimate objectives, glossing over many of the difficulties of achieving them."[73] The project stalled almost immediately. Seeking to arrest inflation, which had risen to 3.5 percent (GDP deflator) in 1969, the Bundesbank had raised the discount rate in March 1970, but higher interest rates attracted short-term capital. Inflation for the year surged to 7.4 percent. Through the first week of May, the Bundesbank had already taken in $5 billion for the year; $2 billion flooded into West Germany between May 3 and May 5 alone. "The dollar exodus from the United States and the supply of credit on the Euro-markets led to a particularly massive swamping of Germany," the Bundesbank noted.[74] Hoping to negotiate a joint float or exchange rate realignment within the European Community, Schiller proposed that "the current situation can become a great moment for further monetary integration and a step forward on the way to economic and monetary union for the Community."[75] With little support forthcoming, however, Bonn resorted to floating the Deutsche Mark unilaterally. The move undermined progress toward EC integration, but the West Germans identified choking the flow of capital as the higher priority.[76] Not wanting the appreciation of the Deutsche Mark to disrupt their trade with West Germany, the Dutch floated the guilder as well. The currency crisis "has once again confirmed how difficult it is to achieve monetary integration between countries with different priorities," Witteveen sighed.[77] More broadly, it illustrated the growing power of short-term capital to dislodge fixed exchange rates.

Nixon had no simple solution to the US balance of payments deficits. He had limited ability to compel other nations to revalue their currencies. US policy-

makers considered introducing border taxes and subsidies, which would dis-
courage the flow of speculative funds while not touching the dollar-gold rate,
but it would only apply to a portion of the balance of payments and thus would
create a confusing system of variable exchange rates. The only real economic
leverage that Washington had was the suspension of gold-dollar convertibility, which was the monetary equivalent of the nuclear option.[78]

Taking office in February 1971, the new Treasury secretary John Connally
pushed Nixon to embrace a hard line. Given his background as a Democratic
governor of Texas and LBJ protégé as well as his lack of economics expertise,
Connally seemed a peculiar choice for the post. "Mr. Connally knows as much
about economics as most economists know about cattle ranching," The Times
scoffed.[79] But what Connally lacked in technical knowledge he compensated
with conviction. Put simply, he believed that "the foreigners are out to screw
us and therefore it's our job to screw them first."[80]

Connally voiced crudely what many US officials already thought, even if they
did not use such colorful language. For a quarter century after World War II,
Peterson wrote in a sweeping evaluation of US international economic strategy,
Washington had "placed security, military-political objectives, and cold war tactics in a dominant position with economic policies largely shaped to serve these
ends." Yet the gap between the United States and the rest of the developed world
narrowed as Western Europe and Japan registered impressive gains in part due
to "discriminatory trading arrangements." While the United States had expected
"that as the economies of other leading industrialized countries became stronger, they would accept an increasing share of responsibility for the maintenance
of security and economic order in the Free World" as well as "gradually open
their markets to suppliers from around the world," neither of these assumptions
proved correct. Peterson argued that the US "willingness to incur perennial balance of payments deficits" and "increasing world liabilities and shrinking
reserves . . . kept the system going as long as it did." The Bretton Woods system
did not "reflect these changes" in the balance of economic power, and US businesses suffered from the overvalued dollar. Since the surplus countries gave
Washington little reason to believe that they would make "adequate, prompt or
equitable" adjustments, the Nixon administration had to act. Otherwise, the deteriorating US position could have led "to a hasty and dangerous reduction of
our military commitments abroad, and an equally ill-considered relapse into the
most short-sighted forms of trade protectionism."[81]

Speculative pressure against the dollar mounted in the summer of 1971 and
emboldened those pushing for action. The US Congress Joint Economic Committee's Subcommittee on International Exchange and Payments under Wisconsin Democratic senator Henry S. Reuss issued a report in early August 1971

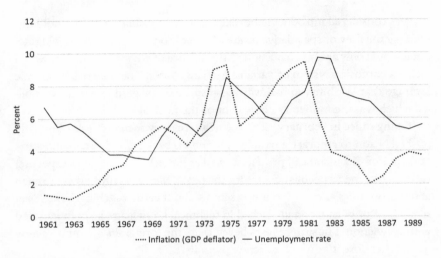

FIGURE 1.2. Inflation and unemployment in the United States, 1961–1989. Source: World Bank, World Development Indicators.

that recommended "the exchange rates of industrial nations should be [realigned] to eliminate the existing structural payments deficit of the United States."[82] In response, some $3.7 billion rushed into non-dollar-denominated assets during the following week, with the Swiss franc taking more than 45 percent of the total.[83] A rumor circulated that the Bank of England had attempted to exchange $3 billion into gold, a charge that British policymakers denied, and fanned fears of a bank run.[84]

As inflation climbed, Republican senators proposed a wage-price review board to manage the problem. Rising unemployment also devastated workers who never really had a problem finding jobs before. "I don't need welfare," maintained the former supervisor of a closed Alabama mill. His wife had also been laid off, and their small town of Roanoke had an unemployment rate above 17 percent. "What I need is a job that would let us keep our dignity and pride, like we had in the mills."[85] The Democrats smelled blood as they prepared to attack Nixon on economic grounds during his 1972 reelection bid.

The administration resolved to act decisively. At a meeting with Nixon and the director of the Office of Management and Budget George P. Shultz in mid-August 1971, Connally argued, "Our problems are basically, to the extent that we have them, right here at home. And when they're solved, your international problems are solved, your international trade problems to a large extent are solved, because it's merely a reflection." What was really important, Connally contended, was "the impact on the American people, and their reaction to you and what you did, and their reaction to your action. . . . The international thing, hell, it's going to be in turmoil or a state of turmoil or semi-turmoil from now on. . . . And I just don't think you ought to worry too much about that." Nixon agreed, adding that his goal remained "a continued upward surge in the domestic economy. And we must not in order to stabilize the international situation, cut our guts out here." He would not sacrifice the domestic agenda to appease international partners and resolved to act sooner than later so that any adverse effects would pass before the reelection campaign heated up the following year.[86]

Nixon whisked his top economic advisers to Camp David for a weekend retreat to hammer out the details. The State Department was sidelined, and even Kissinger was out of the loop.[87] Burns stood as the lone internationalist in the room. On the eve of the meeting, he moaned to his diary, "The gold window may have to be closed tomorrow because we have a government that seems incapable, not only of constructive leadership, but of any action at all. What a tragedy for mankind!"[88] The participants traveled by helicopter, hoping to escape to Camp David undetected. Relishing the moment, Nixon instructed the group not to make telephone calls, and declared that "any leak would be treason."[89] Then the group returned to Washington to "slap 'em on Sunday night," as Nixon put it.[90]

While Connally celebrated the New Economic Policy, the foreign policy team sulked. Kissinger congratulated Nixon over the phone but sang a different tune privately.[91] "We are heading for a catastrophe in Europe," he confided in John McCloy, an original Cold Warrior. "We can't throw away twenty-five years of what has been built up for Treasury reasons." Connally's brinksmanship was "breaking the backs of our closest friends," he griped.[92] The August 15 measures compounded the "mood of depression" in Foggy Bottom in the fall of 1971, the British ambassador Lord Rowley Cromer reported, as monetary upheaval coincided with setbacks in Vietnam and Taiwan's expulsion from the United Nations.[93]

The stock market enjoyed a red-letter day, and Nixon's measures proved popular at home, but the allies scrambled to react to the fait accompli measures for which they had no warning. Most closed their foreign exchange markets for a week and maintained dirty floats of their currencies thereafter. The president "had no specific programme or blue-print for reform in mind," Volcker told his foreign counterparts after taking a red-eye flight to London following Nixon's speech, but rather "had an objective which was that the United States must now be put back into a strong balance of payments position." Nixon would not consider any proposal for changing the dollar price of gold. The onus fell on US partners "to consider what programme of measures, including parity changes, would bring about the necessary strengthening of the

American payments position."[94] Volcker later recalled the "sense of shock, even of betrayal" on their faces.[95]

Over the next few months, the Nixon administration used the closure of the gold window and the import surcharge as leverage to force the other industrial democracies to yield on trade and monetary issues. US officials insisted that a dollar devaluation was off the table. The economic ramifications would be enormous, and it would punish West Germany and Japan, which had held their dollars, and reward France, which had hastened the crisis by converting them into gold. A reduction in the dollar's value would also show that the dollar-gold rate was not sacrosanct, which would encourage central banks and speculators to hedge against additional dollar devaluations down the road.

The other industrial democracies sought to escape the standoff with their exchange rates as close to the precrisis parities as possible. "The smaller the devaluation of the dollar, the larger the compensatory revaluations will have to be," the secretary of the Dutch Economic Affairs Council Ton van de Graaf remarked.[96] The most conciliatory was Schiller. "All countries should . . . take part in such a realignment," Schiller stressed at the G10 summit in London during mid-September 1971, "because otherwise the burden placed on individual countries would become too heavy."[97] Connally refused to budge. The United States needed a $13 billion improvement in its balance of payments, but determining how that would happen was a task for other countries. "The dollar is our currency but your problem," he commented to foreign officials.[98]

With no agreement in sight, Nixon decided in November 1971 that he needed to defuse the crisis. Kissinger had coaxed him to negotiate, and the president wanted to have Western unity before making his historic trip to China at the beginning of the new year. Nixon told Connally that he wanted "progress" at the G10 conference in Rome at the end of the month, and then Nixon would strike a final agreement during talks with Pompidou during mid-December so that he would "get some direct credit."[99] Connally complained that Nixon was letting a good crisis go to waste. "I did not take this apart to put it back at a cheap price," he grumbled, but he accepted his marching orders.[100] At Rome's Palazzo Corsini, the US delegation made its first constructive proposal to resolve the standoff. "Somewhat impatiently," Connally proposed to his foreign counterparts, "Assume a 10 percent devaluation of the dollar against gold. What would you do?" A "long silence" followed.[101] No final agreement was reached, but the participants had not expected one. The point was that the United States would include the dollar as part of a systemic recalibration of exchange rates.

Nixon and Pompidou met in the Azores in mid-December 1971 to negotiate a settlement. International monetary policy fascinated Pompidou, a former

Rothschild investment banker, but bored Nixon.[102] Nixon engaged sufficiently to agree to devalue the dollar to $38 per ounce, and in return Pompidou promised to revalue the franc, provided that the amount was less than the revaluation of the Deutsche Mark. With an agreement with the French in the bag, the G10 met once more in Washington to decide on the final realignment. Under the terms of the Smithsonian Agreement, the Nixon administration lifted the surcharge and promised to ask Congress for an increase in the price of gold to $38 per ounce, a devaluation of nearly 9 percent. Compared with May 1971 rates against the dollar, the major revaluations included the Swiss franc by 13.9 percent, the Deutsche Mark by 13.6 percent, the Belgian franc and Dutch guilder by 11.6 percent, the British pound and French franc by 8.6 percent, and the Italian lira and Swedish krona by 7.5 percent.[103] Since Japan held the largest trade surplus with the United States, the scheme depended on a sizable revaluation of the yen. The Japanese delegation rejected Connally's proposal of 17 percent during the Rome meeting, citing Tokyo's decision in 1930 to devalue the currency by the same amount that had catastrophic economic consequences, and accepted 16.9 percent instead.[104] The margins for acceptable fluctuations also expanded from 1 percent in each direction to 2.25 percent.

While Nixon hailed the Smithsonian Agreement as "the most significant monetary agreement in the history of the world," few shared his confidence. "I hope it lasts three months," Volcker whispered to an assistant.[105] Indeed, it did nothing to solve deeper problems, providing "mere palliatives, one more patch on a system which last year gave every indication of being on its deathbed," concluded Brian Reading, an economic adviser to Heath. The terms did not provide a new source of international liquidity, overlooked the dollar overhang, failed to restrict speculative capital flows, and set parities that were not "likely to be more permanent than in the past." The international monetary system "has suffered a severe fever," Reading described, and while "the doctors have found a way to bring his temperature back to 'normal' . . . they have not found a cure for the complaint which caused the fever."[106] The Bretton Woods system may have been gravely ill, but its caregivers did not want to pull the plug just yet.

While the Smithsonian arrangement provided temporary relief, stakeholders expected another fever soon. The European Community set its sights on integration in the spring of 1972, "once again flogging a horse which had looked convincingly dead," an article in the Economist noted. "Maybe it's a different horse."[107] It was not a horse, as it turned out. Dubbed the "Snake in the Smithsonian tunnel," the arrangement limited the maximum deviation to 1.125 percent in either direction from the existing parities, cutting the Smithsonian allowance in half. The main argument for the Snake's tighter margins was that closer coordination would allow the members to deal with dollar instability as a group.[108] The European Community implemented the agreement in April 1972, and the four candidates Britain, Ireland, Denmark, and Norway joined the following month.

The Snake lasted only a couple months before sterling came under attack in June 1972. Even though the British held a balance of payments surplus, speculators worried about the current account that had fallen into the red, how British businesses would fare against EC competition, and rising labor tensions over the new Industrial Relations Act. After spending a third of the Bank of England's reserves, some $2.5 billion, to defend sterling, London waved the white flag at the end of the month and announced a float. "It must be now clear that further intellectual investment by Great George Street and Threadneedle Street in the conventional wisdom of Bretton Woods is going into a wasting asset," relayed Cromer, himself a former Bank of England governor. The international community needed "some new gospel" to prevent the international payments system from becoming "subject to a series of competitive devaluations as in the 1930s."[109]

Thinking in Western Europe coalesced around using controls to stem the tide of capital flows. The French had long advocated for restrictive measures, and the West Germans became converts after attracting two-thirds of the capital fleeing sterling in June 1972. The Brandt government passed a series of measures causing Schiller, the most enthusiastic among Western European officials for exchange rate flexibility, to resign in disgust. Into his position slid Helmut Schmidt, the minister of defense, who took a hard line. "Billions of dollars are floating around the world and Germany is taking in too many of them," Schmidt argued, causing inflation to rise to 5.4 percent by the summer of 1972.[110] The West German and French positions moved closer together with Schmidt at the helm, as they both advocated decentering the dollar in the international monetary system and relying more on SDRs and gold. They agreed that "freedom of capital movement should not be dogma. . . . If a country has a deficit, it should not allow capital to flee without restrictions."[111] The West Germans imposed capital controls during late 1972 and early 1973 such as imposing a ban on the purchase of West German assets by anyone outside the country and requiring businesses to obtain a permit before using external funds to finance their activities.[112]

Managing inflation took on added importance for West Germany in the fall of 1972 because of the looming federal election. Brandt had lost his Bundestag majority in the spring when several SPD representatives defected to the

CDU in protest of *Ostpolitik*, a new policy that sought to build bridges between East and West, and the chancellor narrowly escaped a vote of no confidence. With a new election scheduled for mid-November, Brandt faced an uphill political battle, and Schmidt said that his chances "would be completely ruined" if the government could not control inflation. Speculative attention on the Deutsche Mark might force a revaluation, which would harm West German exports and lead to a backlash among voters.[113] Bonn's overtures to the Soviet bloc may have commanded the attention of the international press, a foreign correspondent reported, but "the typical German voter . . . seems far more worried about the price of his food, beer, and cigarettes."[114] Brandt's coalition ultimately emerged victorious, but the chancellor knew that the support would crumble if he did not manage the economic problems.

Tighter monetary policy had not reduced inflation in the early 1970s, so governments reoriented toward fighting unemployment with expansionary monetary and fiscal policies. After slumping to 2.7 percent in 1970, growth in the Organisation for Economic Co-operation and Development (OECD) area increased to 3.7 percent in 1971 and 5.4 percent in 1972. Inflation, which registered about 7 percent during 1971 and 1972, accompanied the renewed economic growth.[115] Demand for raw materials from the developing world grew as the industrial boom unfolded in the West. Prices spiked for commodities such as energy, fibers, food, fertilizer, and metals at rates not seen since the Korean War.[116] Food prices jumped 16.4 percent and clothing 18.4 percent in West Germany during 1972. "Car costs are going up so much we may return to our bicycles," a Dutch woman worried. "And we have stopped eating butter. We Dutch produce butter but are forced to eat margarine." Meat shortages in Italy caused beef prices to spike 20 percent, and rent for a two-bedroom apartment in Paris rose by 10 percent. Increased competition in the British housing market led to the neologism "gazumping," which referred to the practice of an owner promising to sell a property to a buyer at a certain price but then using other bids as leverage to demand more money than originally agreed.[117]

While the Western Europeans generally renewed their attempts to regulate capital, US Treasury officials moved in the opposite direction. Connally's resignation and Shultz's appointment to the post of Treasury secretary in June 1972 oriented Washington toward a market-based solution to the Bretton Woods system's travails. Together with Volcker, Shultz developed Plan X, an ambitious blueprint for the international monetary system that envisioned greater exchange rate flexibility. It permitted floating in a few cases, including "indefinitely" if the country pledged not to put in controls on the flow of capital and trade.[118]

Nixon was far less interested in monetary ideology than he was in his political fortunes. Even though the president won reelection in November 1972, he still had to contend with a Democrat-controlled Congress and protectionist labor unions. "I want to see new jobs created all over the world," Nixon declared at the IMF in September 1972, "but I cannot condone the export of jobs out of the United States caused by any unfairness built into the world's trading system."[119] Managing the Bretton Woods system's unraveling required careful diplomacy, but Nixon's nationalist streak irritated the United States' closest allies. It did not help matters that Nixon did not get along with the other leaders. He found Heath too European, Pompidou too doctrinaire and Gaullist, and Brandt too thick and parochial. When word circulated in early 1973 that Brandt may have had throat cancer, Kissinger reported, "Unfortunately, he's likely to hang on in there." Nixon responded, "He is a dolt."[120]

After another round of speculative pressure in the spring of 1973, the Bretton Woods system finally had its terminal bout of fever. Nixon removed wage-price controls at the end of 1972, which the markets interpreted to mean that he no longer saw combating inflation as a priority. Furthermore, the press reported a record U.S balance of payments deficit in 1972 while West Germany enjoyed strong figures.[121] A dollar outflow ensued. West Germany had upheld its responsibilities under the Smithsonian Agreement "to the letter and in spirit," the frustrated Brandt appealed to Nixon. The Bundesbank supported the dollar on the Frankfurt Exchange Market, an intervention that needed to "be supported by corresponding actions of the American monetary authorities."[122] Little US help was forthcoming.

Bonn had to decide between initiating another unilateral float or persuading the EC members to float as a unit. Schmidt preferred the latter, but a de facto Deutsche Mark bloc was difficult to sell to Paris.[123] Pompidou noted that the US trade deficit with Japan totaled $4 billion while the deficit with Western Europe registered $500 million, and he did not understand "why the European currencies, whose countries and governments were not responsible for the deficit, should increase the prices of their exports and hurt their 'terms of trade' in the world economy."[124] Volcker traveled between Western Europe and Japan to facilitate a deal in which the United States would devalue the dollar against gold by 10 percent, the yen would float, the pound would continue to float, and the other Western European currencies would remain unchanged. The West Germans were relieved that they did not need to take unilateral action as they had in May 1971.[125]

The arrangement lasted only a couple weeks. On March 1 alone, the West Germans absorbed another $2.7 billion, the Dutch $500 million, and the French and Danes significant amounts as well. Brandt was "very reluctant to act in isolation" and once again tried to forge a common EC response. State Secretary of the Finance Ministry Karl Otto Pöhl noted that the experience of the Deutsche Mark float in May 1971 "had brought the Community near the breaking point." Floating alone "would be very useful and would reinforce their attempts to contain inflation," but Bonn did not want to postpone the achievement of monetary union.[126] West German and French officials reached a compromise: France participated, and the West Germans appreciated the Deutsche Mark 3 percent against the franc. Six EC countries participated in the joint float in addition to Norway—which had backed out of its agreement to join the European Community after a popular referendum—and Sweden. Not wanting to keep pace with the Deutsche Mark, Britain, Ireland, and Italy elected to stay out.[127]

A meeting of the G10 in mid-March 1973 blessed the passing of the Bretton Woods system. No longer the "pivot" of the international monetary system, the dollar was now simply "the expression of the world's most powerful economy in an interdependent world," a British official wrote. "A dollar is a dollar," a slogan that implied "a great deal of freedom of action for the Americans."[128] Shultz was blunter. "Santa Claus is dead," he celebrated.[129]

The collapse of the Bretton Woods system illuminated a fundamental problem in the US welfare empire: its structure had been based on a distribution of economic power that prevailed in the late 1940s but no longer existed in the early 1970s. "The national security of the United States requires us to play a leading world role," Nixon's international economic adviser Peter Flanigan wrote Shultz in January 1973, "but our economic capacity to do so is being constrained by the present imbalance in the world monetary and trading system." The Nixon administration struggled to reconcile its geopolitical ambitions with diminishing means and public support.

Amid the economic tensions, policymakers could not fall back on the communist threat to rally the West together because détente had made the Soviet Union appear less menacing. In this period of drift, Kissinger believed that "the concept of partnership must be given context. This content had been provided during the 1960s by the defense element. Now, in an era of change, this was not enough. Some new themes on which to work together must be found."[130] Kissinger tried to reinvigorate the West with new purpose by proclaiming a "Year of Europe" in a wide-ranging April 1973 speech to the editors of the Associated Press at New York's Waldorf-Astoria Hotel. Now that Western Europe and Japan had recovered economically and the Soviet Union had reached strategic parity, Kissinger declared that the "era that was shaped by decisions of a generation ago is ending." The situation called for a "new era of creativity in the West." Invoking the Atlantic Charter of August 1941, he proposed that the transatlantic community refocus on shared ideals and interests as well as coordinate more closely with Japan.[131] Behind the initiative stood a desire to recalibrate burden sharing to the new economic balance of power. The Western Europeans "have got to face up to the linking of political, economic and defense factors," Kissinger later said to his staff. "We can't have a trade war and keep troops in Europe."[132]

The Western Europeans paid lip service to the Year of Europe but saw through the rhetoric. Linkage implied that Washington would use the US military commitment as leverage to extract trade and monetary concessions, Overton worried.[133] Western European officials also suspected that the Nixon administration wanted to use the Year of Europe to distract his constituents from the public hearings on the Watergate scandal, which began in the spring.[134] Most of all, they found the initiative patronizing.

The annual rate of real GNP growth reached an impressive 8 percent in the industrial democracies during the first six months of 1973.[135] Yet other indicators portended trouble. Inflation and unemployment rose, intracapitalist tensions increased, and the international monetary system crumbled. "It is a sobering thought that the Civil War under Cromwell, the French Revolution and the appeal of Nazism in Germany were each one the aftermath of financial collapse," Cromer wrote Heath in February 1973 as the Bretton Woods system lay on its deathbed. "I do not mean to sound too gloomy, but time is not on our side at the moment!"[136] The Bretton Woods system, a key instrument of the US welfare empire that had promoted noninflationary growth across the industrial democracies for nearly a quarter century, had unraveled.

CHAPTER 2

Eastern European Development and Soviet Subsidies

The chairman of the Soviet Council of Ministers Alexei Kosygin could not believe his ears. In the summer of 1973, East German officials updated him on their plan to take out loans from Western banks to finance their country's development. When his East German counterpart Willi Stoph estimated that East Berlin would have to pay up to $650 million annually just to service its debt while its yearly exports earned only about $600 billion, the anxious Kosygin noted, "That really is the extreme limit." Even if the East Germans reached their optimistic target of raising exports by 15 percent in both 1974 and 1975, they acknowledged that the debt would still almost double by the end of 1975. "We pay on time and then take out new loans," the East German chairman of the State Planning Commission Gerhard Schürer explained. The worried Kosygin inquired how the East Germans envisioned the end game. "What are you planning for 1980?" he asked. "How much debt will you have? How large will your exports have to be?" Stoph responded pointedly: "That depends on the quantity of raw materials that we receive from the Soviet Union and the rest of the socialist countries."[1] The link between East Germany's development and Soviet resources was clear.

The conversation highlighted the emerging strains in the Soviet welfare empire by the early 1970s. First, the Soviet socialist growth model began to sputter, and the East German decision to take out loans from capitalist banks reflected a solution to this problem. Economic growth had surged during the

1950s and early 1960s behind the Iron Curtain, but opportunities for extensive growth began to dwindle by the mid- and late 1960s. Rather than attempt to transition to intensive growth using their own resources, policymakers across Eastern Europe turned to debt-driven development. They used credits to purchase Western technology and goods with the hope of developing advanced industries of their own and then exporting to the nonsocialist world to earn the necessary hard currency with which to repay their debts. Behind closed doors, some officials expressed fears that if this strategy did not work, the Eastern European regimes would become locked into a dangerous state of financial dependence on the West. Unwilling to contemplate failure, political elites overpowered dissenting voices.

Second, Eastern European plans irritated the Soviet Union not only because of their reliance on Western credits but also because their success turned on the Kremlin's willingness to deliver extensive material support, fuel above all, to power the industries. Production costs for Soviet raw materials increased in the late 1960s, but the Soviet bloc utilized a pricing formula that undervalued commodities and overvalued finished goods. The Soviet implicit subsidy thus began to increase, and the Kremlin's willingness to underwrite Eastern Europe waned. Moscow believed that higher commodity prices could stimulate Eastern Europe's production of quality manufactured goods, reducing the drain on the Soviet economy and creating a more equitable international division of labor.

The political stakes of resolving the rising economic contradictions in the Soviet bloc were high. As a teleological ideology, Soviet socialism had to deliver on its lofty promise to create a prosperous, secure, and egalitarian bloc. If not, then the socialist bloc could justify its existence only on the strength of Soviet tanks and bayonets.

While the Soviet Union asserted hegemonic control over Eastern Europe after World War II ended, the Soviet welfare empire did not form immediately. The victory over Nazi Germany had come at the cost of twenty-seven million dead soldiers and civilians and billions of dollars of property damage, and Moscow plundered occupied Eastern Europe to hasten postwar reconstruction. The Soviets seized reparations, forced Eastern European governments to sign unequal trade agreements, and participated in joint-stock companies through which they claimed Eastern European production. The occupied countries also had to supply provisions for the Red Army and pay the salaries of Soviet advisers. While the exact figure is difficult to calculate, the Soviet Union extracted an estimated $23 billion worth of goods from its sphere of influence (including reparations from occupied Germany) between 1945 and 1960.[2]

Soviet rearmament accompanied reconstruction because dictator Joseph Stalin feared capitalist encirclement. His overriding foreign policy priority was to create an international environment that would protect the Soviet Union and his regime from external threats. The memory of Barbarossa haunted him. If Germany were not "deprived of the possibility of revenge," Stalin told British prime minister Winston Churchill in October 1944, then "every twenty-five or thirty years there would be a new world war which would exterminate the young generation."[3] Stalin sought to maintain the alliance with the United States during the postwar period to maintain access to US economic assistance and to contain the defeated Axis powers. By the spring of 1946, however, Soviet officials had identified the United States as a hostile adversary that sought "world domination," as the Soviet ambassador Nikolai Novikov warned.[4]

Stalin reannexed the Baltic States, eastern Poland, sub-Carpathian Ruthenia, Bessarabia, and northern Bukovina (territories that the Soviet Union had seized between 1939 and 1941 and lost during the Nazi invasion) but initially did not have a blueprint for how to treat occupied Eastern Europe. Although Stalin permitted the Eastern European countries no autonomy in foreign policy, he did not immediately impose the Soviet developmental model within his sphere of influence. The emerging Cold War shaped Stalin's approach.[5] His flexibility evaporated after the Truman administration launched the Marshall Plan and moved forward with plans to establish a West German state. The US initiatives exposed the capitalist plot to encircle the Soviet Union, Stalin believed. He feared that a resurgent and irredentist Germany would endeavor to follow in Hitler's footsteps, and this time Anglo-American financial and industrial power would aid the effort.[6]

Stalin consolidated his sphere of influence in Eastern Europe in response. He established the Communist Information Bureau (Cominform) in September 1947 to increase Soviet control over communist parties in Europe. No longer tolerant of national roads to socialism, Moscow insisted that the communist parties establish dictatorships across Eastern Europe and import the Soviet developmental model, based on industrialization, nationalization, collectivization, and central planning. Socialists viewed Stalin's "revolution from above" during the 1930s as the paradigm for how their own states should proceed. Bulgarian first secretary Todor Zhivkov explained that "it was no coincidence that especially in the first years of our socialist development, almost all of our steps necessarily had to take into account the Soviet experience."[7] Fearing that Yugoslav leader Josip Broz Tito wanted to challenge Soviet primacy in the Balkans, Stalin orchestrated the expulsion of the Yugoslav communist party from the Cominform in June 1948. That same month, he also initiated a blockade of Berlin in a failed attempt to thwart the formation of a West German state and push the

Western powers out of the divided city.[8] The socialist states convened the Council for Mutual Economic Assistance (CMEA or Comecon) in January 1949 to coordinate their economies, but the organization also served as another mechanism through which Moscow could impose its will.[9] To ensure that the next world war would not be fought on Soviet soil, the Soviets secured Eastern Europe as a socialist buffer zone and continued to exploit the region for its resources.

Following the death of Stalin in March 1953, a quartet of potential successors—Communist Party of the Soviet Union (CPSU) first secretary Nikita Khrushchev, foreign minister Vyacheslav Molotov, premier Georgy Malenkov, and KGB chief Lavrentii Beria—signaled a new direction in Soviet foreign policy. They believed that the material demands of waging the Cold War diverted resources away from increasing living standards at home. The production of consumer goods must be given higher priority in the future, Malenkov declared at Stalin's funeral. So that the Kremlin could focus more of its attention on improving conditions at home, he announced that the Soviets sought better relations with the West.[10]

The same logic dictated a reevaluation of Soviet policy in Eastern Europe. Stalin's successors identified a symbiotic relationship between Soviet national security interests and Eastern European material prosperity and political legitimacy; the Eastern European socialist countries could serve as a reliable buffer zone and promote international socialism only if they had a strong economic and political foundation. Continued emphasis on heavy industry did not ingratiate Soviet socialism to the Eastern European people, who had not elected the communists.

The East Berlin uprising of June 1953 reinforced the point. Triggered by a state decree that increased labor quotas, workers took to the streets, and their economic grievances quickly led to political demands as well. They called for the East German Socialist Unity Party (SED) government's resignation, free elections, and the legalization of noncommunist parties. Half a million East Germans participated in the revolt. Unwilling to lose its satellite, Moscow crushed the uprising with tanks.[11] The lesson that Moscow learned was that popular discontent over material conditions endangered political stability, which in turn undermined Soviet hegemonic control over Eastern Europe.

In the mid-1950s, Moscow adopted a new strategy in Eastern Europe known as the New Course. The Kremlin permitted the Eastern European regimes to implement their own modifications to the Soviet model, including reduced emphasis on heavy industry, increased focus on consumer goods, the suspension of collectivization, and a reduction of terror. Quality of life became a key indicator of success in the Cold War. "Now the peasants and the workers need to live better than before the war, under the bourgeoisie," Soviet minister of trade Anastas Mikoyan declared at a CMEA summit in March 1954. "Now the question of who-whom is decided by whether capitalism or socialism will provide a better life for the working class and peasants."[12] The New Course also entailed relating to the Eastern European regimes more as allies than satellites. "In the future we will create a new kind of relationship," Beria promised the Hungarian leadership in June 1953, "a more responsible and serious relationship." Malenkov added, "The comrades will see; this relationship will be entirely different from that of the past."[13] As a countermeasure to West Germany's entry in NATO, Moscow established the Warsaw Pact in May 1955, which represented the Eastern European countries as sovereign nations and enhanced the Soviet bloc's international prestige as a cohesive unit.

The Soviet welfare empire crystallized in the mid- and late 1950s as part of the New Course. Moscow shifted from a policy of exploitation to subsidization. The Kremlin supplied material aid and accepted trade concessions to promote the construction of socialism in Eastern Europe. The allies enjoyed a trade surplus with Moscow in the overpriced categories of machinery and equipment and ran trade deficits in the subsidized areas of fuel and raw materials.[14] As part of the new initiatives, Khrushchev reinvigorated the CMEA, which had remained largely dormant since its creation. Rather than national self-sufficiency, the CMEA sought to increase trade among the socialist states, embracing an international division of labor in which each country specialized in certain products. This arrangement represented a "curious inversion" of European overseas empires, as Tony Judt describes: the "imperial power" (the Soviet Union) provided the raw materials, and the "colonies" (Eastern Europe) supplied the finished goods.[15] Khrushchev's "Basic Principles of the Social International Division of Labor" provided the framework for international coordination between short- and long-term national planning. The transition coincided with Moscow's optimism about the Soviet economy's prospects in the late 1950s and early 1960s, with Khrushchev boasting that "full communism" was just over the horizon.[16]

In a reversal from the Stalin years, resources now flowed from the Soviet Union to Eastern Europe. Beyond the implicit subsidies in international trade, Moscow also served as a backstop for its allies when they ran into financial trouble with the nonsocialist world. The Soviets helped the Bulgarians weather a debt crisis in the early 1960s by agreeing to defer payments to the Moscow People's Bank and Eurobank as well as paying for some Bulgarian imports with convertible currency, for example, which Sofia then used to service its hard currency debt.[17] "When we want help," Zhivkov commented to Leonid Brezhnev, who succeeded Khrushchev in October 1966, "we turn to you."[18] The obsequious Bulgarian leader fawned over his Soviet counterpart and even repeatedly proposed that Bulgaria join the Soviet Union as the sixteenth republic.[19] While Zhivkov was the most sycophantic, the other Eastern European leaders also "used the most shameless flattery," as the longtime member of the Central Committee's International Department Georgy Shakhnazarov remembered, to receive additional credits and resources from Moscow.[20] Soviet political elites often granted their wishes and overruled bureaucrats who had pressed for an advantage in negotiations with the Eastern Europeans. "So what do you think, Bulgaria established the CMEA?" Soviet deputy chairman of the Council of Ministers Mikhail Lesechko challenged a subordinate. "Of course we should pay to support their economies."[21] Eastern European officials had leverage because their political stability was vital to Soviet national security.[22]

Granting a limited subsidy at first was not a large burden for Moscow, which held seemingly endless supplies of raw materials and an insatiable domestic appetite for finished goods. "Our alliance with Moscow was a guarantee of existence and survival," Zhivkov described in his memoirs. "The USSR was for us an inexhaustible source of raw materials and an endless market for the sale of our products."[23] Exchanging raw materials for finished goods "seemed initially to be a rather painless way to support socialism abroad," Randall W. Stone explains, but the arrangement became increasingly disadvantageous for Moscow over time.[24] The quality of Eastern European products vis-à-vis those of the West worsened while the world market value of Soviet raw materials increased in value. Prices for raw materials were low on the world market during the Golden Age, but skyrocketed during the 1970s. Moscow delivered the raw materials to its allies at a growing opportunity cost and served as a safety valve for Eastern European products that would otherwise not find buyers.

The method that CMEA used to determine prices in international trade (*tsenoobrazovanie*) shaped the implicit subsidy. During much of the 1950s, prices for intrabloc trade were fixed at world market prices at the levels of 1949 and 1950 to protect the CMEA from sudden price changes in the nonsocialist world such as the commodity boom during the Korean War. Over the course of the decade, however, the fixed CMEA and current world market prices diverged considerably, and the socialists believed that they needed to create a more dynamic system that would more accurately approximate the costs of production. If the prices could not provide incentives to export goods, then the CMEA could not deliver an efficient international division of labor. Furthermore, each country determined domestic prices differently, and no country wanted to accept another's system for valuing exports and imports.

Established at the CMEA's Ninth Session in June 1958, the solution was the "Bucharest formula," which fixed prices at world market averages between 1957 and 1958. These remained in force until 1965.[25] Thereafter, the CMEA fixed international trade prices for five years according to the average of world market prices over the previous five years. This formula struck a compromise that drew on world market prices to simulate costs of production, but its five-year average insulated the CMEA from abrupt swings on the world market. It "approximately reflected the real relationship [between prices] and the cost of production of individual goods," an East German report explained.[26] In practice, socialist policymakers did not rigidly adhere to the Bucharest formula, and bilateral negotiations determined prices, but they used it as a guide. Trade was conducted on a barter basis, and prices were denominated in "transferable rubles," a unit of account introduced in January 1964 that technically consisted of 0.987 grams of gold. Each national currency within the CMEA had a fixed exchange rate to the transferable ruble, and the International Bank for Economic Cooperation facilitated international settlements.[27]

The nonconvertibility of Soviet bloc currencies made it necessary to conduct trade with capitalist countries in their currencies, which the CMEA countries could earn with its exports or take out loans. Soviet authorities set the official exchange rate in 1961 at $1.11 per ruble, and the ruble was fixed to a basket of Western currencies after the collapse of the Bretton Woods system. The ruble-dollar rates were merely for bookkeeping, however, because the ruble had no value outside the bloc. After buying goods in convertible (also known as "hard") currency on the world market, the Soviet government would sell them to consumers at the domestic price for the closest Soviet substitute. The domestic Soviet price system was fixed arbitrarily and thus did not optimize foreign trade. The impossible task of trying to make world market prices legible in the socialist bloc was known by its German term: *Preisausgleich* [price equalization].[28]

The CMEA's focus on expanding regional trade in the first half of the Cold War did not preclude engagement with the capitalist world.[29] Particularly in the 1960s, as tensions cooled between the two blocs, East-West trade began to increase. Still, the focus within the CMEA remained on intrabloc trade. Exogenous developments, including the Sino-Soviet split, the growing strength of the European Community, the Coordinating Committee for Multilateral Export Controls (COCOM) trade restrictions, and West Germany's campaign to isolate East Germany reinforced the CMEA's concentration on strengthening regional ties.[30]

While Eastern Europe constituted the core, the Soviet welfare empire had a global reach. Moscow extended massive aid to Beijing, for example, that totaled $3.4 billion between 1946 and 1960, averaging a bit less than 1 percent of Soviet GDP each year. Aid peaked between 1954 and 1959, when the proportion was likely much higher. Soviet experts guided the construction of the new communist country, working closely with their Chinese counterparts to implement the

Soviet model.[31] Khrushchev expanded the Soviet footprint in the Third World as decolonization accelerated.[32] As the relationship between Moscow and Beijing deteriorated in the early 1960s, the Soviet Union used economic aid as a tool to support revolutionary nationalists in the Third World and compete with Beijing for leadership of global socialism.[33] Moscow called aid to the developing countries "solidarity" to eliminate the distinction between donors and recipients.[34]

Few in the developing world wanted to replicate the Soviet model, but elements thereof appealed to postcolonial leaders. It had an attractive combination of modernity, justice, technology, and social progress, and the Soviet Union's rapid industrialization during the 1930s provided a blueprint for independent developing countries that wanted to industrialize quickly.[35] Furthermore, aligning with the Soviet Union opened the CMEA's doors for trade. Mongolia joined the CMEA in 1962, Cuba in 1972, and Vietnam in 1978.[36] In contrast to trade with the Eastern Europeans, trade with developing countries gave Moscow markets for its manufactured goods. Soviet exports to North Vietnam consisted primarily of fuel, chemical products, and machinery, for example, while Hanoi sent "traditional" goods such as clothing, bananas, and coffee.[37]

Moscow sustained its welfare empire because it privileged national security interests over domestic economic imperatives. It helped that the burden during the first two decades was not very large. Michael Marrese and Jan Vanous estimate that the Soviet subsidies to Eastern Europe totaled $11.7 billion during the 1960s.[38] Furthermore, Soviet officials had optimism that Eastern European efficiency would improve, and the subsidies would disappear. Adherents to Marxist-Leninist teleology, they believed that their path would ultimately lead to peace and prosperity. During the Kitchen Debate in July 1959 with US vice president Richard Nixon, Khrushchev acknowledged the achievements of US capitalism but pointed out that the United States had a head start on the Soviet Union, which was making up ground rapidly. He predicted that the socialists would soon overtake the capitalists. He boasted, "As we pass you by, we'll wave 'hi' to you, and then if you want, we'll stop and say, 'please come along behind us.'"[39] In the meantime, it was more cost effective to extend limited subsidies and emergency financial and military assistance to support the fraternal socialist regimes than risk social unrest that could undermine the Warsaw Pact or even spread to the western regions of the USSR itself. The arrangement helped maintain Eastern Europe as a buffer zone of socialist states, and a few extra rubles seemed a tolerable price to pay for the time being.[40]

Soviet socialism proved effective at promoting extensive economic development during the first two decades of the Cold War. World War II had decimated the Eastern European and Soviet economies, and economic growth rates in the Soviet bloc soared as the socialists not only recovered from the war but also industrialized. The socialist countries sent peasants to work in factories, mobilized women into the work force, and directed their material resources to support industrialization. They applied the backlog of proven technologies to make gains in the industrial sector. Industry had been virtually nonexistent in some of the bloc's poorer areas at the end of World War II, but by the late 1960s, it supplied half of total output.[41]

The adoption of Soviet socialism accelerated industrialization but also deformed Eastern Europe. The CMEA assigned agricultural roles to Romania and Bulgaria, hindering their manufacturing base. East Germany and Czechoslovakia focused on industrial goods, but Soviet industrialization did not make sense in countries that had a skilled workforce instead of the endless reserves of unskilled laborers that the Soviet Union had when it industrialized in the 1930s. For example, the industrial Czech regions of Bohemia and Moravia had a higher per capita output than France before World War I and boasted a reputation for quality leather goods, automobiles, weapons, and luxury goods. On the eve of World War II, Czechoslovakia was comparable to Belgium and ahead of Italy and Austria in terms of industrial skill, productivity, living standards, and share of foreign markets. By 1956, however, Czechoslovakia had fallen behind each of them and had become poorer and less productive than it had been just two decades prior.[42] The Soviet Union may have subsidized Eastern European socialism after the late 1950s, but Moscow was also responsible for imposing the inefficient developmental model in Eastern Europe in the first place.

Rapid industrialization yielded success in quantitative, not qualitative, terms, but the task grew more complicated once extensive growth ran out of steam. Reconstruction from the war concluded, and there was no longer a large surplus of unskilled laborers to send to the cities or more resources to invest in the system. Mobilizing idle manpower and materials to industrialize was a lever that socialist regimes could pull a single time. In February 1970, the Soviet embassy in Prague estimated that almost 95 percent of the population in the Czech regions was employed and 90 percent in Slovakia. As more workers approached retirement, Czechoslovakia faced a looming labor shortage. Prague, along with its allies, would have to make the transition to intensive development.[43] "The period of extensive development of production is over, now the main task is to increase the efficiency of social production [*obshchestvennoe proizvodstvo*]," Gosplan chairman Nikolai Baibakov declared in January 1971. "This is the main field of economic competition between the two world systems."[44] The outcome of the struggle between the West and the Soviet bloc depended on which side could make this shift.

The structural incentives of Soviet socialism did not encourage intensive growth.[45] Despite successes in the defense sector, Soviet bloc technology lagged far behind the West, particularly in civilian applications. Bloated military budgets, missiles, weapons, and military equipment could guarantee the Warsaw Pact's security but did little to satisfy the material desires of its people. An Institute of Economics of the World Socialist System (IEMSS) report argued that socialist scientific progress was "insufficient both from the point of view of creating the necessary conditions for a sharp increase in social production, and the elimination of the gap behind the developed capitalist countries in a short period of time."[46] The socialists had to shift their focus from heavy machinery to products that would enhance living standards. Poland may have had impressive rates of growth in the first couple decades, a Polish United Workers Party (PZPR) report acknowledged, but "this rapid growth of the economy had a predominantly extensive character, occurring at excessive social costs."[47] The people had sacrificed so that the country could industrialize, but now they needed to reap the rewards of their work.

The Soviet bloc needed better and cheaper everything, and more of it. Leaders believed that raising living standards depended on the transition to intensive development. They did not mince words about the importance of this task. "The issue of increasing living standards of the workers in socialist countries is fundamental," Zhivkov commented to the Soviet ambassador.[48] The Soviet leadership could always fall back onto the victory in World War II for legitimacy, but the Eastern European socialists had no such basis. The Marxist-Leninists claimed that socialism provided a superior standard of living and more equitable society than exploitative capitalism, but their system had been in a state of crisis since it had been imposed after World War II. In Czechoslovakia, there was a chronic "mismatch between incomes and the quantity and range of goods," the Soviet embassy reported. On the internal market, there existed "continuous tension" with periodic drops in living standards. After reversing the Prague Spring reforms, the new Gustáv Husák regime tried to pacify the Czechoslovak people with higher wages, but the combination of higher wages and diminishing labor productivity placed upward pressure on prices and the cost of living. Because increasing living standards played an essential role in the socialist project, correcting the "inflation gap" was even "more a political issue than an economic one," the Soviet embassy pointed out.[49] Regimes wanted to avoid such unpopular measures as raising prices for goods and services, which made the cost of living more expensive and threatened to undermine socialism's egalitarian philosophy. Such was the case when Bulgaria experimented with price increases for basic foodstuffs in 1968.[50]

Nowhere was the transition to intensive development more important than in East Germany. It stood on the front line of the Cold War across from West Germany, which had become one of the most prosperous countries in the world thanks to its rapid reconstruction and economic growth (the *Wirtschafts-wunder*). East Germany was clearly losing the battle for the hearts and minds to its stronger western neighbor. Before the construction of the Berlin Wall in August 1961, hundreds of thousands of East Germans, particularly skilled workers and educated professionals, fled to West Germany. "In the final analysis, we cannot choose against whom we would like to compete," East German first secretary Walter Ulbricht acknowledged. "We are simply forced to square off against West Germany."[51] Furthermore, the East German regime already lacked political legitimacy, and the memory of the June 1953 uprising loomed large in East German thinking. Ever since then, Schürer explained in his memoirs, "the fear of price increases for basic necessities sat so deeply in the bones of policymakers that nobody made a change."[52] Satiating the impatient East German population proved a difficult challenge.

The masses noticed the disconnect between SED propaganda and daily life. When students asked about it, "the teachers would say, 'Well, this is what we are working towards,'" an East German woman remembered. "It will be sorted out in a few years."[53] On a visit to the Soviet Union in December 1970, East German tourists reported to Soviet officials their discontent. "The opinions and desires of several people in the government are passed off as the opinions and desires of the people," a member of the Union of Free German Youth complained. She noted that East Germans could not visit relatives abroad while West Germans could travel freely. "If our government is afraid that the majority will remain in the FRG [Federal Republic of Germany], then this indicates the preference of the people to live in the other part of Germany," she said. "That means that we have it worse in the GDR." It was incumbent on the government to prove "not in words" but rather by "increasing the quality of life" that socialism was superior. "Under the guise of improving the quality of products, prices are rising again," which causes "dissatisfaction."[54] Shortages of consumer goods created discontent around the country in 1969 and 1970, and SED regional bosses from East Berlin to Dresden reported popular discontent with economic policy.[55] Schürer acknowledged "a fundamental divergence" between the desire to raise the East German standard of living and the lack of the productivity gains to achieve this goal.[56]

In the mid- and late 1960s, a wave of reformers across the bloc tried to adapt the system to make Soviet socialism work better. They granted state enterprises more autonomy and introduced more market mechanisms. Such ideas found expression in programs such as East Germany's New Economic System, the USSR's Kosygin reforms, Hungary's New Economic Mechanism, and Czechoslovakia's Action Program. The reform movement stalled, however, after Czechoslovak policies went too far during the Prague Spring of 1968. Soviet leaders feared that Czechoslovak first secretary Alexander Dubček's political and economic decentralization reforms endangered the monopoly of the communist party, and Warsaw Pact armies (except Romania) crushed the Prague Spring. Thereafter, the Soviets and local conservatives compelled a return to orthodoxy and reestablished central control.[57]

With the Soviet response to the Prague Spring effectively closing the road to reform socialism, the Eastern European regimes instead looked abroad for help making the transition to intensive development. Plans differed by country, but they shared two characteristics. First, they called for taking out loans from Western banks. Increased East-West economic ties became possible because of détente, which opened Western credits, technology, and consumer goods to the socialist bloc at an unprecedented pace. The height of the Cold War, "when the capitalist countries imposed an economic boycott against socialist governments," the Hungarian minister of foreign trade József Bíró commented, seemed to have passed.[58] Bilateral trade conditions with most Western countries "have come close to normal in recent years," director of the IEMSS Oleg Bogomolov observed in July 1971.[59] The Eastern Europeans purchased Western technology and tried to apply it to improve their industries. "The Czechoslovak economy . . . has a pressing need for the modernization of its industries and improvement of its infrastructure," the Soviet ambassador Stepan Chervonenko reported. "Because Czechoslovakia itself cannot manufacture many types of equipment and cannot obtain them from other members of the CMEA, it is forced to turn to the West."[60] Most imports of Western capital goods were low-end technology, however. The export of the most advanced technologies remained *verboten*.[61] East Germany had special access to West Germany because the latter considered inter-German trade as "inter-zonal" rather than "foreign." Bonn extended a "swing credit" that provided interest-free financing to help East Berlin cover imports from its wealthier neighbor.[62]

East-West commercial ties thickened as relations between the blocs improved. The Soviet leadership interpreted détente as indicative of a favorable shift in the global balance of power. The first round of the Strategic Arms Limitation Talks (SALT I) and the Anti-Ballistic Missile (ABM) Treaty indicated the US recognition of strategic parity, which the Soviets had long craved. They believed that arms control would restrain US attempts to recapture its strategic advantages, though they saw no contradiction between their own increased spending on the military and détente.[63] Détente also coincided with a West German initiative, known as *Ostpolitik*, to calm Cold War tensions in Europe. Brandt believed that the confrontational strategy of nonrecognition that his predecessors had implemented had failed. Instead, he pursued a strategy of *Wandel durch Annäherung* ("change through rapprochement") that increased cultural and economic ties with the Soviet bloc countries, especially East Germany. He hoped that closer relations would pave the way for German unification in the future.[64] In the early 1970s, West Germany signed treaties with the Soviet Union, Poland, and East Germany that de facto recognized Eastern European borders, which was also a long-standing Soviet objective.[65] By easing tensions with the West, the Soviets could also focus their attention on the threat emanating from China, with which the Soviet Union had fought a border war in 1969.

Second, the Eastern Europeans planned on importing more inexpensive Soviet raw materials. During the 1950s, most of the CMEA countries had met their energy needs by mobilizing their own reserves. According to Soviet Ministry of Foreign Trade statistics, 85 percent of the growth in CMEA energy supplies was provided by expanding the members' own production. The average share of imported energy was 13 percent in 1960, only slightly exceeding the 10 percent in 1950. In fact, Eastern European countries were net energy exporters, mostly to the Soviet Union at preferential prices, through 1960.[66] With the push for industrialization in the 1960s, the energy requirements changed, and imported fuel became far more important for Eastern Europe. Coal was still king in most CMEA countries (even taking an 84 percent share of total consumption in East Germany and 85 percent in Poland), but Eastern European plans called for expanded reliance on imported oil and natural gas, as well as nuclear energy, in the future. Most would come from the Soviet Union.[67] While coal constituted 60 percent and oil 20 percent of the total CMEA energy mix in 1960, the figures changed to 40.8 percent and 31.8 percent, respectively, by 1973.[68] "Everybody expects that the Soviet Union will provide the necessary raw materials," Zhivkov commented.[69] Soviet officials viewed with alarm the claims that the Eastern Europeans placed on Moscow's resources. Bogomolov warned that Sofia "counted on the almost unlimited support of the Soviet Union." Because the plan was "so closely linked with supplies from the USSR," he feared, "we find ourselves in the eyes of public opinion responsible to a large extent for the success of the Bulgarian plans."[70] IEMSS data showed that raw materials constituted 52 percent and 64 percent of total Soviet exports to the CMEA in 1970 and 1980, respectively.[71]

The East German example illustrates how the prongs of the plan interacted. Ulbricht and the SED economics secretary Günter Mittag pursued a seemingly paradoxical strategy of "overtaking without catching up" (*überholen ohne einzuholen*). They hoped to surpass the West in several important industries such as chemicals, machinery, and electronics. They believed that a "great leap" in high-value exports would increase East German labor productivity to levels that exceeded those in the West and would eventually cause living standards to pull ahead as well. Importantly, this plan depended on the expansion of industries that required huge energy inputs to produce capital goods. Ulbricht believed that if East Germany could import Western technology and combine it with Soviet raw materials and superior socialist labor, the country would surge past the industrial democracies within the decade. In 1969, he boasted that East Germany would sell computers to the West by 1975.[72] The East Germans would develop their own robust industries and would then export to the West to earn hard currency and pay off their debts.

The plan contained significant risks. It called for the socialists to run up their debts to the capitalists, creating a state of dependence on the West for at least a short period. Ulbricht outlined his strategy to the horrified Soviet deputy chairman of the Council of Ministers Nikolai Tikhonov in June 1970, telling him, "We get as much debt with the capitalists, up to the limits of the possible, so that we can pull through in some way. A part of the product from the new plants must then be exported back to where we bought the machines and took on debt. In a short time, we must pay for the equipment. . . . We are, therefore, now correcting the lags from the time of open borders."[73] Some officials worried that the debt would give the capitalists leverage over East Germany if the regime could not turn its plans into reality. The strategy was a serious gamble.

Ulbricht did not get the chance to carry out his scheme. He drew Moscow's ire for his resistance to détente and poor economic performance, and the SED's second secretary Erich Honecker pushed him out office in the spring of 1971 with encouragement from the Kremlin. Honecker reversed the New Economic System initiatives of the previous decade, depriving state enterprises of their limited autonomy. He abandoned Ulbricht's hope of unifying the two German states under the socialist banner for the time being, but he, too, articulated an ambitious program of economic and social development that increased consumer and housing subsidies. Rather than seeking to overtake West Germany in living standards as Ulbricht had advocated, which was unlikely anytime soon, Honecker wanted to promote an East Germany based on socialist values that would provide a compelling alternative to capitalist West Germany. "The people need cheap bread, a dry flat, and a job," said Honecker, who had worked as a roofer before World War II. "If these three things are in order, nothing can happen to socialism."[74]

At this point, East German policymakers believed that the integrity of the regime depended on delivering the promises of socialism immediately, not demanding more sacrifices for the future. At the SED's Eighth Party Congress in

June 1971, East Berlin committed to constructing a consumer society with extensive social programs. Maintaining this "Unity of Economic and Social Policy" would be a calling card for Honecker for the rest of his tenure.[75] He may have recalibrated Ulbricht's objectives and tempered expectations about what socialism could deliver regarding catching up to West Germany, but in terms of reliance on the West and the USSR, it was a distinction without a difference.

Plans to shift toward intensive development drove Eastern Europe to reengage global capitalism after a quarter century of relative isolation. Increasing economic ties with the West did not signal a "reorientation" away from the Soviet bloc, the Soviet embassy in Budapest noted, but rather represented a tactic to "solve urgent problems as soon as possible."[76] The share of CMEA trade with the industrial democracies rose from a quarter to a third between 1970 and 1974.[77] Romania even joined the International Monetary Fund in December 1972 to become eligible for financial support. The United States supported Romania's application because U.S. officials hoped that it would bring Bucharest closer to the West.[78]

As the Eastern European regimes increased commercial ties across the Iron Curtain, they confronted the instability in the Bretton Woods system and the rising cost of commodities on the world market. Politically, the socialists took pleasure in the collapse of the Bretton Woods system and the monetary instability that caused it. They believed that the volatility reflected "the aggravation of the crisis in the imperialist system," as the imperialist powers struggled "for domination and access to raw material sources and commodity markets."[79] The Bucharest formula insulated CMEA trade from the inflationary trends on the world market, at least for the time being. Since the formula calculated prices with a five-year delay, capitalist inflation did not carry into the bloc immediately.

Yet the regimes felt the pain of inflation as East-West trade increased. "Prices demanded by Western countries for their export goods are growing much faster than the revenues we generate for our deliveries to these countries," Stoph sighed.[80] Schürer calculated that the "inflationary development of prices in the capitalist countries" alone added an additional Valuta-Mark (VM) 1 billion (about $400 million) to the East German trade deficit.[81] Although the Soviet Union provided the bulk of Eastern Europe's raw materials, the Eastern Europeans had to "run to the Western market" for additional raw materials, as the Hungarian chairman of the Council of Ministers Jeno Fock put it.[82] East German purchases of commodities from the nonsocialist world cost VM 1.8 billion (about $720 million) in 1972, an increase of more than three times in comparison to prices in 1968.[83]

Inflation aggravated the larger issue that the socialists struggled to find buyers for their products, and they struggled to bring their trade accounts with the nonsocialist world into the black. The socialists had hoped to make the turn to intensive growth within a few years, but early returns did not seem promising. "The problem is not just the debt," the East German State Planning Commission explained, "but also the fact that we do not have exports that can immediately generate hard currency."[84] The development plan depended on East Berlin's ability to earn hard currency to repay its debts. As of 1973, however, attempts "have so far been inadequate."[85]

Concerns began to arise about debt even in Bulgaria, the Eastern European socialist country least integrated into global capitalism. Bulgaria's debt was relatively low, but it had the largest debt service ratio (43 percent in 1971) among CMEA countries relative to exports.[86] The chairman of the State Planning Commission Sava Dulbokov, the minister of finance Dimitar Popov, and the chairman of the Bulgarian National Bank Kiril Zarev sounded the alarm about the growing debts to the capitalists. Sofia needed to implement "significant structural changes in production," they implored the chairman of the Council of Ministers Stanko Todorov. They outlined several steps that the country needed to take, including restricting the supply of equipment imported from the capitalist countries and limiting purchases of licenses. "The main task of state-owned enterprises," the memorandum concluded, "must be to enhance the competitiveness of exports on the international market."[87] Zhivkov wanted to purchase technology from the West and Japan in convertible currency and apply them to Bulgarian industries so that Sofia could export goods back to the nonsocialist world to repay the debt. Zarev confided in Soviet officials that "the only thing that calmed" him was that Sofia lacked the funds to carry out Zhivkov's plans. It was also unlikely that the West would sell its "most recent achievements in science and technology." The strategy was "totally unrealistic," Zarev concluded.[88]

The growing debts placed the socialist economies in a precarious position. The danger of growing imports from the nonsocialist world preoccupied Bulgarian economic officials. "The difficulties of covering our deficits in the balance of payments in capitalist currency are high," the Bulgarian State Planning Commission relayed to Zhivkov in April 1971. "We can cope with these difficulties only if the entire government pulls in one direction: pursuing a decisive curtailment of imports from the capitalist countries, increasing exports to these countries, [and] strict control over distribution and most economical use of the raw materials and other products."[89] In its estimates for 1972, the East German State Planning Commission determined that as much as one-third of industrial production could not proceed without imports from the nonsocialist world. For the most advanced industries the dependence on imports was even higher.[90] Developing a solution to the growing dependence on the capitalist world would not be easy. "The problems of foreign trade are not just problems of foreign trade but rather problems of the entire domestic economy," Schürer reminded the Council of Ministers in March 1973. Should East Germany reach its ambitious targets of increasing exports to the nonsocialist world by 20 to 30 percent and decreasing imports by 15 percent, "stable supply" of the domestic economy could not be continued. The country had "extraordinarily large problems," and he brought this issue to the attention of his colleagues "with the utmost urgency."[91]

Reducing imports proved easier to accomplish on paper than in reality. Officials established ambitious export targets but failed to meet them. Socialist policymakers also refused to suppress consumption to reduce the trade deficit. The issue in Hungary, the Soviet Foreign Ministry reported, was simply that the country "consumes more than it produces."[92] Polish labor unrest in December 1970 after a sudden price hike forced Władysław Gomułka's resignation, as if the bloc needed yet another reminder about the link between regime stability and living standards. Werner Krolikowski, the Central Committee's economics secretary, warned Honecker that East Germany risked bankruptcy if it continued down the path. Honecker replied, "Fine, so what?" Krolikowski responded that building socialism on the foundation of loans from the West would cause the GDR to become an "exploitative object" of the West. Honecker stood up, declared that setting policy was his prerogative, and accused Krolikowski of inciting panic.[93] Honecker marginalized Krolikowski thereafter and ensured that discussion of the debt did not take place at Politburo meetings.[94] Political considerations persuaded Honecker to ignore the early warnings about debt.

As debt began to climb in the early 1970s, Eastern Europe's demand for cheap Soviet raw materials caused conflict with Moscow. The CMEA had adopted the Bucharest formula to simulate production costs while insulating the Soviet bloc from instability on the capitalist market. CMEA prices privileged manufactured goods at the expense of raw materials, just as in the nonsocialist world, and by the late 1960s, the Soviets had grown concerned that the Bucharest formula undervalued their raw materials. An IEMSS study in July 1970 calculated that the capital intensity of Soviet exports of raw materials was 3 to 3.5 times higher than for the machinery received from the other CMEA countries. "The financial burden that the Soviet Union bears in the export of raw materials is several times greater than the costs of its partners for the import of raw materials," the IEMSS concluded.[95]

Production costs increased as the center of oil production shifted to the harsh climate and terrain of western Siberia. Although Soviet oil production took years to recover from the shock of World War II (the Soviet Union was a net oil importer until 1954), it grew from just under 3 million barrels per day (bpd) in 1960 to nearly 8.5 million bpd in 1973.[96] Yet production in the southern Caucasus and the Volga-Ural regions decreased in the first half of the 1970s much faster than officials had anticipated, and the Ministry of Oil Industry neglected to develop the enormous reserves in western Siberia. Soviet geologists first discovered oil reserves there in 1953, but institutional inertia and the logistical challenges of moving the production infrastructure away from consumers in the European regions of the USSR meant development in western Siberia lagged. By the mid-1970s, more than two-thirds of new reserves that Soviet geologists identified were in western Siberia, but only about 15 percent of the investment in the countrywide drilling effort to extract oil went to projects in the region.[97]

The isolation of western Siberia meant that the Soviets had to develop infrastructure from scratch. The underpopulation of the Soviet interior presented a chronic problem, and Moscow had little success using material incentives to convince migrants to relocate. The summers were unbearably hot and humid. Operating conditions in Tyumen during the winter posed the opposite problem: severe cold burst pipes and caused other accidents.[98] The earth froze even at depths of three hundred to five hundred meters, posing significant challenges for surveys and pipeline construction. A Soviet oil industry journal, *Neftianik*, commented that the exploitation of Siberian reserves was "comparable to the complexities of space research."[99]

Despite the impressive growth in Soviet oil production, it could not satisfy Soviet domestic and international objectives. "Problem number one," Baibakov remarked in December 1972, "was securing the necessary fuel and energy to supply the rising demand."[100] Oil exports were Moscow's primary source of hard currency earnings, and deliveries to the industrial democracies jumped from 320,000 bpd to 960,000 bpd between 1960 and 1973. Soviet oil exports to the CMEA countries (except Romania, which produced most of its own oil) climbed even higher, from 185,000 bpd to 1.1 million bpd during the same period.[101] Still, Soviet exports could not meet the CMEA's full need, and the Soviets encouraged the Eastern Europeans to seek the balance of their requirements on the world market.[102] The Soviet Union "could not cover the oil deficit without the participation of fraternal countries in the development of oil in third countries," Baibakov told his Hungarian counterpart Imre Padri.[103] Eastern European countries began to collaborate in several long-term energy development projects in friendly Arab countries as a means of diversifying their energy sources.

They also concluded agreements with major Western companies such as British Petroleum, Shell, and ENI.[104] By 1973, the Eastern European countries (minus Romania) imported between 8 percent and 20 percent of their oil from the nonsocialist world.[105]

Similar challenges confronted the Soviets regarding natural gas production. In addition to working in the unforgiving regions of western Siberia, Moscow faced the difficult task of transporting gas over thousands of kilometers to consumers and distributors far to the west, traversing rugged terrain. "The relocation of gas production centers to the harsh climatic and mining-geological regions, which are located at a considerable distance from the main gas-consuming systems, hinders the growth rates of gas production to a considerable extent," Minister of Gas Industry Sabit A. Orudzhev reported.[106] Soviet planners saw cooperation with Western Europe as means to develop the vital but remote natural gas reserves in western Siberia. They signed a pathbreaking agreement with Austrian companies and banks in June 1968 for the delivery of Soviet natural gas and the construction of a pipeline. Agreements with the French, Italians, and West Germans soon followed.[107] Natural gas exports to Eastern Europe remained low in the early 1970s, with only Czechoslovakia and Poland importing small quantities.[108]

The growing production costs weighed on the Soviet Union. "The incoming data again and again confirm the need to improve the organization of foreign economic relations," the head of the CPSU's Central Committee department on relations with the socialist countries Konstantin Rusakov stressed in October 1970. The development of foreign trade "lags far behind the opportunities arising from the economic potential of the USSR" and did not sufficiently increase Soviet "political influence." The Soviet share of world trade totaled only 4 percent, placing it at the level of countries such as Canada and the Netherlands. Within the CMEA, the Soviets exported "low currency efficiency" raw materials: on average, Moscow received sixty-five kopeks per ruble spent on production, with 12 percent of exports yielding below forty kopeks per ruble. In return, Moscow imported goods "that do not meet the requirements of advanced world standards."[109]

The Kremlin needed to recalibrate the relationship between domestic and CMEA prices to promote greater efficiency and profitability. Rusakov advocated more cooperation between the state organs responsible for foreign trade and the state enterprises that produced the goods. State enterprises received a fixed price for their goods sold in foreign markets, meaning that Moscow did not have "sufficiently effective levers to expand exports of the more profitable goods" and do the opposite for unprofitable goods. Furthermore, selling imported goods from the nonsocialist world on the domestic market set at prices for similar Soviet products was "divorced from the cost of obtaining foreign currency to make the purchase" and stimulated greater demand for imported goods. Unlike other sectors of the economy, foreign trade "remained almost unaffected" by measures to increase incentives meant to expand the "initiative and independence of enterprises." This system had formed during the 1930s, when Stalin had focused on self-sufficiency as part of a global turn to autarky. The strategy may have worked then, Rusakov observed, but "does not correspond to the changed conditions."[110]

As production costs grew, world market prices increased much faster than CMEA contractual prices. According to an IEMSS study that used 1960 as a baseline (100), the index of CMEA prices increased only slightly from 1966 (73) to 1972 (78). The index for wholesale prices (*optovaia tsena*) during the same time frame, however, jumped from 117 to 283.[111] As oil nationalists in the developing world began to seize power from the multinational oil companies and increased the posted prices in the early 1970s, oil prices finally began to rise on the world market. The opportunity cost of selling cheap oil to the CMEA rather than the capitalists widened.

Moscow was not the only one to express dissatisfaction with prices. Agricultural producers had similar grievances. "Given the current level of foreign trade prices, it is economically profitable to be importers rather than exporters of agricultural goods," a CMEA report noted. As a result, food prices "do not stimulate the mutual division of labor." Resources in countries such as Bulgaria and Mongolia were "underutilized," and low prices provided incentives to sell food to the nonsocialist world instead and to focus on industrial development.[112] The Romanians balked at a system that locked them into a role of providing their industrial northern neighbors with agricultural goods and elected to expand trade with the nonsocialist world instead.[113] Zhivkov advocated for higher prices in the agricultural sector in the CMEA and approached Brezhnev for help, but the Soviet general secretary demurred, commenting that it would not be "convenient" for Moscow to raise the issue and that it "must be decided by the CMEA."[114] Zhivkov kept pressing. Agriculture "requires more capital investment," and the low prices "do not stimulate production for exports," he complained to the Soviet ambassador. Industrial socialist states took advantage of the pricing imbalance between agricultural and manufactured products. Zhivkov argued that the industrialized CMEA countries such as East Germany exploited Bulgaria by importing cheap Bulgarian agricultural goods and selling them on their own internal market for "a large profit."[115]

The pricing formula placed agricultural exporters at a disadvantage. Agricultural products constituted almost half of Bulgarian exports, for example, and Sofia received between 40 and 60 percent of wholesale costs in payment from the CMEA countries. As agricultural prices rose on the world market, the Bulgarian opportunity cost of exporting to the socialist world grew as well. "We can no longer stand it," Zhivkov complained to Brezhnev during a September 1973 meeting in Voden. He wanted an adjustment that would eliminate what his government calculated to be the 1 billion leva subsidy that Sofia provided to the CMEA countries. If the other states refused to consider higher prices yet demanded more food, Zhivkov complained that Bulgarian development would stagnate. "Bulgaria cannot exist if the current situation continues," he stressed. "The Soviet Union will have to absorb our losses and save us." In contrast to his deflection in the mid-1960s, Brezhnev agreed that CMEA prices needed to change. "I have to say," Brezhnev assured Zhivkov, "that we are ready" to discuss prices. He relayed that the Central Committee already had assigned teams to study the issue.[116]

The push by agricultural and raw material exporters brought them into conflict with the importers. During negotiations about the upcoming five-year plan in the summer of 1970, the Soviets proposed adapting the mechanism to account for the rising prices of raw materials, but every Eastern European country except Poland (which wanted to capitalize on its large coal deposits) opposed the proposal.[117] The Bucharest formula created winners and losers, and Soviet planners concluded that the Soviet Union fell into the latter category.

Moscow also tried to make increases in raw material deliveries contingent on participation in resource development in the Soviet Union. The Soviets promoted the Comprehensive Program in the CMEA, which was conceived to accelerate socialist integration. Established in January 1971, the International Investment Bank (IIB) provided the financial conduit for the Comprehensive Program and extended loans to member countries for investment programs.[118] Moscow hoped that the Comprehensive Program would reduce the burden of extracting capital-intensive resources in remote regions of the Soviet Union. The CMEA operated under an "interested party" principle, meaning that each country had the right to opt out of a project. The organization approved nine projects after 1972, eight of which involved the development of Soviet raw materials.[119] The Soviet Union received commitments to assist in these projects on a bilateral basis as well. Czechoslovakia and East Germany, for example, decided to participate in the production of Soviet oil and natural gas; Poland and Hungary offered to help extend the Druzhba pipeline, which was built in the late 1950s and early 1960s and transported Soviet oil to Eastern Europe; Bulgaria contributed to natural gas, wood, pulp, and ferrous metals; and Romania participated in the development of iron ore.[120]

Despite the rhetoric of integration, CMEA trade remained along bilateral lines. Attempts to accelerate bloc integration were not streamlined and appeared like "separate islands in a large ocean," as one Hungarian official described it.[121] The allies preferred alternative arrangements that did not involve unilateral assistance to Moscow. The East German State Planning Commission, for example, believed that investment in the Soviet Union "cannot be the only way to secure an increased supply of raw materials." The increase in Soviet deliveries should be offset instead by corresponding deliveries of East German goods such as chemical products as well as reciprocal Soviet investment in East German industries.[122] Hungarian experts estimated that Budapest would need to allocate an addition 2.5 billion rubles if it were to participate in the development of Soviet raw materials that the country would receive until 1980. "The Hungarian national economy cannot withstand such a load," Padri told Baibakov.[123]

The Soviets also resented that they traded their raw materials for goods that fell short of world market standards. This was a systemic problem that hurt everybody, and if solved, it could diminish the emerging reliance on Western imports. The socialists needed to approach each other "without concessions," Baibakov told Padri, "supplying and accepting only those products that meet or exceed world standards." If the quality of goods increased, then the CMEA members could forgo the "large frequent purchases on the capitalist market."[124] Moscow hoped that it could recalibrate the CMEA so that the socialist bloc could realize its lofty expectations.

The CMEA international division of labor caused living standards to converge across the Soviet bloc during the first two decades of its existence. According to Gosplan's calculations in 1971, the living standards index of Czechoslovakia and East Germany surpassed that of the Soviet Union by almost 50 percent, but the report did not find that gap "significant," particularly considering Czechoslovakia's lead had been 109 percent in 1950. The Soviet Union lagged only slightly behind Bulgaria, Hungary, and Poland, with Romania marginally behind. Mongolia trailed by a large margin.[125]

The Gosplan report contained a warning, however. It claimed that extending aid to allies "cannot be justified by the need to bring their economies to the Soviet level." Of the seven European members of the CMEA (inclusive of the USSR), the Soviet Union ranked sixth, and it had held that position since the CMEA's creation. "Any unilateral assistance from the USSR to other countries in the socialist commonwealth [aside from Romania and Mongolia] . . . increases the gap between our country and these countries in terms of living standards."[126] Granting credits and providing additional resources to Eastern Europe, in other words, meant depriving Soviet citizens.

The Soviet welfare empire showed signs of stress in the early 1970s. The postwar growth model yielded diminishing returns, and the changing international political economy placed greater strains on Soviet resources. "The burden of fueling a decent standard of living in our allied countries grew heavier for the Soviet people," recalled Anatoly Chernyaev, a longtime official in the Central Committee of the CPSU's International Department. "The connection of economic development of these countries to the Soviet market and the Soviet model of industrial development caused increasing dissatisfaction."[127] Soviet resentment about the material burden that it carried to support Eastern Europe heightened in the early 1970s. Nothing challenged Soviet tolerance more than the global oil crisis of 1973.

CHAPTER 3

The West and the Oil Shock

The quadrupling of oil prices in the fall of 1973 signaled the formal end of the Golden Age. The oil shock fanned inflation, increased unemployment, triggered a sharp recession, created chaos in the international monetary system, and precipitated an enormous transfer of wealth to oil producers in the developing world. The oil shock had the potential, in the words of British foreign secretary Alec Douglas-Home, to "bring down the economies of all or most of the developed countries."[1] Fears pervaded that the sun had set on postwar prosperity.

The oil crisis also struck a major artery of the US welfare empire. During the postwar period, the United States had overseen an international regime that supplied inexpensive oil from the developing world to the industrial democracies, but the oil shock brought the order crashing down. It upended the industrial economies, threatened to divide the allies, and cast doubt on US leadership. "The stakes involved go beyond oil prices and economics, and involve the whole framework of future political relations," Kissinger explained. The oil crisis damaged "the unity and strength of our countries that have been the basis for our resilience to the threats from Soviet power through the years." Social and economic upheaval could reduce public support for liberal parties in the industrial democracies, which would become subjected "to influence from radical left- and right-wing political forces," he warned.[2] The Soviet Union had not caused the oil crisis, but Kissinger feared that the Kremlin would exploit the consequences.[3]

With the Bretton Woods system and the US-led international oil regime each collapsing in 1973, the US welfare empire was in transition. Washington adapted its tactics in the mid-1970s to sustain its community of nations. In contrast to the confrontational approach that the Nixon administration had taken with US allies during the early 1970s, the political and economic consequences of the oil shock persuaded US officials to emphasize multilateral coordination to maintain Western unity. Especially after a changing of the guard in the Western leadership during 1974, the industrial democracies rallied around initiatives such as consumer solidarity and economic summitry to manage shared problems. Even in the backdrop of worsening stagflation, the mid-1970s marked a high point for Western cooperation.

Within that multilateral framework, US officials competed with their international counterparts to shape the contours of the post–Bretton Woods global economy. Reflecting the beginning of an intellectual shift in economic ideology as well as responding to conditions in the global economy, they advocated market-based solutions to manage the economic upheaval. Rather than seek to restore the Bretton Woods system's compromises between domestic autonomy and international openness, US officials believed that their country's interests aligned with the advancement of economic globalization, a process that contemporaries of the 1970s called "economic interdependence."[4]

The United States produced about two-thirds of the world's oil in 1945, but US policymakers understood that they still had significant interests in overseas oil after World War II ended.[5] Supplying Western Europe and Japan with oil from the developing world—and denying the Soviet Union access to those reserves—was a core US strategic objective. Oil from the Western Hemisphere had supplied much of the Allies' needs during the war, but the Truman administration did not want to deplete those supplies further; the United States would need them itself in the event of another global conflict. Instead, oil from the Middle East supported Western European and Japanese reconstruction. Ten percent of Marshall Plan dollars, for example, financed imports of Middle Eastern oil from US companies.[6]

The United States adopted a corporatist approach regarding oil to achieve its strategic objectives. Five of the seven largest oil companies, called the Seven Sisters, were US companies: Standard Oil of California, New Jersey, and New York; Texaco; and Gulf. Anglo-Iranian Oil Company (renamed British Petroleum in 1954) and Royal Dutch Shell rounded out the group. By the early 1950s, the Seven Sisters controlled over 90 percent of oil reserves outside of the United States, Mexico, and the centrally planned economies.[7] The companies set prices and owned the developmental infrastructure, and they generally split half of the

profits with the producer governments. As Washington relied on the oil companies to keep cheap oil flowing to the West, US officials also supported friendly
authoritarian producers such as Saudi Arabia and Iran to thwart oil nationalism
and prevent communist encroachment. Producer governments founded the
Organization of the Petroleum Exporting Countries (OPEC) in September 1960,
but it initially had little power because of a global oil glut during the 1960s, and
political, cultural, and geopolitical differences divided the members.[8]

The energy complement to the Bretton Woods system, the US-led international oil regime helped fuel economic growth across the West during the
Golden Age. Industries relied on cheap raw materials, and a barrel of oil cost
$1.90 in 1947 and $1.80 in 1970.[9] Prices stayed so low that the Eisenhower administration set an oil import quota in 1959 to protect domestic producers from being undercut by cheap imports.[10] Oil powered factories, played an increasing role
in generating electricity and heat, and improved the efficiency of agricultural
production. Western economies also depended on transportation infrastructure
that needed fuel to function. Powered by gasoline, tens of thousands of new cars
hit the road in Western Europe, and the number of motor vehicles in the United
States jumped from 49 million vehicles in 1949 to 119 million in 1972.[11]

The availability of inexpensive oil encouraged an energy transition in the
West. In 1955, coal supplied 75 percent of energy consumption in Western
Europe, but the proportion fell to 23 percent by 1972. The share of oil, con-
versely, rose from 22 percent to 60 percent over the same period.[12] Between 1949
and 1972, consumption jumped in Western Europe from 970,000 to 14.1 million
barrels per day (bpd), and in Japan from 32,000 to 4.4 million bpd. This comported with global trends: world oil demand increased more than five and a half
times between 1949 and 1972.[13]

The international oil regime began to unravel in the early 1970s. A key cause
was the skyrocketing demand in the industrial democracies: OECD oil consumption jumped from 23.2 million bpd in 1965 to 41.5 million bpd in 1973.[14]
Even production in the United States, the world's largest oil producer, could
no longer keep pace with domestic demand. US crude production peaked at
9.6 million bpd in 1970, but demand spiked to 10.9 million bpd and rose for the
rest of the decade.[15] "America's spare capacity had proven to be the single most
important element in the energy security margin of the Western World, not
only in every postwar energy crisis but also in World War II," Daniel Yergin
writes. "And now that margin was gone."[16] The United States turned to foreign supplies. Nixon abolished the quota system in 1973, and imports jumped
from 3.4 million bpd (23.2 percent of total supply) in 1970 to 6.3 million bpd
(36.3 percent of total supply) in 1973. At this point, most of the US imports came
from Canada and Venezuela.[17]

The spike in Western demand coincided with a shift in the global oil map. The Eastern Hemisphere, for the first time ever, produced more oil than the Western Hemisphere in 1963. Ten years later, the Eastern Hemisphere's share of global production surpassed 70 percent, with Middle Eastern and African producers accounting for most of the gains.[18]

OPEC countries also asserted their sovereign rights.[19] The Libyan Revolution in September 1969 was the catalyst. Many Western European countries had turned to Libya as a "short-haul" supplier to evade high transportation costs after Egypt had closed the Suez Canal during the Six-Day War in June 1967. They considered Libya's oil secure because of its conservative monarch and decentralized oil market, but Colonel Muammar Qaddafi's seizure of power transformed the landscape. He insisted on renegotiating the revenue-sharing agreements, and the closure of the Trans-Arabian Pipeline in May 1970 and a tight tanker market strengthened his hand in negotiations with Western oil companies. The dam broke when the small US company Occidental Petroleum signed a landmark agreement in September 1970 for a price hike of thirty cents. The deal also ushered in a new industry standard tax rate of 55 percent.[20]

Libya's success "precipitated [a] flurry of OPEC activity towards the end of 1970" and opened the floodgates for producer governments to demand a greater share of profits and control over their oil industries.[21] In February 1971, the six Persian Gulf members of OPEC and representatives of thirteen companies agreed to increase the posted price of crude by thirty-five cents and adopted the 55 percent tax rate. Two months later, the Tripoli agreement raised the price of crude from Mediterranean producers by ninety cents. Some such as Algeria and Iraq nationalized their oil industries, while others such as Saudi Arabia and Iran insisted on participation agreements that gave them joint ownership with the companies.[22] The collapse of the Bretton Woods system also placed upward pressure on prices; oil was mainly priced and purchased in dollars, which depreciated in the early 1970s. Crude oil prices jumped from $1.80 in 1970 to $3.29 in 1973.[23] An April 1973 article in *Foreign Affairs* captured the changing landscape: "The Oil Crisis: This Time the Wolf Is Here."[24]

The erosion of the US-led international oil regime created friction in the transatlantic alliance over strategy in the Middle East. While the United States remained a staunch ally of Israel, the Western Europeans began to gravitate toward the Arab side after the Six-Day War in June 1967 because of their dependence on oil imports. The outbreak of the Yom Kippur War in October 1973 revealed the new fault lines. The war had regional origins, but the Nixon administration viewed it as a Cold War conflict. "A victory by states perceived to be radical and armed by the Soviet Union would have had a disastrous impact on the US position in the Middle East and globally," Kissinger explained.[25] When Moscow launched an airlift to resupply Syria and Egypt, Washington responded in kind, initiating Operation Nickel Grass to provide a $2.2 billion military assistance package to Israel. Most of the Western Europeans, in contrast, viewed the war through an oil lens, declared neutrality after the war erupted, and called for a ceasefire. "The European view is that relations with the Russians are not automatically at stake in the Middle East," British ambassador Cromer reflected. Consequently, "it is right that we should act to safeguard our own interests."[26] With Arab producers supplying around two-thirds of Western European imports, an Arab embargo would cripple the Western European economy within an estimated sixty days.[27]

The war coincided with price negotiations between representatives of the oil companies and OPEC during mid-October 1973 in Vienna, meetings that had been on the calendar for weeks. Hurting from dollar depreciation and emboldened by recent gains, OPEC demanded a 100 percent increase in posted prices. When the companies refused to accept an increase of more than 15 percent, the meeting adjourned without an agreement. OPEC representatives reconvened in Kuwait City, where they announced an increase in the price of oil by 70 percent, bringing it to $5.11 a barrel.[28] For the first time, OPEC bypassed the oil companies and set the posted price unilaterally. It was an historic moment.

The Arab members of OPEC (OAPEC) also wielded the "oil weapon" against countries that supported Israel during the Yom Kippur War. They imposed an embargo against the United States and the Netherlands, then extended it to Portugal, South Africa, and Rhodesia. Additionally, they announced monthly production cuts of 5 percent until Israel withdrew from the territories that it had occupied since June 1967 and restored the "legal rights" of the Palestinians.[29] The embargo of the Netherlands allowed OAPEC to accomplish two objectives at once: it punished The Hague for opposing the Arabs in the "fight against imperialism and Zionism" and disrupted Western Europe's oil supply without having to embargo each EC country.[30] The port of Rotterdam received 3.8 million bpd and served as the regional hub for refinement and distribution in northwest Europe. Only about a fifth was consumed at home—the rest was either reexported as crude or refined and then sent abroad. In sum, oil passing through Rotterdam represented about one-third of total EC consumption.[31] Although Dutch foreign minister Max van der Stoel conceded that his country's sympathy for Israel "could not be denied," he speculated that the Netherlands had been made a "scapegoat" because of its "special role" in Western Europe's supply chain. Oil imports could plummet by as much as two-thirds, Prime Minister Joop den Uyl worried. "This would be an economic catastrophe."[32]

The rest of the Western European countries clung to their declarations of neutrality, hoping to avoid becoming the next country to come under an embargo. Most NATO members refused to participate in the US resupply mission to Israel and denied permission to use their airspace. "Nobody would give us landing rights on their territory," Kissinger grumbled to his staff. "And this in a matter which at that point was entirely Soviet-U.S. as far as we were concerned."[33] With officials from Arab nations explicitly threatening additional embargoes, the European Community issued a statement in early November 1973 that called for Israel to withdraw from the occupied territories. It hoped that the declaration would curry favor with the producers as well as lift the embargo against the Netherlands.[34] The Nixon administration offered to send oil to the Netherlands, but the Dutch government declined because the Arabs had singled out the Netherlands, and by offering special assistance, "the U.S. was in fact doing the same thing," a Dutch Foreign Ministry report warned. "We would then be in an isolated, vulnerable position, with a degree of uncertainty and pressure to which our people are mentally unaccustomed."[35]

Although the Arab embargo created a supply disruption, it did not cause the long-term crisis. Oil from Arab countries supplied less than 20 percent of US imports, and domestic production still covered nearly two-thirds of US demand.[36] Oil companies circumvented the embargo against the Netherlands, and Dutch stocks began to replenish by January 1974. "The embargo became quite useless," Dutch minister of Economic Affairs Ruud Lubbers later reflected.[37] A consequence of Kissinger's "shuttle diplomacy" in the Middle East and leveraging the US relationship with Saudi Arabia, the Arab oil ministers ended the embargo against the United States in March 1974, even though Israel had withdrawn from just a small part of the Sinai Peninsula. The embargo against the Netherlands dragged on for another few months. While the production cuts eliminated about 5 million bpd in late 1973, the Arab countries also backed off their threat to reduce production until Israeli forces withdrew from the occupied territories. Saudi production, for example, returned to September 1973 levels by April 1974.[38]

OPEC's price increases persisted, however. In late December 1973, the OPEC ministers raised oil prices again to $11.65 per barrel, nearly a fourfold increase since September 1973, and prices climbed slowly during the mid-1970s. Higher energy prices pummeled the global economy, and for the first time in the postwar period the industrial democracies experienced a collective decline in production. After reaching 6 percent in 1973, real GNP growth stagnated in 1974 and contracted 1 percent in 1975.[39] Inflation (GDP deflator) across the OECD area averaged 16.4 percent and 14.5 percent during the same period, with oil prices accounting for a quarter of the increase.[40] After posting a collective

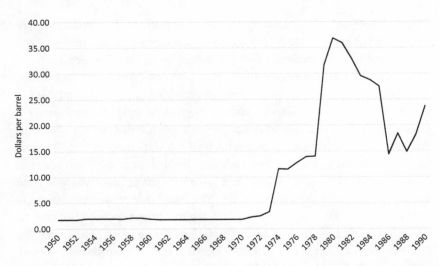

FIGURE 3.1. Crude oil prices, 1950–1990. Source: *BP Statistical Review of World Energy 2022*.

$2.5 billion surplus on current account in 1973, the OECD countries ran a deficit of $36.25 billion in 1974.[41]

The oil crisis tore at the fabric of US society and politics. With early signs of shortages appearing in the summer of 1973, oil companies rationed sales for the first time since World War II. Facing domestic pressure for government intervention, the Nixon administration announced a two-tiered system of price controls in August 1973.[42] Long lines became grim realities after the crisis erupted in the fall of 1973, as were "Sorry, No Gas Today" signs. Motorists rushed to the gas stations long before they opened, hoping to beat the long lines. The crisis "changed my whole life," a southern Californian complained. "I don't even want to go out at night if it means burning a lot of gas." She arrived two hours before her Venice gas station opened in the morning, killing time by doing paperwork while others joined the line and then left their vehicles to search for breakfast.[43] Truckers shut down US highways in a series of strikes in February 1974, protesting rising fuel costs, reduced speed limits, and low hauling rates. Strikers slashed tires, littered highways with nails, and shot or beat fellow drivers who continued their routes. Governors of several states deployed the National Guard to patrol for violent protesters, and five counties in West Virginia even declared martial law.[44]

Already discredited by the Watergate scandal and the Vietnam War, the oil crisis weakened Nixon's political prospects. John A. Love, Nixon's first director of the Office of Energy Policy, warned the president in November 1973 that regardless of how Washington reacted, "considerable public fear and indignation, cries of industry conspiracy and government ineptitude, and possibly real hardships, appear imminent."[45] Nixon came under fire for mismanaging the oil crisis or, worse, for acting in cahoots with greedy oil barons. A December 1973 Gallup poll found that just 6 percent of the US public held the Arab oil producers responsible for the crisis. The oil companies and the US government, in contrast, received 25 percent and 23 percent of the blame, respectively.[46]

The same "panic at the pump" that the United States experienced did not occur in Western Europe and Japan, but Nixon's international peers also found themselves in precarious political positions. Heath's energy conservation initiatives aggravated his already contentious relations with the Trades Union Congress (TUC), and his government toppled in February 1974. Labour Party leader Harold Wilson replaced him and believed that he had to please organized labor to stay in power. Elsewhere, governments "in Italy, the Netherlands, Belgium and Denmark live from day to day," Widman commented. Pompidou confronted "a dangerous build-up of internal pressure," and even Brandt faced criticism for rising unemployment and inflation. "In none of our major allied nations do we find Prime Ministers with the political strength to be able to take the actions likely to be needed to cope effectively with 1974's economic challenges."[47]

The industrial democracies could do little in the short term to mitigate their dependence on imported oil. Lowered speed limits, rationed supplies, driving restrictions, and shortened work weeks only had an impact at the margins. Nixon launched Project Independence in November 1973, which called for the United States to become energy self-sufficient by 1980 by investing in alternative energy sources, reducing oil consumption, and accelerating the development of domestic oil reserves. Yet US officials understood that self-sufficiency was likely unrealistic. Furthermore, it would do little to neutralize the "irreversible dependence of our industrialized allies," NSC staffer Robert Hormats noted in July 1976. "Energy independence" may serve "useful" as a "rhetorical goal," he concluded, but "it is neither an attainable objective nor a basket in which we should put many of our eggs."[48] Dependence on OPEC, at least over the medium term, seemed inevitable. The international oil order, which had fueled the US welfare empire for a generation, was in shambles.

The oil shock compounded the existing tensions in US alliances. US officials fumed that the Western Europeans had refused to participate in the resupply of Israel and failed to appreciate the Cold War stakes of the war. "When I look at the European behavior in this crisis, I ask myself what in God's name is this alliance," Kissinger complained. "They assert the indivisibility of our interest in defense and in every other respect conduct themselves as neutrals." The British and French gave him nearly as much trouble as the Soviets, he claimed.[49]

Secretary of Defense James Schlesinger asked Cromer whether submitting to Arab "blackmail" would "not have made the first Lord Cromer turn in his grave?"[50] For their part, policymakers on the other side of the Atlantic resented "the harsh and unjustified criticism," as Cromer put it, from the Nixon administration.[51] The French characterized the US request to participate in an operation outside of NATO's borders as the "arrogant assumption that it was U.S. role to decide the right course of action and allies' role to follow orders."[52]

The Nixon administration did not forgive the allies for their perceived betrayal but reoriented toward mending transatlantic fences at the end of 1973. While Kissinger had no expertise in economics ("When people tell me we are consuming six million barrels a day, they might just as well say fifty thousand Coke bottles worth of oil," he quipped), he understood that the oil crisis threatened core strategic objectives.[53] Preserving US national security required healthy US allies and propitious conditions in the global economy, but the desperate scramble for oil supplies would create debilitating competition among the capitalist countries. As the Western Europeans and Japanese signed bilateral deals with producer governments in the winter of 1973–74, the specter of beggar-thy-neighbor policies and a closed trading environment that resembled the 1930s emerged.

Yet amid the crisis, Kissinger also saw an opportunity to reassert US leadership by rallying the industrial democracies around consumer solidarity.[54] The oil shock threatened the international architecture of the Atlantic community that had been in place since the end of World War II, he declared at London's Pilgrim Society in December 1973. It presented "a challenge which the United States could solve alone with great difficulty and that Europe cannot solve in isolation at all." Therefore, he argued, "we strongly prefer, and Europe requires, a common enterprise." He proposed the creation of an energy action group to reorient the industrial democracies around a common purpose as well as increase the bargaining power of the consumers.[55]

Despite its growing reliance on imported oil, the United States still had significant geological, economic, political, and technological advantages that would allow it to weather the oil crisis more easily than its allies, except perhaps Canada, which was a major producer itself. Kissinger sought to leverage those assets. His proposal of consumer cooperation offered the carrot of allowing the other industrial democracies to benefit from US strengths. The implicit stick was that if they refused, they would be outmatched and "eaten up by the American wolf," as a French official had characterized it, in the race to secure supplies.[56]

Japan signed on, but Western Europe proved a more difficult sell. Most Western European policymakers supported consumer cooperation in principle. The United States was better equipped to handle the oil crisis, West German Ministry of Economics state secretary Detlev Rohwedder acknowledged, and "the Community cannot afford . . . to turn away this outstretched hand."[57] Western European officials worried, however, that Washington wanted to confront the producers, a charge that Kissinger denied publicly but conceded privately.[58] Although the United States had the resources to play hardball with OPEC, the Western Europeans did not. The Western Europeans were "entirely dependent upon [the Arab producers]," Pompidou commented to Kissinger. "We can't afford the luxury of three or four years of worry and misery waiting for the Arabs to understand the problem." He could not accept a situation that would force France to "forego Arab oil, for even a year."[59] The French ascribed ulterior motives to Kissinger as well, suspecting that consumer cooperation was a vehicle for Washington to reassert hegemony over Western Europe.

Instead, Paris sought a Western European solution to the crisis based on a common EC energy strategy and closer relations with the producers. At the Copenhagen Summit in December 1973, the European Community failed to agree on the former but made progress on the latter. Demonstrating the point, foreign ministers from Tunisia, the United Arab Emirates, Sudan, and Algeria made official visits to Denmark, and the EC's communiqué included calls to support Palestinian rights as well as a proposal for a formal dialogue between the Arab League and the European Community.[60]

Seeking to preempt the French alternative, the Nixon administration extended invitations in early January 1974 to the EC countries, Canada, Japan, and Norway to attend a conference in Washington the following month to discuss the energy crisis. The purpose was to create a Western strategy that would unite the industrial democracies around a common goal. Kissinger wanted to "break this regional autarky concept" and return to "the more cooperative conceptions which underlay our policy at earlier periods and their policy at earlier periods." The conference would also "avoid the sense of panicky impotence . . . in which everyone feels he must run for the nearest exit or assure his own supplies."[61] All invitees agreed to attend the conference but indicated that they saw it as the "first step towards a more comprehensive dialogue with the oil-producing countries," as Brandt responded to Nixon.[62] The conference placed most of the Western Europeans in the awkward position of straddling the line between "keeping the Americans happy" and not alienating the French. The British, for example, sympathized with the French "on most substantive issues," including a belief that bilateral deals were "necessary" and that the Euro-Arab dialogue could exist within "a multilateral framework in which bilateral arrangements can be carried on."[63] Later that month, French foreign minister Michel Jobert proposed a world energy conference under the auspices of the United Nations that would provide a foundation for cooperation between producers and consumers and discuss the global economic impact of the oil shock.[64]

In his opening remarks at the Washington Energy Conference in February 1974, Kissinger dwelled on the lessons of the 1930s. He warned that economic nationalism would lead to a cycle "of competition, autarky, rivalry and depression such as led to the collapse of the world order in the Thirties." He articulated a vision of cooperation that included the conservation of existing energy supplies, the development of alternative energy sources, new research into possible additional sources of energy, sharing schemes for emergencies, and the responsible recycling of oil revenues into Western financial markets.[65] The EC delegations met alone on the second day of the conference to develop a position, and except for the French, they decided to participate in the energy action group. "We need the Americans in a way that they do not need us," the British decided. "It is therefore in our interest to cooperate with them."[66] The conference led to the creation of the International Energy Agency (IEA) in November 1974 and an emergency-sharing arrangement, but the larger significance was that the conference had forced the participants to choose between the US and French approaches. Consumer cooperation, not bilateral deals or a Western European strategy, became the basis for dealing with OPEC. "We have broken the Community," Kissinger celebrated.[67]

Or so it appeared. The following month, the European Community put its plans for Euro-Arab dialogue into motion, seeing no contradiction between this initiative and consumer solidarity. Kissinger fumed. He believed that it undermined both his peace strategy in the Middle East and his plan for consumer solidarity. Nixon gave a thinly veiled threat that the United States might withdraw US soldiers from Western Europe, claiming that Congress would not finance the troops to protect a region whose policymakers undermined US interests.[68] Kissinger urged cooler heads to prevail on the troop withdrawal issue, though he accused the European Community of not consulting the United States before announcing the Euro-Arab dialogue. "Europe seems intent upon taking a path we will not accept," he told West German foreign minister Walter Scheel. "If Europe is determined to float its foreign policy," then the United States would follow suit. "We will then have to see whose specific weight is the greatest," he warned.[69] Kissinger did not "give a damn about energy," he told his staff. The Washington Energy Conference had a "purely political" purpose, but now Kissinger even suggested that he "would rather break the European Community than have it organized against the U.S." When his aides tried to coax him off the ledge, Kissinger shot back, "You are living in the Europe of the '50s not of the '70s. The Europeans . . . oppose us everywhere."[70] Not for the first time Kissinger had an emotional response to unfavorable news, but his anger was directed at substantive issues.

To make matters worse in the spring of 1974, the United Nations General Assembly adopted the "Declaration on the Establishment of a New International Economic Order," an initiative that called for reconstructing the economic system to protect the equality of all states and the "permanent sovereignty over its natural resources and all domestic economic activities."[71] Demands included greater control of foreign investment, increased purchasing power of raw materials, better access to the markets of the developed countries, boosted development aid and technology transfers, alleviation of national debt, and more influence in international institutions such as the IMF and World Bank.[72]

Transatlantic tensions finally calmed in the summer of 1974. An important factor was that within just a few months, Nixon, Heath, Pompidou, and Brandt all left office. Labour leader Harold Wilson replaced Heath and emphasized Britain's traditional postwar role as a transatlantic mediator. Pompidou suddenly passed away in April 1974, and Giscard eked out a narrow victory over the communist-backed François Mitterrand to become his successor. He and new foreign minister Jean Sauvagnargues softened the Gaullist policy of Pompidou and Jobert. Brandt resigned in May 1974 amid an espionage scandal, and his successor Helmut Schmidt had a wealth of experience as former minister of finance, economics, and defense. Finally, Nixon resigned in August 1974 amid the disgrace of Watergate. Gerald R. Ford, a former congressman who had a reputation for working collegially with others, assumed the presidency. International cooperation depends, to a degree, on personal rapport, and this new quartet got along well.

The change in leadership helped Washington and Paris bridge their differences at a bilateral summit in December 1974 on the French-controlled island of Martinique in the Caribbean Sea. Sauvagnargues told Kissinger and Ford that "Giscard comes here with a sort of mandate to reconcile our positions." He said that the French agreed about the importance of the consumers developing a common position but wanted further clarification about what that entailed. Kissinger claimed that "consumer organization is a way to give the consumer nations a sense of control over their destiny." He admitted that consumer solidarity would not lower prices, but it would bring the industrial democracies together. France did not have to join the IEA; "We can work out parallel paths," Kissinger stressed. The United States promised to participate in a preparatory meeting between producers and consumers in March 1975 to develop an agenda and procedures for a main conference later that year. In return, the French accepted the need to take "actions by consumers sufficient to guarantee cooperation," including implicit cooperation on parallel paths with the IEA on the conservation of energy and the development of alternative fuels.[73]

The Martinique Summit marked the beginning of a constructive period in transatlantic relations during the mid-1970s. In the face of global economic disruption, the industrial democracies reaffirmed the importance of maintaining their cohesion. Disagreements persisted about how to combat the instability in the global economy and how to match objectives and tactics during the ensuing North-South dialogue, but the Western nations agreed that they would pursue multilateral solutions to common problems.

The oil crisis also had significant implications for global finance and the post–Bretton Woods international monetary system. "The world oil crisis has suddenly been transformed from a critical *oil supply* problem to a severe, world-wide *financial* problem," the oil consultant Walter J. Levy noted in January 1974.[74] The volume of official foreign exchange reserves increased by half during 1974 and 1975 because of the accumulation of assets by OPEC countries, which collectively ran a surplus of about $60 billion in 1974.[75] Reduced oil consumption during the recession decreased OPEC's current account surplus to $30.8 billion in 1975, which nevertheless represented a large sum.[76] Some policymakers feared that the funds would overwhelm the free market, and the collapse of Franklin National Bank and Herstatt Bank during 1974 confirmed fears about the system's fragility. "The financial markets are close to panic," William E. Simon, who replaced Shultz as secretary of the Treasury, warned. "There are major corporations which are unable to borrow."[77] Others worried that the producers would use their financial clout as a weapon to extract political concessions.[78]

The industrial democracies agreed that they should incentivize the OPEC nations to "recycle" their profits back into the West.[79] Petrodollars could fund Western current account deficits and cushion the blow of the oil crisis. Because the industrial democracies refused to respond to the oil crisis by cutting public spending, they needed to compensate for the outflow of wealth somehow. "To maintain the current level of prosperity," Van der Stoel explained, "net capital exports of around $60 billion will have to come from the oil countries to the rest of the world."[80] Giving OPEC a stake in the Western financial system would also provide the producers with an incentive not to disrupt the Western economies with another price shock. "We've got to come up with ways to soak up their dough," Kissinger argued. "Our principal objective should be to maximize their dependence on us."[81] It would also help combat calls from the developing world to index raw material prices to those of manufactured goods. Indexation was "extremely problematic," as the West German minis-

THE WEST AND THE OIL SHOCK

ter of the economy Hans Friderichs argued, in part because it would arbitrarily link two different types of goods, create inefficiencies, and disadvantage the industrial democracies.[82]

The United States aggressively sought petrodollar investments. Simon shared Shultz's predisposition to deregulating capital, and petrodollar recycling coincided with a change in economic ideology in the Treasury during the mid-1970s. The United States abolished capital controls such as the Kennedy-era interest equalization tax, which had taxed US purchases of foreign stocks and bonds, to attract petrodollars. Direct controls on foreign investment expired in early 1974 as well.[83] Commercial bankers lobbied the Ford administration to remove additional barriers, including withholding taxes on interest and dividends flowing out of the United States. An article in the *Wall Street Journal* queried, "Why should the sheiks cough up 30% of their income from investments here when they can keep it all when their investments are cycled through London?" The Treasury would forgo some $200 million in tax earnings, but "it is small potatoes compared to the tens of billions in petrodollar business that the U.S. is throwing away to foreign capital markets."[84] During 1974, OPEC countries invested about $11 billion in the United States (about 18 percent of the total surplus), particularly in US government securities and bank deposits, by far the largest among the industrial democracies.[85] Fears abated during the second half of 1974 that the Western financial system could not absorb the OPEC surpluses, and the United States became a preferred option for investment.

Reliance on the free market to recycle OPEC's surpluses benefited some but not all. By the end of 1977, 38 percent of OPEC's foreign assets ($160 billion) went to the Euromarkets and more than 25 percent to the United States while just 10 percent were invested in the other industrial democracies.[86] The problem was that the countries that needed the most help were generally the least attractive to investors, and countries such as Britain advocated using international institutions to distribute the petrodollars to ensure that the United States did not crowd out the others. Washington resisted. So too did Bonn, which had also removed capital controls in January 1974 to allow foreigners to purchase West German assets.[87] Reliance on the free market to handle the surpluses rather than channeling them through an international institution such as the IMF would also avoid legitimizing high oil prices. "No one knows when the pressure on OPEC will be intolerable and the price returned to its former level," Assistant Secretary of State Thomas Enders noted. Recycling "offers the best guarantee that prices will be restored and normal price mechanisms will come into play."[88] While Washington won the battle, US officials acquiesced to the creation of safety nets to assist the most distressed countries. The IMF created two oil facilities through which OPEC countries would direct part of their revenues to help distressed countries. The OECD also created a fund to help members that struggled to make energy payments.

OPEC investment in the West elicited fears in some quarters. When Iran purchased a quarter share of the legendary West German firm Krupp and Kuwait bought just under 15 percent of Mercedes-Benz, apprehension grew about OPEC using its wealth to gain control of major industries. Ohio senator Howard Metzenbaum pointed out that it would take only three-quarters of OPEC's surplus in 1974 to purchase a controlling interest in eleven giant US corporations, including AT&T, Boeing, General Motors, IBM, U. S. Steel, and Xerox.[89] While "spectacular investments" proved "few and far between," concerns persisted about the potential, particularly when Arab investors attempted, but failed, to purchase a controlling share of Lockheed Aircraft Corporation.[90]

Petrodollar recycling fed the explosion of global liquidity in the post-Bretton Woods world. In an environment in which capital became increasingly liberalized and links to precious metals did not constrain the growth of the money supply, banks facilitated petrodollar investment as well as created new assets through massive credits. The value of the Euromarkets jumped from about $188 billion in 1973 to $305 billion in 1976. Most of the expansion occurred in the dollar sector of the market, which accounted for just under three-quarters of the total Eurocurrency assets.[91]

Against the backdrop of New York City's fiscal crisis and social upheaval, Wall Street reemerged as the center of global finance after capital controls expired in January 1974. International lending provided only one-third of the profits of major US banks in 1973, but that proportion surged to three-quarters by 1976.[92] Foreign banks also established a greater presence, with twenty-one opening offices in New York during 1976 alone. "New York has become the major international marketplace as a result of the guidelines being abolished," commented the New York branch manager of the Westdeutsche Landesbank Girozentrale. "Before that, you had to go to London."[93]

Developing countries needed loans to sustain import-substitution industrialization amid high prices for raw materials, and commercial banks eagerly accommodated their needs. Collectively their current account deficit increased from $4.8 billion in 1973 to $38.5 billion two years later.[94] With inflation pushing interest rates very low or even negative, borrowing was attractive. In this "international lending orgy" of the mid- and late 1970s, as the former traveling loan officer for Cleveland Trust Company Samuel Gwynne described it, banks leapfrogged each other to cut interest rates and attract sovereign borrowers, with 13 percent of loans during 1977 fetching a spread of 0.75 percent or less. Regional banks with little experience in foreign lending hastily created international departments to join the bonanza.[95] The Soviet bloc countries became major sovereign borrowers as well, which is a topic covered in chapter 4.

The oil crisis and explosion of global liquidity shaped debates about reforming the international monetary system. A patchwork system without blessing from the IMF had existed since the collapse of the Bretton Woods system. The dollar, pound, and yen floated. The Snake floated as a unit, although it had lost "ribs."[96] The major blow came when France spurned Schmidt's offer of $3 billion to support the franc and chose to withdraw from the Snake in January 1974.[97] Most policymakers concluded that the upheaval from the oil crisis meant that floating exchange rates should continue for the immediate future, frustrating the work of the IMF's Committee of Twenty as it contemplated a new monetary architecture.

The future role of gold in the international monetary system marked an important point of debate. The convertibility of the dollar into gold had been the lynchpin of the Bretton Woods system, but gold's place was now unclear. On one hand, Washington sought to phase gold out. The Western Europeans had a larger share of global gold reserves; indeed, France alone owned more gold than the United States in 1975 for the first time in the postwar era.[98] US officials feared that Western Europe therefore had "the dominant position in world reserves and the dominant means of creating reserves."[99] On the other hand, Paris wanted maximum flexibility for authorities to deal in gold. This preference stemmed from a belief that states should be able to use their gold to finance current account deficits and reflected the engrained French belief that gold constituted the safest hedge against monetary instability.

Countries' positions on gold influenced their preferences on the exchange rate regime. While Washington wanted to legitimize floating, Paris returned to the Snake in July 1975 and hoped to reestablish a system of fixed exchange rates.[100] The French believed that it would restore "order" amid the "state of confusion we are nowadays facing."[101] Giscard thought that floating exchange rates aggravated the instability in the commodities markets, but fixed rates would impose discipline. Floating exchange rates also removed "certain constraints on governments to pursue anti-inflationary policies," but fixed exchange rates would force governments to restrain the growth of the money supply.[102]

In July 1975, Giscard floated the idea of a summit of the major industrial democracies to discuss the global economy, moving the disagreement about the monetary system out of the hands of technical experts and into the hands of political leaders.[103] Giscard found "little enthusiasm" from his international partners for his suggestion, however.[104] Simon considered it a ploy to "restore the conditions which prevailed before August 1971, when there was an overvalued and noncompetitive dollar, as well as a system of rigid exchange rates which kept the monetary system subject to continuous uncertainty, speculation and recurrent crisis."[105] Most Western European officials preferred a return to a system of fixed yet adjustable rates but believed that market volatility precluded it for the moment. Flexible exchange rates could deal with hot money better than fixed, a West German Ministry of Finance report determined. Rather than causing the "anarchy" and chaos," as the French saw it, flexible exchange rates did the opposite in Bonn's view, acting as "a brake against excessive capital movements" and tamping down inflation.[106]

Leaders agreed to participate in Giscard's summit, discussed below, though they shared British foreign minister James Callaghan's sentiment that the summit could have value only if it did not "develop into the pursuit of fetishes about the monetary system."[107] Rather than at the summit, the fate of the international monetary system was determined during bilateral negotiations between Washington and Paris. After a flurry of meetings in the fall of 1975 between French deputy finance minister Jacques de Larosière and US undersecretary of the Treasury Edwin Yeo III, the French abandoned their hopes for a fixed-exchange rate system while the United States accepted that gold would play a limited role in the system, giving states the ability to use it in official transactions at market prices. Countries could choose the exchange arrangement that they wanted if they behaved responsibly, although what exactly constituted a responsible policy was left undefined. The IMF Interim Committee accepted the agreement in January 1976, amending Article IV of the Fund Agreement to enact the "first sweeping revision of our international monetary arrangements" since the Bretton Woods system, Simon bragged.[108] He "came back from the . . . meeting . . . with everything except the proverbial kitchen sink," the *Washington Post* reported.[109]

The Jamaica Accords marked a significant victory for proponents of market-based international monetary reform. The patchwork system that had emerged after the collapse of the Bretton Woods system endured. A de facto dollar standard reigned; during the mid-1970s, the dollar's share of official holdings of foreign exchange approached 80 percent.[110] The proportion owed much from not only the inertia of the Bretton Woods system but also the postwar US-led international oil order because producers still priced and sold much of their oil in dollars. The US relationship with Saudi Arabia played a key role in ensuring that OPEC did not stop this practice. In return for security assistance as well as the ability to purchase advanced US weapons, the Saudis supported the dollar as the pivot of global finance and international trade and were a moderating voice in OPEC against large price increases.[111]

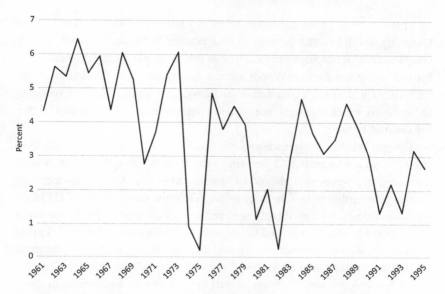

FIGURE 3.2. Annual average GDP growth in the OECD area. Source: World Bank, World Development Indicators.

The post–Bretton Woods system contained a new set of benefits and vulnerabilities for the United States. Washington still enjoyed seigniorage and now had no formal responsibility for maintaining a gold-based system. Untethered to gold, the dollar had freedom of action. Without its special status enshrined in international agreements as under the Bretton Woods system, the dollar's position now depended on international confidence. While the dollar accounted for the lion's share of official reserves and served as the currency of choice for trade in the commodities markets, that could change if dollar holders believed that their dollar-denominated assets would be worth less in the future.

The debates about the future of the international monetary system unfolded against the backdrop of the longest and most severe recession since the Great Depression. At the sharpest period during the second half of 1974 and the first half of 1975, US industrial production dropped 12.3 percent, Japanese 13.9 percent, West German 8.7 percent, and British 8.5 percent.[112]

Western governments counteracted the downturn with a Keynesian prescription. Governments pumped billions of dollars into their economies with the hope of jump-starting stagnating industries and limiting unemployment numbers. As a percentage of GDP, public expenditure jumped between 1970 and 1975 from 31.9 percent to 35.2 percent in the United States, from

18.5 percent to 25 percent in Japan, from 36.9 percent to 46.7 percent in West Germany, and from 38.5 percent to 46.1 percent in Britain.[113] Labor also received additional employment protections and unemployment insurance. The breakdown of the Bretton Woods system and transition to floating exchange rates eliminated implicit constraints on the money supply, and public spending fed inflation, which averaged more than 14 percent in the OECD countries during the mid-1970s.[114]

The gap between wage increases and productivity gains also widened. During 1975, wages increased 7.1 percent in the United States, 8 percent in West Germany, 20.3 percent in Italy, and 20.7 percent in Britain. These wage increases had no relationship to productivity gains. While the productivity of US labor, for example, increased by about 3 percent annually during the first two decades of the postwar period, it slowed to less than 2 percent during the third. The oil crisis "accentuated the decline in the real rates of return on capital investment that most countries had experienced since the 1960s," the Bank for International Settlements annual report noted. Profit rates on investment dropped from 22.7 percent to 14.4 percent between 1970 and 1974 in West Germany.[115] The commodity price boom became "built into domestic cost structures," and the OECD calculated that labor costs rose an estimated 10 to 15 percent across its member states.[116]

Unemployment increased to postwar highs. On one end of the spectrum was the United States, where unemployment jumped from 4.9 percent in 1973 to 8.5 percent in 1975. On the other stood countries such as Britain and France, where unemployment rose from 2.6 percent to 4 percent and from 2.7 percent to 4.1 percent, respectively, during the same period.[117] Part of the reason that unemployment did not go even higher was that many governments accepted higher levels of inflation as the cost.

The transition to prioritizing the fight against inflation at the expense of rising unemployment numbers unfolded at different speeds during the second half of the 1970s. The Ford administration pursued a restrictive fiscal policy, allowing unemployment to hit nearly 9 percent in the United States in 1975, up from 5.6 percent the year before.[118] It was a jaw-dropping figure by postwar standards. Whip Inflation Now (WIN) became a bumper-sticker slogan for a call to action, and when the US economy began to lift itself out of recession the following year, inflation did not rise substantially. With the legacy of the Weimar hyperinflation ever present, West Germany also focused on reducing inflation. "Keynes' methods worked in the 1930's; they don't today, and there is no new Keynes," Schmidt argued.[119] West Germany weathered the storm perhaps better than anybody, with inflation peaking at 7.6 percent in

1971, two years before the oil shock.[120] Other countries that remained in the Snake such as the Netherlands and Denmark also performed relatively well in part because they had to maintain the pegged exchange rates, which acted as a brake against inflationary domestic policies.

No countries found accepting unemployment as the price for battling inflation a more difficult pill to swallow than Italy and Britain. They struggled with an annual average increase in the consumer price index of 16.7 and 13.5 percent, respectively, between 1973 and 1983.[121] "Weak governments needed to spend as a way of buying popularity and thus fueled nominal demand," Harold James explains, "while at the same time being unable and unwilling to curb the monopolistic positions of unions."[122]

With industries in the transatlantic community struggling, the oil crisis hastened the relocation of manufacturing from the transatlantic community to East Asia. Among the most vulnerable of the industrial democracies to the oil crisis because of its almost complete dependence on imports, Japanese companies shifted from energy-intensive industries such as steel, chemical, cement, and aluminum in favor of the electronic and precision machinery sectors. While in 1974 it took 82 percent of Japanese export income to pay for imports of raw materials, food, and fuel, within three years this ratio declined to 68 percent.[123] Japan applied new technology to manufacturing earlier than its international peers and used the industry's new products to compete on the world market. Japan exported manufactured goods such as automobiles and consumer electronics to the United States and Western Europe, and its surplus with the transatlantic countries offset its oil bill with the Middle East. This flow of resources constituted what Kaoru Sugihara dubs the "oil triangle."[124]

The decline of manufacturing fanned social tensions as workers and union leadership looked for scapegoats. Migrant workers had always been treated as second class (entrance signs to Swiss public parks instructed, "No entry for dogs and Italians") and now became even more vulnerable.[125] During the postwar period, migrants from southern Europe had found employment in northern European countries. They worked in the factories and performed menial labor such as cleaning the streets. During the mid-1970s recession, however, these foreign workers found themselves in the crosshairs of public criticism and took abuse for "stealing" jobs. "Why should we have a short work week at my plant?" a West German machinist asked. "Why don't they just send the *Gastarbeiter* (guest workers) home and give us Germans their work?"[126] When industrial production slowed, migrants often found themselves first on the chopping block. Four out of five BMW employees who lost their jobs, for example, were foreign. With job opportunities hard to find, many workers returned home. In

1975 alone, almost three hundred thousand workers and their families departed West Germany for Turkey, Yugoslavia, Greece, and Italy.[127]

Stagflation also took a toll on NATO. "The single factor weighing most heavily on Allied activities was inflation and the need to compensate for it," a US report noted. Many NATO countries boosted their defense budgets in nominal terms, but inflation wiped out the increases. Policymakers faced public calls to redistribute funds from defense to social needs. "Crippling economic pressures have forced both Britain and Italy to initiate measures that seem certain to result in major, permanent military retrenchment."[128] With plans to cut defense expenditures by 1.5 percent of GNP within a decade, Kissinger warned Ford, "the British will largely abandon their ability to intervene militarily even on a token scale, anywhere outside of Europe." Tensions flared between Greece and Turkey after a coup d'état in Cyprus, and rising support for far-left parties in countries such as Portugal and Italy compounded tensions in the southern flank of the alliance. NATO countries accepted "the thesis that national security and economics are so closely intertwined" that only through international cooperation could the West cope with the problems, Kissinger noted, but the horizon promised no relief "from the consequences of the energy crisis, from sagging economies, strained government revenues and rising unemployment."[129]

In this precarious situation, Schmidt saw value in Giscard's proposal for an economic summit.[130] While Giscard had wanted to concentrate on monetary affairs, Schmidt refashioned the idea to include a wide-ranging discussion of the economic and political challenges facing the West. The chancellor had been an early proponent of multilateralism and was by his own account "obsessed with the idea" that the industrial democracies faced "a situation reminiscent of the early 1930s." Though the problem in the Great Depression had been deflationary whereas in the 1970s it was inflationary, "it all added up to a situation of world-wide recession and depression which, in the 1930s, had only been ended by war."[131] Many critical issues needed attention, including inflation, unemployment, energy, international monetary policy, North-South relations, and international trade. Schmidt had no illusions that a summit alone would resolve these problems, but it could demonstrate a commitment to international cooperation. "If we could create the impression we intend to work together and coordinate our policies," he suggested, "that will be enough."[132]

Schmidt expected that a summit would support his domestic agenda as well. Under fire at home for relatively high unemployment numbers and budget deficits, he hoped that a major summit could boost his domestic standing, particularly with upcoming federal elections. Furthermore, Schmidt's push for international coordination was "really an appeal to the United States to take the lead with strong economic measures aimed at rapid recovery from recession," the director of the State Department Policy Planning Staff Winston Lord suspected.[133] The growth of US demand could stimulate the global economy and create opportunities for West Germany's export-driven economy.

France hosted the economic summit in mid-November 1975 at the Château de Rambouillet, the French president's summer residence located southwest of Paris. Participants in this "G6" summit included Britain, France, Italy, Japan, the United States, and West Germany. The summit had an atmosphere of a "house party," the British ambassador reported, and the cozy setting meant that the British delegation was relegated to working in Napoleon's bathroom and Sauvagnargues prepared at a table in a corridor.[134] Fundamental issues divided the leaders, ranging from monetary policy to North-South issues. The *tour d'horizon* summit concluded with no concrete agreements, but that was not really the point. Talks had the "spirit of a shared responsibility . . . for the common fate of an indivisible global economy and with it, the democratic social order," the West German report noted.[135] The summit served a psychological purpose of showing the commitment of the industrial democracies to work together to solve global issues, even if they disagreed about how.

But there was only so much that the summit could do. The industrial economies began their uneven recovery from the recession by the second half of 1975, but the conditions of the Golden Age did not return. The political positions of Western leaders weakened. "There is a serious question as to whether political democracy will survive over most of Western Europe," Widman warned.[136] Communist participation in Western European governments had "not been a lively prospect since the onset of the Cold War in the late forties," a State Department report summarized, but it resurfaced because of "the widespread lack of direction and disintegration resulting from . . . the severe pressures of simultaneous unemployment and inflation in the post-Keynesian West; the acceleration of modern technology and communications; the widespread decline of authority in executive branches of government; the fading of the idea of progress and lack of genuine energizing ideals; and the buffeting of the individual in the face of political corruption, economic decline and personalized wars."[137] Inflation remained in the double digits across most of the region, and unemployment stayed high relative to Golden Age levels. "When [the communists] say the capitalist system doesn't work," British foreign minister Callaghan acknowledged, "they seem to have a good case when there are six million unemployed."[138] Eurocommunists remained a minority everywhere, but US officials feared that further economic and social dislocation would increase their popularity, echoing the fears of the Truman administration when communist parties in Italy and France received 20 percent of the vote during the immediate postwar years.[139]

Although communist parties earned less than 5 percent of the total vote across Western Europe, they grew in strength in a few key countries. The situation was most alarming in Italy, where the communists trailed the Christian Democrats by only four percentage points. "The likelihood of continued weak government is made to order for the large, well-disciplined Italian Communist Party," Yeo summarized.[140] A French "Union of the Left," consisting of the socialists, communists, and other leftist parties, posed a serious threat to Giscard, who had only defeated Socialist Party leader François Mitterrand in the 1974 presidential election with 50.8 percent of the vote, and popular frustration with stagflation hindered the consolidation of a center-right coalition.[141] In elections during 1976, the communists took 34.4 percent in Italy, 23 percent in France (not to mention the 26 percent won by the socialists), 17 percent in Finland, 18 percent in Iceland, and 14.5 percent in Portugal. Western European communist parties advocated a democratic path to power and declared their independence from Moscow after being disillusioned by the Soviet suppression of the Prague Spring, but nobody knew whether this new line reflected "considerations of tactics or convictions," Bonn noted, and whether they had truly severed ties with Moscow.[142]

As economic interdependence accelerated, it became even more important to figure out how to discipline countries in disequilibrium so that instability in one country did not infect the others. Italy and Britain seemed the most vulnerable. "Both Italy and the UK threaten France and through her, Germany and the rest of [Europe]," Yeo argued. "From an economic and financial standpoint, the disequilibrium in both the UK and Italy has to be dealt with." Italy and Britain needed to take steps at home but also required help from their international partners. Surplus countries such as the United States, West Germany, the Netherlands, and Japan needed to "see their current account surpluses erode . . . so that the weaker countries can earn current account surpluses." The international community also had to "come up with sizable transitory and conditional financing for Italy and perhaps the UK if the adjustment process is to proceed on an orderly basis."[143]

Recognizing the high geopolitical stakes for managing economic interdependence, Washington pushed for a second economic summit to discuss how to sustain a noninflationary recovery. Ford sent Shultz abroad to make the case for another meeting to foreign leaders; they agreed but took some convincing.[144] As the host, Ford invited Canadian prime minister Pierre Trudeau, whom Giscard had excluded from Rambouillet despite protests from the others, so the G6 became the G7. Held in Puerto Rico in June 1976, the second summit showcased the difference between the stimulators such as Britain and Italy, who championed public spending to reduce unemployment, and the stabilizers such as the United States and West Germany, who advocated restraining public expenditure to choke inflation.[145] The summit adjourned without any major initiatives, although the Ford administration believed that it had value because it reflected a sustained dialogue among the major industrial democracies. "We may have developed a new form of international institution," Council of Economic Advisers chairman Alan Greenspan commented.[146] Indeed, while it emerged out of a narrow French desire to return to a fixed-exchange rate international monetary system, the G7 summit became an annual fixture for the major industrial democracies to have sweeping discussions about international political economy.

Washington grappled with how to close the gap between the stimulators and the stabilizers, and US Treasury officials began to view the IMF as an instrument that could impose discipline by making financial aid conditional on structural adjustments. Not only did the United States have great influence in the IMF, but working through the institution would give policies international legitimacy and provide the Ford administration with political cover from Congress, which did not want the United States to bear a disproportionate burden for providing aid to distressed countries. While the Truman administration had extended financial assistance directly to struggling countries in the late 1940s, the IMF began to take on this expanded role in the mid-1970s.

Both Italy and Britain turned to the IMF for loans, accepting conditions that reduced government budgets. The Italian economic situation was delicate in terms of the growing support for the Eurocommunists. There was no comparable revolutionary movement in Britain, but the specter of British neutralism made Washington sweat in the fall of 1976. When sterling's exchange rate plummeted in September 1976, the Callaghan government approached the IMF for a standby loan. "We used to think that you could just spend your way out of a recession and increase employment by cutting taxes and boosting spending," Callaghan admitted at a Labour Party conference in September 1976 as he tried to prepare the country for spending cuts. "I tell you in all candor that option no longer exists and that insofar as it ever did exist, it only worked by injecting a bigger dose of inflation into the economy, followed by a higher level of unemployment."[147] As protracted negotiations between the IMF and London stalemated, the danger was that the IMF's demands could force spending cuts on national defense or even empower the Labour Party's left wing to withdraw from NATO and transform Britain into a siege economy. Although Ford and Schmidt refused to extend bilateral loans or intervene with the IMF to reduce the conditions, they helped avert disaster when they provided Callaghan with political support by promising to help fund a safety net to support sterling after Britain came to terms with the IMF. When Britain, the bastion of the welfare state, reduced its budget and sold public holdings of British Petroleum as conditions for an IMF loan in December 1976, the symbolism reverberated across the globe.[148]

The industrial democracies were stronger "by far" in comparison to the Soviet bloc, Kissinger declared in June 1976. The West's "problem is a problem of concept, of will, of domestic support," he argued. "That is our problem—not a problem of strength."[149] The postwar international economic architecture had broken down and compounded stagflation, and the industrial democracies scrambled to maintain allied cohesion. "It is just not enough to cooperate in the field of security and foreign policy," Schmidt argued at the NATO summit in June 1974, "if the imminent dangers are waiting for us in the economic, monetary, and financial fields."[150]

The choices that officials made in response to the oil crisis had lasting effects. First, amid the worst economic crisis of the postwar period, the industrial democracies decided that their national interests were best served through international cooperation. They resolved that there would be no return of the autarkic 1930s. Second, continuing the ideological shift that had taken place when Shultz became Treasury secretary, the Nixon and the Ford administrations fought against proponents who wished to return to fixed exchange rates to legitimize the patchwork international monetary system that would support floating currencies and encourage the freer flow of capital. The post–Bretton Woods system was still organized around the dollar, which ensured that the United States retained the privileges of seigniorage, but the greenback was no longer supported by its convertibility into gold at a fixed rate.

After contracting nearly 1 percent in 1975, real GNP growth during 1976 shot back up to 5.2 percent in 1976 in the OECD countries but petered out by the end of the year.[151] Inflation and unemployment remained above Golden Age levels. Productive capacity remained underutilized, and current account deficits persisted in many countries. Western governments seemed brittle, and the prosperity of the postwar period appeared a relic of the past. Put simply, as Lord commented in November 1976, "all is *not* well among the industrial democracies."[152]

CHAPTER 4

Twin Oil Crises behind the Iron Curtain

As the world's largest oil producer by 1974, the USSR appeared at first glance well situated to capitalize on the oil crisis.[1] Yet Soviet policymakers did not bask in abundance; they spoke of shortages instead. Supply certainly outpaced domestic demand, but Soviet planners did not think in just national terms. Moscow bore responsibility for its welfare empire and came under pressure to cushion its allies from the worst of the oil crisis.

The oil crisis forced Moscow to make difficult decisions about how to rank its priorities as production costs in the energy sector rose, Soviet agriculture slipped into crisis, inefficiencies in the CMEA became more apparent, and resentment grew that Eastern European living standards outpaced the quality of life at home. On one hand, the Soviets needed hard currency to pay for imported Western technology and food. Oil exports to the West were the biggest Soviet source of hard currency, and the potential profits from oil sales at world market prices were tantalizing. On the other hand, Moscow knew that Eastern European development depended on the Soviet Union delivering the lion's share of the bloc's energy needs. If the socialist states could not realize their economic goals, the political instability that would inevitably follow would threaten the integrity of the Soviet bloc.

In a decision that represented its growing discontent about bearing the rising costs of its welfare empire, the Kremlin promoted exports to the West and imposed price hikes within the CMEA. Moscow still traded energy to its allies at rates below those on the world market, but the Soviets insisted on revising the Bucharest formula to adjust terms of trade more in their favor. The conditions of the late 1950s that had persuaded the CMEA countries to establish the pricing mechanism no longer existed, and Moscow decided to adapt the Bucharest formula to accommodate the new realities. The Soviets made this decision with their eyes open to the danger that it posed to their hydrocarbon-dependent allies.

Indeed, the Eastern European regimes had to contend with two oil shocks. First, they each bought a fraction of their oil from producers in the developing world at world market prices, and they fell deeper into debt as they struggled to finance the imports. Second, the revision of the Bucharest formula created large trade deficits with the Soviet Union as well. The command economy insulated the Soviet bloc from the immediate upheaval that plagued the industrial democracies, but the socialist economies nevertheless strained as the twin oil shocks exposed the structural shortcomings of Soviet socialism and its energy-guzzling industrial model.

While Eastern European officials publicly trumpeted the superiority of Soviet socialism at a time when the West struggled with stagflation, they scrambled to respond to the twin energy shocks. Socialist officials shuddered at the thought of embracing austerity to reduce their trade deficits, a tactic that would shift the burden of adjustment onto their populations. The Soviet bloc's numerous uprisings in its brief history had demonstrated that decreases in living standards could trigger popular uprisings. Like the industrial democracies, the Eastern European regimes did not want the economic consequences of higher energy prices to undermine their political legitimacy.

The socialists looked to the West for financial assistance. Fortunately for them, commercial banks eagerly extended loans to the socialist states. Eastern European governments drew on these funds to maintain, and in some cases raise, the standard of living in their countries. Access to Western credits masked the exhaustion of the Soviet socialism developmental model. As their sovereign debt soared, the Eastern Europeans ironically found themselves dependent on the inflow of Western credits to subsidize their development.

Many Soviet political elites believed in the mid-1970s that the global balance of power was shifting in their favor. After the success of SALT I, Brezhnev and Ford achieved a breakthrough that established a framework for SALT II during a summit in the Far Eastern Soviet port of Vladivostok in November 1974. The Soviets interpreted the US willingness to engage in arms control as evidence of US weakness, and members of the Politburo considered détente to be a part of the "inevitable course of history" that would lead to the disintegration of the capitalist bloc.[2] Following a summit on European security, known as the Conference on Security and Cooperation in Europe (CSCE), countries from both blocs signed the Helsinki Accords of August 1975, which asserted the inviolability of the postwar European international boundaries—a long-standing Soviet objective. In addition, the Helsinki Accords called for greater economic and cultural exchanges across the Iron Curtain and respect for human rights.[3]

Seeing no problem with simultaneously pursuing détente and supporting revolutionary nationalists in the Third World, the Soviet Union expanded its presence in the developing world during the mid-1970s, making notable gains in sub-Saharan Africa.[4] The United States, in contrast, appeared on its backfoot, still licking its wounds after the withdrawal from Vietnam in early 1973. Left to fend for itself, Saigon fell to North Vietnamese forces two years later. "The capitalists have gone on the defense," asserted East German propagandist Paul Markowski. "They are losing in Europe, Asia, and Latin America" and were forced to take "defensive positions" across the globe.[5]

Socialist policymakers initially celebrated the eruption of the oil crisis as evidence of the West's decay. "For the first time in their history," the Department of International Relations of the SED's Central Committee declared, "the capitalists have lost full control of the production and the price of raw materials, above all oil. This will lead to a decrease . . . in the profits and the power of international monopoly capitalism."[6] The oil crisis aggravated the existing symptoms of the "contradictions of the imperialist system" such as high levels of inflation and unemployment, monetary instability, and trade tensions between the capitalist powers.[7] The upheaval might even serve as the spark for the long-awaited terminal postwar collapse of capitalism and reopen a window of opportunity for the Soviets to extend the revolution into the industrial democracies. "The imperialists are mired in crisis," crowed Hermann Axen, director of the International Relations Department in the SED's Central Committee. As unemployment increased in the West, "class consciousness" among the workers was reawakening.[8] "We are now witnessing the crisis of the economic foundation of imperialism," CMEA secretary Nikolai Faddeev boasted. "The future lies not with capitalist integration," he said, "but with socialist."[9] Despite the economic inefficiencies and political oppression, conditions in the Soviet bloc appeared steady.

Behind the veneer of stability, however, high-ranking socialist officials worried about how the oil crisis would impact their own countries. While they took pains to declare the opposite publicly, they knew that they were not immune to the upheaval underway in global capitalism. The Soviet bloc confronted two energy shocks during the mid-1970s. First, the Eastern Europeans suffered from the price hikes on the world market. The Soviet Union supplied each CMEA member, except Romania, with much but not all of its oil. Every Eastern European country, including Romania, imported supplies from the nonsocialist world. With the growth of Eastern European demand outpacing the planned increases in Soviet deliveries, the financial burden of importing oil from outside the bloc was only expected to get heavier as the decade wore on.[10] This meant that the sudden hike in world market prices hit the Eastern Europeans hard. The oil crisis "did not leave us untouched," admitted the chairman of the Bulgarian Council of Ministers Stanko Todorov in December 1973. Only weeks after Sofia had supplied weapons, food, and medicine to the Arab side during the Yom Kippur War, he complained, Arab oil producers had the audacity to demand world market prices. Instead, Zhivkov submitted a request to Moscow for an additional two million tons of Soviet crude oil, among other items, for which he offered to pay convertible currency. Bulgaria had not fulfilled its agricultural quotas during 1973, and Sofia could not afford to purchase energy as well as additional food, the prices for which had also risen on the world market. Bulgarian policymakers turned to the Soviets for help. "The Soviet Union is our only hope," Todorov implored the Soviet ambassador.[11]

Moscow could understand Sofia's frustration. Soviet policymakers themselves grumbled that friendly OPEC countries asked for nearly world market prices for their oil, offering only a small "confidential discount." This disrupted Soviet plans for 1974 to export almost twenty-nine million tons of oil to Western Europe because this figure depended on the purchase and re-export of nearly fifteen million tons from the Middle East, mostly Iraq. The strategy was now "unprofitable," Soviet officials informed the Central Committee.[12]

Second, the global oil crisis spread to the Soviet bloc through the Bucharest formula, which had a baked-in relationship with global capitalism. In 1973, Soviet oil prices for exports to other CMEA countries varied: 14 rubles (Bulgaria and East Germany), 15 rubles (Poland), to 15.89 rubles per ton (Czechoslovakia and Hungary). At the official dollar-ruble rate, which grossly overstated the value of the ruble if it had been convertible, the world market price of oil checked in at 22.35 rubles per ton in 1973 but spiked to 60 rubles per ton the following year.[13] Because the Bucharest formula used a delayed average of world market prices, it deferred the worst of the energy shock to later years. When prices were set for the next term, adherence to the formula meant that world market prices during the early 1970s would weigh down the inflated prices after 1973. Thus, the Bucharest formula would ensure that the full weight of the oil shock would only be felt behind the Iron Curtain in the early 1980s.

Soviet officials refused to wait that long. With prices quadrupling on the world market, the Soviets now sold oil to the CMEA states for a fraction of what they could receive at market prices. Discontent about the subsidies had already been building in Moscow, and the oil crisis marked the breaking point in Soviet patience. In November 1973, only weeks after the price hikes in the capitalist world, Soviet minister of foreign trade Nikolai Patolichev informed East Berlin that the two sides would have to renegotiate energy prices.[14] "In many capitalist countries the prices of gas, oil and other raw materials are rising," Brezhnev told Honecker in June 1974. "We must find a way to deal with this problem in the world economy because it affects us all in certain ways."[15]

In August 1974, the Soviets distributed proposals about a revision to the Bucharest formula that would take effect at the beginning of 1975.[16] Under this new "Moscow Principle," prices would change each year instead of every five years. In 1975, CMEA prices would reflect the average of world market prices over the previous three years; thereafter, the time frame would extend to five years. The Kremlin had initially wanted to use 1973 and 1974 prices as the basis for 1975 but yielded to Eastern European protests that the transition would be "too difficult."[17] In the case of East Germany, oil prices jumped from 14 rubles in 1974 to 35 rubles per ton in 1975, and in Hungary, they rose from 15.89 rubles to 37 rubles per ton. CMEA prices still trailed those on the world market (1.5 to 2 times lower at the official dollar-ruble rate, but the annual recalculation meant that prices began to track inflationary capitalist trends more closely.[18]

The Soviets insisted on revising the Bucharest formula to solve several problems at once. Developing Soviet raw materials became far more expensive as the center of the energy industry continued to shift farther east into Siberia. Moscow lacked the technology to extract oil and natural gas efficiently, and the harsh climate of western Siberia—a "giant snow-driven cemetery," as one tsarist official had characterized it—compounded the technical problems of transporting resources over thousands of kilometers. The summers were unbearably hot and humid. "The tundra, bogs, swamps . . . It's one thing to hear about that or see it in the cinema or magazines, but it's quite different to experience it yourself," Baibakov recalled. "I still remember the attacks of gnats and midges from which neither mosquito nets nor fumigators saved." After touring the reserves in Siberia, the Czechoslovak State Planning Commission chairman Václav Hula sent Baibakov a carton of insect repellent on which he placed a label: "anti-Tyumen."[19] Even though Soviet oil and natural gas deliveries to Eastern Europe rose during the 1970s, Baibakov reported to the Central Committee that Moscow could not meet its obligations because of the "depletion of developed fields in the central parts of the USSR" and "delays in the construction of pipelines" farther into the Soviet interior.[20]

Production costs and CMEA prices diverged rapidly. The CMEA used the Bucharest formula to insulate the system from disruptions in the nonsocialist world, but prices had no relationship to the rising costs of production in the Soviet Union. Raw material exporters in the CMEA "suffer great losses because the production costs . . . are not balanced by these prices," the deputy chairman of the Soviet State Committee for Prices Anatoly Komin explained.[21] The high cost of energy production contrasted with the lower investments that the Eastern Europeans needed for their industries. Gosplan estimated that the average cost of producing one ruble of exports of finished goods totaled sixty kopeks, but the investment that was needed to do the same for raw materials exports was four times as high.[22] More than 70 percent of Soviet imported machinery and equipment came from the CMEA countries, with East Germany as the largest supplier by a fair margin. According to the Hungarian economist Sándor Ausch, the CMEA inflated the prices for machinery and equipment by 25 percent and for certain products by more than 200 percent.[23] In the backdrop of climbing oil prices on the world market, the situation looked even worse when Soviet planners considered the opportunity cost of shipping inexpensive energy to their allies.

Moscow believed that the inequity not only disadvantaged the Soviets but also deformed the economic development of the whole socialist bloc. Countries without domestic sources of fuel could count on cheap Soviet energy and focus on "material-intensive" rather than "labor-intensive" production. This "exacerbated the shortages of fuel" and led to "low efficiency in the international division of labor." In contrast, machinery and equipment were set at prices "significantly higher than the prices earned in capitalist markets," Komin wrote. "This does not stimulate the modernization [of production] or removal of obsolete equipment." It also meant that the Soviets purchased finished goods at prices that dwarfed the cost of production. The Soviets bought products from their allies at prices two or three times more than the prices at which they could be produced at home. "Therefore, purchasing products and spare parts from the CMEA countries is unprofitable for the USSR," Komin concluded, "since it leads to the overpricing of finished products or the need to subsidize them." Resolving this discrepancy would facilitate a more equitable and efficient division of labor, and improved material conditions would strengthen the socialist bloc and enhance popular support for Soviet socialism.[24]

Soviet Politburo minutes from August 1974 indicate that rectifying this imbalance was a primary objective of revising the Bucharest formula. The Soviets wanted the new pricing mechanism to reflect the "internal conditions of development in the socialist countries," hoping that it would play a "stimulating role" in the CMEA's development.[25] Moscow hoped that the price shock would stimulate a more equitable division of labor in the socialist bloc and assist in the transition to intensive growth. "This is not just in the interest of the USSR," Patolichev assured his skeptical East German counterpart Horst Sölle.[26] It would also gradually phase the global oil shock into CMEA pricing so that the socialists would not have to contend with a huge price increase a few years later.

More efficient energy utilization would not only lead to better developmental outcomes but also free more Soviet oil to ship to the West. Above all, the Soviets needed cash to pay for grain imports. A series of poor harvests substantially raised the Soviet hard currency import requirements; in 1975, the Soviets spent $14.2 billion, creating a trade deficit with the West of more than $6.3 billion.[27] "Bad harvests have been a millstone around our necks," Kosygin admitted.[28] Weather helped account for some variety in the annual harvest yields, but overshadowing everything was the inefficiency of the collective farming system in which unproductive, underresourced, and depopulated state farms failed to live up to expectations. Soviet farms even suffered from fuel shortages for tractors and trucks. This forced Moscow to sell even more oil to the West for grain, creating a vicious cycle that exacerbated both problems.[29] The Soviet Union sold gold, whose dollar-denominated value spiked after Bretton Woods collapsed, for hard currency. Yet Moscow could not depend on gold sales to accumulate the funds required to keep the Soviet people fed, particularly as global food prices rose.[30] Oil was the only resource that could bring in the necessary hard currency, and oil exports to the nonsocialist world leaped from 897,000 bpd in 1974 to 1.3 million bpd in 1976.[31] Oil export earnings jumped from $1.25 billion to $4.5 billion during the same period.[32]

When Soviet policymakers negotiated the revision to the Bucharest formula, resentment of the Soviet subsidies bubbled to the surface. During September 1974 talks in Prague, Patolichev argued that Moscow had long subsidized its allies at the expense of its own citizens. "I don't want to name a figure" for the total, he said, "but that is a fact that one cannot dismiss."[33] Patolichev asked the Czechoslovak foreign trade minister Andrej Barčák "how the Soviets should explain to their people" that they traded oil for only fifteen rubles per ton in the CMEA. The Soviets sent oil at prices more than three times lower and purchased finished Czechoslovak goods at prices at least two times higher than on the world market. Patolichev claimed that the standard of living in the USSR was lower than all other CMEA countries except Mongolia.[34] "There is . . . the question," Patolichev grumbled during a meeting in East Berlin, "as to why the standard of living in the USSR must be lower than, say, Hungary. It is not enough to say that the USSR bears the military burden or that it helps the developing countries. . . . The USSR had accepted this situation long enough."[35]

The Soviets still subsidized Eastern European energy because they did not demand world market prices. They resented that their allies did not appreciate it. The Soviet Union used a lot of its own resources "for the benefit of the other CMEA countries," Baibakov noted pointedly to Honecker.[36] "If the USSR did not have such obligations," the Soviet deputy foreign trade minister Vladimir Alkhimov asserted, "it could release these quantities to sell on the free market at the current high world market prices."[37] Moscow estimated that the Soviet energy subsidy to the CMEA countries registered in the billions of rubles.[38] The revision of the Bucharest formula impacted all prices, including those of manufactured goods, so the Eastern Europeans did see some benefits, but its significance rested in the oil price shock.

The Soviets extended low-interest loans to facilitate the transition to the new pricing mechanism ("You are not alone," Patolichev assured), but the price increases created a second energy shock for Eastern Europe.[39] As the nonsocialist world struggled to adapt to the rising price of commodities, the Eastern Europeans had taken comfort in their reliance on the Soviet Union to supply raw materials at fixed prices. "With the speculative price movements of commodities on the capitalist world market," Schürer had pointed out in December 1973, "one cannot estimate this fact highly enough."[40] The Soviet decision to raise prices removed that advantage for the Eastern Europeans. Patolichev tried to sell the Moscow Principle as the "anti-imperial price" for raw materials, but Eastern European officials did not view it in those terms.[41] Instead, they interpreted it as threat to internal stability.

Higher energy costs threatened to stunt industrial production at a most inopportune moment. Formulated in the late 1960s and early 1970s, the Eastern European debt-driven developmental strategy was "connected to a sudden increase in the need for energy resources," a Bulgarian report explained, particularly inexpensive oil and natural gas from the USSR.[42] Now that energy prices had risen, the Eastern European regimes had the unexpected burden of directing more goods to the Soviet Union to pay for the same imports. This was a major problem because they needed to swing their trade accounts into surplus with the nonsocialist world and earn hard currency to pay back their loans. Their greatest fear was that rising trade deficits with both the West and the USSR would impact consumption at home. They did not want their people to have to tighten their belts in the name of balancing external accounts; austerity would betray the promises of Soviet socialism and trigger popular protests.

Officials in East Germany, one of the largest CMEA importers of Soviet oil, worried what higher energy prices would mean for their energy-guzzling industries.[43] East Berlin had charted an ambitious developmental plan in the late 1960s that depended on combining cheap Soviet raw materials and imported Western technology to develop robust East German industries in several key sectors. Higher energy prices threw a wrench into those plans. While coal was still the primary energy source in East Germany, imported hydrocarbons fueled its primary industries, including its chemical, machine, and metallurgical industries, on which the plan's success depended. Higher energy prices "on this scale represent a significant increase in the cost of all stages of production in the GDR," the East German State Planning Commission warned.[44] The East Germans wanted the CMEA to continue using the Bucharest formula, believing that the current rise in raw materials prices reflected "speculative and inflationary factors . . . that we should in no circumstance transfer into CMEA prices."[45]

In August 1974, Honecker convened a meeting with his top economic advisers to discuss how to respond to the Soviet proposal. GDR estimates indicated that the higher energy prices would lead to trade deficits with the USSR that dwarfed the "expected increase in national income." Changing prices every year shook the foundation of central planning, transferring the impact of inflation on the world market into the CMEA. "This measure would practically mark the end of the CMEA's pricing principle," Günter Mittag worried. "Planning without fixed prices is not possible." The East Germans resolved to fight the change because accepting the revision to the Bucharest formula "would mean a large decrease in the standard of living in the GDR."[46]

It was obvious that East German living standards trailed those in the West, but the SED also claimed that it provided a more equitable and ethical alternative to the materialist and exploitative capitalist world. Lower economic growth and more shortages would mean that the promise about material prosperity would ring hollower and cast further doubt on the party's ideological claims. "World market prices must not have an effect on the inner fabric of the GDR," Honecker decreed. "Otherwise we might as well resign right now, and naturally we do not want that." The task, however, was monumental. Under the new pricing regime, East Germany would need to export 20 percent more just to tread water. "That's not at all possible," Honecker worried.[47]

The East Germans raised these concerns at multiple levels in talks with the Soviets in the fall of 1974, but they failed to sway Moscow. As the benefactors, the Soviets asserted their "legitimate claim to charge realistic prices," in Patolichev's words.[48] Honecker waived the white flag. "The basic decision has already been made," he conceded. Frustrated, the East German leader commented to

Patolichev that both sides must remain vigilant in the battle against imperialism but remarked that the price changes hindered East Germany's ability to do so. Fighting imperialism "requires a certain standard of living," Honecker argued. "The GDR has proven to be stable for 25 years and must prove to be so in the next 25 years. . . . We had stability even in difficult times, in contrast to Poland and Czechoslovakia." Patolichev expressed sympathy and commented that the present task was the "hardest job" of his life.[49]

The Hungarians had similar fears. They estimated that the revised Bucharest formula would cost Budapest almost 1.5 billion rubles over the next five-year plan that, combined with losses from trade with the industrial democracies, would impose "an unbearable burden on the Hungarian economy."[50] Some 70 percent of Soviet exports to Hungary consisted of energy and other raw materials.[51] The Hungarian permanent representative to the CMEA György Lázár wrote that integrating world market prices and "the harmful effects of capitalist inflation" into socialist-bloc trade would create "an undue burden for CMEA members" that had developed manufacturing industries and had to import raw materials. "This would slow down the pace of development of their entire economy and jeopardize the successes achieved in the field of socialist industrialization and in the area of living standards."[52] In 1974, the Soviets traded one million tons of oil for 800 Hungarian Ikarus buses, but by 1981, the same amount of oil equaled 2,300 buses, and by the mid-1980s, 4,000 buses.[53]

Budapest attempted to use its trade deficit to extract concessions from Moscow. The Hungarians argued that their exports of machinery to the Soviet Union contained materials obtained with hard currency, and they could not close the trade gap without Soviet assistance. Yet the Soviets said, "Export more, but we cannot increase our exports," the Hungarian chairman of the State Planning Commission István Hetényi remembered. Budapest responded "that under those conditions, we could not increase our exports. So we built up debts between 1975 and 1980."[54]

On the agricultural side of the spectrum, Bulgaria saw the revision to the Bucharest formula as a major threat as well. The Bulgarian minister of foreign trade Ivan Nedev put up a fight with Patolichev, and the permanent representative to the CMEA Tano Tsolov also sounded the alarm, but the Soviets dismissed these fears. "Tsolov not infrequently dramatizes the situation and baselessly argues that a decrease in the deliveries of oil [and] gas [and] the increase in price would be catastrophic for the Bulgarian economy," Soviet ambassador Vladimir Bazovsky commented to Zhivkov during an October 1974 meeting. "It's simply not so." Zhivkov agreed that Tsolov "sometimes succumbs to emotions" but called him a "good worker" before changing the subject.[55] A week later the Bulgarian Politburo approved the Soviet proposal to begin negotiating new contract prices for the next five-year period, adding that Bulgarian officials should lobby their Soviet counterparts to increase prices for agricultural products.[56]

The year 1974 "was extremely difficult for us," Zhivkov summarized at the November 1974 plenum of the Central Committee. In addition to a drought that "caused significant losses" in agricultural production, the "increase in the price of raw materials and energy products on the world market had a negative impact on the country's development." After warning his colleagues that the information "should not be spread," he reported that Bulgaria had a deficit of $700 million to $800 million, which was "a colossal amount for a country of our size." It was crucial that the imbalance should "not impact the standard of living of the people."[57]

The twin oil shocks strained the Bulgarian economy. "Our exports cannot cover the costs" of importing oil at world market prices, Zhivkov admitted to his Romanian counterpart Nicolae Ceaușescu in July 1975. "These crisis phenomena in the capitalist countries cannot help but cause us great harm."[58] Bulgarian officials estimated that more than half of the trade deficit with the Soviet Union of 3 billion rubles could be attributed to the price increases.[59] The global oil shock and the revision of the Bucharest formula burned Bulgaria from both ends. The revision of the Bucharest formula may have been conceived to respond to the "great price dynamics" on the capitalist market and coordinate CMEA planning, Zhivkov wrote Brezhnev in 1976, but "we want to inform you that, in practice, this was not the case." "There is a paradox," he pointed out, because Bulgarian "exports to the socialist countries, including the Soviet Union, are greatly increasing, and yet at the same time Bulgaria is becoming ever more indebted to them." The ramifications of the price increases "have shaken the entire planning of our development for the forthcoming period until the 1980s."[60]

Increased costs for energy could further hinder Bulgaria's economic development, Zhivkov feared. Bulgaria specialized in agriculture within the CMEA, which "has created considerable tensions in our economy, holding back the development of other important industries." In the context of rising prices for fuel, machinery, and chemical products, this concentration on agriculture was becoming an even bigger disadvantage. Agricultural prices had not risen as quickly. "This is an overwhelming burden for us. . . . We are at a dead end. We do not see an exit from the current situation." The Bulgarians had developed industries in mechanical engineering, metallurgy, energy, and chemical products (largely achieved with Soviet aid and equipment), but their exports were "quoted at low prices or not at all." Zhivkov pleaded for help changing the balance between agriculture and industry in the country; otherwise, "Bulgaria will

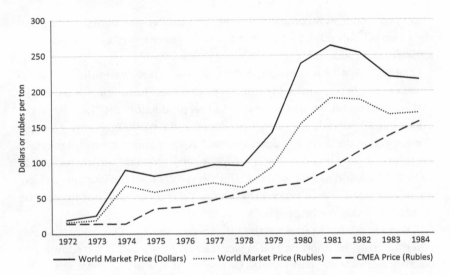

FIGURE 4.1. Soviet oil subsidies to East Germany, 1972–1984. Source: "Übersicht über die Preisentwicklung für Erdöl ab 1972," no date (1985), BAB, DE 1/58747.

continue to develop with a deformed economic structure, an inefficient economy." The national income per capita in Bulgaria was lower than that of almost all other CMEA countries, and the changes in the conditions of trade in the socialist community would "inevitably lead to the continuation of this trend."[61]

Despite the Eastern European protests, the Soviet Union muscled through the revision to the Bucharest formula. The CMEA formally approved it by a unanimous vote at the seventieth meeting of the Executive Committee in January 1975, but, as the Hungarian Party secretary Károly Németh put it to the Soviet ambassador, "you cannot expect us to show great enthusiasm about this decision."[62] It transformed the balance of CMEA trade; while the Soviets had a collective trade deficit with the Eastern Europeans of 700 million rubles in 1973, the change in oil prices turned that deficit into a peak surplus of 1.4 billion rubles by 1977.[63] Moscow still subsidized trade within the CMEA, but the Soviets' increasing desire to play hardball with the Eastern Europeans marked an important turning point. Moscow had to make a choice between pursuing its own economic advantage or cushioning the ballooning costs to its allies, and it chose the former.

Nevertheless, the Eastern European leaders expected that the Soviet welfare empire was still in force. The Soviet Union was the "big oak," Hungarian first secretary János Kádár remarked at a March 1975 summit of Soviet bloc leaders in Budapest, and the Eastern European countries were "the young shoots that grow up around it." While the allies "must not become a parasite at the expense of the USSR," he said, "this does not mean that we will not continue to make various demands of the USSR." On the contrary, Kádár claimed that the Soviet Union's "destiny" was "to support all of us." For the past three decades, "when we had difficult problems, we turned to the USSR."[64] Though the Soviet Union had sought to reduce the burden of its welfare empire, the Eastern European leaders still viewed Soviet assistance as their entitlement.

While the Moscow Principle revised prices, the issue of quantities remained a sticking point in bilateral negotiations. Even at the higher rates, importing Soviet oil was still cheaper than buying from OPEC. Furthermore, the Soviets accepted Eastern European goods—which struggled to find buyers on the world market—as payment. The Eastern European countries sought to obtain as much of their raw material needs from the Soviet Union as possible and conserve their own reserves to pay for imports from the other CMEA states. "The Soviet Union was the exception," commented an official in the Czechoslovak State Planning Commission. "It was the only country willing to tolerate an unbalanced trade structure. All the other countries were careful not to export more than they imported in the crucial categories."[65] Soviet oil exports to Eastern Europe jumped from 807,000 bpd in 1970 to 1.6 million bpd in 1980.[66]

Soviet deliveries doubled during the 1970s, but the Eastern Europeans pressed for more. "Oil is very economical for you," Kosygin grumbled to Stoph in December 1976. "All you have to do is turn on the tap." The East Germans pleaded for more energy, but Moscow refused. "You must get your head out of the clouds," Kosygin instructed. "We cannot meet such demand. Nobody in the world can."[67]

Invoking the Comprehensive Program, the Soviets renewed calls for the Eastern Europeans to assume greater responsibility for developing their raw materials. The Soviets saw CMEA cooperation as a means of exploiting their reserves more rapidly as well as compensation for past expenses and subsidized energy. An increase in natural gas and oil deliveries "can only happen with the direct participation of the socialist countries concerned," Soviet officials told Bulgarian leaders in July 1973.[68] The Eastern Europeans had no real alternative to the Soviet offer. "Because there is at the moment no other way to cover the growing oil and natural gas needs of the GDR after 1975," Schürer noted, "we must take this suggestion very seriously."[69] In 1972 and 1973, the CMEA Commission for Oil and Gas resolved to construct a unified system of pipelines to transport natural gas to Eastern Europe, and then on to the new Soviet customers in Western Europe.[70] The push for multilateral projects had mixed results. By 1973, Moscow secured commitment from its allies to participate in producing 55 percent of the Soviet natural gas that they would receive by 1980 but only 13 percent of the oil.[71]

The construction of the Soyuz pipeline constituted the best example of CMEA multilateralism. The CMEA agreed in the summer of 1974 to build a pipeline that would transport natural gas from Soviet reserves in Orenburg to Uzhgorod, and then on to Eastern Europe. The Soviet Reserves Committee estimated that reserves totaled 1.66 trillion cubic meters and that the field could yield about 60 billion cubic meters annually.[72] After the completion of the project, the Eastern Europeans received compensation: 2.8 billion cubic meters of gas per year in exchange for building their *pod kliuch* ("turn-key") section.[73] The CMEA utilized an "interested party" principle, meaning that individual countries could opt out of any collaborative project, and the Romanians did so here.[74] The Soyuz pipeline initiated "a qualitatively new stage in the cooperation of the socialist countries" in the energy sector, Oil and Gas Industry official Boris Shcherbina declared in November 1975. He touted "the perfect organization, labor enthusiasm, and close cooperation of the builders of the Orenburg . . . pipeline."[75]

The Soyuz pipeline may have served as the "showpiece" of CMEA integration, but the Eastern Europeans balked at the costs of participating in the development of Soviet resources.[76] The pipeline placed pressure on Eastern European resources that were needed at home. The Eastern Europeans had to provide skilled workers to build their sections of the pipeline. "Removing this workforce from our sites in Bulgaria for a long period of time, with our limited labor resources, will lead to difficulties in the fulfillment of our annual plans," the chairman of the Bulgarian State Planning Commission Ivan Iliev worried.[77] Constructing their portion of the Soyuz pipeline also contributed to the sovereign debt trap that ensnared most of Eastern Europe. The Eastern Europeans borrowed from Western banks, with CMEA's International Investment Bank serving as the intermediary, to purchase machinery, pipes, and equipment from the nonsocialist world. The inflation in the capitalist world added to the cost. Rising prices in the capitalist world increased costs by a quarter, a Hungarian State Planning Commission official calculated in July 1976. "The profitability of Hungary's participation in the pipeline construction is no longer what it would originally have been."[78] In sum, the countries spent roughly $1.75 billion, with each country contributing between $290 million (Bulgaria) and almost $400 million (Czechoslovakia).[79] For countries that struggled to earn hard currency, this was a lot of cash.

The revision of the Bucharest formula worked to Eastern Europe's disadvantage as well. When the project began, the Soviets sold natural gas to East Germany, for example, for 14.50 rubles per cubic kilometer. When the pipeline became fully operational in 1980, East Berlin paid 56.40 rubles per cubic kilometer, an increase of almost 400 percent in comparison to 1974.[80] Credits for natural gas imports were calculated when each country completed its portion of the pipeline. Deliveries of natural gas would continue for more than a decade, and they paid contractual prices in effect at the time of delivery. Thus, the Eastern Europeans received less natural gas than they would have if there had been fixed prices at the time of the original agreement.

Moscow's hope that the CMEA would relieve the burden on Soviet resources by promoting integration failed to materialize. Rather than pooling resources as envisaged in the Comprehensive Program, the structure of CMEA trade remained along bilateral lines. The Eastern Europeans objected to what they saw as unequal investment obligations, and the joint-project movement lost steam by the late 1970s. The construction of the Soyuz pipeline was "a serious, real form of participation," Kosygin said to Stoph in December 1978, but such participation was rare because the Eastern European interest in cooperation essentially amounted to "a purchase and a sale," which was "the exact same thing as when we sell something on the capitalist market." The Soviet premier lectured, "I would like to say that the whole economy of the GDR is in a rather privileged position. You will not think about that much, but I would like to remind you. . . . Where do you find, Comrade Stoph, such a place in the world where oil and gas come directly through pipelines practically to your front door? You don't need transport or tankers. . . . The economy of the GDR is in paradise and in a rather privileged and better position than the economies of Italy, France, and West Germany. . . . You have a favorable situation, a very favorable position." Calculating the difference between CMEA and world market prices, Kosygin estimated that the East Germans saved $2.4 billion over the past three years by relying on oil from the Soviet Union instead of purchasing it on the world market.[81] With its large implicit trade subsidy, the Soviet Union had bargaining leverage over its allies but failed to translate it into greater Eastern European investment in developing Soviet resources. While the revision of the Bucharest formula and the Soyuz pipeline represented two cases in which the Soviet Union used coercion to get its way, they were exceptions rather than the rule.[82]

While the trade deficits within the socialist bloc could be handled internally, imbalances with the capitalists could not. The Eastern Europeans adopted a debt-led developmental strategy at the beginning of the 1970s, believing that they would be able to develop strong export industries of their own that would allow them to repay their debts. Some officials took the gamble of accumulating debt because they believed that the strategy would work. Others did so because they thought that they had no alternative besides suppressing consumption at home and this was the path of least political resistance.

The plans failed. Rising trade deficits with the West were symptoms of the larger issue that the socialist bloc produced goods that neither satiated its own people nor enticed Western buyers. "The intensive economic development of the Socialist countries has not yet enabled them to produce goods of a quality satisfactory to the West," Italian prime minister Aldo Moro observed.[83] Soviet socialism had industrialized agrarian societies, but it could not make the transition to the information age. Ulbricht's boasts from the late 1960s that East Germany would sell computers to the West failed to materialize. "The capitalists have already taken a step forward," Kosygin acknowledged.[84] Soviet socialism's claims that it represented the paradigm of the future rang increasingly hollow.

The twin oil shocks exposed, but did not cause, the structural inefficiencies of Soviet socialism and the contradictions in its growth model. "The changed external economic conditions did not cause but only exacerbated the problems of the development of the Czechoslovak economy that have accumulated over many years," Soviet ambassador to Czechoslovakia Vladimir Matskevich reported in November 1975.[85] The command economy's inability to transition from extensive to intensive growth represented a core problem. The Soviet bloc followed multiyear plans and used quantitative indicators to measure progress, and consequently, as André Steiner notes, innovation was disruptive. Planned economies created a division of labor that limited opportunities for the cross-pollination of ideas as bureaucracies jealously guarded their turf. On the ground, laborers and farmers had few incentives to increase performance.[86] Soviet socialism promised full employment as part of its social contract, but technological progress and heightened labor productivity could create a "contradiction," as the Hungarian chairman of the State Planning Commission Imre Padri observed. "It is necessary to ensure full employment" on one hand, but on the other, technical development would lead to "a reduction in the number of employees." Hungarian enterprises generally preferred to hire additional labor to boost productivity, a tactic that was "cheaper than introducing scientific and technical advancements."[87] While the industrial democracies developed computers and microchips, the socialists struggled to move beyond heavy industry.

Developments in Western Europe also limited opportunities for Eastern European exports. The oil crisis–induced recession of the mid-1970s reduced Western demand for imports. To make matters worse, the European Community did not open its arms to the CMEA.[88] The European Community needed to eliminate the tariffs to "establish a level playing field," Zhivkov complained, and then the socialists would prove their value. "We can compete with the capitalists" if only they played fairly.[89] The socialists wanted to make most-favored nation (MFN) status the bedrock of Basket II of the CSCE and eliminate barriers to East-West trade, but this proposal found few Western supporters. With the CMEA countries unwilling to grant reciprocity, the fear was that the socialists would dump their products at artificially low prices.[90] While some Western companies wanted to do business with the socialists, others were skeptical. "In the USSR, money is treated with no less respect than in Germany," Patolichev reassured the West German economics minister Hans Friderichs, but some Western businesses remained unconvinced.[91]

Eastern European fortunes would have been different had it not been for the willingness of Western commercial banks to extend loans. The capitalist world fell into a deep recession after the oil crisis, and banks initially wanted to limit their exposure to risk. Obtaining credits "on the capitalist money markets have become much more difficult," Staatsbank president Horst Kaminsky reported.[92] After the Western financial system endured the initial shock and global liquidity exploded, however, the situation changed.

Eastern Europe beckoned to Western investors for several reasons. First, bankers believed that the Soviet Union took its hegemonic responsibilities seriously. They had faith in the "umbrella theory," which posited that the Soviet Union would bail out its allies should one of them approach bankruptcy. Second, they expected that the structure of the command economy meant that it would be easier for governments to pay off their debts in the event of a crisis because they could move goods around more easily than market economies. Third, Eastern European countries had an excellent record of meeting their debt obligations. Fourth, socialist countries used the loans to purchase Western goods, adding a stimulus to the capitalist economies. Finally, the recession dampened demand for credit in the industrial democracies, and lenders, particularly in the Euromarkets, began to focus on sovereign borrowers instead. The banks and the regimes had overlapping interests, and the socialist countries enjoyed "an enviable credit rating in Western financial circles," a Chase Manhattan Bank official commented. They commanded favorable interest rate spreads on their Eurodollar credits, ranging from 1.25 to 1.5 percent over the London Interbank Offered Rate (LIBOR).[93]

The CMEA countries became major players on the Euromarkets in 1975, taking more than 10 percent of syndicated medium-term loans. The volume of loans only continued to grow. "1976 proved to be a vintage year," described an article in *Euromoney*, a respected Western journal that reported on the Euromarkets. Eurocurrency credits of $3.2 billion were a third larger than in 1975, and four times as much as in 1973. While all socialist countries accepted loans, their levels of exposure varied by country. On one side of the spectrum was

Poland, whose debt service ratio reached 30 percent by 1976. On the other side was Czechoslovakia, which had thus far approached Western credits with suspicion. Prague's debt of $1.8 billion was less than its annual hard currency earnings. Total CMEA indebtedness was difficult to calculate because the member countries jealously guarded their financial data, but Western estimates placed it between $45 billion and $48 billion by the end of 1976.[94]

Western European banks, and West German in particular, eagerly offered credits to the Soviet bloc countries. "Go East, Young Man," instructed the July 1975 cover of *Euromoney*, with a line of eager bankers and the brilliant onion domes of St. Basil's Cathedral visible in the distance. US law limited the freedom of US banks to lend to Soviet bloc countries (US banks held only 13 percent of total socialist debt), but Western Europeans operated under no such restrictions. Frankfurt and London emerged as the primary syndicate centers.[95]

Western policymakers viewed the accumulation of Eastern debt as a threat as well as an opportunity. The flow of goods and credits across the Iron Curtain reinforced détente. Because the Soviet bloc relied on East-West trade far more than the industrial democracies, economic relations provided the West with leverage. The West could make access to technology, manufactured goods, grain, capital, and markets conditional on political concessions. Western leaders did not develop a coherent strategy to utilize this leverage, but socialist interest in engaging capitalist markets paid dividends at times.[96] In the midst of the mid-1970s recession, the industrial democracies also enjoyed the stimulus that Eastern demand for their goods provided.

What the debt meant in the long term was unclear, particularly with reliable data about the Soviet bloc finances in short supply. Few worried about the Soviet Union's ability to repay its debt; Moscow's vast reserves of gold, energy, and other raw materials gave creditors confidence that it could meet its obligations if it ran into trouble. Nobody really knew what debt meant for Eastern Europe, however. "In the end," Callaghan said at the Puerto Rico G7 summit in June 1976, "the Soviet Union will bail out Eastern Europe or impose discipline."[97] Poland and Romania were already "in serious trouble," Schmidt noted, and the rest approached "desperate situations." The chancellor feared that if the Eastern Europeans drowned in debt, they would "draw back into a closer relationship with the USSR," which would undermine the West's goal of driving a wedge between the Soviet Union and Eastern Europe. Furthermore, Schmidt called the credits "a net outflow of real resources from West to East," and therefore there was the question of why Western governments should burden their taxpayers in the name of improving life behind the Iron Curtain. "How much do we want our citizens to work to help the consumers of Leningrad?" Schmidt asked.[98]

Western bankers pondered similar questions. As the debts mounted, they grew frustrated that the socialist states did not release financial information. "In almost every conversation with leading bank representatives," East German Außenhandelsbank (DABA) vice president Werner Polze reported that "it became clear that many . . . are worrying about the future solvency of socialist countries." The bankers knew that the East Germans had a rising trade deficit, and "nobody knows what [they] did with the loans in the previous years."[99] Many bankers warned that future loans would depend on how transparent the socialists were about their finances. A US official told Polze that he found it incomprehensible that the Soviet Union and the other socialist states publicized little about their balance of payments, currency reserves, and foreign debt. Polze "must understand that somebody who grants credits needs the information to understand how the credits will be repaid," they maintained.[100]

Socialist bankers also realized that the availability of credits could soon cease. In the fall of 1976, DABA officials met with representatives from thirty-one US banks, including Citibank, Chase Manhattan, Bank of America, and Wells Fargo. "The trip came at an advantageous time for us," the report stated, "because U.S. banks are currently in a favorable liquidity situation on account of the unexpectedly low demand of large U.S. firms for loans." The banks warned "very openly" that this would change as soon as demand in their own countries rose again.[101]

As Eastern European sovereign debt increased, a state of interdependence emerged between the regimes and capitalist banks. On one hand, the Eastern Europeans needed the loans to pay for imports from the nonsocialist world. If they could not prove their solvency, the flow of credits would stop. On the other hand, the banks had invested billions of dollars in the region. If the Eastern Europeans did not, or could not, pay it back, the banks had no recourse. "Make a small loan, and you have created a debtor," a Swiss banker noted. "Make a large loan, and you have created a partner."[102] Western governments guaranteed some loans in the hopes of facilitating more East-West contacts, but the banks nevertheless assumed risk.

The credits played a paradoxical role in the Eastern bloc. They permitted the socialist economies to develop a "dual-character," in the words of Gosbank deputy chairman Yuri Balagurov.[103] Western loans allowed the Eastern Europeans to maintain and even raise living standards in their countries. During the first half of the 1970s, economic growth in Eastern Europe (inclusive of Yugoslavia) increased by an average of 5 percent annually.[104] Credits masked the inability to increase efficiency and allowed the regimes to avoid decreasing wages and raising prices to suppress consumption, measures that surely would have an "undesirable political response" from below.[105] At the same time, the Eastern Europeans became reliant on credits and conditions in the markets. While these loans delayed the ultimate reckoning, they placed the bloc at the mercy of the markets.

The Soviet bloc consumed more than it produced, but provided the Eastern European countries could rely on a stream of credits from Western banks, the countries could delay making domestic adjustments to bring down their debt. Officials knew that the tap could turn off. "Inevitably, the time will come when the GDR will not have the necessary cash in convertible currency to meet its external economic obligations," warned Günter Ehrensperger, the head of the SED's Department of Planning and Finance, "which would trigger an intrusion into the internal balance sheets and a chain reaction that would cause great political and economic damage."[106] Nobody had a concrete solution to this emerging dependence. In East Berlin, a few officials such as Schürer, Ehrensperger, and Staatsbank president Margarete Wittkowski sought to convince Honecker that relying on loans to subsidize domestic consumption was unsustainable. "The magnitude of the . . . problem requires action," Schürer stressed. If the party did not do something to manage the trade deficit, the East German living standards would no longer "be affordable." If the country sunk deeper into debt, Schürer believed that it would be even more difficult to reverse the situation. In the past, credits paid for imports. Now, much of the cash raised in the industrial democracies went to paying off old loans and interest.[107]

Honecker worked hard to prevent open discussion of the growing debt and avoided making difficult decisions about how to reconcile the debt with the need to preserve the East German standard of living. At a meeting of high-ranking East German officials in November 1976, Schürer, Stoph, Mittag, and others warned about the trade deficits and mounting debt. Honecker acknowledged the severity of the problem: "this is a question about the existence of the GDR. . . . We can only achieve our objectives if we have a strong economic base." He also indicated, however, that he would not sacrifice short-term domestic objectives. "We have to stick to our course," Honecker decided. Economic growth needed to speed forward but not "over the bones of the workers." Industrial exports provided the key to earning hard currency, he believed, particularly to the developing world.[108]

The East German tactic of drafting plans that called for an increase of exports to the West by as much as a third reflected the path of least political resistance.[109] When exports failed to bring in the necessary hard currency, the East German regime elected to take out loans rather than suppress consumption. The same story played out elsewhere across the bloc. "There is no balance in the economic development," the Soviet embassy reported from

Budapest in October 1975. "The plan provides for obtaining long-term loans in the West in substantial amounts . . . to repay previously received credits." And "even such attraction of external sources from the West" would not balance the budget; should Hungary's exports exceed imports by 20 percent, "which is an extremely difficult task with the current structure of Hungarian exports," the debt to the West would nevertheless continue to rise.[110] To different degrees, the plans amounted to a Ponzi scheme.[111]

This strategy deferred a reckoning that could antagonize restless populations. Events in Poland provided the cautionary tale. As the country that inspired the concept of the "Polish disease," Poland accumulated the highest debt. Rising to power in December 1970 in the wake of a failed attempt to raise prices, Polish first secretary Edward Gierek took out loans from the West with the goal of investing in the Polish economy and improving the quality of Polish exports and increasing productivity. Polish industries remained uncompetitive, however. Warsaw's strategy had precisely the opposite of the intended effect: the Poles imported an increasing amount of manufactured goods from the West and exported "traditional Polish goods" such as food and artisan products.[112] The problem was compounded in the mid-1970s when an agricultural shortage swept the Eastern bloc, forcing Poland to turn to the nonsocialist world for imports. By the end of the 1970s, Poland was the world's third largest wheat importer.[113]

Warsaw balked at implementing austerity measures to limit imports. "Knowing well the level of political consciousness of our population," a Polish official cautioned, "it is important to use any means necessary to avoid price increases."[114] Debt forced Warsaw's hand. In June 1976, Gierek experimented with lowering the state's subsidy for food, and the government increased the price of meat and fish by an average of 60 percent. The action caused strikes at 130 factories around the country. Responding to this public pressure, Prime Minister Piotr Jaroszewicz went on television and called off the price adjustment the very next day, and the regime reverted to its Ponzi scheme of debt accumulation.[115]

The Polish case was more explosive than anywhere else, but the dilemma was ubiquitous across Eastern Europe. A coffee crisis in East Germany was suggestive. Prices for coffee and cacao more than tripled on the world market between 1975 and 1977.[116] When an official suggested that East Berlin introduce rationing or simply explain the problem to the people and raise the price of coffee, Honecker refused to consider it. If the price of coffee rose, Honecker feared that the public would link that change to other price increases across the economy. "Others have already tried that," he noted, and worried that it would lead to "general restlessness" among the East German public.[117]

Recalling the *Ersatzkaffee* improvisations during World War II, the regime introduced an alternative called "Kaffee-Mix," which was a blend of 51 percent real coffee and 49 percent grain. The reaction against Kaffee-Mix was swift. The East German people dubbed it "Erichs Krönung," a play on the popular West German coffee brand Jacobs Krönung. The regime received so many complaints that East Berlin yielded to public pressure and increased coffee imports, but the trade deficit and domestic coffee prices rose as a result. "What the 'coffee crisis' revealed was a vicious circle of rising world market prices, supply disruptions and loyalty losses," André Steiner summarizes, "a vicious circle from which the Party was unable to escape right up to its end."[118]

The Soviets watched with concern as the Eastern Europeans accumulated debt. "Economic development cannot be healthy if it is based on external loans," Baibakov lectured a Bulgarian official. "A country should live within its means. . . . You should not overextend the economy by increasing debts to the capitalist countries." In the event that the socialists ran into problems, "the capitalists will not sympathize with us and we cannot compromise our development."[119] Plans to overcome indebtedness were worthless unless they were realistic. Upon learning that the East Germans planned to pay their debts to the West by increasing exports by 18 percent annually, Kosygin sarcastically remarked, "Gosplan must learn how to do that because Comrade Baibakov has never once dared to plan 10 percent export growth." After Kosygin insisted that the East Germans take steps to lower their debt, Stoph quipped, "Give us a prescription, then." Kosygin retorted, "We could give you one, but would you then follow it?"[120] The Soviets had no easy answer, either.

The West and the Soviet bloc suffered from a common crisis, and the stagflation that mired the industrial democracies added to the confidence that most socialist officials had in their system, even if a few began sounding the alarm behind closed doors. "We understand that things are not easy for you," Kosygin reassured Stoph. "But the position of the socialist countries is a thousand times better than in the capitalist world. All deliveries of raw materials are clear here for five years . . . but in capitalism nobody can see three months into the future."[121]

Scholars tend to portray the Soviet Union, seemingly awash in hydrocarbons, as a primary beneficiary of the 1973 oil shock. Moscow certainly enjoyed a windfall of hard currency, but the story is more complicated. Although the Kremlin wanted to promote the health of its Eastern European allies while meeting its own needs, it struggled to reconcile the competing claims on Soviet reserves. The quadrupling of prices on the world market caused the Soviet implicit subsidy to the CMEA countries to increase exponentially, and their need for assistance increased precisely when Soviet policymakers began to feel the acute weight of that burden. The Soviet revision of the Bucharest formula marked an important step in Moscow's reevaluation of its welfare empire.

The revision of the Bucharest formula delivered a body blow to the Eastern Europeans, but a large gap persisted between CMEA and world market prices. As the rest of the world struggled to finance oil imports from OPEC countries, the Eastern Europeans had the luxury of relying on the Soviet Union as their primary supplier. The subsidized prices stifled the impetus, which was strong in the capitalist world, for Eastern Europe to use energy more efficiently. Reliance on the Soviet Union remained a substitute for economic reforms.

Although increasingly resentful, the Soviet Union provided a lifeline for Eastern Europe, and the capitalist banks extended another. Faced with the twin oil crises, the Eastern Europeans drew on more credits from Western banks to sustain their debt-developmental model and attain their growth targets. Western credits concealed the fundamental problem that the Soviet bloc could not adapt its postwar growth paradigm to new conditions, but the strategy made the bloc vulnerable to changes in lending patterns. Rather than force their countries to live within their means and lower living standards for the working class, Eastern European officials preferred to kick the proverbial can of adjustment down the road.

CHAPTER 5

The Travails of Jimmy Carter

By the time that Jimmy Carter became president in January 1977, the recession of the mid-1970s had ended and the emergency phase of the oil crisis had passed. Yet inflation and unemployment remained high, and the global recovery proved weak. The stubborn persistence of stagflation undermined public confidence in democratic capitalism and sapped the ideological and material strength of the West. "Stagflation may not pose as dramatic a danger as the Great Depression did in the 1930s," Carter's special representative for economic summits Henry Owen summarized in November 1977, "but it could eventually do as much to weaken moderate political forces in Europe and Japan, and thus to unhinge the existing international order."[1] The vexing question of how to reignite noninflationary growth had first-order strategic implications but no clear answer.

To restore Western strength and self-confidence, Carter proposed a new brand of US leadership that moved beyond the welfare empire framework. Rather than the United States carrying the burden for systemic stability, as it had since the late 1940s, the Carter administration sought to unload some of the responsibility onto its strongest allies. Known as the "locomotive theory," this strategy called for West Germany and Japan to join the United States—all countries with relatively low levels of inflation—to expand their economies so that the weaker industrial democracies and developing countries could benefit from an external stimulus without having to abandon their anti-inflationary policies at home.

International coordination failed, however, not only because West German and Japanese officials resisted the program but also because the US locomotive accelerated too quickly, accumulating a massive current account deficit and fanning inflation. With global liquidity increasing exponentially after the collapse of the Bretton Woods system and the oil crisis, hundreds of billions of dollars circulated outside of the United States. Concerned about the direction that the United States was heading, official and private holders of dollars began to sell their assets. The exchange rate of the dollar slid in late 1977 and plummeted in 1978. Dollar depreciation fanned inflation, reduced US defense spending in real terms, discredited US political leadership, and portended another oil price hike. It called into question the very integrity of the post–Bretton Woods international monetary system, even persuading the European Community to reinvigorate its push toward monetary integration to reduce dependence on the dollar.

The Bretton Woods system had generally insulated domestic policy from external pressures, but the global financial markets acquired increasing power to influence domestic decision-making. The assault on the dollar compelled Carter to abandon the locomotive strategy and his expansionary program in November 1978. Instead of pressing for others to join the United States as locomotives, Carter focused on monetary stabilization at home, and he appointed Paul Volcker as chairman of the Federal Reserve with the expectation that he would take a harsh stance toward tackling inflation. The eruption of the second oil shock derailed the anti-inflationary project, however, sending inflation soaring during Carter's final two years in office.

Amid the instability, Carter accepted the need for discipline as the cost of renewed price stability and weaning the country off OPEC oil. Carter's policies during the second half of his presidency set the United States, and the West more broadly, on the path to recovery. Yet they took time to work, and the US electorate did not give Carter a second term to reap the fruits of his labors.

A graduate of the US Naval Academy with a degree in engineering, Carter had a keen mind for detail and the Puritan work ethic to match. Fashioning himself a fiscal conservative, the former Georgia governor wanted a balanced budget, lower inflation and unemployment rates, reduced taxes, deregulation, and stronger safety nets. Some of these objectives contradicted others. "Yet he wanted it all," his first Treasury secretary W. Michael Blumenthal later commented, "and as he considered each issue separately, the connections were often lost on him."[2] Carter inundated Congress, which had little input, with proposals during his first months in office, giving observers the impression that his vision lacked cohesion. The president proposed a tax rebate of $50 per person in

January 1977, for example, but reversed his position three months later after growing concerned about its impact on inflation and the budget deficit. Carter insisted on mastering technical points and making decisions himself, an ambitious tactic that led to contradictions in strategy that a more streamlined organization might have prevented. During his first six months, Carter even reviewed all requests to use the White House tennis courts.[3]

Carter planned to reduce unemployment, which stood at 7.8 percent in December 1976, by reflating the economy. Annualized inflation had dropped to 4.7 percent in the United States by the end of 1976, and Carter believed that it had sufficiently decreased for him to focus on reinvigorating the recovery from the oil shock–induced recession.[4] Carter introduced a stimulus package that included tax relief for individuals (including the $50 rebate) and businesses as well as a jobs program that enlarged the public sector, expanded training programs, and introduced public works projects. He also supported the deregulation of major industries such as airlines, trucking, railroads, and financial institutions.[5]

Restoring sustainable noninflationary growth required tackling the energy problem. In an April 1977 address, he described the effort to reduce energy consumption as the "moral equivalent of war." Considering the drop in domestic production and anticipated global shortages during the following decade, he warned that the growth in US demand was unsustainable. Increasing dependence on foreign oil compromised US economic and political independence, he cautioned, and circumscribed "our freedom as a sovereign nation to act in foreign affairs." Should the United States not take steps immediately to conserve energy, the country would "feel mounting pressure to plunder the environment," suffer further from stagflation, compete with other nations for resources, and confront "an economic, social, and political crisis that will threaten our free institutions." The crisis had become acute, but Carter assured the country that there was still time to act.[6]

Later that week, he introduced legislation that included decontrolling oil and natural gas prices, imposing taxes on crude oil and automobiles, raising efficiency standards for industry, and extending tax credits to reward consumers for conserving energy and transitioning to renewables.[7] To spearhead the government's energy policy, he proposed the creation of the Department of Energy to replace the Federal Energy Administration. Carter appointed the former secretary of defense James Schlesinger to lead the new department, established in August 1977. "The closing of the frontier in 1890 was in some sense a shock to the American system," Schlesinger declared. "And similarly, as we face a future with constraint in the area of oil and gas, we are going to have a similar transition for the American society to go through."[8]

Limiting oil imports had national security implications. Western Europe and Japan remained far more reliant on foreign oil than the United States, National Security Adviser Zbigniew Brzezinski argued, and the Carter administration needed to show leadership by reducing its own dependence. "Europe's high-level energy dependence . . . competes with its political, economic and security relationships with the U.S.," he wrote. "This tension creates the potential for serious strains on Alliance cohesion in the event of a supply emergency like the Arab oil embargo of 1973–74." The failure of the United States to reduce its dependence on foreign oil would create "suspicion of U.S. motives and a resentment of the economic strength that permits the U.S. to indulge its current pattern of energy use." Higher energy costs also made the adoption of "assertively nationalist economic policies" more likely and would upset the international monetary system. The energy problem could further "spill over into the field of Atlantic security policy" with economic problems placing limits on NATO defense budgets.[9]

The program failed to garner support from Congress, however, even with Democratic supermajorities in both chambers. Few elected officials had the appetite to pass legislation that required their constituents to pay more for less oil. Many US citizens doubted that an oil crisis even existed, suspecting instead that the big companies, which had lobbied against the program, withheld supplies to keep prices high and maximize their profits. "The influence of the oil and gas industry is unbelievable," Carter wrote in his diary, exasperated as his program stalled in the Senate, "and it's impossible to arouse the public to protect themselves."[10] The United States consumed a record nineteen million barrels of oil per day in 1977, 47 percent of which were imported.[11] When Congress finally passed the National Energy Act in October 1978, it had gone through so many revisions that it was a shell of Carter's original package. Carter was forced to play the role of Cassandra, and his warnings about the interlocking dangers of dependence on fossil fuels went unheeded.

Carter complemented his initiatives at home with bold departures in foreign affairs. Rather than using the Cold War as the lens for US foreign policy, the Carter administration initially focused on "world order politics," as Carter's advisers described it during the presidential campaign. World order politics sought to initiate "a new phase in U.S. foreign policy" that went "beyond the Atlanticist/East-West Cold War framework of the years 1945–1976."[12] In his first major foreign policy address at the University of Notre Dame in May 1977, Carter promised to reinfuse US foreign policy with moral purpose. "For too many years, we've been willing to adopt the flawed and erroneous principles and tactics of our adversaries, sometimes abandoning our own values for theirs," he declared. With dozens of new independent postcolonial nations and the world becoming more interdependent, the emerging new world order transcended Cold War bipolarity, Carter believed. The United States needed to forge a new strategy that accounted for the new conditions in the international system.[13]

Cooperation among the core industrial democracies played a key role in the world order politics framework. Carter and his vice president Walter Mondale had been early members of the Trilateral Commission, an organization that advocated close cooperation among the major industrial regions to solve common economic and social issues. US and Western European elites had a long history of collaboration; the novelty was integrating their Japanese counterparts more explicitly into the club. Carter appointed Trilateral Commission veterans to key posts in the administration, including Brzezinski as national security adviser, Cyrus Vance as secretary of state, W. Michael Blumenthal as secretary of the Treasury, and Harold Brown as secretary of defense.

Carter applied the trilateral formula to manage economic interdependence and restart economic growth. The question of how to reinvigorate the noninflationary recovery from the mid-1970s recession, which had stagnated during the second half of 1976, preoccupied officials around the world. Weak demand kept unemployment rates above Golden Age levels, but governments feared that stimulating their economies would rekindle inflation. "We should be cautious about calls for expansion," Dutch prime minister Joop den Uyl commented. "A revival of inflation would be dangerous for all."[14] Inflation had fallen from its 1974 peak but remained at an elevated rate of 7 percent (GNP deflator) in the industrial democracies during 1977.[15]

Carter's solution was to coordinate an expansion of the world's strongest countries. The United States, Japan, West Germany, the Netherlands, and Switzerland had been among the most vigilant in choking inflation in the mid-1970s while others such as Britain, France, and Italy had prioritized limiting unemployment. The locomotive theory called for the two groups to switch places. As weaker countries that had struggled with current account deficits and high levels of inflation now adopted restrictive monetary and fiscal policies, they needed a demand boost from the stronger economies.

The locomotive theory acknowledged the limits to US power in an interdependent global economy. The United States remained the most powerful country in the world, but the margin had shrunk considerably since the US welfare empire formed in the late 1940s. "Unlike times in the past, the *relative* economic and political weight of the United States is not enough on its own to carry the day," Brzezinski cautioned Carter. Instead, "U.S. leadership must involve prodding, cajoling, consulting—and a lot of stroking."[16] Under the protection of the US welfare empire, West Germany and Japan had become economic powerhouses on the strength of their export-driven development. Now the Carter administration asked them to increase demand, draw down their trade surpluses, and help fuel global growth.

Shortly after his inauguration, Carter sent Mondale to Western Europe and Japan to coordinate the locomotives. The new administration planned to provide the US economy with a stimulus, Mondale told Schmidt, and "hoped for parallel and coordinated efforts by the German and Japanese governments . . . to stimulate the global economy."[17] Yet the West Germans were skeptical. They did not want to upset their own monetary stability. The problems of the weaker countries could not be solved through misguided expansion of the stronger countries, the West Germans maintained. Greater macroeconomic stability was the precondition for noninflationary growth. There "was only limited room for further economic growth without reigniting inflation," State Secretary in the Ministry of Finance Karl Otto Pöhl cautioned.[18] Despite the chilly reception in Bonn, Assistant Secretary of the Treasury for International Affairs C. Fred Bergsten suggested that the administration nevertheless "must continue to hit the Germans, and the Japanese and Dutch to lesser extents, to expand more rapidly." Bergsten speculated that Schmidt "might move" after the wage negotiations ended in the spring.[19] The Mondale team had a warmer reception in Tokyo, where the Japanese reaction was favorable but noncommittal.[20]

The London summit of the G7 in May 1977 gave Carter his first opportunity to discuss the locomotive theory with his international peers. While the debates about macroeconomic coordination were technical, they had grand strategic implications. "The underlying mood of the forthcoming Summit meetings is one of anxiety," Brzezinski primed the president. "That anxiety pertains to the quality of leadership, to the viability of the social systems, and to the West's staying power particularly in the East-West competition."[21] Each major Western European government "is a near political minority . . . and neither Japan nor Canada can be considered in good shape," Brzezinski noted. "The democratic 'Establishment' is in decline, the Communist Parties and those of the extreme right have growing public acceptance and legitimacy." The summit must "show results both in overcoming the 'crisis of capitalism' and imparting new momentum to the political strength of our allies and the cohesion of the Alliance."[22] Communists had already joined in the Italian government, and French public opinion polls indicated that while the majority opposed a communist president, twice as many (43 percent to 20 percent) would accept communist ministers in the government than not.[23] Growing support in Italy and France for the Left "could endanger confidence and stability in neighboring Germany," Owen added. Economic stagnation and political disruption also impacted security and "hinder defense efforts in some European countries, and an evident weakening of European defense could hinder European recovery."[24] The geopolitical stakes of reinvigorating the global recovery were high.

Carter had no expertise in international economics. In contrast, Schmidt, Callaghan, Giscard, Andreotti, and Japanese prime minister Takeo Fukuda had sharpened their teeth as finance ministers before becoming heads of government, and Trudeau had been prime minister since April 1968. Displaying some rookie humility at the first session, he admitted that he came to the summit "not as an economist . . . but as an eager student."[25]

Despite support from Callaghan and Andreotti, Carter could not persuade Schmidt and Fukuda to commit to formal growth targets. Schmidt stressed the importance of price stability, and Fukuda even remarked that Carter's withdrawal of the tax rebate undermined the US calls for others to expand their economies.[26] Instead of announcing new annual targets, which would have been difficult because the year was almost half over, the United States, Japan, and West Germany reaffirmed their existing growth forecasts of 5 percent, 6.7 percent, and 4.5 to 5 percent, respectively. Britain, France, and Italy also committed to maintaining their stabilization policies.[27]

Early returns on the informal deal were "disquieting," Owen reported. While the weaker countries maintained their stabilization programs, it already appeared by the summer of 1977 that West Germany would fall short of the target.[28] After reassuring Schmidt that the United States would not try to impose any policy on West Germany, Carter stressed that "with 7 percent unemployment [in the United States] it is difficult to explain a $25 billion trade deficit to Congress, especially while the Germans have a $9–10 billion surplus." The chancellor responded that the Deutsche Mark had appreciated by about two-thirds since 1970. "That had been the German contribution to recovery."[29] Washington also grew frustrated that the Japanese did not "assume the international role their economic weight both entitles and obligates them to adopt."[30] Despite "nice communiques," Brzezinski described the Japanese as "derelict in meeting their international responsibilities in the economic field." He complained that Japanese officials offered "cheap palliatives which will get us off their backs for a while in hopes that some other issue will emerge to divert our attention."[31] West Germany ultimately missed its growth target by half, and Japan fell 1.7 percent short. Furthermore, their current account surpluses persisted, even though the Deutsche Mark and yen each appreciated. From 1976 to 1977, West Germany's surplus increased slightly, but Japan's spiked from $3.7 billion to $11 billion.[32]

The United States was the only locomotive to achieve its target. After running current account surpluses of $18 billion in 1975 and $4.2 billion in 1976, a deficit of $14.5 billion appeared in 1977. Yet a rise in oil imports accounted for much of the deterioration, so it did little to stimulate activity for the countries that most needed help.[33] The swing of the US current account into deficit also encouraged the depreciation of the dollar, which fell about 7 percent between September and December 1977.[34] Contemporaries worried that the US locomotive was unsustainable because the Carter administration might have to sacrifice its expansionary domestic agenda to address the large current account deficit, weak dollar, and rising inflation. Without the US locomotive, the global recovery could stall further.

The president addressed dollar depreciation publicly for the first time at the end of December 1977. Carter assured the nation that the "American economy and the dollar are fundamentally sound" and that the "recent exchange market disorders are not justified."[35] The White House established a swap line between the Bundesbank and the US Treasury but determined that the time had not yet come to make policy changes at home.[36] The dollar incurred losses against the Deutsche Mark, yen, and Swiss franc but had not moved much against the other OECD currencies, so the administration did not think that it needed a new economic strategy.[37]

The situation appeared more urgent in the spring. Between September 1977 and March 1978, the dollar dropped 14.6 percent against the Deutsche Mark, 24.7 percent against the Swiss franc, and 12.5 percent against the yen.[38] Saudi officials warned that OPEC might cease denominating oil in dollars if the greenback kept falling, and US officials began to acknowledge that they could not rely on the market to reverse the losses. "I have come to the conclusion that things have reached a point where it is essential for you to take vigorous action to halt the drift of events on energy and on the dollar," Blumenthal wrote the president in February 1978. "The cost of going as we are is now dangerously high and I urge that you act now."[39]

Concern grew in Washington about the dollar's continued slide because it threatened the West's entire international economic architecture and posed a national security threat. If in response OPEC increased oil prices to regain lost profits, the United States "would be blamed for converting a slow but steady recovery to a world-wide recession," cautioned Assistant Secretary of State Julius Katz. The Tokyo Round of trade liberalization negotiations would likely fail as a result. The dollar costs of maintaining the US military presence overseas would climb, leading to questions about Washington's commitment to defend its allies against Soviet aggression. The "burden of maintaining these forces would face us with difficult decisions: to curtail domestic social programs, to retrench on our defense expenditures, or to increase our budgetary deficit with adverse effects on domestic inflation."[40]

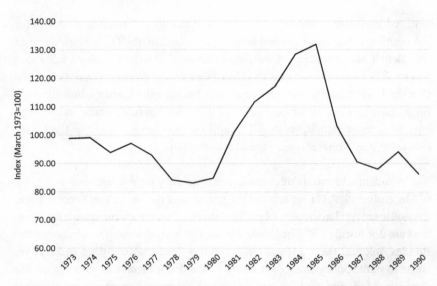

FIGURE 5.1.   Trade-weighted value of the dollar. Source: *Economic Report of the President*, 1991, 410.

The United States found itself at a crossroads. Under the Bretton Woods system, Washington had "encouraged other countries to be in surplus," the governor of the Bank of England Gordon Richardson explained. After 1973, it "abdicated from that role and took part in the game with everybody else under a regime of floating rates." The dollar became the global reserve currency, elbowing out alternatives such as gold, SDRs, and other national currencies. The problem was that the patchwork post–Bretton Woods system provided no rules for how the dollar should behave, and US authorities had not shown a willingness to "shoulder the responsibilities of running the only reserve asset in the system." The Carter administration had to make a choice: "Either the U.S. explicitly shoulders the burden of running a stable reserve currency for the world—a course which could involve at times some difficult decisions in domestic policy; or the world will hunt . . . for other currencies to share with the dollar the reserve and vehicle functions and burdens."[41] Maintaining the Bretton Woods system had thrust US economic and security objectives into conflict by the 1960s, and the current system presented Washington with similar tradeoffs.

Instead of sacrificing his domestic program to aid the dollar, Carter renewed his efforts to make the locomotive theory work. The problem was that the United States could not "continue with fast growth in a slow growth world," as Under Secretary of the Treasury for Monetary Affairs Anthony Solomon put it, and the president sought to speed up the latter rather than moderate the former.[42] The strategy garnered international support because global growth had dropped from 5.3 percent in 1976 to 4.1 percent in 1977.[43] US spending on oil was destabilizing, IMF managing director Johan Witteveen acknowledged at an April 1978 meeting of the IMF Interim Committee, but growth rates outside of the United States were too low. Representatives at the meeting singled out West Germany and Japan for their large trade surpluses. "Of the three locomotives, only one has functioned up to this point," Italian treasury minister Filippo Maria Pan criticized.[44]

With the Japanese agreeing in the winter to adopt new growth targets, the US focus turned to the West Germans.[45] "Action by the United States, alone, will not be enough," Carter lobbied Schmidt. "Indeed, there is a real question as to whether we can make meaningful progress in improving our current account position in the absence of faster growth abroad."[46] For their part, the West Germans were in the "uncomfortable position in the international debate" because they missed their 1977 growth target, Foreign Office official Hans Werner Lautenschlager admitted, but he lamented that Bonn had become a scapegoat for "unsatisfactory global economic development." The international community ignored West German contributions to the global recovery such as a reduction of the current account surplus and low rates of inflation, he griped, successes that were "hardly considered" in the press. "Unfortunately, the U.S. is trying to blame the weaker growth in Europe and especially [in West Germany] for its balance of payments deficit and the dollar rate, and thus to divert attention away from the main cause: the enormous increase in oil imports to the United States," he concluded.[47]

Bonn saw the locomotive theory as Washington's attempt to shirk responsibility for its profligacy. West Germany should not have to compensate for the United States' irresponsible spending. "It was up to the U.S. to promote growth," Schmidt argued. He accepted that he may eventually be forced to "take some measures" at home but suggested that "he might even resign rather than do so."[48] The US appetite for foreign oil was "dangerous for Western Europe as well," an economics ministry report added. "The more that the U.S. imports, the more problematic the long-term supply/demand situation is on the world market, and the more dangerous the latent danger of bilateral protection of U.S. oil imports with the OPEC countries . . . could become."[49] Bonn also speculated that Carter cared more about demonstrating to the US people that "the Germans also did something" than that West German measures made a difference.[50]

The chancellor did not want to let Carter off the hook, but domestic pressure to reflate reinforced the international calls. Not only had Bonn come up short on its London summit target, but West German growth in the first quarter of 1978 was an anemic 0.4 percent, and analysts forecasted annual growth under 3 percent.[51] Schmidt indicated his willingness to participate in a multilateral deal, brokered by Callaghan, in which each of the G7 countries contributed to systemic stability. Schmidt told the British prime minister in April 1978 that he would "pay a very high price if the United States . . . took action on energy and inflation." He wanted Carter to deregulate oil so that US consumers would pay more at the pump and reduce their consumption. "If President Carter would only do that," the chancellor promised that he "would go on his knees and praise God."[52] Schmidt faced opposition from within the SPD on tax cuts, while the SPD's coalition partner, the Free Democratic Party (FDP), supported them, so passing the stimulus package would be difficult politically. To square the circle, Schmidt wanted to make his domestic audience believe that West Germany's international partners had forced the program on him so that he could accept the deal and blame it on external pressure.[53]

In contrast to the informal growth targets in London the previous year, the G7 countries concluded the Bonn summit in July 1978 "with concrete agreements for each country."[54] Carter pledged to reduce oil imports by 2.5 million bpd by 1985 and eliminate price controls on domestic oil by the end of 1980. In return, West Germany promised to implement an additional fiscal stimulus program that totaled 1 percent of its GNP, and Japan set a target of 7 percent growth in real GNP. The remaining countries committed once more to their stabilization programs, and all agreed to conclude the Tokyo Round of trade talks as soon as possible to combat protectionism.[55] The Bonn summit marked a high point of multilateral coordination, but the agreement, even if implemented in full, would take months to make an impact. "We are not doing well," NSC staffer John Renner admitted to Brzezinski shortly after the summit.[56]

There was no love lost between Schmidt and Carter. "The American leadership does not know what it is doing," Schmidt groused.[57] The inexperienced Carter was "idealistic and fickle," he later claimed, not least for his dogmatic promotion of human rights, which antagonized the Soviet bloc and made it more difficult to maintain détente.[58] The animosity was mutual. In his diary, Carter described Schmidt as "strong, somewhat unstable, [someone who] postures, drones on and on, giving economic lessons."[59] When Carter complained that Schmidt had "been quite obnoxious," Brzezinski responded, "You have been quite obnoxious to him."[60] The late 1970s marked a low point in US–West German relations as Carter and Schmidt clashed on issues such as East-West relations, international economics, and nuclear technology transfers.

Schmidt may have been the most vocal, but the other Western European leaders had reservations about US economic policy as well. Recalling the unraveling of the Bretton Woods system, they viewed the slide of the dollar and Carter's stance of benign neglect with an exasperated sense of déjà vu. The European Council expressed concern about the level of US oil imports, a burden on the US balance of payments that "led to a breach of trust in the exchange rate of the dollar."[61] The dollar also impacted the sluggish recovery in the European Community. In June 1978, unemployment ranged from West Germany's 4.4 percent to Belgium's 9.9 percent, which were figures that "would have been thought revolutionary in the Europe of the 1960's," a State Department official noted. These numbers resulted from the deflationary and slow-growth policies that Western European capitals had implemented to fight inflation, a war that was going well in only a few places. "No one has found the key to a return to high growth and employment at tolerable levels of inflation," he observed. "The great economic puzzle of the 1970's remains unsolved." Fears still pervaded that Eurocommunists would make gains, particularly in Italy and France.[62] The kidnapping and murder of former Italian prime minister Aldo Moro in May 1978 by the far-left Red Brigades amplified fears of what communist governance would mean for Western Europe.

As it had in the early 1970s, the European Community turned to monetary integration to shelter itself from dollar instability. During the mid-1970s arguments in favor of monetary cooperation had focused on protecting the common market and achieving political objectives, but concerns about the dollar moved to the front of the line in early 1978.[63] Schmidt and Giscard proposed the formation of a regional monetary system at the European Council in April 1978. If the European Community "acted together," Giscard explained, "then it could create a European Bretton Woods with a European exchange rate against the dollar."[64] After years of false starts, the European Community at the Bremen Summit of July 1978 declared its intention to establish the European Monetary System (EMS). Stable monetary relations would minimize currency fluctuations and provide a greater measure of certainty in a region with a high volume of trade. "The time has come for a stable monetary zone in Europe," a West German official noted, "if one wants to limit the dangers of unstable exchange rates on economic growth and the fight against inflation."[65]

The EC countries had a common objective but differed on how to achieve it. As the abortive experience of the early 1970s had shown, the challenge of achieving monetary integration was formidable, and many financial officials expressed skepticism. Pöhl commented on the difficulty with an anecdote about World War II. Someone came to the British Admiralty, he told a Dutch official, with a plan to neutralize the German submarine threat by heating the ocean to 100 degrees Celsius. When the Admiralty asked the man how he planned to raise the ocean's temperature, he responded that he did not know; the technical experts at the Admiralty would have to figure that out themselves.[66]

The EC battle lines were drawn between the members of the Snake and nonmembers, and between countries with strong and weak currencies. As the leaders of the Snake, the West Germans promoted the expansion of the Snake into a parity grid, a structure that meant countries with weak currencies would bear the burden of adjustment to keep pace with the stronger.[67] Bonn preferred this method because it would keep its currency from appreciating too far against the dollar. The other members of the Snake, including Belgium, Luxembourg, the Netherlands, and Denmark, supported the West German position. The Snake had "proven itself to work well in practice," concluded the Dutch finance ministry, which saw no reason to abandon it.[68] This group believed that it benefited from the certainty that exchange rates among its members would stay constant. The group also wanted to limit pooling resources so that its taxpayers would not have to bail out countries struggling with balance of payments deficits.

States with weaker currencies, in contrast, feared that joining the Snake would mean that they would have to deflate to keep pace with West Germany. Under the terms of the Snake, when one currency reached its intervention margin, there would always be another currency at its intervention margin at the opposite end. The burden of adjustment would fall on the country with the weaker currency.[69] Britain worried that sterling's weak position meant that it would "likely be the first to attract speculative attention." Sterling would be the "lead in the balloon," the Treasury warned, anchoring the Deutsche Mark and other strong currencies from drifting too high. The Treasury was skeptical about a system that placed "pressures on all participating countries to appreciate at the speed of the D-mark against non-participants, especially the dollar, and does not therefore contain a deflationary bias."[70] Paris and Rome harbored similar concerns. They supported a basket system in which each currency would fluctuate within an agreed band of its exchange rate against the average of all the members of the system. This meant that if the Deutsche Mark appreciated too far, the burden of adjustment would fall on Bonn.[71]

A "Belgian compromise" bridged the gap. It blended the Snake with an "indicator of divergence," a mechanism to determine which currency was deviant. When a currency exceeded its threshold, the central bank would be obligated to intervene in the exchange markets to correct the change in parity.[72] The EMS used the new European Currency Unit (ECU) as a unit of account for payments within the zone, a development that made it possible to decrease reliance on the dollar. The British joined the system but refused to participate in the exchange-rate intervention obligation, which some charged "as analogous to trying to play Hamlet without the Prince."[73]

The EMS further solidified the European Community as a coherent entity in international economic affairs, signaling the "growing power of Europe" on the world stage, as the West German Finance Ministry noted in November 1978.[74] The Western Europeans had never been comfortable with the post–Bretton Woods system and had expressed their desire to return to a fixed exchange rate system. Absent US cooperation in reforming the international monetary system and with dollar instability illustrating the dangers of the current patchwork system, the European Community sought to carve out an area of regional stability.[75]

The formation of the EMS occurred in the backdrop of the dollar's largest and most sustained decline since the collapse of the Bretton Woods system. The dollar dropped 13 percent on a trade-weighted basis between May and October 1978, including 23 percent against the yen and 18.5 percent against the Deutsche Mark.[76] Analysts agreed that the dollar was now undervalued, but it fell because of the widespread anxiety about the United States' willingness and ability to tackle its own problems. Bergsten wrote Blumenthal in August 1978 that the fall of the dollar "indicates a lack of confidence in the U.S. Government's ability to deal with the fundamental U.S. problems of inflation, energy policy and trade. Monetary policy is regarded as no longer effective, fiscal policy moves as unlikely in the near future, and the anti-inflationary program as a failure. The market sees the Administration as resigned to await future developments, which may, over the horizon, be helpful but which offer no present incentive to hold dollars." Bergsten added a handwritten note at the top of his memorandum: "Mike—this is rough but, I'm afraid, an accurate picture."[77] Carter had committed to reducing US oil consumption and decontrolling domestic energy prices at the Bonn summit, but Congress had dragged its feet on passing energy legislation and had removed the teeth of the administration's program. Inflation surged to 10.4 percent during the first six months of the year, in comparison to just 3 and 4 percent in West Germany and Japan, respectively.[78]

Dollar depreciation made US exports more competitive at a time when the current account deficit spiraled, but the weaker dollar also presented serious problems. The dollar crisis was tied to broader questions of monetary stability, global growth, and the maintenance of the open world economy. First, the Federal Reserve increased interest rates to protect the dollar, which threatened the economic expansion at home. Second, it empowered OPEC countries that wanted to increase oil prices to compensate for the lost purchasing power of their oil income. OPEC countries invested about 60 percent of their $160 billion in foreign holdings in dollar-denominated assets, but by the spring of 1978 their value had depreciated to 72 percent of what it had been in 1974.[79] "We can no longer make the case that OPEC is no worse off than in early 1974," Widman warned Solomon in August 1978.[80] Even Moscow, which exported energy in dollars and generally imported in Western European currencies, felt the squeeze. "The scissors are expanding, export revenue is falling, and import costs are increasing," the Soviet deputy minister of foreign trade complained.[81] Third, OPEC had agreed in June 1975 to use SDRs to denominate oil prices but did not implement the agreement because the dollar began to appreciate. The question now reemerged of whether OPEC might finally shift away from the dollar. Fourth, it threatened the dollar's position as the world's reserve currency and lowered US prestige and political influence. More than half a trillion dollars circulated overseas, and unless the private and public owners of these bills were satisfied that the Carter administration had taken steps to defend the dollar, the assault would continue.

The Carter administration refused to intervene directly into the markets, believing that such an action would have little impact with hundreds of billions of dollars floating beyond US borders. Noting that US inflation was "not much higher than the average level among our major trading partners" and that the current account deficit was beginning to shrink, the White House blamed the crisis on "uncertainty in foreign exchange markets" and believed that the dollar's decline "was not justified by fundamental economic conditions."[82] Carter announced voluntary price and wage controls and reductions in federal spending in late October 1978 to show that he took the fight against inflation seriously. The announcement, which did nothing to support the dollar in the short term, "went over like a lead balloon," chairman of the Council of Economic Advisers Charles Schultze recalled.[83] "I would rather not take any dollars at all," a West German taxi driver commented. "If somebody offered me dollars, I would drive him to the nearest bank to check the rate. . . . I don't know what it's going to be tomorrow, do I?"[84]

The tepid market response compelled the Carter administration to do more. US officials resigned themselves to intervening in what they interpreted as disorderly markets. "Leaving it to Adam Smith doesn't work anymore," Solomon conceded. "The old invisible hand is just not there."[85] On the first day of November 1978, Carter and Blumenthal introduced a dollar rescue package. In addition to announcing that the Federal Reserve would raise the discount and federal funds rates, they publicized a $30 billion intervention package to support the dollar in the exchange markets. This included drawings from the

US reserve tranche in the IMF; sales of SDRs; increasing the Federal Reserve swap lines with West Germany, Japan, and Switzerland; and a commitment to issue foreign currency–denominated securities.[86] Carter's package of measures did not "remove all reasonable doubts," the British embassy reported, but it made "the administration's policies look more coherent and vigorous."[87] The markets agreed. By January 1979, the dollar had appreciated 7.7 percent above its October 1978 low.[88]

The dollar crisis of 1978 presented the United States with the most severe external challenge to its monetary autonomy in the postwar period.[89] The Bretton Woods system had insulated domestic policies from external balances, but the current system provided no such protection. Financial globalization circumscribed Carter's freedom of action and compelled him to subordinate domestic policy to external pressures.[90] After nearly two years of seeking to create an international environment that would accommodate his expansionary domestic program, Carter reversed course. He told his Cabinet that "the problem of inflation was his most pressing concern."[91] Rather than trying to stimulate growth and creating jobs, he would discipline the economy. He took some heat at home for it. "Future Mortgaged to Defend Dollar," read a headline in the *Washington Post*.[92] The long-term implications of this decision were not yet clear, but the Volcker shock the following year must be viewed as part of a longer trajectory that began with Carter's choice to abandon economic expansion in favor of monetary discipline.[93]

Those who doubted the de facto dollar international monetary system felt vindicated. Under the Bretton Woods system, central banks held dollars because the dollar had a fixed relationship with gold, but now they had no guarantee of the future value of their dollar holdings. "What is now dangerously at risk is the role of the dollar in international finance and as the world's banking currency and with it all the world's trading arrangements," warned Harold Lever, Callaghan's economic adviser.[94] The proportion of official reserves held in dollars dropped from 78 percent in 1977 to 72.9 percent in 1979.[95]

Yet the existing de facto dollar standard had also shown resilience. For starters, there did not appear to be a compelling alternative. "The talk about lessening the burden on the dollar by other currencies (or artificial reserve units) taking over part of the reserve currency role is a waste of time," Bundesbank president Otmar Emminger commented. "For there are no sufficiently strong candidates for this role available."[96] The Deutsche Mark share of official holdings increased from 9.1 percent to 12.5 percent between 1977 and 1979, but it remained a very distant second place to the dollar, and the West Germans discouraged the broader use of the Deutsche Mark as a reserve currency.[97] Furthermore, the Carter administration's response demonstrated the US commitment to an open trading system and the existing order. Foreseeing tight US monetary policy, a corrective recession, and an end to US oil price controls, the British ambassador Peter Jay predicted that the dollar would soon become "embarrassingly strong." "The things-that-go-bump-in-the-night-school, with its talk of the collapse . . . of the dollar and underlying capital account problems, will then seem implausible."[98] He was right.

The outbreak of the second oil crisis disrupted Carter's anti-inflationary program. Dollar depreciation had overdetermined at least a modest price increase during 1979. At the urging of Saudi Arabia, OPEC had respected a "price freeze" after January 1977. Riyadh wished to maintain good relations with the United States and retain access to its weapons dealers, and the Carter administration reciprocated by muscling an arms package through Congress in the spring of 1978 that included the sale to Saudi Arabia of sixty F-15s (the F-15 was one of the most advanced fighter jets in the world) over objections from the pro-Israel domestic lobby.[99] OPEC nations grew frustrated, however, that their moderate position had not protected the purchasing power of their earnings. "All signs point to an increase in the dollar-oil price," the West German Foreign Office warned in November 1978.[100] In December 1978, OPEC announced that it would raise the price of crude oil from $13 per barrel to $14.50 in stages over the course of 1979.[101]

Upheaval in Iran turned a modest price increase into the second oil crisis. As the Iranian Revolution erupted, strikes in the Iranian oil fields began in October 1978. Iran was the world's second-largest exporter of oil with a total of more than 5.5 million bpd, but by mid-November, that figure had fallen to fewer than 1 million bpd. Domestic oil production ceased completely in late December 1978 and did not restart for more than two months.[102] Recalling the shortages during the winter of 1973–74, traders scrambled to secure supplies and bid up prices on the spot market. The British Department of Energy noted that "the oil market is very dependent on perceptions." Even though supply exceeded demand by about 1 million bpd, the market reacted because it feared "a possible permanent change for the worse."[103] OPEC ignored its earlier plans for moderate increases and raised the posted price by 14.5 percent in December 1978 and an additional 9 percent in March 1979. Exploiting the widespread anxiety about shortages, individual OPEC countries sold oil above those prices.[104]

The industrial democracies were better prepared for it than met the eye. Through a combination of domestic measures, some of them had been able to reduce the amount of oil they consumed while others had slowed annual increases. From 1969 to 1973, Britain's oil consumption increased 4.7 percent per year, but from 1974 to 1978 it declined 3.2 percent annually. France, Italy, and West Germany also achieved yearly reductions. US and Japanese consumption increased, but only 0.4 and 1.8 percent per year, respectively.[105] OPEC still produced about 55 percent of the oil outside of the Soviet bloc in 1978, in comparison to 59 percent in 1973, but investors poured resources into developing new sources of oil in Alaska, Mexico, and the North Sea that began to come on line.[106] With their balance of payments problems during the second half of the 1970s, the British took comfort that "a rainbow spans the somber horizon of the next few years: the prospect of off-shore oil" from the North Sea.[107] Between 1974 and 1979, British oil production spiked from 10,000 bpd to 1.6 million bpd.[108]

New non-OPEC supplies threatened OPEC's stranglehold on the oil market in the medium term, but OPEC still called the shots for the moment. A disaster at the Three Mile Island power plant at the end of March 1979 fed popular doubts in the United States about the safety of nuclear power and amplified the despair about the dependence on foreign oil. In an address the following month, Carter announced that he would decontrol the prices of domestic oil in phases, beginning on the first day of June. "Federal Government price controls now hold down our own production, and they encourage waste and increasing dependence on foreign oil," he explained. Claiming that the oil companies would "reap huge and undeserved windfall profits" on domestic oil as the prices increased, he also asked Congress to impose a windfall profits tax "to capture part of this money for the American people," the revenues from which would be spent on cushioning the blow of the crisis on low-income families, building more efficient mass transportation, and investment in solving the long-term energy problems. "The energy crisis is real," Carter stressed. "Time is running short." He alerted the public that it would "use less oil and pay more for it," but "that is the cost we must pay to reduce our dependence on the foreign oil cartel."[109]

Bringing domestic oil prices in line with those on the world market incentivized domestic production, reduced dependence on imports, and lowered consumption. During 1979, demand for petroleum products dropped by 4.2 percent and gasoline by 9.3 percent.[110] Imports as a percentage of total supply dropped from 44.7 percent in 1979 to 40.2 percent in 1980 and to 37 percent in 1981.[111]

These positive developments offered little comfort to US consumers who craved relief now. Long lines at gasoline stations reappeared in the spring and summer of 1979. "If this is a free country," a New Yorker griped, "then why can't we get gas?"[112] At a Texaco station in northeastern New Jersey, a queue of three hundred cars began to form well before 3 a.m. Some drivers had parked overnight and returned to their cars before the sun had come up. Each driver received a maximum of five dollars' worth of gasoline per visit, but supply dwindled within just two hours, so the cap was lowered to four dollars.[113] The average sale of gas in the United States fell from eight gallons to three.[114] There simply was not enough to go around. California governor Edmund Brown Jr. demanded that his state receive a greater supply; otherwise, he threatened to go to Washington himself to "rattle a few cages." California cast the largest number of electoral votes of any state, Brown warned, "and if Carter wants to be re-elected in 1980, he better listen to us."[115]

Just as Nixon's political standing had taken a beating from the first oil crisis, the second shock hurt Carter's reelection prospects. Many US citizens even doubted the legitimacy of the crisis. "No one believes there is really a shortage," White House public opinion pollster Patrick Cadell reported. "The Administration's credibility is low. The public is now unwilling to pay higher prices to solve what they regard as a trumped up crisis."[116] Some took the crisis seriously, making "a long list before driving to the market," skipping vacations, and then lining up at gas stations "for hours at unbelievably inconvenient times as a reward for their energy consciousness." Others were still joyriding, taking trips to the beach, and "zip[ping] down to Safeway just for a loaf of bread," a Maryland man complained.[117] US consumers did not want to sacrifice; they demanded a quick fix.

Western policymakers understood that a solution to the second oil shock required the cooperation of Saudi Arabia, which had replaced the United States as the world's swing producer. This meant that of the world's producers, Saudi Arabia alone had "the spare capacity to provide significant immediate relief on the supply side."[118] Riyadh had imposed a production ceiling of 8.5 million bpd since 1974, but Finance Minister Mohammed Ali Abalkhail indicated that Riyadh was ready to "do its share" to cover the Iranian shortfall. In return, he asked the industrial democracies for concessions in the form of energy conservation measures.[119] Saudi Arabia increased production to 10.5 million bpd. Other members of OPEC, particularly Kuwait and Iraq, also increased production to take advantage of higher prices, and Iran resumed oil shipments in early March, albeit at a lower level.

Carter's initiative to convene a peace conference with the Arabs and Israelis complicated matters, however. He brokered the Camp David Accords in September 1978, which provided a "peace for land" agreement between Israel and Egypt in which the former withdrew from the Sinai in exchange for the latter signing a formal peace treaty in March 1979. Important issues endemic to the broader Arab-Israeli conflict remained unresolved, including the status of the Golan Heights, Gaza Strip, West Bank, and Palestine. The rest of the

Arab nations denounced the peace treaty, and the Saudis "were not prepared after Camp David to allow themselves to be seen to be the friends of the United States."[120] The Saudis lowered their production back to the self-imposed 8.5 million bpd ceiling to protest the treaty.[121]

The G7 Summit in Tokyo in June 1979 provided a forum for the industrial democracies to demonstrate that they were serious about energy conservation and regain Riyadh's help. The mood at the meetings was agitated. "The first day of the economic summit was one of the worst days of my diplomatic life," Carter wrote in his diary. "Schmidt got personally abusive toward me, alleging that American interference in the Mideast on a peace treaty had caused problems with oil all over the world."[122] Energy dominated the summit agenda. The G7 now vowed to reduce oil imports through 1985. The EC countries promised to freeze their consumption while the United States and Japan promised to limit imports to 8.5 million bpd, and 6.5 million bpd, respectively, through 1985.[123] In return, Saudi Arabia indicated in early July 1979 that it would increase production. The gasoline lines in the United States began to disappear, but the high prices remained. By mid-1979, the official price for Arabian marker crude had risen to eighteen dollars per barrel, 42 percent above its end-1978 price.[124]

Pessimism reigned as the second oil shock took its toll on Western economies and societies. Carter captured the zeitgeist in a remarkable address to the nation in July 1979. He shared that over the previous two weeks, he had met with business and labor leaders, teachers, politicians, and private citizens at Camp David to listen to their stories. Reflecting on their insights, Carter concluded that the problems confronting the United States went deeper than gasoline lines, inflation, and recession. "All the legislation in the world can't fix what's wrong with America," he admitted. This threat to US democracy was one of confidence. "It is a crisis that strikes at the very heart and soul and spirit of our national will," he declared. "The erosion of our confidence in the future is threatening to destroy the social and the political fabric of America." For the first time in US history, he noted, more people in the United States believed that the next five years would be worse than the previous five years.

This crisis of confidence had accumulated over many years, he said. The productivity of US workers was dropping, and investment rates lagged those of other Western countries. Respect for public, religious, and other institutions waned. The assassinations of John F. Kennedy, Robert Kennedy, and Martin Luther King Jr.; the agony of the Vietnam War; and the stain of Watergate had shaken the nation's faith in its political institutions. The optimism and prosperity of the postwar period had disappeared. "We remember when the phrase 'sound as a dollar' was an expression of absolute dependability, until ten years of inflation began to shrink our dollar and our savings," Carter lamented. "We believed that our nation's resources were limitless until 1973 when we had to face a growing dependence on foreign oil." The "wounds" to US confidence cut deep, the president asserted, and "they have never been healed."[125]

Carter voiced hard truths as he looked into the soul of his country, but he also outlined a path to restore the nation's "common purpose" and values. It started with resolving the "energy problem." He set a goal that the United States would never import more oil than it did during 1977 and announced new investment into developing domestic reserves, alternative energy sources, and a conservation program.[126] The speech was remarkable for its honest assessment of the problems plaguing the country, but Carter's call for sacrifice and moderation did not resonate with most of the public. He received a temporary boost to his approval rating that quickly disappeared.[127]

His next move gave ammunition to critics who charged that the administration lacked stability and coherence. Two days after his speech, Carter dismissed five of his cabinet members. Among those on the chopping block was Blumenthal, whom Carter replaced with Federal Reserve Board chairman G. William Miller. "When the falling curve of the President's popularity intersects with the rising curve of interest rates," Blumenthal quipped, "it is time for the Treasury Secretary to go."[128] With Miller taking over at Treasury, Carter had to fill the open position at the Federal Reserve.

Paul Volcker emerged as the favorite among those surveyed by the president's staff. A figurative and literal giant (he stood six-foot-seven) in the field of economics, Volcker had served at Treasury as the undersecretary for monetary affairs and had been described as the "Henry Kissinger of international monetary diplomacy" for shuttling around Western capitals "as a traveling salesman for the American dollar" in the early 1970s. He served as president of the New York Federal Reserve after leaving the Nixon administration and earned the respect of colleagues across the political spectrum. Volcker "is a pragmatist's pragmatist," reflected former Treasury official Robert Roosa. "He really isn't doctrinaire."[129] Understanding that Volcker would discipline the economy, many White House advisers and Mondale opposed Volcker because they feared that harsh monetary medicine would dim Carter's chances for reelection. Carter shared the concern and first offered the position to Bank of America president Tom Clausen, who promptly put the president on hold to consult his wife. Clausen returned a few minutes later to decline. Still in bed when Carter called with the job offer the next morning, Volcker accepted.[130]

It was a fateful decision. During his first confirmation hearing before Congress in July 1979, Volcker emphasized price stability, contending that he did not "think we have any substitute for seeking an answer to our problems in the context of monetary discipline." When Volcker accepted the position, he received a promise that the White House would respect the Federal Reserve's independence, and he fiercely guarded it throughout his tenure. "Decisions on monetary policy are those of the Federal Reserve," he told Congress. "We have to call the shots as we see them."[131]

The core task, he believed, was to eliminate the inflationary expectations that had accumulated over time and show the Federal Reserve's resolve to choke inflation, even at the cost of economic hardship in the short term. Volcker rejected the Phillips Curve, which described the conventional postwar wisdom that there existed a trade-off between inflation and unemployment. "I simply am not sure that this 'either-or' doctrine is a valid guide to public policy in the current circumstances," he explained to Republican senator Jacob Javits. He suggested that "inflation may have gone too far for too long," that efforts to "'buy' less unemployment by 'accepting' more inflation may ultimately result in more, not less, unemployment."[132]

Volcker prioritized monetary discipline over boosting economic growth and employment, believing that only after the country had mastered inflation should it reorient toward expansion. After holding a secret meeting of the Federal Open Market Committee (FMOC) on October 6, 1979, Volcker announced a stabilization program that would focus on managing the growth of the money supply rather than monitor interest rates. The strategy provided political cover because it obscured the relationship between regulating the money supply and interest rates. By controlling the former, Volcker influenced the latter, and thus rates of inflation, economic growth, and unemployment. Yet he could claim that the market bore responsibility for hardship.[133] "There really is only one reason why we should have abandoned the federal funds target procedure to go to the [nonborrowed] reserve target," explained Lyle E. Gramley, a governor on the Federal Reserve Board. "And that is because if we operate on federal funds, we explicitly take responsibility for what is happening to interest rates and then this becomes a very difficult world to live in."[134] With the Federal Reserve no longer targeting the federal funds rate, the rate became erratic and jumped from 11.4 percent in September 1979 to 17.2 percent in March 1980, dipped under 10 percent in the summer, and then surged again to nearly 19 percent by the end of the year.[135]

Interest rates rose not only because of Volcker's tight monetary policy but also because the markets became anxious when news broke in early 1980 that the estimated federal budget would be nearly 50 percent higher than anticipated.[136]

Most of the increase came from pressure on social safety nets in response to the economic downturn and larger interest payments. In sum, the budget deficit increased from $41 billion (1.6 percent of GDP) in 1979 to $74 billion (2.6 percent of GDP) in 1980.[137] Fearful that the budget indicated that the White House would not exercise fiscal restraint, the markets demanded high interest rates because they believed that inflation would continue to grow.

Expanded defense expenditures pushed the budget further into the red. Carter increased defense appropriations in response to the Soviet invasion of Afghanistan in December 1979. Brzezinski had identified Afghanistan as part of what he called an "arc of crisis" that stretched "from Chittagong . . . through Islamabad to Aden." Comparing the situation to Western Europe in the late 1940s, he warned that fragmentation across this large area could create a "political vacuum" that might "be filled by elements more sympathetic to the Soviet Union."[138] Events appeared to confirm Brzezinski's fears. With Iran in the throes of revolution, Washington's twin pillars strategy in the Middle East faltered and the security of Persian Gulf reserves came into question. Angry about economic stagnation, inequality, and the shah's close association with the United States, radicals sacked the US embassy in Tehran in November 1979 and took sixty-six hostages. The Carter administration's inability to free them symbolized the United States' diminishing position in the region.

Although declassified Soviet documents have since proven otherwise, the White House feared that the invasion of Afghanistan was part of Moscow's larger plan to expand its sphere of influence. "A successful take-over of Afghanistan would give the Soviets a deep penetration between Iran and Pakistan," Carter later wrote, "and pose a threat to the rich oil fields of the Persian Gulf area and to the crucial waterways through which so much of the world's energy supplies had to pass."[139] In what became known as the Carter Doctrine, the president announced during his State of the Union address in January 1980 that "an attempt by any outside force to gain control of the Persian Gulf region will be regarded as an assault on the vital interests of the United States of America, and such an assault will be repelled by any means necessary, including military force."[140] The Carter administration imposed a grain embargo against the Soviet Union, reduced trade, boycotted the summer Olympic games in Moscow, recalled the US ambassador, asked the Senate to cease its consideration of SALT II, and boosted defense expenditures.[141] Real defense spending increased 5.7 percent during 1980.[142] What was left of superpower détente collapsed.

Much of the new defense spending went to building US military infrastructure in the Persian Gulf, where US officials acknowledged that US forces would be outmatched by Soviet forces in the event of a war. The Carter administration began to negotiate with regional governments to house US bases and procured new ships and weapons that would allow US forces to deploy to the region on short notice.[143] The other industrial democracies were content to have the United States take responsibility for protecting the oil regions that were so vital to their own economies and security. Although "Western European and Japanese dependence on Persian Gulf–Southwest Asian oil dwarfs that of the United States," the Department of Defense noted in its annual report, "yet we have assumed the overwhelming bulk of the renewed effort to defend the flow of oil." The Department of Defense estimated that its Rapid Deployment Force (RDF) programs, most of which focused on Southwest Asia, would cost $17.4 billion over the next four years.[144]

While claiming that the United States enjoyed advantages vis-à-vis the Soviet Union in technology, economics, political institutions, and military-related technology, US officials believed that there was "essential equivalence" in the military balance and the trend lines were "adverse."[145] The Department of Defense estimated that the Soviet Union dedicated between 11 and 14 percent of its GNP to defense, and Soviet spending on the military was about 50 percent larger than that of the United States. It assumed that the difference in investment was even larger. Moscow had overcome its strategic inferiority in just over a decade and had the "potential for strategic advantage if we fail to respond with adequate programs of our own," Brown warned.[146] Inflation sapped the impact of defense increases. "We keep running faster just to stay in place and can't catch up with the Soviet effort," remarked Under Secretary of Defense Robert Komer.[147]

With setbacks abroad and stagflation compounding the "crisis of confidence" at home, Carter took shots from both the Republicans and the left wing of the Democratic Party as the November 1980 presidential election approached. His GOP opponent Ronald Reagan accused him of being weak on national security issues, and inflation and a recession in the first half of 1980 cast a shadow over everything else. "A recession is when your neighbor loses his job, a depression is when you lose your job, and recovery is when Jimmy Carter loses his," Reagan jabbed.[148] The outbreak of war between Iraq and Iran in late September 1980, less than two months before the election, removed about 4 million bpd from the world market and helped push oil prices to thirty-five dollars per barrel by the end of the year.[149]

Despite the political costs, Carter believed that the nation needed a disciplinary program, even if he knew that it darkened his prospects for reelection. The US GNP dropped at an annual rate of almost 10 percent in the second quarter of 1980.[150] "Rarely has a recession been as eagerly awaited as this one, nor as carefully nurtured by an administration," noted an article in the *Washington Post* in August 1980. "Presidential encouragement for this year's economic slowdown was . . . all the stranger since 1980 is an election year."[151] After Volcker informed Carter just two months before the election that he would raise the discount rate, the president reflected, "This will hurt us politically, but I think it's the right thing to do."[152] Reagan won the election in a landslide.

The inversion of the US welfare empire was contingent on key events and decisions. The 1980 election marked one such moment. While Reagan ultimately found a way for the United States to spend more than it produced, Carter offered an alternative model that required the country to confront limits. Inflation, the second oil shock, and the lack of productivity growth were "all related to each other," Carter wrote in his final *Economic Report of the President* in January 1981. The country could overcome them, but the problems were "so deep-seated that progress will come slowly, only with persistence, and at the cost of some sacrifice on the part of us all."[153] The inverted US welfare empire, which entailed living beyond the means of the United States by drawing on foreign resources, was precisely what Carter did not want. The counterfactual of a second Carter term is not too far-fetched; although polls indicated a sizable lead for Reagan in the battle for the electoral college, surveys completed just days before the election showed a tight race for the popular vote.[154]

Carter nevertheless helped create structural conditions that contributed to the resurgence of US economic and military power during the first half of the 1980s. First, he initiated the military buildup that Reagan would expand. Second, Carter waged a deregulation campaign to make the economy more efficient. This was particularly important in the energy sector. By late 1980, the United States imported nearly 30 percent less oil than it did two years prior, and gasoline consumption had dropped more than 10 percent.[155] Third, Carter's support of the dollar helped ensure that the de facto dollar standard endured. Although it was not an uninterrupted rise, the dollar crossed the 2 Deutsche Mark threshold in December 1980 for the first time since September 1978.[156] A strong dollar emerged, as Jay had predicted, in the first half of the 1980s and the continued centrality of the dollar in global finance and trade served as the pivot of the US welfare empire's inversion. Finally, Carter's transition to promoting monetary discipline over expansion played a key role in taming inflation over the next few years. His decision to appoint Volcker as Federal Reserve chairman was "an act of presidential courage," notes Kai Bird, because Carter understood that it would help the country reduce inflation but harm his own political fortunes.[157]

The Volcker shock stands out as pivotal in the arc of US power in the late twentieth century. It was oriented toward domestic issues but had global re-

THE TRAVAILS OF JIMMY CARTER   135

percussions. High US interest rates imposed monetary discipline around the world and transformed transnational lending patterns. Although the breakdown of détente grabbed the headlines about East-West relations during the late 1970s and early 1980s, the Volcker shock had an unexpected Cold War utility as well: it struck a body blow against the Soviet bloc.

Chapter 6

The Soviet Umbrella and the Volcker Shock

In late October 1980, Brezhnev told the Politburo about his recent meeting with Polish leaders Stanisław Kania and Józef Pińkowski. The Polish regime was locked in a struggle with a new independent trade union, known as Solidarity, that had emerged a few months earlier in response to an unpopular increase in food prices. While Kania and Pińkowski tried to wear a brave face, they "did not hide their alarm" about the opposition's strength, Brezhnev reported, and "vacillation crept into their utterances" when discussing how to crush the counterrevolution. As the battle raged between the regime and Solidarity for the hearts and minds of the Polish nation, they worried that the people would revolt if the regime used force.[1] Socialism in Poland hung in the balance.

The Solidarity crisis was different from previous crises that had threatened the integrity of the Soviet bloc. Whereas flashpoints such as the Hungarian Revolution and the Prague Spring had taken place when the West had little leverage over events, Poland's external debt forced the leadership to formulate policy with an eye on how Western creditors and global financial markets would react. "Poland is bound by debts hand and foot," Kania and Pińkowski claimed. "Poland's economy has become dependent primarily on the West." Given this dependence, they feared, "any exacerbation of the situation in the country could create grounds for the capitalists to refuse further deferment of credits and Poland . . . would be brought to its knees." Debt had become a tool for the West to intrude on internal decisions behind the Iron Curtain.[2]

The Solidarity uprising was an explosive manifestation of a debt crisis that swept across Eastern Europe in the wake of the Volcker shock. While the twin energy crises of the mid-1970s had exposed the CMEA countries' inability to transition to intensive economic development, the Volcker shock removed the lifeline that capitalist banks had extended to them to compensate. Although directed toward choking inflation at home, the Volcker shock triggered a series of paralyzing jolts to the Soviet bloc in the late 1970s and early 1980s, bringing several socialist states to the brink of bankruptcy. The CMEA countries struggled to find creditors, and when they did, could not afford the high interest rates.

The crisis was ubiquitous across Eastern Europe, but nowhere did the Volcker shock spark a more volatile situation than in Poland. Officials in Warsaw believed that they had no other choice but to suppress consumption to stay solvent. Austerity forced simmering political and economic frustrations to the surface, and the establishment of Solidarity in the summer of 1980 threatened to bring down the PZPR government. As the debt crisis spiraled and threatened to spread across the Soviet bloc, *Euromoney* wondered whether "economic ills may yet rot the guts out of the East European economy in a way that no political subversion could."[3]

The Solidarity crisis presented Moscow with the legitimate possibility that socialism in Poland might collapse. The logic of the Soviet welfare empire demanded a strong response from the Kremlin to secure the PZPR's position, but new economic limitations closed off options. Poland's needs spiked at the same time that the Soviet economy took a turn for the worse. "In practice," *Euromoney* described in August 1981, "the Soviet umbrella is providing only partial cover."[4] The Soviets ruled out the use of force and resolved to allow events in Poland to run their course, tacitly acknowledging a new hierarchy of Soviet interests that privileged the domestic over the international.

The Polish regime's declaration of martial law in December 1981 defused the immediate political crisis, but a tectonic shift in the Cold War balance of power occurred in the early 1980s. In previous years, the Soviet Union had provided emergency financial aid and military support to protect an ally, but Moscow no longer had the margins. Into the vacuum stepped Western international institutions and governments, providing bridge loans to keep the struggling regimes solvent in return for political concessions. As many of the Eastern European states turned to the West to stay solvent, they surrendered some of their sovereignty. The Soviet welfare empire was beginning to unwind.

Many Soviet political elites believed that they still had the advantage in the Cold War in the late 1970s. Moscow continued its military buildup and made advances into the Third World, while the industrial democracies staggered from a wave of domestic and international crises. The West remained mired in stagflation, but the Soviet economy "develops dynamically, free from such inherent ailments of the capitalist system as economic recessions, inflation, and unemployment," Baibakov, who sang a different tune behind closed doors, bragged to the Japanese ambassador.[5] After meeting with Soviet officials in Bonn, Schmidt reported the "feelings of superiority among the Soviets" as well as their "general uncertainty about U.S. staying power."[6] West German public opinion surveys in early 1980 indicated that a majority believed that the Soviet Union enjoyed a military advantage over the West. More than a third expected that by the end of the decade, communists would seize power in some Western European countries.[7]

These perceptions did not match reality. The small circle of policymakers who understood the extent of the socialist world's economic woes knew better. In Brezhnev's final years, Moscow struggled to balance upholding its international responsibilities while managing an economic crisis at home. Soviet policymakers always longed for the day that they could redistribute resources from guns to butter, but they believed that the hostile international environment required privileging the military-industrial complex, which commanded three-quarters of all investment.[8] Waging the Cold War "limits our opportunities to allocate additional funds for the development of the national economy," Brezhnev observed. "We cannot allow our sword to be shorter than the American one, or our shield to be insufficiently reliable."[9] The United States had refused to negotiate in the early Cold War because it did not look at the USSR as an equal, he reasoned, so the only way to get Washington to take Moscow seriously was to eliminate the United States' sense of superiority.[10] The Kremlin fumed that the Carter administration insisted on the insertion of human rights provisions into arms talks, contributing to the breakdown of détente. After years of negotiations, the two sides agreed to SALT II at the Vienna summit in June 1979, but Carter withdrew the treaty from Senate consideration after the Soviet invasion of Afghanistan. The tit-for-tat deployment of intermediate-range missiles in Europe in the late 1970s and early 1980s confirmed that the arms race remained very much on.

Heightened superpower tensions contributed to the Kremlin's choice in December 1979 to invade Afghanistan, which bordered both the Soviet Union as well as revolutionary Iran. The People's Democratic Party of Afghanistan (PDPA), friendly to Moscow, had struggled to govern ever since it seized power in April 1978. As protests erupted across the country, the Afghan government requested Soviet help to restore order. Whether Moscow should intervene divided the Soviet leadership for months. Intervention would have great international costs, dashing any hope that détente with the United States could be repaired. Yet the collapse of PDPA rule could bring a hostile new government to power, giving the United States a foothold right on the Soviet doorstep. Moscow doubted the loyalty of President Hafizullah Amin, the former second-in-command who killed his superior Nur Muhammad Taraki in October 1979, and worried that he was making a backdoor deal to align with the United States.[11]

With deteriorating health effectively sidelining Brezhnev (he "cannot even read what's at his fingertips" and even if he could, "would hardly be able to comprehend the significance of his decisions and actions—because of dementia," Chernyaev scoffed), the hawkish troika of Foreign Minister Andrei Gromyko, Defense Minister Dmitry Ustinov, and KGB chairman Yuri Andropov seized the reins of Soviet foreign policy.[12] They overcame Kosygin, chief of the General Staff Nikolai Ogarkov, and other dissenting voices to commit a garrison of seventy-five thousand Soviet troops in December 1979 and install a new regime under Babrak Karmal. During the worst crisis in the Soviet Union's backyard since the Prague Spring, Moscow elected to send in the troops once again.

The troika expected that the Soviet deployment would give the Afghan government support to reestablish control rapidly, but just as the US military fell victim to mission creep in Vietnam, so too did the Red Army in Afghanistan. Some members of the Politburo got cold feet, but after committing Soviet troops, Moscow resolved not to withdraw until the job was done. The war became a quagmire and cost Soviet blood, treasure, and international prestige.[13]

Supporting the PDPA with military and financial aid was the most visible example of Moscow's continued support of revolutionary nationalism. The Soviets "devote a significant part of our resources . . . to assisting countries that urgently need it," Brezhnev explained.[14] Indeed, the 1970s marked the height of Soviet involvement in the Third World. In addition to Afghanistan, the Kremlin intervened in conflicts in Angola, the Horn of Africa, and Nicaragua toward the end of the decade, sending hundreds of military advisers and providing financial assistance. More than half of the $85 billion in military aid that Moscow extended to the Third World between 1955 and 1984 was distributed in the final six years of that period.[15]

China's defection from the socialist camp in the late 1970s delivered an enormous blow to international socialism's credibility as a coherent movement. Deng Xiaoping introduced market reforms to raise living standards after the devastating Cultural Revolution. Economic development, not class struggle, defined Deng's outlook. The Chinese reforms allowed the Kremlin to reassert the leadership role of international socialism, but Beijing's reversal weakened Moscow's contention that socialism provided a superior alternative to capitalism. China's attack on Vietnam in early 1979 symbolized how fractured international socialism had become.

To make matters worse, Washington normalized relations with Beijing in January 1979, further altering the geometry of the Cold War. Along with the Treaty of Peace and Friendship between Japan and China in August 1978, Moscow believed that the Pacific powers were conspiring against the Soviet Union. Ogarkov claimed that they indicated the "creation of military alliance" among the United States, China, and Japan "similar to the 1930s Rome-Berlin-Tokyo 'axis.'"[16]

Eastern Europe drained Soviet resources as well. Soviet officials had hoped the revision of the Bucharest formula would stimulate a more equitable division of labor and incentivize energy-saving practices, but nothing of the sort had materialized. As the industrial democracies transitioned to the information age, the energy-guzzling factories behind the Iron Curtain fell further behind. The Soviets grew frustrated that their allies seemed interested in expanding trade with the West at the expense of "weakening cooperation with the USSR," selling their more valuable products to the nonsocialist world and using the USSR as a safety valve to dump their unprofitable goods.[17]

The second oil shock caused Soviet subsidies to spike. At the official dollar-ruble rate, world market oil prices clocked in at 65.34 rubles per ton in 1978 but jumped to 93.29 rubles in 1979, 154.81 rubles in 1980, and 190.13 rubles in 1981. During the same intervals, Soviet oil prices to East Germany totaled only 57.70 rubles, 66 rubles, 70.74 rubles, and 91.10 rubles.[18]

The Eastern Europeans and Soviets debated about whom the revised Bucharest formula disadvantaged. Zhivkov was already complaining about the "paradoxical situation" that the more agricultural products that Bulgaria exported, "the more we lose, as the state subsidies and the production costs increase. The bulk of this export goes to the Soviet Union. The situation over the next five years will become even more complicated. The increase in exports will mean new losses . . . due to the further increase in prices of fuels, materials, machinery, and equipment."[19] In contrast, the Soviets pointed out that they charged prices that fell well short of those on the world market. "One must not only judge this problem from the perspective of the buyer, for whom the price of imports has naturally increased," Patolichev argued to Sölle in November 1979, "but also from the perspective of the seller, who receives far less currency for this critical resource than could be obtained on the world market." The argument that the revised Bucharest formula burdened Eastern Europe by raising prices found little sympathy with Patolichev. "That the Soviet Union loses 20 to 30 rubles per ton of oil in comparison to world market prices is not even considered," he fumed. "The Soviet Union can no longer bear such a disadvantage, that is completely out of the question."[20]

Soviet analysts calculated that Moscow subsidized its allies with energy to the tune of 15 billion rubles during the second half of the 1970s and would rise to almost 30 billion rubles during the first half of the 1980s. "There are sometimes voices that the Soviet Union provides 'insufficient assistance' to the socialist countries, that it could provide assistance on a larger scale, that 'too many' goods are exported from the socialist countries to the USSR," Brezhnev commented to Zhivkov. "The importance of Soviet assistance is sometimes downplayed," but the prices of many of our goods are lower than on the world market."[21] Soviet policymakers marveled at how cheaply they sold their energy to the CMEA countries. "We could sell all that oil for hard currency," First Deputy Premier Ivan Arkhipov sighed, "and our earnings would be colossal."[22]

Moscow also continued to serve as a backstop for its bloc, with Eastern European indebtedness to Soviet banks almost doubling between 1976 and 1982.[23] The Kremlin did the same for hard currency debt. Bulgaria had one of the lowest levels of debt among the Warsaw Pact states, for example, but the relatively small $4 billion in liabilities loomed large because of Sofia's limited capacity to earn hard currency. With growing debt to both the West and the USSR, Bulgarian deputy prime minister Andrei Lukanov described Bulgaria as "trudging in place, equivalent to a man running up an escalator that's moving downward."[24] The revision to the Bucharest formula created a trade deficit of 4 billion rubles from 1975 to 1980. Considering that Bulgarian exports to the USSR totaled only 3 billion rubles annually, Zhivkov wrote Brezhnev, "it becomes clear how difficult it is to cover this negative balance with additional goods."[25] At an August 1978 meeting in Yalta, Zhivkov appealed to Brezhnev for help. Treat Bulgaria as Moscow would "any of [the Soviet] republics," he begged. Sofia was "simply paralyzed," and assisting would not "require special sacrifices from the Soviet Union."[26] The Soviets granted the Bulgarians licenses and technology transfers, at no cost, and provided a credit of $400 million in transferable rubles during 1979 and 1980.[27]

These international commitments became particularly more burdensome because the Soviet economy took a turn for the worse in the late 1970s. The overall state of the economy was a well-guarded secret, but a small cadre of Soviet elites understood the magnitude of Soviet economic problems. Economic growth stagnated, and social tensions began to bubble to the surface. Laborers protested poor working conditions, the lack of accountability, outstanding wages, unpaid work on holidays and weekends, and poor living conditions, among other grievances. Instances of strikes jumped across the republics in 1980. The murmurs of unrest across the Soviet Union signaled that the superpower might not be immune from the social restlessness that enveloped its allies.[28] The "shadow economy" thrived as the official economy stagnated. With grim prospects, many turned to the bottle. Alcohol sales provided a whopping 15 percent of budget revenue.[29]

A string of poor harvests afflicted the country at the end of Brezhnev's tenure. Shortages were ubiquitous, and grocery stores became impenetrable on the weekends as people jostled to buy whatever they could find. People in the provinces took "sausage trains" to the urban centers in search of food. As the Soviet economy stagnated, the Soviet people resorted to leveraging personal connections to obtain goods and services, a long-standing practice known as *blat*. "We couldn't buy a thing in the stores," a woman from Saratov recalled, "beginning with food and ending with everything else. Everything had to be gotten hold of through *blat*. That's how we lived."[30]

The Soviet leadership, particularly the agricultural lobby that had a vested interest in the existing system, refused to countenance limited market reforms like those that China would adopt. Instead, Moscow used the familiar solution of throwing more resources at the problem. Beginning in 1976, the Soviet Union poured manpower and materials into the Russian Nonchernozem Zone (RNCZ), a project spanning Russian territory roughly the size of Western Europe. The idea was that each province needed to become self-sufficient in food, and Soviet policymakers believed that the fifteen-year project could transform infertile soil with low potential into productive farmland. The RNCZ claimed a fifth of the agricultural budget, marking the most ambitious Soviet agricultural program since Khrushchev's failed Virgin Lands initiative in the 1950s. Operating in a tough climate in isolated regions with low-quality soil, labor shortages, and dated technology, the RNCZ flopped. Output in the RNCZ declined after 1977 at a higher rate than across the rest of the Soviet Union.[31] While the Soviet Union purchased only 2.2 million tons of grain on the world market in 1970, it had to buy 29.4 million tons in 1982 and an astounding 46 million tons in 1984.[32]

Soviet agriculture became a matter of Cold War politics after the invasion of Afghanistan. As part of its retaliatory measures, the Carter administration announced a grain embargo against the Soviet Union. "Unless the Soviets recognize that [the invasion] has been counterproductive for them," Carter explained, "we will face additional invasions or subversion in the future."[33] Imports from Canada and Argentina increased slightly but could not compensate for the loss of US supplies. In sum, the Soviets lost about 17 million tons.[34]

The Soviets did not have a range of competitive products that they could sell on the world market. Arms sales to Middle Eastern oil producers brought in some hard currency, but Moscow relied on energy exports to earn the necessary cash. The Soviets received $15 billion for oil and natural gas exports between 1976 and 1980 and $35 billion between 1981 and 1985. The Soviets used $14 billion and $26.3 billion, respectively, of this income to import grain.[35] "Of course, it's better to export VCRs, airliners, and if worse comes to worst, cars, lathes, and instruments, rather than oil," the director of the Institute of the USA and Canada Georgii Arbatov commented in his memoirs. "But if you don't have competitive, high-tech goods or even industrial end products, then there's no alternative."[36] By 1980, energy accounted for 67 percent of Soviet exports to OECD countries.[37]

Since the energy industry was Moscow's cash cow, its long-anticipated crisis raised alarm. "We stand at the threshold of stagnation in the production of oil, a bit later perhaps even a reduction," Baibakov's deputy Nikolai Vorov described in August 1977. The Soviets expected a growth in the production of oil from 500 million tons to 640 million tons during the five-year-plan of 1976–1980, but a third of the 140-million-ton increase assumed production in the Barents Sea oil fields that had still not been developed at that point, in part because that area was frozen for most of the year. The situation would worsen the following decade, when Vorov anticipated an increase of only 20 or 40 million tons.[38] The Soviets struggled to recruit workers and develop areas near the isolated reserves. "Those wishing to live in northwestern Siberia are few," Tikhonov admitted.[39]

The stagnation of the Soviet economy forced Moscow to make tough decisions about how to prioritize its competing obligations. Eastern European policymakers appealed for help, but with greater frequency, the Kremlin turned them away. "I must say to you frankly that we are not at the moment in a position to grant any more large credits," Kosygin told Stoph in December 1978. "We have considerable spending on the military, and besides that we have to spend a lot on agriculture."[40] The Soviet invasion of Afghanistan demonstrated that for the moment at least, security concerns still trumped domestic economic imperatives, but the deepening crisis across the Soviet bloc presaged a change.[41]

With the Soviet Union overextended, the Volcker shock pummeled Eastern Europe. The socialist countries were vulnerable to the interest rate hike because they had become dependent on Western credits during the 1970s to finance imports from the nonsocialist world. They had known that this arrangement could not last indefinitely. "No country can live off attracting foreign loans forever," Baibakov warned. "It is necessary to have a concrete plan for the future to normalize the situation, to develop the economy in such a way that will allow you, over time, to cover both current needs . . . and pay off debts."[42] His counterparts could solve the problem on paper, but translating ambitious export targets into reality was more difficult. "Our plans for exports to the non-socialist world must be credible," Honecker said. "What does it mean for an enterprise to target an increase [of production] by 30 percent without having the means to do so?"[43] Even so, Honecker refused to adjust his domestic plans to account for the external constraints. "Ideological positions and illusions made it incredibly difficult to develop an economic plan that was based in reality," Mittag later explained. "Existing realities . . . were simply ignored or suppressed."[44] The CMEA's collective debt rose quickly in the second half of the 1970s.

The Volcker shock transformed international lending patterns. Commercial banks suspended in-progress negotiations, and reevaluated deals or offered short-term credits with interest rates that surpassed 20 percent. Loans to the socialist countries in 1980 fell to a third of the volume in 1979.[45] Tightening market conditions reinforced bankers' skepticism about the Soviet bloc, which did not provide detailed information about their finances, and the secrecy about the intended use of the borrowed funds did not inspire confidence. The possibility that China would emerge as an attractive alternative for investment as it reengaged the nonsocialist world fed the anxiety.[46]

Alarm bells rang. Servicing the interest payments alone demanded two-thirds of East German hard currency earnings every year. "If capitalist banks no longer grant credits to the GDR, in a few months . . . the GDR will no longer be solvent and cannot pay for imports," a State Planning Commission report warned.[47] Bulgaria had drawn down its liabilities after its debt crisis the previous year but still had to pay $400 million in interest annually. "For a country of our scale, with our capabilities, this is a lot," Zhivkov feared.[48] Before 1979, Gosbank noted, "Hungary was viewed by Western creditors as a first-class borrower." With the new global financial conditions, however, Budapest struggled to raise new funds to service its debt, contributing to "the reassessment by Western creditors of . . . its solvency."[49] The shock even hit Romania, which until then had kept its debt low on the strength of its oil. Production slumped, however, from 14,600 tons in 1975 to 11,500 tons in 1980. Moscow refused to cover more than a fraction of Romanian oil needs, so Romanian oil imports from the nonsocialist world nearly tripled during the second half of the 1970s.[50] Romanian debt consequently jumped from $500 million in 1976 (3 percent of GDP) to $10.4 billion (28 percent of GDP) in five years, with interest payments alone totaling $3 billion in 1981.[51]

Poland was in a class by itself, with its debt registering more than $17 billion in 1979 and interest payments due in 1980 totaling $2 billion.[52] Recent history had shown that the regime needed to consider consumer expectations when

Table 6.1   National reserves as a share of debt maturing in one year (percent)

COUNTRY	1979	1980	1981	1982
Eastern Europe	28.8	29.0	26.3	22.1
Bulgaria	31.0	53.5	55.4	68.7
Czechoslovakia	46.8	65.3	55.7	53.4
East Germany	46.7	45.2	40.7	42.5
Hungary	27.2	34.0	23.6	32.0
Poland	14.7	7.5	9.7	9.0
Romania	9.6	9.4	8.9	9.5
Yugoslavia	46.3	36.9	35.5	15.9
Developing countries excluding Middle Eastern countries	119.8	100.6	91.4	78.2

Source: CIA Directorate of Intelligence, "Eastern Europe: Facing Up to the Debt Crisis," September 1983, CIAERR.

formulating economic plans, so Warsaw had tried to buy political legitimacy with higher living standards during the 1970s, using Western credits to finance imports of consumer goods. Shops were filled with Western food, jeans, radios, and cassette-players. The average per capita consumption of meat rose from 53 kg in 1970 to 70 kg in 1975.[53] Following a string of disappointing harvests between 1977 and 1980, Warsaw used a third of the credits to subsidize consumption, and Poland clocked in as the world's third largest wheat importer.[54] Seeing little reason to expect a change in Poland's economic fortunes, creditors began to sour on the country. "In their hearts, banks and governments sense that Poland's problems will get worse, not better," a *Euromoney* article warned in March 1980. For a country with a history of food riots, a fall in national income "portends poorly for economic stability in the future."[55]

With most of its debt maturing in the next year or two, Warsaw had to make domestic changes to ensure its solvency. Yet placing the burden of adjustment onto the people was probably more dangerous in Poland than anywhere else in the CMEA. Poland had a maturing opposition counterculture, which had gained strength after the June 1976 uprisings. Intellectuals, led by Jacek Kuroń, formed the Workers' Defense Committee (KOR) several months later to support labor. The Catholic Church also increased its support of the workers, and the election of Cardinal Karol Józef Wojtyła, the Archbishop of Kraków, as pope (John Paul II)—the first non-Italian since the sixteenth century—in October 1978 offered a source of strength to the Polish people beyond the reach of the state. His visit in the summer of 1979 attracted adoring crowds of millions chanting, "We want God, we want God."[56] The election of John Paul II provided a symbol of renewed religious faith and contributed to the resurgence of Polish national identity.

Polish prime minister Edward Babiuch knew that austerity would spark unrest, but with the crushing weight of the debt, he believed that he had no other choice. Warsaw could not regain the confidence of the markets without demonstrating that it was serious about paying its creditors. The regime raised the price of food in July 1980 to suppress consumption and limit imports. Officials hoped that summer vacation planning would distract the population and allow the price hikes to fly under the radar, but just as they had in response to price hikes in 1956, 1970, and 1976, Poles immediately took to the streets. The size and intensity of the protests, however, were unprecedented. The Lenin Shipyard in Gdańsk emerged as the epicenter of the strikes where the young electrician Lech Wałęsa, who had been a leader during the 1970 strike and had lost his job for his role in the 1976 uprising, played a leading role. The catalyst for the strikes was economic, but the protests turned political. Demands included the right to independent trade unions, the right to strike without reprisals, and the right to freedom of expression, wage increases, and others.[57]

The scale of the unrest shook the Polish regime. Hoping that negotiating with Solidarity, combined with a propaganda offensive, could satiate the restless masses, the regime acquiesced to some of Solidarity's demands. "We are suffering material and moral losses," Defense Minister Wojciech Jaruzelski conceded. "We have to display our good will."[58] Outlined in the Szczecin and Gdańsk Accords, the concessions included the right to form independent trade unions, the release of political prisoners, and many of the economic requests. Strike committees united under the banner of Solidarity, whose membership ballooned to nearly ten million by the following year, roughly a quarter of Poland's entire population. When Wałęsa announced the deal with the PZPR to an exhilarated crowd as state television cameras watched, he downplayed the historic victory. "There are no winners and no losers," he said. Wałęsa's statement fooled nobody. The symbolism of the PZPR, a Marxist-Leninist party whose very legitimacy rested in its claim to represent the workers, conceding the right of independent union representation echoed around the world.[59] The regime and Solidarity coexisted in a stalemate for the next sixteen months, exercising dual power and competing for the loyalty of the people.

Poland's neighbors watched anxiously. The anti-socialist forces had learned from their failures in 1956 and 1968 and applied "new and much more flexible and dangerous tactics," Zhivkov concluded, duping the working class by "covering up their counter-revolutionary goals."[60] Success there could inspire similar movements across the bloc, even in the USSR. Belorussian villages picked up Polish-language radio and television signals, and anti-Soviet demonstrations broke out elsewhere, notably in the Georgian republic.[61] Moscow resolved to hold the line. "We cannot lose Poland," Gromyko asserted. "In the battle with the Hitlerites, while liberating Poland, the Soviet Union sacrificed 600,000 of its soldiers and officers and we cannot permit a counter-revolution."[62] With the Kremlin's approval, the PZPR replaced Gierek, whom the party used as the scapegoat, with the security secretary Stanisław Kania in the fall of 1980. The Politburo appointed a committee under ideology secretary Mikhail Suslov tasked with devising a strategy to reverse Solidarity's gains. One of the Suslov Committee's first decisions was to mobilize three Soviet tank divisions and one mechanized rifle division. The Warsaw Pact conducted military exercises on Polish soil during the winter of 1980–81, sending a clear message that if the Poles could not resolve the problem, the Warsaw Pact would.

PZPR officials knew that restoring living standards to pre-1979 levels would go a long way toward defusing the situation, but there was little reason for optimism. "Today, the difference between demand and supply is about twenty percent, and it is rising permanently," Kania told the other Warsaw Pact leaders in December 1980. The following year would be the third consecutive year in which the national income decreased. "Poland is still very strongly dependent economically on capitalist countries," Kania admitted. "This situation gives rise to certain threats of a political character."[63] Poland's debt, which now totaled about $26 billion, brought it to the brink of bankruptcy. In Poland's ruinous financial situation, "it is not easy to speak with the capitalist countries," said Jaruzelski, who would also assume the position of prime minister in February 1981. The Poles had to restore economic order. "That includes a correction of the pricing system, however we have to take into account all previous 'attempts,'" he said. "Certainly unpopular measures will be necessary." Everything must be done quietly, because the "patience of the society has already been strongly tested. Beyond that Poland must reclaim its trustworthiness in the international community."[64]

Warsaw had one big advantage: nobody on either side of the Iron Curtain wanted Poland to default on its debt.[65] "If a bank lends you less than a million dollars the bank has leverage over you," a New York Times journalist pointed out, "but if it lends you more than a million dollars you have leverage over the bank."[66] The commercial banks had invested too much money in Poland. Western governments had focused on driving a wedge between Poland and the Soviet Union, but bankruptcy could push Warsaw back into Moscow's hands.

The financial crisis came to a head when Warsaw suspended principal payments in March 1981, and Poland's Bank Handlowy requested to reschedule its debt with its official and private creditors. Poland held by far the highest proportion of government-guaranteed debt to total debt among the socialist countries, at 40 percent.[67] Rescheduling offered the West an opportunity to "get off the escalator," in British cabinet secretary Robert Armstrong's words, of extending further loans for Poland to cover interest on previous credits.[68] Official creditors allowed Poland to defer payment of 90 percent of maturities coming due during 1981, payable over the next eight years. The only condition attached was known as the "tank clause," which stipulated that the governments could suspend the agreement in "exceptional circumstances" such as a political crackdown or a Soviet military intervention. Striking an agreement among the commercial creditors, which totaled several hundred banks, was more difficult. The resulting "Polish Memorandum" rescheduled 95 percent (some $2.5 billion) of the Polish debt that came due until the end of 1981 but demanded that Warsaw pay $500 million in interest by the end of the year. Mostly at US insistence, the terms also stipulated that the Polish government accept oversight from a Western advisory committee as well as permit a technical adviser to collaborate with Polish authorities.[69]

Western bankers and policymakers hoped that Moscow would help Poland as well. Lenders had extended credits in part on the strength of the umbrella theory, which posited that the Kremlin would act as a financial backstop for the socialist countries, but they worried that the Polish debt could overwhelm Soviet resources. "The Soviet Union had so far provided considerable support for the 'umbrella theory' but it was simplistic to suppose . . . that one could simply leave the problem for the Soviet Union to solve," a British official noted. "The simple answer was that the Russians could not cope with a burden of this scale."[70] Moscow itself poured cold water on the idea. The Soviets had never endorsed the umbrella theory, the deputy chairman of Gosbank Valeri Peshkev reminded a US official, and therefore it was "speculative." The Western banks and Eastern European regimes needed to handle their financial relationship themselves, he said; Moscow was not involved.[71] The Soviets played ball to some extent, granting a moratorium on Polish debt and providing Warsaw with hard currency and credits, but the aid fell far short of what Poland needed. Some suspected that Moscow's refusal to pull Poland out of its hole was diplomatic maneuvering, but the lack of massive assistance indicated Soviet weakness rather than posturing. "We give Poland a limited amount of raw materials because we simply cannot give any more," the deputy prime minister Ivan Arkhipov explained at a March 1981 Politburo meeting. The Poles asked for $700 million. "Of course, we cannot find that kind of sum."[72]

Given the domestic strain on Soviet resources and the magnitude of the Polish crisis, Moscow could not reach into its pockets to bail out Poland. It permitted Warsaw to run a trade deficit, but spare hard currency was in short supply. The Politburo resolved in October 1980 that Soviet allies, with the exceptions of Cuba, Mongolia, and Vietnam, would shoulder some of the burden by relinquishing a percentage of their planned oil imports from the USSR. Moscow would sell it for hard currency instead and then transfer the cash to Poland. The allies would object to this plan, "that is for sure," Baibakov knew. "But what is to be done? We have no other way out and we will . . . have to use the one we have."[73] Brezhnev penned letters to Budapest, East Berlin, Prague, and Sofia, asking each regime to waive the contractual delivery of several hundred thousand tons of Soviet oil "without touching" corresponding exports to the Soviet Union.[74] The Eastern Europeans reluctantly acquiesced. "Of course, this is not easy," Zhivkov responded.[75]

Soviet resources were even tighter the following year. Moscow asked the allies to release more fuel in August 1981, but this time it needed to pad *its own* coffers. The agricultural shortages had become so acute that Moscow would have to redistribute energy shipments from Eastern Europe to the West "to obtain currency to purchase grain and foodstuffs that we cannot do without," Brezhnev explained.[76] The Politburo commissioned Baibakov to consult his foreign counterparts about the composition of the cuts among crude oil, oil products, and natural gas ("products that can be sold at short notice for free currency"), but "the quantity of the reduction" was not up for discussion. Baibakov explained to the East Germans that "the 1981 harvest will be the worst in the USSR in years. . . . It is an open question how the food supply will be secured." Bulgaria, Czechoslovakia, East Germany, Hungary, "and, to a lesser extent, Poland are asked to release fuel to solve the food problem."[77] It was a striking acknowledgment of economic weakness. Soviet oil exports to Eastern Europe peaked at 1.61 million bpd in 1980 and dropped to 1.42 million bpd in 1984, reversing two decades of steady increases. In contrast, Soviet oil exports to the industrial democracies jumped from 1.08 million bpd to 1.71 million bpd during the same period.[78]

The East Germans threw a fit about what amounted to an 11 percent reduction of their oil supply. Their prized chemical industry relied on oil for 60 percent of its production, and analysts estimated that replacing the supplies on the world market would cost East Berlin almost $1 billion annually.[79] The credit conditions after the Volcker shock were already squeezing East Germany, and the loss of energy added to the pressures on the accounting books. When Schürer asked whether a strong socialist East Germany still played a role in Soviet plans, Baibakov snapped, "[I have to think about] the People's Republic of Poland! When I cut back on oil there (I am going next week) that would be unbearable for socialism. . . . And Vietnam is starving. . . . Should we just give away South East Asia? Angola, Mozambique, Ethiopia, Yemen. We carry them all. And our standard of living is extraordinarily low. We really must improve it."[80] At another meeting with Rusakov the next month, Honecker howled that

East Germany was surrounded by West German imperialists and Polish counterrevolutionaries, and without the oil, he could "no longer guarantee the stability of the GDR" (nor, so he claimed, sleep at night). Soviet living standards already ranked near the bottom of the socialist countries, Rusakov countered, and the Soviets "could not go still lower." "If we tighten our belts even more, our people could ask us . . . why the Soviet people always have to live at such a low level." The Soviets had "provided assistance so many times in such difficult situations" over the past three decades. But now the Soviets needed to ask the allies for their understanding.[81]

East Berlin took the news particularly hard, and the other socialist capitals reacted with similar dismay. "If not directly, then in their soul they are unhappy with this decision," Brezhnev admitted.[82] Bulgarian officials called their slated fuel decrease "unbearable." Why could the Soviets not come up with the extra energy themselves, they asked Baibakov. "For the Soviet side these quantities are insignificant and could be realized without additional restrictions in the national economy," they pleaded. Baibakov noted that Moscow had no such spare capacity and remarked that Bulgaria "would not suffer at all" because the reductions would only impact the quantity that Sofia reexported for hard currency. "The Soviet Union has never provided resources for anyone to export to third countries," he sneered. When Zarev tried to negotiate quantities of natural gas deliveries the following day, the deputy chairman of the Soviet Council of Ministers Nikolai Talyzin lost his patience. "Seemingly forgetting for a moment that he was speaking to Bulgarians," he muttered, "Here is the Bulgarian trick: they offer to decrease what they will not receive in the first place."[83]

Moscow simply did not have the means to keep its allies afloat. "Our position is not to sustain the Polish economy," Brezhnev summarized. "Some assistance will have to be provided, but we cannot plug holes. They need to do it themselves."[84] Moscow prioritized domestic needs, even as Solidarity threatened socialism in Poland. The IEMSS identified two possible outcomes: "The West will assume the role of savior to the Polish economy, with all of the resulting economic and political consequences, or the Soviet Union will be forced to assume the remission of Polish indebtedness upon itself."[85] The Soviets hated the idea of the former but ruled out the latter.

The Soviets placed their hopes on a political solution to the Polish crisis. The question was whether it would come from Warsaw or Moscow. With the integrity of the Soviet bloc at stake, many on both sides of the Iron Curtain expected Moscow to crush Solidarity under the Red Army's tank treads. The possibility that Brezhnev would deploy Soviet forces, as he had in Czechoslovakia in 1968 and Afghanistan in 1979, to restore order hung over the Polish crisis.

Fearing Solidarity could inspire similar movements in their own countries, most Eastern European leaders pressed Moscow to select the military option. Czechoslovakia's conservative leader Gustáv Husák compared the situation in Poland to the Prague Spring in 1968 and called for the Warsaw Pact to respond to the "threat to our joint interests."[86] Honecker feared that the fall of the PZPR would isolate East Germany on the western flank of the alliance. Zhivkov implored Brezhnev that the question of *koi-kogo* (Bulgarian for Lenin's famous "who-whom") was "directly raised in Poland." The allies needed to "exert decisive pressure on Cde. Wojciech Jaruzelski to take the necessary political and military measures to defeat the counter-revolution" as well as "strengthen our socialist community."[87] Only Kádár and Ceaușescu advocated restraint, recommending maximum political pressure instead.

The Soviets intimidated the Poles to take decisive action. Moscow made a point of reminding them what had happened to Czechoslovakia during the Prague Spring.[88] At an April 1981 meeting in Brest, Kania and Jaruzelski assured Andropov and Ustinov that they would impose martial law. Tensions were high at the meeting; the Polish leaders even feared that they would be taken to Moscow and arrested, or that their plane would not arrive safely.[89] Despite the promise, the Polish leadership continued to drag its feet, causing further exasperation in Moscow. According to Georgy Shakhnazarov, then a staffer in the Central Committee's International Department, internal Soviet conversations were full of "alarming statements that the situation is constantly getting worse [and] complaints about the helplessness, spinelessness, or even opportunism of the Polish leaders." Many Soviet policymakers were "burning with righteous anger at the ungrateful Poles, whom we saved from the fascists, to whom we returned western territories, to whom we supplied millions of tons of 'black gold' for peanuts, and they try to go to the West." The Soviets became so disillusioned in Kania, whose negotiations with Solidarity and the Church were "seen as cowardice, if not collusion with the class enemy," that they arranged his ouster in October 1981 in favor of Jaruzelski.[90] Within weeks, Brezhnev grumbled that Jaruzelski, too, was "not showing any initiative."[91]

Despite doubts about the PZPR's ability to restore order, the Soviets excluded deploying their own forces to subdue Poland. They adhered to this line all the way up until Jaruzelski imposed martial law in December 1981. Unlike debates about whether to commit Soviet forces to Afghanistan, which had divided the Soviet leadership, Soviet officials had a consensus against military intervention in Poland. At a Politburo session just three days before Jaruzelski's declaration, Andropov, Gromyko, and Ustinov—the very same troika that had taken the country to war in Afghanistan—resolutely came out against launching an invasion. Suslov summarized, "I think that we all share a unanimous opinion here that there can be no discussion of any introduction of troops."[92] Moscow understood that the PZPR could lose its monopoly on political power, which would have undermined Poland's commitment to the Warsaw Pact. Yet confronted with this unconscionable possibility—the same that had led to military interventions in Hungary in 1956 and Czechoslovakia in 1968—Moscow preferred accepting a Solidarity-led Poland over committing Soviet forces to protect PZPR rule.[93]

The potential economic consequences of an invasion played a key role in Soviet calculations. First, if the Red Army occupied Poland, Moscow would have to assume responsibility for Poland's deteriorating economy. According to a US estimate, it would cost Moscow an estimated $10 billion annually to keep Poland afloat.[94] Second, the Soviets feared that the West would impose economic sanctions against the USSR itself, and they knew that they needed to ensure that they had access to Western goods. Reagan had lifted the grain embargo in the spring of 1981, believing that it hurt US farmers more than the Soviet Union. The renewal of sanctions could have a devastating impact on the Soviet economy, exacerbating food shortages and even portending social unrest. Well informed about the state of the Soviet economy from his perch as KGB chairman, Andropov resolved that "even if Poland comes under the authority of Solidarity that will be one thing." The larger problem was if the capitalist countries, in retaliation for the invasion, would "fall upon the Soviet Union . . . with various kinds of economic and political sanctions, then that will be very difficult for us. We must show concern for our country, for the strengthening of the Soviet Union. That is our main line."[95]

The Soviet Union and Poland had each become too entangled in global capitalism for Moscow to risk using force. During 1956 and 1968, Khrushchev and Brezhnev had dwelled on the geopolitical consequences and worried that the invasions of Hungary and Czechoslovakia would spark a third world war. The Kremlin contemplated the Western reaction during the Polish crisis as well, but this time focused on the economic consequences. A Soviet invasion would exacerbate the emerging "second Cold War" and choke East-West commercial relations, forcing the socialists to provide for their restless populations without Western imports. The Soviet bloc could not retreat into autarky; its growing dependence on the West meant that it needed to keep trade and credits moving.

Beyond the postinvasion costs, Moscow also knew that the fight itself to subdue Poland would be difficult. Given the frosty history of Russian-Polish relations, occupying Poland would have presented a greater challenge than perhaps anywhere else in the bloc. "Poland is neither Czechoslovakia nor Hungary," Shakhnazarov later reflected. "Here you can prepare such a murderous porridge that you will choke on it yourself."[96] The Soviets could expect a bitter fight. The Polish army was "battle-ready and patriotic," General Anatoly Gribkov warned. "They will not fire on their own people."[97] Particularly as the Red Army struggled in Afghanistan, Moscow did not have the stomach or resources to wage bloody military campaigns on two fronts.

The Soviets let out a sigh of relief when Jaruzelski finally imposed martial law, but the Polish crisis nevertheless indicated a transformation of Soviet strategy. For the first time during an existential crisis in the Soviet bloc, domestic concerns overrode international responsibilities. Moscow had to prioritize objectives that had not really come into conflict before. The Politburo's unwillingness to defend a fraternal socialist country in the most important theater of the Cold War stemmed from a sober evaluation of Soviet means and ends. Socialism in Poland would have to survive, or crumble, on its own.

Martial law extinguished the political threat for the moment, but the financial fallout of the Polish crisis paralyzed the Soviet bloc as Western creditors withdrew short-term deposits and refused to extend new loans. Banks have "almost completely stopped providing foreign currency," Staatsbank president Horst Kaminsky worried.[98] The socialists could still draw on old lines of credit, but new offers were almost impossible to come by. "A cold blizzard of insolvency" swept the region, *Euromoney* reported.[99]

Soviet policymakers blamed Washington for "artificially" creating the financial crisis.[100] Now the Gosbank chairman Vladimir Alkhimov declared at an April 1982 meeting of the International Investment Bank in Moscow that "with a total credit boycott, the largest possible deductions of money deposits, and the ruthless violation of contracts, the goal is to bring about the insolvency of the socialist countries, create economic and political difficulties in these countries, and discredit the Soviet Union and the other socialist countries."[101] The socialists expected Washington to bully its partners into falling in line. Even though they did not want to agree with the boycott, Schürer predicted, "the other capitalist countries will submit to the diktat of the United States."[102]

Yet the Western Europeans resisted US attempts to restrict credits to the Soviet bloc. More invested in East-West trade, the Western Europeans did not want to abandon détente or reduce Soviet bloc orders for their products, which would hurt their industries in a time of global economic downturn. Furthermore, the Reagan administration itself backed away from using the financial nuclear option. The White House decided to make payments to Poland's creditors for guaranteed loans rather than have the banks make claims, which would have triggered a default that nobody wanted. The Reagan administration understood that the ripple effects of Poland's bankruptcy would destabilize the global economy and that action against Poland would hurt relations with their

NATO allies because Western European banks held most of the debt. Applying pressure on Poland to make payments also provided leverage that Washington needed to use wisely. "We want to preserve our flexibility on the issue of Polish debt," National Security Adviser William Clark explained.[103] The West German Foreign Office concurred, believing that "our influence is greater as long as there is the threat" of declaring Poland in default. Bankruptcy might also "bind Poland even more tightly to the Soviet Union."[104]

Investors turned away from Eastern Europe because the socialist bloc simply no longer offered bankers the safe investment that it had seemed in years prior. The Polish crisis showed that the umbrella theory did not work in reality. "In the case of Poland, the theory of a watertight Russian umbrella now seems to have been discredited," a British Treasury report explained, "and it can no longer be taken for granted in the case of the others."[105] Fears abounded that the other Eastern European countries might not be far behind Poland. "The entire Eastern bloc is under economic pressure," reported Alan Whittome, the director of the IMF's European Department. "The trust of Western banks is declining."[106] Sure enough, in September 1981 Romania became the second Eastern European country to seek rescheduling of its debt. When Romanian officials tried to reassure their creditors that Bucharest's financial difficulties were only temporary, a Western banker mocked, "With a $10 billion hard currency deficit, poor agricultural production, a flagging oil industry, limited coal reserves, the increase of trade with Comecon, and certain political developments which must be taken into account, to say the problem is temporary is stretching optimism to the limits."[107] Afraid of exposing themselves further to what could be a sinking ship, banks took "a wait-and-see approach," a Western banker told Alkhimov. They indicated that they needed to see the situation, particularly in Poland, stabilize before they could put their trust in the Soviet bloc again.[108] There were greener pastures in the West, anyway. For the moment at least, "the door of the Euromarket had closed on Comecon," *Euromoney* observed, "quietly, politely, but firmly."[109] Mexico's default in August 1982 and the eruption of the sovereign debt crisis in the developing world made investors became even more reluctant to extend loans to the Soviet bloc.

The Eastern Europeans struggled to adapt to life without credits. "Things at the beginning of the eighties stood on the edge of a knife," Mittag later wrote.[110] The potential consequences of bankruptcy were too terrible to contemplate, so the Eastern Europeans mounted a desperate "export offensive" between 1980 and 1984, Iván T. Berend writes, in a bid to remain solvent. This "last, bitter attempt to change the economic trend" increased exports by 25 percent across the region, but they scraped the bottom of Eastern European reserves.[111] "We cannot discuss whether we will meet the plan, we have to fulfill the plan," Stoph barked at a subordinate. "If exporting doesn't work, we will have to carry out further import cuts, which is not possible and is not up for discussion."[112] The economic downturn in the West as well as the developing world during the early 1980s limited export opportunities. Traditional trade partners such as Libya, Syria, Mozambique, and Angola struggled to pay for CMEA goods in cash. They needed loans that they likely would not be able to repay.[113] CMEA exports of manufactured goods rose 16 percent between 1981 and 1987, less than half of the growth rate of world trade in manufactured goods.[114]

The regimes increased consumer prices and imposed rationing across the bloc, and real incomes dropped. With the notable exception of Romania, which pursued a draconian austerity program, the regimes wanted to minimize cuts to state subsidies and social programs to the extent possible. They knew that such a strategy would lead to social unrest, particularly since officials refused to countenance seeking popular support for austerity by making political concessions. Nobody wanted to be the next Poland, and they saw how grim austerity already made life in Romania. When the deputy chairman of the East German State Planning Commission Heinz Klopfer advised cuts to consumption to compensate for coming up short on export targets, Honecker put his foot down. "You should not be so light-hearted in the State Planning Commission about providing for the people," he scolded. "One such . . . interference in supplying the people is intolerable."[115]

Most regimes decided instead to mortgage future economic growth to insulate their people from the credit drought. With Western loans providing the necessary breathing room, the socialist states during the 1970s had increased the percentage of utilized national income dedicated to investment projects in almost every year.[116] Between 1975 and 1985, however, the ratio of investment to GDP dropped from 35 percent to 15 percent in Bulgaria, 24 percent to 17 percent in Czechoslovakia, 25 percent to 16 percent in East Germany, 34 percent to 21 percent in Hungary, 34 percent to 25 percent in Poland, and 34 percent to 24 percent in Romania.[117] The redistribution of resources prevented the people somewhat from feeling the full weight of the shock, but it came at the expense of investment in the future.

Moscow's economic troubles and the magnitude of the Eastern European needs overwhelmed the Soviet umbrella. Moscow faced a "very complicated situation" that squeezed Soviet resources, Alkhimov warned his CMEA counterparts in April 1982. High grain imports "placed a heavy burden on the balance sheets," while the falling prices of gold and oil led to severe losses. Alkhimov advised that Eastern European regimes needed to "prepare their populations ideologically and psychologically" for the "unavoidable" drop in living standards.[118] "The USSR can no longer intervene," a Gosbank official told his Czechoslovak counterpart. "The Soviet people do not understand any more why we are lending to all countries, but the shelves in their own shops are empty." Czechoslovakia had the highest standard of living in the bloc, he said, but "now the belt has to be tightened a bit, even if it is not pleasant."[119] The International Investment Bank also turned down applications for hard currency loans.[120]

After Brezhnev passed away in November 1982, Andropov assumed the role of general secretary and took responsibility for reversing the stagnation. "Soviet leaders have reached the point of banging and shaking the ketchup bottle to get out a few more drops," the CIA concluded. "The Soviet economic bottle is not yet empty," but there was precious little ketchup left.[121] Andropov admitted that the Soviet Union faced serious domestic problems. His prescription was familiar: increase labor discipline to reduce truancy and idleness. The new general secretary also, however, experimented with granting state enterprises more autonomy and flexible pricing rules.[122] As Andropov tried to reinvigorate the Soviet economy, he grumbled that the Soviet Union "unjustifiably diverted resources from our economy to countries that declare their socialist orientation." He became "firmly convinced" that the Soviets needed to reduce assistance to the fraternal states. "This is not a commonwealth," he sighed, "but vulgar robbery."[123] Yet Andropov died in February 1984 before he had a chance to implement his reforms. The party's second secretary Konstantin Chernenko succeeded him but served only thirteen months before he too was laid to rest beside the Kremlin wall.

With Moscow preoccupied with its own problems and recognizing the new material limits to its hegemony in Eastern Europe, an important transfer of power took place. Western governments and institutions began to act as the lender of last resort for the bloc, wrestling control away from Moscow. Joining the IMF and World Bank beckoned as a pathway to regain access to financial markets. Romania already had membership, but the IMF suspended its stand-by assistance because of arrears. Bucharest imposed austerity rather than acquiesce to structural adjustment or trying to prolong its Ponzi scheme.[124]

Other socialist countries eyed admission into the IMF and World Bank. Moscow had blocked repeated Hungarian attempts to join since 1967 but could do little more than grumble when Budapest announced its application in November 1981.[125] The Soviets had, in fact, only been informed of the Hungarian application just two days prior.[126] Hungary submitted its application "to secure better conditions for the necessary economic and financial relations with the non-socialist world," Kádár explained.[127] The country teetered on the brink of bankruptcy in early 1982 as lenders withdrew short-term funds, and the Bank for International Settlements cobbled together a series of bridge loans of more than $500 million to keep it solvent.[128] Upon earning admission into the IMF and World Bank in May 1982, Budapest renewed efforts to decentralize the economy, pushing greater autonomy in enterprise management, pricing, wages, and the use of labor and capital. The deputy chairman of the Council of Ministers Jóysef Marjai told British prime minister Margaret Thatcher, "Profit must be the incentive. It was not for the Government to hand out money. The Government did not have money." Thatcher responded that "these remarks could have been made in one of her own speeches."[129]

Poland submitted applications to the IMF and World Bank as well in November 1981. The Polish economy was suffering a "downright break-down," in the words of a Polish representative in the summer of 1982. Living standards plummeted by 20 percent during the first half of 1982. Steel production dropped by 30 percent, machinery by 43 percent, and car output by 50 percent.[130] Plans for the economy were "unrealistic," the Polish ambassador admitted to Baibakov.[131] Warsaw appealed to its allies for assistance, but they had their own challenges to meet. The Soviets allowed the Poles to reduce coal deliveries and granted credits but refused requests for grain, petroleum products, and the extension of the Kobryn-Brest natural gas pipeline, among others.[132] With the dust still settling from martial law, Brezhnev believed that the "decisive condition for fully stabilizing the situation in Poland must be the rebirth of the economy," but he acknowledged that the Kremlin was already "at the limit" of its ability to assist. "Perhaps we still have to do something, but we can no longer afford major advances," Brezhnev told the Politburo in January 1982.[133] Moscow provided credits of $690 million and allowed the Poles to defer payment on debt to the Soviets, but these did not resolve the problem.[134]

Western European governments agreed to accept Poland into the IMF, but the Reagan administration blocked the application and took a hard line on rescheduling Polish debt, hoping to use its financial leverage to force Warsaw to make political and human rights concessions. The West needed to "keep the heat on," US Treasury Secretary Donald Regan stressed in May 1982. "Poland should remain faced with the threat of a default."[135] After Jaruzelski lifted martial law and granted a mass amnesty in July 1984, the United States ended its opposition to Poland's accession as well as the ban on LOT Airlines and reestablished scientific exchanges. The Reagan administration still maintained leverage by withholding most-favored-nation status and credits.[136] IMF membership followed a couple years later.

The East Germans denounced membership in Western institutions, convinced that they were instruments of US imperialism. As East Germany's financial situation deteriorated, it was nevertheless running out of options.[137] "You did not need to be a prophet to predict that less oil would lead to massive production shortages and therewith export losses," state secretary in the East German Ministry of Foreign Trade Alexander Schalck-Golodkowski later reflected. "Insolvency loomed—we knew that we could no longer fulfill our credit responsibilities."[138] "In the era of the Kaiser or the tsar in Russia," Krolikowski added, "officers used to shoot themselves when they found themselves in this position."[139]

East Germany, however, had one advantage that the other Eastern European countries did not: it had a powerful neighbor that had a special interest in ensuring that it did not go bankrupt. A consortium of West German banks extended a credit of DM 1 billion to East Berlin in June 1983, guaranteed by the West German government. Bonn did the same for another loan of DM 950 million the following summer.[140] These *Milliardenkredite* restored East Germany's creditworthiness in the eyes of global financial markets but came at a steep price. Bonn demanded allowances that intruded on East German domestic policy, including greater freedoms for East German people to emigrate and visit the West. The credits showed that "the CMEA was no longer the stimulator [*Impulsgeber*]," Mittag wrote in his memoirs. "The only way forward was closer cooperation and contact with the Federal Republic, even under the tacit acceptance of the fact that the Federal Republic always offered assistance on the premise that it was preparing for reunification in the future."[141] Few expected that unification was on the horizon anytime soon, and the West Germans extended the credits as part of the *Wandel durch Annäherung* strategy. Yet the *Milliardenkredite* inaugurated a new era in inter-German relations, crystallizing a relationship in which Bonn traded financial aid in return for more access to East Germany's people. "'Seismographic developments are taking place," West German chancellor Helmut Kohl described in March 1984, pointing to the increasing number of East Germans whom the regime now allowed to leave. "Pressures are building up, and it is clear that the ideological basis for communism has gone to pieces."[142] The keys to the East German economy were no longer in East Berlin and Moscow but in Bonn and Frankfurt.

Soviet policymakers worried that growing financial influence in Eastern Europe provided the imperialists with the opportunity, in the words of a Soviet Central Committee official, to "estrange and wrench the socialist states away from the USSR and to try and change their socioeconomic system."[143] Chernenko denounced the *Milliardenkredite*, railing at Honecker in August 1984 that he had made "unilateral concessions" to Bonn.[144] The Soviets objected to Hungary's entry into the IMF and screamed at their allies to sever their dependence on the West. In years past, the Soviets had a variety of tools to enforce their will, but those days were coming to an end.

The scale of the domestic and international economic problems facing Moscow overwhelmed its resources during the early 1980s. "The umbrella theory . . . has apparently failed a test," commented a Federal Reserve staffer.[145] Upholding the welfare empire required that Moscow privilege security concerns over domestic needs, but the Soviet decision to stand aside during the Polish crisis marked the first time that Moscow reversed the equation as it contemplated how to react to an existential threat to a socialist state within its sphere of influence. The Soviet umbrella had ripped.

With the Volcker shock deepening the cracks in the Soviet welfare empire, the debt crisis also hastened Eastern Europe's pivot to the West. Banks now insisted on seeing tangible signs of improvement in the balance of payments before they would extend credits. The risks were too great, and there were far more profitable investment opportunities in the industrial democracies. In the absence of commercial loans and with Moscow unable to meet Eastern European needs, Western institutions and governments began to provide temporary lifeboats to ensure that no sovereign borrower defaulted on its loans. They accumulated power over Eastern European domestic policy by signaling that the socialists needed to take steps at home to fix the problem.

Deflationary measures at home to prevent financial collapse aggravated the structural problems that had led to the accumulation of debt in the first place. The export offensive bought Eastern Europe a few more years before another crisis reappeared. When debt began to spike again in the mid-1980s, they had already exhausted their reserves. Absent comprehensive reforms, which socialist policymakers refused to make, it was simply a matter of time before the debt would rise once more to crisis proportions, forcing Eastern European policymakers to make agonizing decisions about how to balance the demands of their restless people with those of their creditors. With Moscow incapable of providing a lifeline, this constellation of forces primed Eastern Europe for its terminal crisis.

CHAPTER 7

Managing the Inversion

"The familiar objective of monetary policy is to foster sustained economic growth and employment in a context of reasonable price stability," Volcker stated before the House Subcommittee on Domestic Monetary Policy in February 1985. By this standard, 1984 was an unequivocally good year for the US economy. After the United States endured a sharp recession in 1982, GNP growth surged in real terms for the second year in a row, the unemployment rate dropped, and real incomes increased. Furthermore, Volcker pointed to "encouraging signs" that inflationary expectations had diminished, and businesses and organized labor no longer seemed to "anticipate inflation in their pricing and wage decisions."[1] Noninflationary growth had finally returned.

Yet Volcker did not celebrate. Instead, he dwelled on the contradictions of the recovery. Unprecedented budget and trade deficits accompanied the expansion. The only reason that they did not undermine the economic revival was that foreign capital, attracted by high interest rates and the dynamic US private sector, flooded into the United States. "The stability of our capital and money markets is now dependent as never before on the willingness of foreigners to continue to place growing amounts of money in our markets," Volcker warned. The country was "in a real sense living on borrowed money and time." High interest rates and the inflow of foreign funds, in turn, caused the dollar to appreciate, which disadvantaged US farmers and manufacturers in relation to their foreign competitors. The nation needed "a sense of urgency," he stressed, to deal with the forces that simultaneously contributed to the recovery and threatened to undermine it.[2]

Although not labeling it as such, Volcker described the inverted US welfare empire. The United States had become a net importer of goods and capital to lubricate its economy, fund social safety nets, and sustain the US military umbrella. The new international political economy provided benefits as well as problems for the United States.

This chapter examines how the Reagan administration navigated the US welfare empire's inversion. Reagan had not planned it. The president claimed that he could balance the budget after cutting taxes and increasing defense spending, but his fiscal policy introduced historic deficits that he had not expected. They pushed interest rates even higher, and the US economy fell into a sharp recession that acted as a brake on global growth and created tensions between the United States and its allies. In the backdrop of declining oil prices on the world market, however, the unexpected interaction of high interest rates, capital inflows, a strong dollar, and trade and budget deficits fueled a noninflationary recovery in the mid-1980s. By further aligning US interests with economic globalization and promoting capital account liberalization, the Reagan administration accessed the world's savings and loosened the fiscal constraints.

The US expansion acted as "the 'locomotive' for growth in the West," as British official Alan Walters described, during the mid-1980s.[3] The US locomotive under Reagan differed from that under Carter in two significant respects. First, it imparted a much more powerful stimulus abroad because oil constituted a significantly smaller proportion of US imports than it had during the late 1970s and the appreciating dollar made foreign products inexpensive for US consumers. US trade deficits now ballooned with Japan, Western Europe, and the developing countries but shrunk with OPEC. Second, whereas Carter's locomotive fanned inflation, Reagan's had a deflationary impact because the Volcker shock kept pressure on monetary authorities to maintain their tight policies even as economic activity recovered. The resurgence of noninflationary growth strengthened the West's material power and ideological authority to wage the Cold War.

The new imbalances among the industrial democracies created winners and losers, however, and the White House came under domestic pressure to provide relief to US workers whom inexpensive imports displaced. The Reagan administration began to compromise on the market ideology that had characterized its first term. This chapter identifies a Reagan international economic "reversal" that occurred during Reagan's second term when US officials turned to multilateral coordination as they scrambled to redistribute the burden of the US welfare empire's inversion.[4]

Although foreign policy figured prominently in his presidential campaign, Reagan focused on domestic affairs when he entered the White House in January 1981. The US economy had contracted 0.3 percent in 1980, and unemployment registered more than 7 percent. Inflation, which preoccupied US citizens more than any other issue, ran over 9 percent.[5] After cutting household expenses to a minimum, a mother of three children who lived in the Chicago suburbs confided in an emotional letter to Reagan, "I feel that we are just existing and not really living." Her husband's wages at a General Motors dealership were cut "because people can't afford new cars and aren't even getting the ones they own fixed. So job wages don't increase as everything else continues to increase." With little money in the bank and local dealerships laying off workers, "it's scary." This was just one story of a self-described "average American family," she wrote, "but most everyone I talk to has the same problems."[6] The US people craved relief.

Reagan believed that the remedy was simple. A crippling tax burden and unrestrained public spending had mortgaged the country's future and crippled prospects for long-term growth, he asserted in his inaugural address. "Government is not the solution to our problem," Reagan declared; "government is the problem."[7] The solution could be found only in reducing the state's footprint in the economy and society.

Reagan identified cutting taxes as one of his first priorities. He was influenced by supply-side economics and the work of University of Southern California economist Arthur Laffer, whose "Laffer Curve" posited that there existed an optimal rate of taxation that would maximize government revenue. After passing that point, every dollar that the state spent on nondefense outlays would reduce GNP by $1.30. The prescription was that taxes needed to come down immediately, even before the government balanced the budget.[8] In July 1981, the administration muscled through Congress the Economic Recovery and Tax Act (ERTA), which slashed income tax rates by an average of 23 percent, decreased the highest tax bracket from 70 percent to 50 percent, cut the bottom rate from 14 percent to 11 percent, and reduced the capital gains tax from 28 percent to 20 percent.[9] The White House believed that the laws of the Laffer Curve would bring the federal budget into balance, even though Reagan promised to raise defense spending. "How this fits together will give them quite some trouble for digestion," Schmidt remarked to Thatcher shortly after the election.[10]

Early returns confirmed Schmidt's suspicions. The budget deficit ballooned to unprecedented levels, increasing from $79 billion (2.5 percent of GDP) in

1981 to $208 billion (5.9 percent of GDP) in just two years.[11] The increase had several causes. First, government receipts simply did not compensate for the tax cuts. It became clear that the figures that the administration had paraded in support of its budget had no basis. "None of us really understands what's going on with all these numbers," the director of the Office of Management and Budget David Stockman admitted to journalist William Greider in the December 1981 issue of *Atlantic Monthly*. "People are getting from A to B and it's not clear how they are getting there."[12] The interview fed public doubts that Reagan's team knew what it was doing, and it almost cost Stockman his job.

Second, the Federal Reserve's war against inflation magnified the revenue problem. Higher inflation pushed taxpayers into higher tax brackets, but the Federal Reserve's successful fight against inflation meant that revenue estimates had little basis in fact. With the tax system not indexed for inflation, the end of "tax bracket creep" accounted for an estimated 40 percent of the reduction in income tax revenue.[13]

Third, Congress refused to support the White House's plan to decrease public spending by slashing social programs. Often invoking the trope of the "welfare queen" who defrauded the government, Reagan maintained that he wanted to eliminate the waste and inefficiency of welfare programs, not reduce aid to people who needed it. The specter of alienating senior constituents who depended on government assistance (and participated more consistently in elections than younger generations) persuaded members of Congress on both sides of the aisle to protect the programs. Some programs suffered cuts—housing subsidies for low-income families, for example, fell from $84.7 billion in 1979 to $26 billion in 1984—but Congress ensured that the welfare state endured.[14]

Finally, a massive military buildup also pushed the budget deficit deep into the red. As a proportion of federal budget outlays, defense took 48.2 percent in 1960 and 38.7 percent in 1970 but had dropped to 21.5 percent by 1980.[15] In the wake of the Soviet invasion of Afghanistan, the Carter administration called for a 5 percent increase in defense spending. Reagan deemed the rise insufficient.[16] His demand for a military buildup aligned with public sentiment. A 1981 poll showed that 51 percent of US citizens believed that Washington spent too little on defense compared with 15 percent who said too much.[17]

The military buildup was an expensive instrument that placed Reagan's security and economic priorities in conflict. A former budget hawk who became known as "Cap the Knife" during his tenure as Nixon's OMB director, Secretary of Defense Caspar Weinberger insisted on unprecedented investment in the military. "We must now pay the bill for our collective failure to preserve an adequate balance of military strength during the past decade or two," he asserted.[18] While drafting his first defense budget, Weinberger asked the service chiefs to submit "wish lists." The submissions totaled a 9 percent real increase in defense spending, but Weinberger insisted that it was "not enough." The defense secretary instructed them to turn "their wish lists to their dream lists," remembered Colin Powell, then an aide to Deputy Secretary of Defense Frank Carlucci. Again, "the word came back, not enough." The "White House was simply telling the Pentagon to spend more money," Powell recalled, and the "military happily obeyed. Manna, they realized does not fall from heaven every day." Weinberger increased the inherited Carter defense budget by 11 percent. To critics, the stingy "Cap the Knife" had become the spendthrift "Cap the Ladle."[19]

Announced in March 1983, the Strategic Defense Initiative (SDI) constituted the centerpiece of the military buildup. Appealing to Reagan's desire to eradicate nuclear weapons and place pressure on Moscow, SDI aimed to use space-based lasers as an antiballistic missile system to repulse a nuclear attack. The program presented the Soviet Union with a dilemma. The Kremlin could respond with its own defense system or increase its stockpile of ICBMs with the hope of overwhelming SDI, but both courses would strain Soviet resources and exceed their technical capabilities.[20] But turning the fantastic program into reality presented a litany of challenges for the United States as well. Indeed, SDI remained as much fantasy as the 1977 blockbuster from which its "Star Wars" nickname derived.

Reagan envisioned using the military buildup as a lever to achieve a strategic realignment. While the president claimed that the Kremlin had seized the initiative in the arms race, he had supreme confidence that the United States would overtake the Soviet Union. "The Soviets recognize . . . that when we mobilize our industrial base—as we did in World War II—that they cannot compete," he boasted.[21] Reagan wanted to negotiate with Soviet leaders, he often said, but only from a position of strength. His ultimate objective remains elusive. Some scholars contend that he wanted to place relentless pressure on the Soviet Union until it collapsed, while others argue that he aspired to reduce the threat of nuclear war and negotiate with the Kremlin.[22]

The unprecedented budget deficits exposed Reaganomics as "voodoo economics," in the immortal words of the then–Republican presidential candidate George H. W. Bush.[23] "We really are in trouble," groaned Reagan. "Our one time projections—pre recession are out the window & we look at $200 [billion] deficits if we can't pull some miracles," he worried.[24] He had denounced the Carter administration's budget deficits, which had registered in the tens of billions of dollars, as evidence of reckless big government. The irony was clear.

The budget deficit became a target for domestic and foreign criticism. The administration closed ranks in support of Reagan's policies, but the Council of Economic Advisers became a squeaky wheel. The first chairman, Murray Weidenbaum, an economist from Washington University in St. Louis, never bought into the program and resigned in frustration after eighteen months. Reagan appointed Harvard economist Martin Feldstein as the successor. "They don't actually believe this mumbo-jumbo, do they?" Feldstein asked Stockman of the supply-siders, hoping that the OMB director "might reassure him that he had not signed on for duty in a lunatic ward."[25] Known as "Dr. Gloom" for his pessimistic forecasts, Feldstein pleaded with the president to close the budget deficit.[26] "A tax increase to deal with the projected deficits will eventually be needed," Feldstein stressed to Reagan. "The longer we wait, the greater will be the added national debt and the higher will be the extra interest costs that have to be paid."[27] His views antagonized the Treasury secretary Donald Regan, who was the unofficial spokesman of the administration's economic policies. He "ridiculed Feldstein as an ivory-tower professor who has spent too much time in the library," *Time* magazine reported. Feldstein, in turn, dismissed the secretary as "a slow, recalcitrant student who must be patiently tutored and humored." They clashed over the relationship between the budget deficit and interest rates: Regan claimed there was no connection, while Feldstein insisted that the budget deficit kept interest rates higher than they would be otherwise.[28]

While most economists agreed with Feldstein, Regan's arguments appealed to the president. Reagan became so annoyed with Feldstein for his public calls to increase taxes, which the president considered a nonstarter, that he excluded him from strategy meetings. White House spokesman Larry Speakes even purposefully mispronounced his name at press conferences to belittle him.[29] Feldstein resigned in July 1984, and almost a year passed before Reagan appointed Undersecretary of the Treasury for Monetary Affairs Beryl Sprinkel as the successor.

Silencing Feldstein was one thing, but Congress was wary of the deficit as well. Even GOP members of Congress were "[hell] bent on new taxes & cutting the defense budget," Reagan wrote in his diary.[30] Having fought for the largest tax decrease in US history in 1981, totaling $435 billion, the Reagan administration assented to the Tax Equity and Fiscal Responsibility Act (TEFRA) in the summer of 1982 that raised taxes by $99 billion.[31] After failing to persuade the White House to lower the defense budget for the coming year, the GOP-controlled Senate Budget committee voted in April 1983 to trim additional military spending for 1984 in half. "The President has shown courage worthy of the Founding Fathers . . . in refusing to compromise the safety of the American people and our vital interests," grumbled NSC staffer Richard Levine. But "senators from his own party have cut him down."[32] It was not just the Senate. A 1983 Gallup poll indicated that 45 percent of US citizens believed that the defense budget was too large, whereas 14 percent said that it was too small. It was a striking reversal of popular sentiment from just two years prior.[33]

Congress ultimately lacked the political stomach to close the budget deficit, however. Legislators did not want to face the backlash of slashing social entitlements or calling off the military buildup. And there was little appetite to raise taxes beyond TEFRA. The budget deficit continued to climb.

The gap placed pressure on the Federal Reserve to maintain its tight monetary policy. Monetary discipline limited the inflationary impact of the tax cuts and military buildup at a time when the second oil shock had pushed inflation to a postwar high. The core problem was that "expectations about what we are able to produce for individuals for consumption purpose has been running consistently ahead of what we are willing or able to produce," explained the director of the Federal Reserve's division of international finance. "Inflation is only a symptom of that problem." Fortunately, it was a symptom about which the Federal Reserve "could do something."[34] With the federal funds rate climbing to more than 19 percent during 1981 and remaining just under 10 percent in 1983, inflation (GDP deflator) dropped from 9.5 percent to 3.9 percent.[35]

As the White House and the Federal Reserve pursued their agendas, US economic policy lacked coherence. The budget deficit compelled the Federal Reserve to keep interest rates higher than they would have been otherwise, which caused the dollar to appreciate 80 percent nominally between 1978 and 1985.[36] The strong dollar, in turn, hurt US exporters, and the trade deficit increased from $19.5 billion to $106.7 billion between 1980 and 1984.[37] "The primary reason for the high value of the dollar relative to foreign currencies is the high level of U.S. interest rates," Feldstein explained. "As long as the United States has very large budget deficits, we are likely to have high real interest rates, a very strong dollar, and sizeable trade deficits."[38] The White House claimed that the appreciating dollar reflected the United States' strength, but the reality was more nuanced.

Washington assumed a stance of benign neglect toward the dollar, which aligned with Reagan's broader ideology of limited government interference in markets. Intervention, the administration asserted, would only reduce pressure on governments to change the monetary and fiscal policies that had caused the currency to become over- or undervalued in the first place. The United States would consider "limited interventions" in key currencies such as the Deutsche Mark and yen, Sprinkel privately told West German officials in March 1983, but "convergence of economic development is the key to greater exchange rate stability." The markets could judge exchange rates better than governments, he asserted.[39]

The strong dollar clobbered US exporters. "It all seemed to happen in a single night," labor attorney Thomas Geoghegan recalled. "All the mills I lived near . . . gone, or mostly gone, in just one night, in '81, '82, '83, one long night, when the dollar got jacked up artificially and it was all so quickly and casually done."[40] The world's largest agricultural exporter, the United States supplied almost 20 percent of the global agricultural trade in the early 1980s, but the appreciating dollar caused the country to lose global market share.[41]

To make matters worse, unions struggled to combat an administration that endeavored to reduce workers' protections. In August 1981, the Professional Aircraft Traffic Controllers Organization (PATCO) launched a strike over wages, and Reagan fired more than eleven thousand of them, which encouraged private employers to stand firm against labor demands. The early 1980s were a particularly difficult period for organized labor, and they accelerated existing trendlines as the US economy continued its long-term transition from being an industrial superpower to becoming service oriented. Union membership plummeted from 29 percent of the national workforce in 1973 to just over 16 percent by 1991.[42]

Resentment about the decline of US manufacturing fanned anti-Asian racism because the largest trade deficit was with Japan. When a bar fight broke out between industrial draftsman Vincent Chin and local autoworkers during June 1982 in Detroit, one of them yelled, "It's because of you [Japanese] . . . that we're out of work." Three men beat Chin, a Chinese American whom they incorrectly believed was of Japanese descent, to death with a baseball bat. "300,000 laid off UAW members don't like your import," a sign at the Detroit headquarters of the United Auto Workers cautioned. "Please park it in Tokyo." Many union workers were World War II veterans who had seen action in the Pacific, the public relations chief explained, and they resented Japanese industrial success while US workers pounded the pavement.[43]

The trade deficit sparked accusations that Japan did not play fairly. Some commentators alleged that Tokyo kept the yen artificially low to make its products more competitive, but the issue was more the "overvalued dollar than an undervalued yen," Council of Economic Advisers (CEA) staffer Paul Krugman countered.[44] It was inappropriate to criticize the trade deficit between the United States and Japan "in isolation," Feldstein added, since "Japan . . . has a trade deficit with the rest of the world because Japan must import all of its oil and much of its food."[45] US officials had a better case when they complained that the Japanese protected their domestic market from foreign competition. As Japanese businesses penetrated global markets, Tokyo placed restrictions on imports and direct investment into its own. "Japan does not provide much participation in its market to any country," the US trade representative William Brock noted. "Japan's economy does not respond to international market forces as it should under free trade circumstances."[46] Washington also protested that the Japanese government provided its businesses subsidies that allowed them to undercut US firms.

After growing 2.5 percent in 1981, the US economy contracted 1.8 percent in 1982. Unemployment hit a postwar high of nearly 10 percent in 1982 and 1983.[47] High interest rates choked growth, and the president's program did not seem to be working. Even the Sun Belt, which had generally been spared the worst of the industrial crisis that plagued the Midwest and Northeast, felt the squeeze. Florida was the "kind of place you could always come to find work, sort of an insurance policy," an ironworker from Illinois sighed. He hoped to find some work but found "it's no better than it was back home—zip."[48] Country singer Johnny Paycheck's 1977 song "Take This Job and Shove It" had described the thankless labor of blue-collar workers, but Detroit radio stations played a new song for their unemployed listeners: "I Wish I had a Job to Shove."[49]

While the White House blamed the Federal Reserve for hindering the recovery, the latter accused the former of profligacy. Tensions spiked when the Federal Open Market Committee raised its targeted federal funds rate above 14 percent in February 1982, 2 percent higher than December 1981. The federal funds rate dropped under 10 percent by autumn, but with unemployment high and the recession biting, the damage was done.[50] Volcker "looked into the abyss and flinched," Bailey complained. "That the country's, not to mention the Western world's economic (and therefore social and political) future should be subject to the personal whim of Volcker and his colleagues is simply unacceptable."[51] Republicans paid the price at the polls during the 1982 midterm elections as the Democrats gained twenty-six seats in the House of Representatives and one Senate slot. Reagan's approval rating sank to 35 percent.[52]

The stalled US locomotive caused friction within the transatlantic relationship. "The world economy depends on the USA," Schmidt griped in October 1981. "The failure of Reagan's economic policy could turn the world recession into a world depression."[53] Growth across the OECD area dropped to an anemic 0.2 percent in 1982.[54] "For the first time since taking over at the finance ministry in 1972," Schmidt admitted that "he did not know what to do internationally to avoid economic misery."[55] Considering that the chancellor had spent the last decade lecturing about international economics, this was saying something.

Criticism of US policy in Western Europe focused on the "awful trinity," as Walters dubbed it, of large US budget deficits, the strong dollar, and high interest rates.[56] Together, they amounted to a "third oil shock," in the eyes of Western European officials, that constrained economic growth and kept unemployment high in their own countries.[57] Western European governments could have kept interest rates low with the hope of avoiding recession, but with the dollar surging, monetary authorities felt pressure to keep their interest rates high to prevent their currencies from falling too far against the dollar. "German credit policy must follow American interest rates to avoid further depreciation of the DM and the associated import of inflation," Pöhl explained.[58] In 1983, unemployment hit 12.2 percent in Belgium, 12.4 percent in Britain, 9 percent in France, 9.9 percent in Italy, 17.1 percent in the Netherlands, and 9.2 percent in West Germany.[59]

Monetary instability complicated efforts to solidify the European Monetary System. In its first two years, the system worked relatively well. "The EMS has functioned up to this point much more smoothly than most experts and politicians expected," Pöhl commented in July 1980, in part because of the "relative weakness of the D-Mark" and "surprising" strength of the French franc and Italian lira. But nobody knew yet, he warned, whether the system could make "timely exchange rate adjustments" in response to "serious tensions."[60] Indeed, strains emerged during the early 1980s as monetary policies diverged, the dollar rose, and the recession hit. Seven parity realignments occurred in the first four years of the system's existence, most of which came after the West German current account swung back into surplus in late 1981 and the socialist François Mitterrand was elected French president in May 1981 on a platform of expansionary Keynesian economics. As French inflation rose and the current account deficit increased 2.5 times between 1981 and 1982, however, speculators fled the franc.[61] In 1983 and 1984, Mitterrand yielded to market pressure and implemented an "economic U-turn" that froze prices and wages and cut public spending. Paris deregulated its financial markets, bringing them more in line with those in the other industrial democracies.[62]

Western European officials feared that economic stagnation would spark social unrest, which in turn posed a threat to democracy. Governments everywhere faced "a credibility problem," Schmidt observed. The masses would "begin to draw parallels" with the early 1930s. "Europe had, after all, not seen unemployment at present levels since 1946." The Cold War stakes were clear. "It was impossible to believe that the Soviet Union would fail to exploit the present situation," Schmidt lamented.[63] The chancellor became a victim of the overlapping crises of the early 1980s when a Bundestag vote of no confidence in October 1982 removed him from office after the FDP defected from its coalition with Schmidt's SPD over disputes about economic and foreign policy. With the FDP now lending support to the conservatives, CDU chairman Helmut Kohl assumed the position of chancellor.

Economic anxieties enflamed diplomatic strains in the Atlantic Alliance. Cold War tensions reached fever pitch in the early 1980s as the Soviet Union waged war in Afghanistan, the arms race escalated, Able Archer 83 raised the specter of nuclear war, and the Soviets shot down the civilian airliner KAL 007, killing more than 250 passengers including a sitting US congressman. The White House took a confrontational approach to the Soviet Union in the early 1980s, with Reagan even branding the Soviet Union as the "evil empire" in a March 1983 speech. The Western Europeans, in contrast, sought to uphold détente and maintain economic and cultural ties.[64]

The transatlantic conflicts about economics and security merged during a spat over the Siberian pipeline, conceived to transport Soviet natural gas from the Yamal Peninsula to Western Europe. In May 1980, Bonn gave the "green light" to a consortium of energy companies to engage Moscow on the condition that Soviet gas did not constitute more than a 30 percent market share in West Germany.[65] Companies from Austria, France, and Italy also joined the venture. Amid the second oil shock, the Western Europeans saw Soviet natural gas as an essential part of their effort to diversify energy sources and viewed the deals as export opportunities for domestic manufacturers. With Dutch reserves dwindling, Norwegian fields at capacity, Algerian exports uneconomical, and Nigerian supplies unrealistic at the moment, there was "no short- or medium-term alternative" to Soviet imports, Bonn determined.[66]

While Reagan opposed the pipeline on the grounds that it would provide the Kremlin with a windfall of hard currency and increase Western European dependence on Soviet imports, he initially refrained from imposing sanctions. Jaruzelski's imposition of martial law in December 1981 changed his calculus. At the end of the month, among other punitive measures against Warsaw and Moscow, Washington prohibited US companies from exporting oil and natural gas technology and equipment to the Soviet Union.

The sanctions created a transatlantic rift. They also caused confusion because they left ambiguous whether they impacted US foreign subsidiaries and licensees. Reagan himself admitted that he had been "careless" in announcing the sanctions because he had mistakenly "believed that the United States was the dominant factor in what went into the production of the pipeline." Secretary of State Alexander Haig floated an alternative that might allow the

Reagan administration to save face. "If the Europeans will cooperate with us in choking off the flow of credits," he proposed, "this would represent a trade-off for our willingness to go easy on signed contracts and on the issue of retroactivity."[67] After months of negotiations in the spring of 1982, however, the Western Europeans declared their unwillingness to "take part in an economic war against the Soviet Union," as Schmidt put it to his advisers.[68] His patience expiring, Reagan renewed the sanctions in June 1982 and extended them to US subsidiaries and licensees.

Infuriated Western European officials resolved to press ahead with the pipeline anyway. US sanctions would not impact the West German government's position, Schmidt informed Reagan two days after the decision.[69] The European Council issued formal statements contesting the extraterritorial and retroactive legality of the sanctions, and the British and French governments instructed their companies to ignore the restrictions.[70] When the United States and the Soviet Union signed a new grain deal in July 1982, the Western Europeans could only marvel at the hypocrisy.[71]

The crisis defused soon after George Shultz replaced Haig as secretary of state in July 1982. With a distinguished resume and reputation as a bridge-builder, Shultz earned the trust of Western European officials and reoriented the administration's focus from stopping the pipeline to forging an allied strategy for East-West trade.[72] In return for Western European commitments on restricting additional natural gas imports from the Soviet Union, cooperating in the development of alternative energy sources, imposing stricter export controls on technologies and equipment, and tightening the terms of loans to the Soviet Union, Reagan lifted the sanctions in November 1982.[73]

The economic downturn of the early 1980s also made it more difficult to implement NATO's dual-track decision. In response to the Soviet deployment of SS-20 missiles to Eastern Europe, NATO resolved in December 1979 that the United States would engage in arms control negotiations with the Soviet Union but would station Pershing II and cruise missiles in Western Europe if they could not strike an agreement by 1983. A massive antinuclear movement erupted in the early 1980s as millions of people across Western Europe marched to protest the deployment of US missiles to their countries. Bundeswehr soldiers marched in Hamburg with a banner: "Soldiers against a Euroshima: No new atomic bombs."[74] In the largest public demonstration in Dutch history, a half million people rallied in the Hague in October 1983, including two hundred uniformed soldiers.[75]

The alliance exhaled when the Bundestag ultimately voted in November 1983 to accept the weapons, and the protest movement splintered thereafter.[76] Still, denuclearization remained a powerful political force, particularly among Western Europeans between fifteen and twenty-four years old who also accounted for 40 percent of the unemployed.[77] With no memories of the Golden Age, they rebelled against the Cold War politics of their parents, which they believed provided them with neither security nor economic opportunity.

The clouds began to clear as the US economy recovered in the mid-1980s. In one of the longest US expansions of the postwar period, economic growth hit 4.6 percent in 1983 and 7 percent in 1984 and remained above 4 percent for the rest of the decade. Inflation dropped from its apex of 9 percent in 1981 to just 2 percent in 1986. Unemployment, which sat at 9.5 percent in 1983, fell annually for the rest of the decade and reached a low of 5.5 percent in 1989.[78]

While Reagan claimed that his program of unleashing the power of the free market had worked, the recovery stemmed from the unplanned interaction of different forces. As the Reagan administration empowered the free market by liberalizing international trade, lowering taxes, and deregulating and privatizing industries, the government still retained crucial responsibilities to regulate the economy.[79] Social expenditure as a proportion of GDP increased during the 1980s, as did spending on Social Security and Medicare.[80] The free market drove technological innovation, but federal spending on research and development nearly doubled in the 1980s.[81] The military buildup increased economic activity and provided job opportunities. Because the programs required investment in new programs rather than expanding existing manufacturing bases, those positions went to well-educated and nonunion workers in the West and Sunbelt rather than the industrial Midwest and Northeast.[82] Reagan's stimulus was expensive, however, and the budget deficit peaked at $221 billion (4.9 percent of GDP) in 1986.[83]

Although the Federal Reserve had helped cause the 1982 recession, it also unexpectedly fueled the recovery. High interest rates not only smothered inflation but also attracted foreign capital to compensate for the budget shortfalls. Budget deficits traditionally pit government and private borrowers against each other in search of capital, and the former "crowd out" the latter. The results are higher interest rates and reduced economic activity. However, the rise of global finance meant that the old rules no longer applied. Borrowers were not dependent on national markets; they could engage lenders from all over the world. By the early 1980s, global financial markets had increased ten times in value since 1973, and capital account liberalization made the funds available for investment in the United States.[84]

Foreign investors had plenty of reasons to place their assets in the United States. The US government had a sterling reputation for paying its debts, and interest rates were historically high. Foreign holdings of US debt rose from

$129.7 billion in 1980 to $393.4 billion in 1989.[85] The debt crisis in the developing world and the Soviet bloc in the early 1980s also encouraged investors to seek safety in US assets, and the US private sector sizzled. More broadly, the flow of capital to the United States reflected confidence in the direction that the country was going. "Where else would you put your money?" an Argentine businessman asked.[86] Capital inflows rose from $6 billion in 1982 to $99 billion in 1984 and reached $160 billion in 1987, representing 3.5 percent of GDP.[87] The foreign capital directly and indirectly funded the budget deficits and kept investment strong at a time when the national savings rate was low.

To make foreign capital available for investment in the United States, US officials thus accelerated their campaign, which had begun in the wake of the collapse of the Bretton Woods system, to deregulate financial markets. After failing to prevent offshore capital from disrupting US monetary policy, the Federal Reserve introduced tax- and regulation- free international banking facilities in 1981 to redirect Euromarket activity to US soil. In July 1984, the Treasury repealed the 30 percent withholding tax on interest paid to foreign bond holders.[88] A dollar-yen agreement in early 1984 liberalized the Japanese financial markets, and Japanese capital flooded into the United States thereafter. "The lowering of the barriers in the financial markets created pools of capital deep enough for American companies to swim in," a Goldman Sachs banker added.[89]

Advances in telecommunications facilitated transnational capital flows. Banks tore out the hard-wired telephone lines soldered on dealers' desks and replaced them with computers, which provided data and financial models almost instantaneously. New software not only permitted traders to visualize information but also analyzed it for them in real time.[90] Computers shrank the globe in time and cost, and New York, Tokyo, Hong Kong, and London became the global hubs of finance.[91]

The decrease of oil prices also aided the recovery. Several factors combined to place downward pressure on prices. First, within a week of taking office, Reagan eliminated remaining oil price controls, already due to expire in September 1981, which allowed domestic prices to fall in line with world market prices. Imports as a percentage of total consumption dropped from 47 percent in 1977 to 33 percent in 1983.[92] Second, the recession stifled demand. Consumption across the OECD area dropped from a peak of nearly 45 million bpd in 1979 to 37 million bpd in 1983.[93] Third, while dollar depreciation in the 1970s had placed upward pressure on prices, dollar appreciation in the first half of the 1980s placed downward pressure on prices. Fourth, the oil shocks had stimulated investment into alternative energy sources such as nuclear power and natural gas that diversified the energy mix. Oil as a percentage of energy consumption in the industrial democracies declined from 53 percent in 1978 to 43 percent in 1985.[94] Fifth, new supplies from Alaska, Britain, Mexico, and Norway undercut OPEC, which implemented production caps in a failed attempt to stabilize falling prices. Sixth, financial innovations such as the rise of futures contracts and "paper barrels" as well as greater use of the spot market weakened OPEC's ability to control prices.[95] "OPEC's biggest enemy is the market—it's working," an NSC staffer explained.[96] OPEC slashed prices by 15 percent in March 1983. The bottom fell out during the countershock of 1985–86 when prices dropped by half.

With the economy humming, Reagan won reelection decisively in November 1984. The gloom of the early 1980s disappeared. "My job is very secure," commented a Reagan supporter from Ohio who worked as a toolmaker. "I've been working 70 hours a week for the past several months compared with 32 hours a week four years ago." During his campaign, Democratic candidate Walter Mondale argued that the recovery was based on unsustainable deficit spending and advocated for a tax increase, but his platform did not resonate with the electorate. In an October 1984 poll, 84 percent of US citizens identified the budget deficit as a topic of "serious" or "very serious" concern, but 64 percent said that Congress should not levy additional taxes to fix it. They even blamed Reagan's predecessors more than him for the budget deficits by an almost three-to-one margin.[97] The debt would have to be repaid someday, but the continued inflow of foreign capital gave the United States the luxury of deferring the problem. The US welfare empire had completed its inversion.

The US welfare empire's inversion in the first half of the 1980s was a boon for US allies. While authorities overseas had their own reasons to implement a tight monetary policy, the strong dollar and high US interest rates placed additional pressure on other countries to raise their own rates and stabilize their currencies. Inflation across the OECD dropped from 13.2 percent in 1980 to 4.8 percent in 1987.[98] As the Volcker shock helped reduce inflation rates worldwide, the growth of US domestic demand and dollar appreciation provided "an unusually large stimulus to the rest of the world," the BIS annual report in 1985 explained.[99] The United States provided 70 percent of the growth in demand in the OECD area between 1982 and 1984 despite accounting for only 40 percent of its GNP.[100]

No country profited more from access to the booming US market than Japan. Japanese growth had slowed in the early 1980s, but Japanese GDP per capita growth rose from 2.6 percent in 1982 to 6.2 percent in 1988.[101] Driven by US demand, the appreciation of the dollar against the yen, and quality of Japanese products, the US trade deficit with Japan ballooned from nearly $16 billion to about $50 billion during the Reagan years.[102]

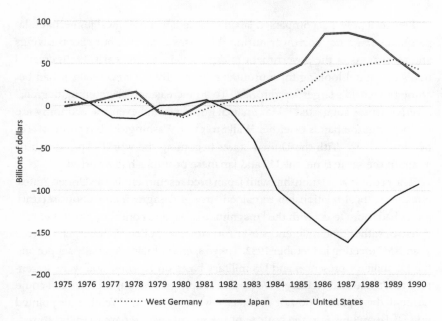

FIGURE 7.1.   Current account imbalances, 1975–1990. Source: IMF, International Financial Statistics: Yearbook 1991.

The trade imbalance raised the specter of Japanese economic dominance in the United States. While "Made in Japan" used to be a synonym for "cheap," Japanese companies such as Sony and Nikon now offered industry-leading products at inexpensive price points.[103] In the critical metal oxide semiconductor (MOS) global market, the US share dropped from 75 percent in 1980 to 46 percent in 1985. "Much of the U.S. industry's problems are tied to the rapid additions in Japanese capacity for the production of MOS devices, especially memory chips," an NSC report concluded in January 1986. The relative decline of the semiconductor industry posed a national security threat because the US military depended on superior technology to offset Soviet advantages in conventional forces. The deterioration of the "U.S. capability to produce the next generation of memory chips will undermine the industry's rate of technological innovation among the wider range of semiconductor products," the report warned. "This decline in the rate of innovation in the U.S. semiconductor industry . . . could then harm the technological base of certain sectors of [the] U.S. economy and create bottlenecks in the modernization of U.S. forces."[104] US chipmakers complained that Japanese companies received government subsidies, and they struggled to access the protected Japanese domestic market, which consumed a quarter of the world's semiconductors.[105]

Financial power accompanied Japan's rise as a technological juggernaut. Japan had been a net borrower during the postwar period, but excess savings and reductions in the government budget deficits by the early 1980s created pools of capital looking for a profitable home. By the mid-1980s, it had become the world's largest creditor.[106] "To an increasingly frightening degree," a *Forbes* article suggested, "U.S. financial markets and even the economy are no longer in the hands of either Wall Street or Washington, but those of Tokyo instead."[107] With the United States becoming the world's largest debtor at about the same time, the US and Japanese positions had reversed.

The economic relationship with Japan bred resentment in the United States, but the political relationship remained strong. Disagreements about security issues had more to do with the "magnitude of Japan's contributions to her self-defense" rather than differences over fundamental policy, Weinberger asserted at an NSC meeting in October 1982. Tokyo spent $1 billion annually supporting the US military presence, and US military bases on Japanese soil were "essential" to US national security. "We cannot simply pick up our marbles and come home if the Japanese do not do exactly what we want," Weinberger pointed out. "If Japan sank into the bottom of the sea, we would have to spend considerably more on defense than we do now," added the chairman of the Joint Chiefs of Staff General John W. Vessey Jr.[108] Economic interdependence and mutual security objectives brought the two countries into a tight embrace.

Other export-oriented East Asian countries such as Taiwan and South Korea took advantage of the US locomotive as well. They enjoyed a boom in manufacturing, trade, and investment during the 1980s. As the first wave of Asian Tigers transitioned from producing simple manufactured products such as textiles and toys to more advanced products such as computers and cars, living standards rose and labor become more expensive. Poorer Southeast Asian countries such as Malaysia, Thailand, and Indonesia took over these labor-intensive manufacturing industries.[109]

With their industries oriented toward exporting to the West, export-oriented industrializing (EOI) countries solidified their geopolitical alignment with the United States. Market-led development "multiplies many times over the effect U.S. policy can have on the basic foreign policy orientation of third world countries," NSC staffer Henry Nau commented in January 1983. "Is there one country among the so-called newly industrializing countries . . . that is a member of the Communist camp?" He could not name one.[110] As EOI countries reaped the benefits of economic globalization, they gravitated toward the United States.

Compared with the United States and East Asia, the recovery in Western Europe was "rather modest," in the words of a Bundesbank official.[111] The assistance that the EC members derived from the US locomotive had less to do with bilateral trade with the United States (which constituted less than 10 percent of EC exports) than the macroeconomic benefits that the US expansion provided, particularly exchange-rate competitiveness.[112] Although Western European governments had their own domestic reasons for hiking interest rates, the Volcker shock kept pressure on their central banks to maintain tight monetary policies. With positive real interest rates, the average annual increase in the consumer price index in Western Europe dropped from 11.2 percent between 1973 and 1983 to 6.9 percent between 1983 and 1993.[113] Reagan's liberal reforms also encouraged a conservative movement across Western Europe that cut taxes, deregulated markets, and privatized industries. The resurgence of the Western European economies coincided with the expansion and coherence of the European Community. The Single European Act 1986 outlined a path toward a single Western European market that would provide for the free movement of goods, services, capital, and people.

The return of noninflationary economic growth did not mean the restoration of Golden Age conditions. The European Community never recaptured the historic growth rates. While the owners of capital flourished, the working class suffered. Unemployment increased, averaging 6 percent between 1974 and 1983 but 9.2 percent between 1984 and 1993.[114] Because their welfare states remained strong, Western European countries generally avoided social unrest. Flashpoints such as the British miners' strike in 1984–85 illustrated the agonizing pain of deindustrialization, but they were rare. West German unemployment insurance replaced 68 percent of workers' previous pretax income for the first two years and 50 percent thereafter, for example. In Belgium, the Netherlands, and Denmark, unemployment compensation provided up to 90 percent of lost income with no time limit.[115]

US policies had a "favorable impact" on the industrial democracies, West German foreign minister Hans-Dietrich Genscher commented to Shultz in June 1984. Yet for developing countries they were "a heavy burden."[116] Debtors sought to devalue their currencies to boost exports, but that made servicing the dollar-denominated debt, the value of which the Volcker shock had also increased, more expensive. After Mexico declared in August 1982 that it could no longer meet its debt obligations and appealed to the IMF for assistance, capital fled from the developing world.[117] "Japanese banks are out of the market, European banks are scared, regional U.S. banks do not want to hear about Brazil, and major U.S. banks are proceeding with extreme caution," the US embassy in Brasilia reported the following month.[118] By 1983, thirty-four countries in the developing and socialist world were renegotiating their debts, with others expected in the near horizon.[119] Left unresolved, the debt crisis "presents an enormous chance for social and political upheaval, and with it the possibility of Soviet encroachments which undercut the entire social structure in the Third World, especially Latin America," Schmidt warned.[120]

Washington focused on ensuring that the debt crisis did not cause a global financial meltdown and create opportunities for the Kremlin to expand its influence. Issued in June 1983, National Security Decision Directive No. 96, "US Approach to International Debt Problem" (NSDD 96), outlined US strategy for the debt crisis that relied on the IMF to impose structural adjustment programs and stabilize debtor countries.[121] From the US perspective, structural adjustment had mixed results. On one hand, the global economy averted a financial panic because the IMF served as the system's lender of last resort and kept debtors solvent. The imposition of the "Washington Consensus" of market-oriented policies unwound import-substitution industrialization (ISI) in the developing world and eliminated the Third World as a coherent political project. On the other hand, structural adjustment programs exacerbated social pain. The burden of austerity fell on the most vulnerable groups that depended on the state for employment and welfare. And many economies, particularly in sub-Saharan Africa, found themselves worse off after the structural adjustment programs than before.[122]

The inversion of the US welfare empire reinvigorated the US system of alliances and struck a massive blow against the Second and Third Worlds. As discussed in the following chapter, it also placed pressure on the Soviet bloc and emboldened Reagan in negotiations with Gorbachev. With the historically large twin US deficits and US dependence on foreign capital, however, contemporaries worried that the new international political economy was unsustainable. In his bestseller *The Rise and Fall of the Great Powers*, published in 1987, Yale historian Paul Kennedy identified the United States, not the Soviet Union, as the better candidate for imperial overstretch. "The United States today has roughly the same massive array of military obligations across the globe as it had a quarter-century ago, when its shares of world GNP, manufacturing production, military spending, and armed forces personnel were so much larger than they are now," he pointed out. The United States suffered from relative industrial decline, and its agricultural exporters faced growing competition from the developing world and the European Community. It relied on "importing ever-larger sums of capital" to close the gap between US means and geopolitical ends.[123]

Domestic calls for protectionism grew louder in response to the trade deficit, which hit a record $150 billion in 1987.[124] The United States was suffering from a cousin of the Dutch disease in which the strong dollar strangled US exports, and the US economy lost an estimated two million manufacturing jobs during the

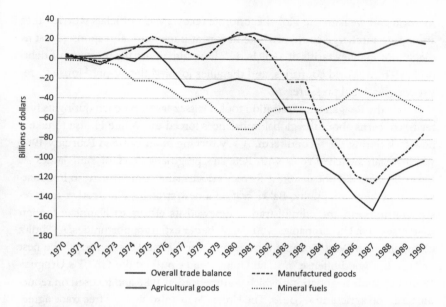

FIGURE 7.2.   US trade balance, 1970–1990. Source: *Historical Statistics of the United States: Millennial Edition Online*, Tables Ee 387, 390, 393, and 396.

first half of the 1980s.[125] During most of the 1960s and 1970s, the United States had a positive trade balance in manufactured goods, but it plunged into a large deficit during the 1980s.[126] Proponents of imposing an import surcharge complained that other governments, particularly in East Asia, unfairly subsidized their industries and erected barriers to foreign competition. The largest trade deficit remained with Japan, and the US cumulative deficit with Taiwan, South Korea, and Hong Kong outweighed that with the European Community members.[127]

The oil industry also demanded a tariff on imports. While the United States ranked as the second largest producer in the world, the price collapse of 1985–86 crushed domestic companies because production was comparatively expensive in the United States. Cheap foreign oil encouraged consumption, while "the suddenness and severity" of the countershock "devastated significant segments of the U.S. petroleum industry," Secretary of Energy John Herrington warned Reagan.[128] Domestic production decreased 18 percent between 1985 and 1990, while imports as a percentage of total supply increased from 32 percent to 47 percent, a proportion that even slightly surpassed the United States' peak dependence on foreign oil in 1977.[129]

The trade deficit put the Reagan administration into an uncomfortable position. On the one hand, the domestic pressure for action was unrelenting. On the other hand, protectionism would betray the administration's market rhetoric and weaken the global economic recovery. US officials worried that an import surcharge could provoke tit-for-tat international responses, just as the Smoot-Hawley tariffs of 1930 had.[130] It would hinder the recovery of debt-ridden Third World countries, and the allies lobbied the White House to resist congressional pressure.

While the Reagan administration took a laissez-faire approach during its first term, concerns about the global imbalances forced the White House to take a new tack during the second term. A key turning point came in February 1985 when Regan switched roles with Reagan's pragmatic chief of staff James A. Baker III, who did not share the former's doctrinaire commitment to free markets. Together with Shultz, Baker crafted a new strategy. First, rather than restricting imports, the administration renewed its efforts to liberalize foreign markets so that US companies would have better export opportunities. As Shultz commented to West German finance minister Gerhard Stoltenberg, "the best defense is a good offense."[131] The United States pushed the GATT's Uruguay Round of trade negotiations, which commenced in 1986 and focused on reducing tariffs on agricultural goods. The United States also signed a free trade agreement with Canada in 1987 that evolved into the North American Free Trade Agreement (NAFTA) when Mexico joined the following decade.[132] The Reagan administration leveraged the threat of tariffs to extract trade concessions from other countries. Japan, for example, agreed to impose an informal quota on its exports of automobiles to the United States as well as to end discrimination against US firms and the practice of dumping in the semiconductor industry.[133]

Second, Washington ended the policy of benign neglect toward the dollar, whose rise climaxed in February 1985. Market forces as well as a more activist stance from key monetary authorities such as the Bundesbank and the Federal Reserve, whose "impressive scale of intervention" totaled $10 billion in the late spring and $13 billion in the fall, caused the dollar to depreciate gradually thereafter.[134] Western European and Japanese officials wanted to halt the rise of the dollar as well; they did not like to see their country's savings invested abroad. After months of negotiations, the Group of Five (G5) met at New York's Plaza Hotel in September 1985 to coordinate exchange rate policies and arrest the rise of the dollar. The Plaza Accord did not establish new exchange rates, but it sent a signal to the markets that governments would take a more interventionist stance.[135]

The Plaza Accord spelled the end for the US locomotive. The "super dollar" disappeared, and the Reagan administration made managing the dollar's exchange rate a matter of policy. The subsequent depreciation of the dollar in the second half of the 1980s helped reduce the trade deficit but also diminished the stimulus that the US recovery had provided the global economy. The

Reagan administration ended its unilateral approach and instead embraced a multilateral line.

The US role in international coordination entailed, above all, reducing its budget deficit, which kept interest rates in the United States—and thus the world—stubbornly high. To force the issue, Congress passed in the summer of 1985 the Gramm-Rudman-Hollings Balanced Budget and Emergency Deficit Control Act, which mandated automatic sequestration and called for a balanced budget by 1991. The Supreme Court removed the teeth of the legislation the following year when it ruled that the provision for automatic budget cuts was unconstitutional, however, so Congress passed an amended bill in 1987. Claiming that it would be revenue neutral, Congress also passed the Tax Reform Act of 1986 with bipartisan support, which closed tax loopholes and lowered the highest tax bracket from 50 percent to 28 percent while raising the bottom rate from 11 percent to 15 percent.[136] After reaching a record $221 billion (4.9 percent of GDP) in 1986, the budget deficit dropped to $149.7 billion (3.1 percent of GDP) the following year and remained steady for the rest of the decade. The reductions were not insignificant, but Congress never met the Gramm-Rudman-Hollings targets.[137]

While Japan took steps to reduce its trade surplus, West Germany resisted calls to serve as a locomotive. Kohl cited the Bonn summit in 1978 when Schmidt "gave in" to international pressure to reflate the West German economy as a cautionary analogy.[138] "Rather than 'taking up the slack' left by the weakening in overall growth in the United States," the Bank for International Settlements annual report in 1987 noted, "other large economies appear to be in difficulties with their attempts to maintain earlier growth objectives."[139] Between 1985 and 1987, the dollar fell about 40 percent in real terms.[140] The dollar fell so far that fears of a recession emerged, and the G5 countries plus Canada gathered in Paris to strike the Louvre Accord in February 1987, which established narrow exchange rate bands that would be maintained through fiscal and monetary policies of the participants.

The Louvre Accord did not stop the dollar's fall, however, because the enduring twin US deficits made the markets nervous. Dollar depreciation in turn disincentivized investors, particularly Japanese, from purchasing US Treasury bonds. The value of Japanese-held bonds fell by $10 billion during 1986, and Japanese purchases waned the following year.[141] Foreign investors had become "increasingly uneasy and fearful as we ask them to lend us more and more money to pay for a problem we cannot seem to solve," Baker informed Reagan. "Like any debtor living beyond his means, it is getting harder and harder for the U.S. to persuade the 'bank' to come up with more money to pay the bills." Dollar depreciation would reduce the trade deficit but would also decrease the value of bonds. "To compensate for this risk the investors want even higher interest rates." The United States confronted a "real Catch-22," the secretary submitted, "which starts with the perceived inability of the U.S. Government to keep at the arduous task of budget deficit reduction."[142] The June 1987 resignation announcement of Paul Volcker, whose leadership at the Federal Reserve had given credibility to US policy, added to the angst about the dollar's future.

Foreign investors turned instead to the US private sector. Dollar devaluation made US assets relatively cheap for them. "Viewed from abroad, the United States is a huge, wonderfully stocked discount store, overflowing with bargains," the *Washington Post* reported in October 1987. Foreign investors had a particular appetite for US real estate, and by then owned, for example, nearly half of the office space in downtown Los Angeles. West Germans "don't see the United States as safer in the short term, but they do see it as safe in terms of longer-term commitment to capitalism," a banker at Frankfurt-based Commerzbank commented. "There is no danger of nationalization. There is no danger of socialist government." A manager of Japan's Long Term Credit Bank added, "The variety of the possibilities—stocks, bonds, real estate—cannot be matched anywhere else and the volume is so good."[143] The largest direct investor in the United States between 1982 and 1987 was Britain, which accounted for a quarter of the total. The Netherlands came in second at 20 percent, the rest of Western Europe totaled 22 percent, and Japan provided 11 percent.[144]

Confidence in the United States over the long term did not preclude upheaval in the short term. The dollar's decline, concerns about the reappearance of inflation, and massive foreign investment created a bubble. On Monday, October 19, 1987, a day that would become known as "Black Monday," the bubble popped, and the New York Stock Exchange plunged a record 508 points. Stocks, options, and futures virtually ceased trading the following day as a credit squeeze threatened to paralyze the financial system. "Tuesday was the most dangerous day we had in 50 years," commented US banker Felix Rohatyn.[145] The memory of 1929 hung over the crisis, but unlike the Great Crash, when adherence to the gold standard handcuffed monetary authorities, the Federal Reserve now had a variety of monetary tools that it could use to backstop financial institutions. Volcker's successor Alan Greenspan declared the Federal Reserve's "readiness to serve as a source of liquidity to support the economic and financial system."[146] With the Federal Reserve promising to serve as the fire department, the financial system avoided a meltdown, and the global economy dodged a recession.

Although the financial system showed resilience, the crash symbolized the challenges of international policy coordination in the age of financial globalization. It showed that the broader issue remained unresolved of how much of the burden for fueling global growth US allies should assume as US economic power continued its relative decline. While Western European and Japanese officials blamed the US budget deficit for the crisis, White House senior policy analyst Bruce Bartlett, who was appointed deputy assistant secretary of the Treasury the following year, claimed the stock market crash demonstrated how "parochial" Bonn and Tokyo were:

> One of the most important problems we face in the coming years is that the U.S. is losing its ability to shoulder the entire burden of Western defense and maintaining economic prosperity in the West. It is not so much that our absolute position in the world has declined as that our relative position has declined, due to the extraordinary success of Germany and Japan in the postwar era—a policy which the U.S. actively encouraged. But the time has come for our allies to recognize that certain responsibilities come with being a world power—responsibilities which are at times very difficult to bear. . . . The Germans and Japanese need to be more aware than they seem to be that their own economic health ultimately depends to a large extent on the economic health of the U.S. and that the U.S.'s ability to shoulder the burden of Western defense is ultimately tied to the health of the U.S. economy.

Unless West Germany and Japan assumed some of the burden, the United States would have to retrench as it reconciled geopolitical ends with diminishing means.[147]

Congress shared these concerns. After years of consecutive trade deficits, the House Ways and Means Committee proposed the Omnibus Trade Bill in the spring of 1986, which mandated retaliation against foreign countries with trade policies that the United States deemed unfair, including the imposition of quotas against exports from countries with large persistent trade surpluses such as Japan, Taiwan, and West Germany. Debate on the contentious bill pitted Congress against the White House, but the sweeping bill passed in August 1988. By embracing protectionism, the legislation sidestepped the sources of the US trade deficit: the budget deficit and the reduced competitiveness of US exports.

Arguments about rectifying economic imbalances mapped on to debates about NATO burden sharing. Playing to popular sentiment, candidates on both sides of the aisle during the 1988 US elections declared that the allies must do more to carry their "fair share" of transatlantic defense. "We are subsidizing the security of our major trading partners while they are cleaning up in international markets," US Congresswoman Patricia Schroeder declared. NATO had agreed in 1977 that each member must increase real defense spending by

3 percent annually, but while US spending increased in 5.7 percent in real terms between 1978 and 1985, the average allied spending had never met the target.[148]

Reflecting a lack of consensus about which indicators mattered most, the Western Europeans pointed to alternative data that highlighted their contributions. In terms of combat-ready troops in Western Europe, for example, their nations provided 90 percent of the manpower, 85 percent of the tanks, 95 percent of the artillery, and 80 percent of the combat aircraft.[149] They implored the Reagan administration to resist congressional isolationism. The worst mistake that the United States made during the twentieth century was retreating across the Atlantic after World War I, Kohl stressed to Bush in October 1987, an error for which the United States "paid dearly" during World War II. The US public needed to understand this lesson. Bush agreed but noted that "isolationist arguments will not be easily dismissed."[150]

Gorbachev's "peace offensive" further complicated alliance management. The personal rapport between Reagan and Gorbachev helped bring superpower relations to the best that they had been during the Cold War, but ambassador Jack Matlock warned in February 1989 that "our alliances will become more difficult to manage" because the fear of Soviet aggression would no longer force the Western Europeans into US arms. The "smiling [Soviet] face will have a more divisive effect than the belligerent growl."[151] Indeed, Gorbachev's policies encouraged the denuclearization movement on both sides of the Iron Curtain and put Western European governments in a tight spot. They worried that if the superpowers agreed to withdraw short-range nuclear forces from Europe, then the United States might withdraw its troops as well, believing US forces would be too vulnerable to the Warsaw Pact's conventional superiority.[152]

Nowhere was the pressure greater than in West Germany. Kohl found himself in the awkward position of having to appease his coalition partner Genscher, whose FDP embraced the politics of denuclearization, by dissenting from NATO's decision to modernize its short-range nuclear forces (SNF).[153] "Managing our relations with Germany is likely to be the most serious geopolitical challenge our country faces over the next decade," National Security Adviser Brent Scowcroft warned President Bush in August 1989. "Bonn's public repudiation of the Alliance position on SNF was unprecedented" and "threatened the very basis of extended nuclear deterrence." West Germany's "geopolitical situation as a divided nation in the middle of Europe, coupled with its growing economic and political power, means that any basic change in its security orientation would disrupt the post-war security order in Europe." The danger was that "Genscherism," as Scowcroft described it, "a vision strong on disarmament and détente, but devoid of a security dimension," would take hold in West Germany and spread elsewhere.[154] Indeed, in public opinion surveys shortly before the Berlin Wall fell in November 1989, roughly equal percentages of West Germans supported unification as opposed it if it meant withdrawing from NATO.[155]

Two contradictory narratives about the United States' trajectory existed on the eve of the Cold War's end. Pessimists noted the reduced US proportion of global production, reliance on foreign capital, and budget and trade deficits as evidence of decline and overstretch. Optimists, however, pointed to the extended noninflationary economic expansion and durability of US alliances. The United States had supported the development of Western Europe and Japan since the early Cold War, and their long-term successes vindicated US strategy.

The declinist school lost adherents as the structural changes that had taken place during the 1980s became clear. The US system of alliances faced challenges, but the eruption of the Eastern European revolutions in the fall of 1989 put them in perspective. NATO's "basic problem is . . . that of coping with success," commented Michael Alexander, the British permanent representative on the North Atlantic Council.[156] Similarly, Japan showed no indication of wanting to translate its economic might into political power. "Japan will remain firmly attached to its alliance with the United States and retain its strong identification with the West," the CIA concluded in April 1988.[157] No disagreement existed about the core objectives such as ensuring the physical defense of Western countries, cooperating with the other industrial democracies, and strengthening democratic capitalism. The differences were in tactics and burden sharing. The challenges that the Soviet bloc confronted in the late 1980s, however, were existential.

CHAPTER 8

The Collapse of the Soviet Welfare Empire

At the beginning of November 1989, Gorbachev met Egon Krenz, whom the SED had recently elected general secretary. The day before and "perhaps for the first time," Krenz told Gorbachev, the Politburo had a "frank" discussion about East Germany's escalating economic crisis. "And it turned out that the financial situation is extremely difficult." Politburo members recognized that the "crisis has not emerged in the last several months," he explained. "Many problems have accumulated over the years." Gorbachev responded that he had a similar experience himself. As agricultural secretary in the early 1980s, he had inquired about the state budget, but Andropov told him, "Do not get in there, it is not your business." When Gorbachev reviewed the books after becoming general secretary, he understood why Andropov did not want him poking around. "It was not a budget," Gorbachev realized, "but hell knows what."[1]

The Soviet leader grasped that East German debt had implications beyond economics. Gorbachev pointed to developments in Hungary and Poland as cautionary tales. "The situation in Hungary and in Poland today is such that they have nowhere else to go . . . because they have drowned in their financial dependence on the West," Gorbachev warned Krenz. The IMF demanded structural adjustments as a condition for loans, for which Warsaw and Budapest knew they needed some degree of popular acceptance. They negotiated with opposition groups to pave the way for austerity, with Moscow providing advice but watching from the sidelines. Some criticized Moscow for "allow-ing Poland and Hungary to 'sail' to the West," Gorbachev continued. "But we cannot take on the support of Poland. . . . Poland has already paid off $49 billion, and it still owes almost $50 billion." The "International Monetary Fund had already dictated its harsh ultimatum under Kádár." When Krenz pointed out that East Germany did not have IMF membership, Gorbachev re-sponded, "You need to take this into account in your relationship with the FRG."[2] The message was clear: West Germany held the keys to the East Ger-man economy, and East Berlin should not expect a bailout from Moscow.

Gorbachev's admission to Krenz indicated the frailty of the Soviet welfare empire in the late 1980s. For the previous two decades, internal stagnation and exogenous shocks had compelled Soviet policymakers to reassess the burden that they were willing to carry. The Politburo had even resigned itself in 1981 to accepting Solidarity rule as the preferable alternative to taking Poland as a dependent, assuming the full burden of rebuilding the debt-ridden country, and likely ending access to Western imports. With Gorbachev's reforms push-ing the Soviet economy to the verge of collapse and Eastern European debt skyrocketing, the same constellation of forces that had compelled the Polit-buro in 1981 to stand aside reappeared on a much grander scale in the late 1980s. The Eastern European regimes confronted an inexorable pincer move-ment: the pressures of global capitalism required economic restructuring, pro-testers demanded political changes, and Moscow could not throw a lifeline. Eastern Europe was no longer the Kremlin's to save. The Soviet refusal to in-tervene in the 1989 revolutions marked the final evolutionary step in the col-lapse of the Soviet welfare empire.

Gorbachev had to play the hand that he was dealt. The stagnation of the Soviet economy and the deterioration of Eastern European finances narrowed Gorbachev's options at every turn and limited his room for maneuver. Gor-bachev's worldview reinforced, rather than initiated, the policy of retrench-ment that material and financial constraints had forced on his predecessors. The Soviets had "buried [the Brezhnev Doctrine] even before Chernenko was buried," Gorbachev later acknowledged.[3] It is doubtful that another Soviet leader would have imposed a 1956 or 1968 solution in 1989.

Structural limitations still left room for creative policymaking, however. Gorbachev tried to move beyond the welfare empire framework and create a new international architecture that reached across the Iron Curtain. In place of the Cold War, he proposed a third path that rejected both US capitalism and Stalinist socialism. The geopolitical division of Europe would disappear, and Eastern and Western Europe would unite under what he called a "com-mon European home." He sought to coopt the revolutions and align them with his vision of a new world order. This strategy aligned with Gorbachev's values, but it also reconciled Soviet objectives with material weakness.

By the time that Gorbachev took office in March 1985, alarm bells had been ringing in Moscow for years about economic decline. Issues ranging from technological lag, supply bottlenecks, the divergence between production costs and prices, and consumer shortages had preoccupied his predecessors. As the capitalist world transitioned into the information age, the Soviet rust belt—much of which had been built during the Stalinist era—fell further behind. Demographic and public health indicators provided additional causes for concern. In the backdrop of decreasing oil prices on the world market during the early 1980s, it is no surprise that Gorbachev, even more than those who held the office before, worried about the atrophy and the continued downward economic trajectory.[4] Having served as the Central Committee secretary for agriculture, Gorbachev understood the shortcomings in that sector, but he did not learn the full extent of the Soviet problems until he became general secretary. While officials and workers along the supply chain confronted the system's inefficiencies, each touched just one part of the proverbial elephant, and only a small number of elites could see the full picture.

Unlike many of his colleagues, Gorbachev had traveled to both socialist and capitalist countries. He confronted the sobering reality that most CMEA countries enjoyed higher living standards than the Soviet Union and that the industrial democracies far outpaced the Soviet bloc. "My previous belief in the superiority of socialist democracy over the bourgeois system was shaken," he remembered. "People there lived in better conditions and were better off than in our country." Gorbachev grew frustrated that the Soviet gerontocracy had rested on its laurels rather than implement structural reforms "to prevent the country and system from sinking deeper into a state of crisis."[5] He reported to the Politburo about a trip to a garment factory in Kuibyshev, located along the Volga River. It looked like a relic of the eighteenth century, he complained.[6]

Gorbachev believed that he had to reinvigorate the Soviet system, but he did not have a blueprint. "The experiment will not develop for a year or two," Baibakov relayed to a Polish official in May 1985. "Many of the provisions have yet to be finalized."[7] The Gosplan chairman scoffed at Gorbachev and other reformers who viewed scientific and technological progress as tantamount to an increase in production rates. Gorbachev may have had big plans, Baibakov later wrote, but he had no understanding of how the command economy worked and "hardly a clear idea" about how to achieve his goals. When Gosplan submitted an outline for the new five-year plan, the party's second secretary Yegor Ligachev asked, "How will we look in comparison to America?" Baibakov responded bluntly, "We won't catch up." It took the industrial democracies many years to transition into the information age, and now Gorbachev demanded doing so in an "unprecedented" amount of time. Baibakov resigned in October 1985. He had been on the job exactly twenty years.[8] Nikolai Talyzin, who had served as the Soviet representative to the CMEA, took the reins of Gosplan.

Gorbachev's initial reforms attempted to make the existing system work more efficiently. He called for greater worker discipline and the *uskorenie* ("acceleration") of production. To aid the endeavor, Gorbachev launched an antialcohol campaign, hoping that purging Soviet society of alcohol abuse would increase productivity. While the policy reduced alcohol-related deaths, it blew a hole in the budget. Vodka sales dropped from 54 billion rubles in 1984 to 11 billion rubles in 1985.[9] Furthermore, Moscow did not provide the masses with replacement consumer products to absorb the displaced purchasing power. Gosplan First Deputy Chairman Lev A. Voronin warned, "We literally will have nothing to provide for the cash that is held by the population."[10] The antialcohol campaign earned Gorbachev the tongue-in-cheek nickname "General Secretary Mineral Water."[11]

More substantive changes came after Gorbachev's speech to the Central Committee plenum in June 1987. His program of perestroika ("restructuring") outlined a transition toward a market socialist economy. Decentralizing decision making and transferring more power to state enterprises gave them greater autonomy to set prices and salaries. The Law on State Enterprises transferred more authority to factory managers and allowed state enterprises to keep profits that would have previously been transferred to the state. The Law on Cooperatives the following year legalized private enterprises, permitting them to employ an unlimited number of workers. The reforms would promote what he called a "scientific-technical revolution" that would close the gap between the Soviet Union and the West. He set a goal of making at least 80 percent of Soviet products meet world standards by the end of the decade. "Without quality products, there is no technical progress and no high standard of living," he declared.[12]

Gorbachev's belief that economic changes alone would prove insufficient to reinvigorate the socialist project marked a point of departure in comparison to other reformers in Soviet history. He concluded that previous attempts had failed "because the political system suffocated everything."[13] Economic reform could succeed only if political reform accompanied it, and vice versa. "We want more socialism and, therefore, more democracy," he liked to say.[14] In Gorbachev's eyes, the two could not be disentangled. He wanted to eliminate the cronyism and corruption in the government and ensure that the party had legitimacy in the eyes of the Soviet people.

The April 1986 disaster at the Chernobyl nuclear power station had a profound effect on how Gorbachev and his advisers viewed the Soviet system. The disaster demonstrated not only the danger of nuclear war but also that Soviet infrastructure required an overhaul and officials needed to have honest discussions about their problems.[15] "Chernobyl opened our eyes to many things," Ligachev acknowledged.[16] Gorbachev promoted glasnost ("openness"), which encouraged Soviet society to discuss the country's policies and history more openly.

Achieving Gorbachev's domestic objectives necessitated changes in foreign policy. Moscow needed to liberate human and material resources from the defense sector, which gobbled up somewhere between 20 and 30 percent of Soviet GDP and employed the best scientists.[17] Gorbachev also understood that the Soviet Union could not afford another round in the arms race. In order to put those resources to work to improve living standards, Gorbachev knew that he needed to negotiate an end to the arms race, which he was naturally predisposed to do. He felt comfortable engaging Washington because he believed that Moscow had more than enough weapons to guarantee its security. Furthermore, Chernobyl provided a glimpse of what nuclear war would look like, and the Barbarossa Syndrome did not afflict Gorbachev. He "did not think anyone was going to attack us," Chernyaev later explained.[18] Gorbachev replaced old guard diplomatic elites such as the longtime foreign minister Andrei Gromyko and ambassador Anatoly Dobrynin and appointed advisers who shared his philosophy to important posts, including Georgi Shakhnazarov, Chernyaev, Vadim Medvedev, and Eduard Shevardnadze to promote his new intellectual framework for Soviet diplomacy, known as *novoe myshlenie* ("new thinking").

Reconfiguring relations with Eastern Europe constituted a key part of Gorbachev's plans. The Soviet leader did not fear war with the capitalists nearly as much as his predecessors did, but he still considered Eastern Europe vital to Soviet security and wanted the region to serve as a model of socialism for other parts of the world to follow. Drawing on the democratic mantra of perestroika, he argued that Moscow needed to treat the other socialist countries as equals, as "full-fledged states," as he put it in a May 1986 speech to Soviet foreign ministry officials. "We cannot lead them by the hand to kindergarten as we would little children."[19] He renounced the use of force as a tool in Soviet foreign policy and stressed that Moscow should not view the Eastern European countries as satellites. Jaruzelski became Gorbachev's "star pupil" for his embrace of perestroika, but Gorbachev regarded the old guard Eastern European elites such as Honecker, Ceaușescu, and Zhivkov as anachronisms and urged them to initiate reforms in their own countries.[20]

Gorbachev also endeavored to reduce the burden that supporting Eastern Europe placed on the Soviet Union. Soviet leaders long had serious concerns about this. Indeed, Chernenko called a CMEA summit of the general secretaries in June 1984 to demand that the Eastern Europeans contribute more to the Soviet economy.[21] The Soviet delegation to the summit outlined four objectives: reduction in Eastern European trade deficits with Moscow, improvement in the terms of trade, increased participation in Soviet raw materials development, and changes in the Eastern European economies to meet Soviet needs. Outstanding loans to the Eastern European states totaled almost 15 billion rubles in 1983 and more than 17 billion rubles in 1984.[22]

Echoing complaints of the past, Gorbachev grumbled that the CMEA division of labor required the Soviet Union to provide valuable raw materials in exchange for poor-quality goods from its allies. "In the beginning," he wrote in June 1986, "the Soviet Union, the largest and most experienced socialist state, led the fraternal countries by the hand. . . . Economic relations developed with an accent on the USSR providing resource support through raw materials and fuel, and developing primary industries."[23] He even described the USSR as "actually hired into slave labor—to get raw materials and supply them to other countries."[24] The growing crisis in the Soviet economy made the margins even tighter. "We must be extremely careful about providing assistance to other countries," Gorbachev concluded after surveying Soviet economic woes in October 1986. "No promises to anyone."[25]

Still, a stable Eastern Europe meant too much for Soviet national security and international socialism for Gorbachev to turn his back on the bloc, and the Soviet Union was too intertwined economically with the CMEA countries. "We cannot take the path of turning off the tap" of cheap oil and gas, Gorbachev resolved.[26] Instead, he tried to figure out a way to make the CMEA more efficient and productive. Taking inspiration from Western European integration, Gorbachev articulated an ambitious but imprecise program to transform the CMEA into a socialist common market. The Comprehensive Program for Scientific and Technical Progress, initiated in December 1985, outlined a series of large projects, supervised by Moscow, to accelerate scientific progress across the bloc. Many of these entailed developing Soviet reserves of raw materials. Participation in the Soviet energy industry became a precondition for the Eastern Europeans to receive the same volume of deliveries.[27] The construction of the Yamburg pipeline followed the model of the Soyuz pipeline the previous decade, with the Eastern Europeans having to purchase expensive equipment on the world market.[28]

Rather than exchange finished products, the socialist countries would co-operate at the production stage. "You are pushing for trade," he told Ceaușescu, "but we are for industrial cooperation." The barter system had not achieved the desired results. Instead, Gorbachev proposed a different model: "not the exchange of goods, rather cooperation in production."[29] This entailed decentralizing international trade, forging connections that empowered the enterprises and decentered the bureaucracy. Gorbachev hoped that this tactic would eliminate the many redundancies within the CMEA. Each of the Eastern European countries except Hungary and Bulgaria developed its own automobile, for example. The new and improved CMEA would have "less administration" and pay "more attention to economic levers, initiatives, socialist enterprises, and involvement of labor collectives in this process."[30]

The socialist common market would create a more efficient and equitable international division of labor that would redress the chronic Soviet complaint that the allies took advantage of the USSR's role as a safety valve for inferior products. The Soviet Union did not depend on foreign trade nearly as much as its partners did, but the opportunity costs of participating in the system—the loss of hard currency earnings and quality imports by trading with the allies rather than the capitalist world—contributed to low Soviet living standards. "We are now in last place among the countries of CMEA with regard to the standard of living," Gorbachev noted. "Fifteen years ago, this level was higher than Bulgaria and Romania."[31] When the Red Army had liberated Eastern Europe during World War II, the soldiers had marveled at the disparity in living standards between the USSR and the European countries through which they marched. Four decades later, the gap endured. On vacations to Hungary, Soviet tourists gaped at the stocked shelves in shops and wondered why life was so different back home.[32]

The Cold War had forced hundreds of millions of people to live under the threat of nuclear war, Gorbachev lamented. He did not want to win the Cold War, which he defined in military terms. He wanted to end it so that the larger struggle between East and West, which turned on matters of political, economic, and social systems, could continue peacefully. His vision for the post–Cold War world included the disappearance of NATO and the Warsaw Pact and in their place the emergence of a common European home under the aegis of the CSCE. The Soviet Union would join a unified Europe that coalesced around social democracy, blazing a third path beyond US capitalism and Stalinism. As it enjoyed unfettered access to European markets and technology, the Soviet economy would resurge and reclaim its position as a model for the world. Gorbachev had absolute confidence that given a choice, people around the world would adopt his reformed Soviet socialism over the Western alternative. He overflowed with the conviction that history was on his side.

International and domestic constraints crushed Gorbachev's idealistic plans. Reagan and Gorbachev shared the vision of a world free of nuclear weapons, but material considerations also pushed them toward ending the arms race. Reagan believed that the United States had sufficiently enhanced its power to dictate terms to Moscow, and Gorbachev knew he could not implement perestroika without a relaxation of superpower tensions. If another round of the arms race commenced, "we will lose!" Gorbachev acknowledged.[33] When Gorbachev in January 1986 called for the abolition of nuclear weapons by the end of the century, Reagan grumbled that the Soviet leader received the credit for nuclear abolitionism.[34] Yet Gorbachev's posturing revealed the fragility of the Soviet position. "Gorbachev gets more than his share of applause for 'initiatives' because he is the one who must try to revive a stagnant system, activate a weak foreign policy, and assault strong American positions," National Security Adviser Frank Carlucci explained in April 1987. "Superficial impressions disguise the fact that the US is historically strong and the USSR historically weak and more deeply troubled."[35] In December 1987, Reagan and Gorbachev signed the Intermediate-Range Nuclear Forces (INF) Treaty, the first arms reductions agreement between the two superpowers. Gorbachev claimed that the INF Treaty was "even more powerful evidence that the course that we are taking is correct."[36] Adoring crowds across Western Europe chanted his name. Gorbachev claimed that his plan was working.

Yet Western admiration and a nuclear arms agreement did little to reverse the deeper problems that plagued the Soviet bloc. Perestroika proved nothing short of an economic disaster. After stagnating under Brezhnev, the economy crashed under Gorbachev. His policies were often incoherent or incomplete. While Gorbachev pushed decentralization, he did not create market mechanisms at the lower levels to compensate. Decentralization without parallel price liberalization and encouragement of competition doomed the reforms. Soviet institutions and bureaucrats also served as a brake on Gorbachev's reforms. Given that half of the roughly twenty departments of the Central Committee bore responsibility for the economy, Gorbachev could not change policy quickly and replace tens of thousands of officials who had a stake in the bureaucratic behemoth.[37] He had to work against political lobbies with entrenched interests in maintaining the status quo. Top Soviet agricultural officials such as Viktor Nikonov resisted structural reforms that decentralized authority, arguing instead that more capital investment was the proper solution to the chronic agricultural problems. In the face of opposition, Gorbachev had to compromise, agreeing to extend higher agricultural subsidies in exchange for the legalization of individual farming and leasing. Officials obstructed the initiative, refusing to provide land for leasing and stalling changes with bureaucratic red tape.[38]

The Soviet Union might have weathered the storm more easily had it not been for a multifaced energy crisis. The price of oil on the world market fell by about half between 1985 and 1986, dropping in real terms close to pre-1973 levels. Triumphalists have claimed that the United States schemed with Saudi Arabia to create a glut in the oil market in a bid to decrease Soviet income.[39] Gorbachev himself believed a derivative of this interpretation.[40] The available archival evidence does not reveal a conspiracy, but the countershock nevertheless hit the Soviet Union hard.[41] In the fall of 1985, Moscow sold oil abroad for 172 rubles at the official dollar-ruble rate. By June 1986, the price had fallen to 52 rubles. The countershock cost the Soviet Union billions of dollars in export earnings.[42] The budget deficit totaled 5 to 6 billion rubles for the year. "This has never happened before in the history of our country," Gorbachev worried.[43]

At first glance, the CMEA appeared to cushion the blow of the oil countershock. Even as world market prices collapsed, CMEA prices stayed high because the revised Bucharest formula calculated prices based on a five-year average. Soviet oil prices to Eastern Europe fell by an average of 10.5 percent in 1987 and dropped another 10 percent the following year, but they were still nominally higher than on the world market. A closer look at the numbers, however, tells a different story. At the official dollar-ruble rate, the Soviets sold oil to the CMEA for $32 per barrel, nearly 74 percent more than the average export price to nonsocialist countries. But the official rate bore little resemblance to reality. Based on Hungarian commercial exchange rates that valued the ruble at $0.55, the price of Soviet oil deliveries totaled about $12 per barrel in 1987, in comparison to the $17 per barrel imported from OPEC. Soviet oil "is not such a bad deal after all" for Eastern Europe, noted *PlanEcon*, one of the most respected Western publications on Soviet bloc economic affairs.[44]

To make matters worse, the countershock arrived alongside the long-anticipated decline in the Soviet oil fields. Oil production had plateaued in the final years of Brezhnev's tenure and dipped from 613 million tons in 1984 to 590 million tons in 1985.[45] Ministry of Oil Industry officials counted on the oil fields in western Siberia to continue carrying production but yields from the Tyumen reserves fell for the first time in 1982, though they recovered slightly under Gorbachev. The failures of the Soviet oil industry stemmed from a lack of drilling, inadequate infrastructure and housing, poor quality equipment, and mismanagement.[46] Existing reserves depleted quickly, and Soviet planners failed to open new fields efficiently. According to Baibakov, up to 90 percent of investment in the Soviet oil industry went to maintain existing production levels rather than developing new areas.[47] Even as the Soviet Union ranked as the world's largest oil and natural gas producer, the energy sector suffered from inefficiency and production disruptions, a paradox that Thane Gustafson describes as "crisis amid plenty."[48]

Deliveries to Eastern Europe dropped from a peak of 1.6 million bpd in 1980 to 1.38 million bpd in 1985 as the crisis intensified.[49] Baibakov apologized to Schürer: "Oil supplies from the USSR cannot be increased in the future."[50] The East Germans emphasized energy conservation to reduce dependence on Moscow, which, as *PlanEcon* pointed out, "was no longer willing to supply them anyway." East Germany turned to brown coal as a substitute, and by 1985, it still accounted for 70 percent of energy consumption in East Germany.[51]

Olga Skorokhodova provides a useful framework for thinking about stagnating domestic production and the world price collapse as a "double shock" for Moscow.[52] But it may be more appropriate to call it a "triple shock." As illustrated in Figure 8.1, not only did Moscow earn fewer dollars from its exports, but the dollars that it received had less value because the countershock coincided with the end of the super dollar of the first half of the 1980s. The Soviet Union received dollars for its energy exports but paid for its imports in other currencies. The upshot was that within eighteen months, the purchasing power of a barrel of Soviet oil against a generic article of West German machinery declined by three-quarters.[53] In an effort to recoup some of the lost hard currency earnings, Moscow increased its energy exports to nonsocialist countries by about 60 percent.[54]

The resource curse reared its ugly head. High oil prices in the 1970s and early 1980s generated a windfall of hard currency, allowing the Soviets to defer difficult decisions about domestic reform. As Arbatov notes in his memoirs, "the old adage that nothing corrupts as much as unearned wealth applies to countries as well as individuals." Why make drastic changes to the agricultural sector, for example, when Moscow could buy millions of tons of grain from the United States, Canada, or Western Europe? Rather than use the energy income "as a chance to put [the Soviet] house in order," Moscow had stayed its course.[55] When oil prices fell, the Kremlin did not have a range of competitive products that could make up the difference; Soviet analysts estimated that only 12 percent of domestically produced industrial goods could compete on the world market.[56]

Moscow no longer had a petrodollar slush fund to compensate for its agricultural woes. The Soviet Union bought more than 16 percent of the world's grain imports between 1980 and 1990, diverting resources and cash that Soviet

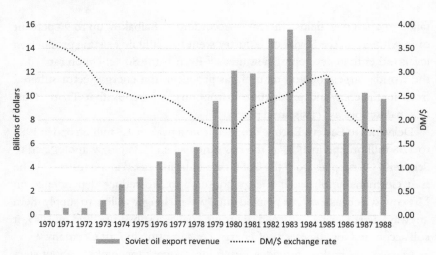

FIGURE 8.1. The Soviet Union, the oil countershock, and the depreciation of the dollar in the mid-1980s. Source: *BP Statistical Review of World Energy 2022*; CIA, *Soviet Energy Data Resource Handbook*, May 1990, CIAERR.

policymakers wished to invest elsewhere.[57] "Importing grain exhausts resources that we need for the scientific revolution," Gorbachev griped.[58] The resource-rich Soviet Union was the largest grain importer in the world, purchasing a whopping 70 percent more than second-place Japan, a resource-poor nation that compensated by ranking among the world's leaders in high technology.[59] As a point of comparison, the Russian empire had been the world's largest grain exporter at the beginning of the twentieth century.[60] The scale of Soviet agricultural inefficiencies was staggering.

These internal and external shocks pushed the Soviet Union into the debt trap. Trying to make up for lost earnings, Moscow "really hit the road" to peddle arms, but the buyer's market limited export opportunities.[61] Fortunately, Moscow had a sterling reputation among capitalist bankers in the mid-1980s and could take out credits from capitalist banks.[62] By 1988, an estimated 66 percent of Soviet hard currency earnings were immediately shipped back to the West to pay for debts.[63] Soviet debt jumped from $22.5 billion in 1984 to $41.5 billion in 1988. By the end of the decade, Western banks began to think twice about extending further loans.[64]

The state budget began to sink deep into the red, but Gorbachev did not want to make the Soviet people bear the burden of closing it. He shuddered at the thought of cutting subsidies and raising prices. "The people have still not received anything from *perestroika*," he worried.[65] Instead, Moscow managed the budget deficit by printing money. Kremlin officials understood the link between the money supply and prices and recognized that inflationary pressure would result. Entrenched political interest groups within the Soviet government, however, meant that spending cuts were off the table.[66] "The main issue was the loss of control over the money supply, over the monetary income of the population, and that gave a major impetus to an inflationary spiral that became more and more difficult to stop," Vadim Medvedev recalled.[67] In a system where "people pretended to work and the government pretended to pay them," as the joke went, too many rubles chasing too few goods made shortages an even bigger problem.

While the debt trap was new for Moscow in the late 1980s, it had ensnared Eastern Europe the previous decade. After launching an export offensive in the early 1980s, the region flipped its trade deficit into surplus, an achievement that came at the cost of exhausting what remained of Eastern European reserves. As some regained the confidence of commercial bankers in the mid-1980s, loans began to flow once again, and Eastern European debt spiked.[68] According to Gosbank statistics, the socialist bloc's debt (including Cuba and Vietnam) rose from $87.5 billion in 1984, to $121.1 billion in 1986, to $142.6 billion in 1987.[69] "All [the Eastern European countries] are in debt," Ryzhkov summarized. "Poland: everybody sees what happened there. Now Hungary is on the cusp. Bulgaria stopped in front of the abyss. We saved them. They are climbing to the West—into a trap."[70] When the Eastern European revolutions erupted, most of the regimes teetered on the verge of bankruptcy.[71]

Several exogenous factors caused the debt to jump. First, Eastern Europe held most of its debt in nondollar currencies, so the depreciation of the dollar caused the dollar-denominated debt to rise. Second, the effects of the Soviet oil "triple shock" trickled down. For years, a few socialist countries had sent a portion of their subsidized Soviet oil to the West for a profit. Reexported crude and refined oil constituted nearly half of Bulgaria's and 30 percent of East Germany's exports to the nonsocialist world in the early 1980s.[72] The decrease in Soviet oil imports and falling oil prices on the world market limited hard currency earnings. Third, participation in the construction of large projects in the Soviet Union such as the Yamburg pipeline compelled participating countries to purchase equipment on the world market, draining hard currency reserves. Finally, weakened demand in the developing world, which stumbled through its own sovereign debt crisis, reduced export opportunities.

The most important issue, however, was that their economies simply did not produce goods that the rest of the world wanted to buy. "The most important question lies in front of us," Zhivkov declared. "Will we be competitive on the international market or not?"[73] The answer was a clear no. The reasons were familiar. The system's "excessive desire for secrecy" hindered its scientific

Table 8.1   Estimated external debt in convertible currency (in billions of USD)

COUNTRY	1980	1985	1988	1989
Bulgaria	3.5	4.0	7.7	10.8
Czechoslovakia	4.9	4.6	6.7	7.9
East Germany	14.4	13.2	19.8	20.6
Hungary	9.1	14.0	19.6	20.2
Poland	24.1	29.3	39.2	41.4
Romania	9.6	6.6	2.9	0.3
Soviet Union	27.5	25.2	46.8	49.2
Total	**93.1**	**96.9**	**142.7**	**150.4**

Source: BIS, *Annual Report*, 1990, 48.

progress, Kádár acknowledged. Military technology found its way into the consumer economy in the United States within a year, he said, but in his country, it took almost a decade.[74] In the all-important computer sector, by the 1980s the Soviet Union had only two hundred thousand microcomputers in comparison to the twenty-five million in the United States.[75] East Germany managed to produce its own version of the "Walkman," a mobile cassette player that became a consumer staple among Western youth. Yet it cost East Germans the equivalent of $400 if they wished to purchase it, and the government spent more on importing the Japanese parts to construct one than the cost of just buying the finished product.[76] Unable to promote innovation at home, the socialists even hoped that Beijing, undertaking its own opening to the West in the 1980s, would become a bridge for technology transfers to the Soviet bloc.[77]

Gorbachev expected that his reforms would reorient the socialists back to the CMEA and end the dependence on the capitalists. Because the socialist states could not purchase necessary products or goods from their allies, they instead bought them on the world market. "Centrifugal tendencies began to appear," Medvedev wrote, as many CMEA countries searched for a "solution to their domestic problems" in the nonsocialist world.[78] In an October 1987 meeting at the Kremlin, Gorbachev pointedly asked Zhivkov, who had boasted that he would turn Bulgaria into the "Japan of the Balkans," whether the Bulgarian leader had "pro-Western" advisers who sought to turn the country into a "mini-FRG" or "mini-Japan." Get rid of them, Gorbachev advised. "All the answers to the questions and all the solutions to the tasks," he stressed, "must be found in socialism, in its dynamic development."[79]

Other leaders welcomed in principle Gorbachev's initiative to rework the CMEA but not in substance. "Our friends already say: if you want to drown an issue, send it to the CMEA," Medvedev said.[80] All bemoaned the "bureaucratic machine" that swallowed reform initiatives, as Zhivkov put it, but the trick was finding a solution on which all agreed.[81] Gorbachev's push for a socialist common market proved stillborn because policymakers disagreed on the content of the reforms. Each country opposed the substance of the Soviet proposal—some for going too far, others for not going far enough—because it aimed to receive the maximum level of Soviet subsidy and had little interest in selling its goods for nonconvertible currency.[82] Many also wondered how Gorbachev would reconcile his desires for closer cooperation between state enterprises and coordination between nations, and they worried about their diminished control over domestic and foreign economic policies. The decentralization of trade won supporters in Hungary and Poland, particularly the push for establishing links between state enterprises. "Determining who will supply whom with what kind of tires should not be the prerogative of Gosplan," said Károly Grósz, the new general secretary of the Hungarian party.[83] East Germany and Romania, in contrast, worried that decentralizing decision-making would undermine domestic priorities. The move toward market conditions would hurt exports and lead to "incalculable economic disadvantages," the East German State Planning Commission summarized.[84] In the end, the CIA concluded, Gorbachev's initiative was "more smoke than fire."[85]

Gorbachev could not wave a magic wand and eliminate decades of rusty infrastructure, inefficiency, bureaucratic red tape, and entrenched interests. The structural obstacles were too formidable to overcome in just a few years, and Gorbachev could not compel his foreign counterparts to follow his lead. The debt burden forced them to focus on meeting the demands of foreign creditors, and they saw engagement with capitalists as the key to modernizing their industries. The Eastern Europeans sold their most valuable products to the nonsocialist world, Gorbachev grumbled, and sent their poorer-quality products to the USSR.[86] "It is time to stop releasing triumphant information about the relationships in the CMEA," he conceded in March 1988. "Everyone knows what the situation is really like."[87] The Soviet Union had viewed the Comprehensive Program as a path toward socialist integration that would yield an equitable and efficient international division of labor. But now, Gorbachev admitted, the initiative was "dead."[88] The CMEA had not improved; it had only deteriorated further. The Soviet Union remained a supplier of cheap raw materials and a safe market for distressed goods. The Eastern Europeans also flipped Soviet fuel for a quick profit. "They resell the specially priced resources they get from us to the West for hard currency," he grumbled to the Politburo. "This is where I turn into a nationalist!"[89]

The Kremlin muscled through a price reform to reduce the implicit subsidy. On the surface, it disappeared after the oil countershock caused the Soviet terms of trade to fall nearly 5 percent in 1987 and a further 6 percent in 1988, and the Soviet Union ran an aggregate trade deficit with its allies in 1988, the first time in fifteen years.[90] Nevertheless, the subsidy remained in place because Soviet resources had value on the world market while most Eastern European products did not. In response, the IEMSS suggested that "the formation of contractual prices on the basis of world market prices remains not only the most expedient, but also the single possible solution."[91] The Soviet Union proposed at the January 1989 session of the CMEA that it should formulate contractual prices with a one-year base period for international trade—a practice that would adopt world market prices with only a slight lag. Further, the transferable ruble worked "under conditions of planned and administrative management," a Gosbank official explained in December 1989, but it "does not fully meet the new conditions of cooperation." Instead, the Soviets pushed for the introduction of "freely convertible currencies for products whose quality corresponds to the world level."[92] This was a major departure that portended the end of the CMEA.

Gorbachev believed that the structural inefficiencies of the CMEA inhibited socialism's ability to realize its potential, just as the rustbelt at home did the same for the Soviet economy. Yet as the fateful year of 1989 approached, Gorbachev still valued Eastern Europe. "The stability of the socialist countries is our vital interest from the perspective of both security and our economic interests," he explained. "If the situation begins to crack, the very idea of socialism will be discredited. The socialist countries are a kind of forward defensive position for us."[93] Granting subsidies to the CMEA countries also provided an incentive for them to remain in the Soviet sphere of influence and slow the pace of domestic reform. "We need the goods from the socialist countries," he said. "We should hang on even though the situation is strangling us."[94]

The same could not be said about Soviet policy toward the Third World. Moscow had supported revolutionary nationalists since the 1950s, providing financial and technical assistance. "The Soviet Union always extends aid to its friends to the extent that it is able," Baibakov had assured a Sandinista official in May 1982.[95] Yet economic limitations and conditions in the international system necessitated a reduction of assistance, and the loss of confidence around the world in state-led modernization efforts began before Gorbachev even took power.[96] "We must put an end to 'revolutionary solidarity' and . . . set conditions for our assistance," Gorbachev decreed.[97] In a December 1988 memorandum, Shakhnazarov argued that supporting revolutionary nationalists presented an "uncompensated economic burden." Whenever "leaders of an underdeveloped country proclaim themselves Marxist-Leninists, they receive the right to unlimited access to our wallet." Many of these regimes were an ideological handicap, he claimed, given their human rights violations.[98] Others played double games. Just look at Angola, Shakhnazarov complained, where Moscow had invested its resources. Now US companies were developing the oil fields.[99]

The Soviet withdrawal from Afghanistan in February 1989 after almost a decade of bloody and costly warfare symbolized the larger retrenchment.[100] The war had cost not only billions of rubles but also killed and maimed thousands of Soviet soldiers. It damaged Moscow's reputation in the developing world and created a hurdle in improving relations with the United States. Gorbachev could not preach *novoe myshlenie* at the same time that the Red Army was fighting a war in Afghanistan. To make matters worse, the campaign did not even achieve its objectives. "We have lost," conceded Marshal Sergei Akhromeyev. "Most Afghans today support the counterrevolutionaries."[101]

With Reagan's second term expiring in January 1989, Gorbachev sensed an opportunity to preempt the new president George H. W. Bush and set the agenda for international politics.[102] Gorbachev shocked the world in a sweeping December 1988 speech to the United Nations that he conceived as "Fulton in reverse." He announced unilateral cuts to Soviet conventional forces as well as the withdrawal of tens of thousands of Red Army soldiers from East Germany, Hungary, and Czechoslovakia. Perhaps the most striking component of the speech was his declaration that the promotion of human rights—not class struggle— lay at the heart of his new world order. After four decades of Cold War, his initiatives were jaw-dropping. Gorbachev believed that his speech had its intended result. "The concern of Western leaders is evidence that the Soviet Union is firmly in control of the initiative," Gorbachev boasted to the Politburo when he returned from New York.[103]

Reality moved in the other direction. The crisis in Eastern Europe was coming to a head. In an October 1988 memorandum to Gorbachev, Shakhnazarov urged that Moscow reevaluate its policy toward the socialist bloc. He observed that "similar problems are increasingly plaguing the fraternal countries," including "some factors rooted in the very economic and political model of socialism as it had evolved over here." The USSR needed to retain its position of leadership within the socialist community, but its means were diminishing. "Whenever any of them was in crisis, we had to come to the rescue at the cost of huge material, political and even human sacrifice," he wrote. Military measures to solve problems were off the table, but this was not unique to the Gorbachev years; "even the old [Brezhnev] leadership seemed to have already realized this, at least with regard to Poland." Shakhnazarov urged Gorbachev to "reflect on how we will act if one or even several countries become bankrupt simultaneously? This is a realistic prospect, for some of them are on the brink of monetary insolvency," and social instability could lead to "another round of trouble-making in Poland" and elsewhere.[104]

Gorbachev never called a meeting to discuss the matter, but he did commission a study in January 1989. He asked that the reports "look at what processes are going on [in Eastern Europe] now—the economic and the political—and where they are drifting."[105] At least two reports were submitted to Aleksandr Yakovlev, whom Gorbachev tapped to coordinate the effort. First, the International Department of the CPSU's Central Committee's February 1989 memorandum admitted a mismatch between Soviet means and ends. It advocated "a balanced approach" to the question of intervening in the affairs of the socialist countries, simultaneously affirming their freedom of choice while maintaining "a certain vagueness" as far as how Moscow would react. The memorandum curiously claimed that Eastern Europe served as an economic asset for the Soviet Union, which was an anomalous view that most Soviet officials, including Gorbachev himself, rejected. In any event, the International Department provided no prescription for how to strike this delicate balance and acknowledged that Moscow had little leverage to dictate the course of events.[106]

The second study came from the IEMSS, which had Gorbachev's ear. Its analysis painted a bleak picture:

> We face a dilemma: to thwart the evolution described above or take it in stride and develop the policy accepting the probability and even inevitability of this process. Attempts to thwart emerging trends would be tantamount to fighting time itself, the objective course of history. In the long term, these kinds of steps would be doomed and in the short run would mean wasting means and resources for an obviously hopeless cause. Attempts to preserve in Poland, Hungary and Yugoslavia the status quo that has lost its objective foundations, as well as the support of conservative forces in the GDR, CSSR, Romania and Bulgaria will weigh as an excessive burden on our economy, for the price of maintaining existing relations will increase in time.[107]

The Eastern Europeans would abandon Soviet socialism, the IEMSS determined, but it was unclear what would replace it. "The model of economic and political development imposed on these countries after 1948 has clearly exhausted itself," the memorandum concluded. This evaluation acknowledged that there would be little opportunity for Moscow to change the course of events. It warned that any attempts to reestablish the status quo "could have the gravest consequences," including "the inevitable slide of the East[ern] European countries back to the ranks of the poorly developed" as well as the return of "quasi-dictatorial regimes which would continuously deplete the material resources of the Soviet Union."[108] Even if Moscow had wanted to prop up the regimes, such an outcome exceeded Soviet means.

When the revolutions erupted later that year, the Soviets had no policy for how to handle the instability. Gorbachev could not even dedicate his attention to international affairs in 1989 because the upheaval coincided with escalating economic and political crises on the home front. The chairman of the Council of Ministers Nikolai Ryzhkov summarized the dismal situation at a Politburo session in February 1989: after tallying losses from falling oil prices, reduced vodka sales, agricultural losses, and cleanup after Chernobyl, among other issues, Soviet government spending had exceeded revenue by 133 billion rubles over the previous three years. With an overhang of 40 billion rubles, the Soviet people had a lot of notes but nothing to buy with them. Price increases "cause social tensions, which threaten *perestroika*," he worried. Instead, Ryzhkov called for reduced government spending across a variety of sectors, including defense, manufacturing, and state enterprises. The Soviets "must go through a difficult school," he said, "and learn to live within our means." In response, Gorbachev admitted that maybe he had "underestimated the depth of the pit from which we had to get out when beginning perestroika. . . . We overestimated our capabilities and our ability to reach a level that would free us from the accumulated burden of stagnation within a short period of time."[109] It was a telling moment of self-reflection.

While Gorbachev inherited a stagnating economy and made it worse, he created the political disaster himself. He believed that the regime needed to democratize the CPSU, so the Soviet Union held contested elections in March 1989 to the Congress of People's Deputies that Gorbachev expected would provide popular support for the party. He also hoped that this new body would provide him with a popular mandate for his policies and allow him to circumvent conservative elites. The results were disastrous. Party favorites suffered shocking losses, particularly in Moscow and Leningrad.[110] Glasnost empowered nationalist movements across the Soviet Union, and Moscow had to contend with new challenges in the republics almost every month in 1989, not least a violent clash between Soviet soldiers and protesters in Tbilisi in April.[111] When the Berlin Wall fell, the escalating crisis in the Baltic republics preoccupied Moscow. Policymakers feared that nationalist movements there could inspire similar movements in Ukraine and Russia. "I smell an overall collapse," Ryzhkov feared.[112]

Events in Poland and Hungary had already overtaken Moscow. Poland had the dubious distinction of accumulating the highest gross debt in the region and had been in de facto default since 1981. Cut off from credit markets, Poland's living standards plummeted. "Warsaw, Western creditors, and the USSR will find no escape from the dilemma posed by Poland's economic weaknesses," the CIA concluded.[113] After releasing political prisoners as a US requirement, Poland received IMF membership in 1986. The IMF demanded structural adjustments as a condition for the credit, requiring among other things that Poland decrease public spending and bring its current account into surplus. This meant austerity.

Jaruzelski knew the threat that carrying out structural adjustment posed to his regime. He understood that suppressing consumption and reducing state subsidies would infuriate and embolden the masses to challenge the regime, but he also acknowledged that the financial situation left no alternative. Increases in the prices of food in the summer of 1988 brought protesters into the streets, just as they had in 1970, 1976, and 1980. The wave of strikes the following month proved particularly effective as they brought the coal and steel industries, key industries that produced exports, screeching to a halt. Believing that austerity needed some degree of popular support, the regime invited Solidarity to participate in roundtable discussions. A Polish official explained, "The main purpose of the roundtable talks is to offer a *political* concession so as to facilitate the implementation of the authorities' *economic* plans."[114] In February 1989, the first roundtable talks took place, leading to an agreement to hold free elections, though a significant proportion were reserved for PUWP candidates. Solidarity nevertheless won a smashing victory, steamrolling the PUWP and electing Tadeusz Mazowiecki as prime minister in August 1989. He became the first democratically elected Eastern European leader since the beginning of the Cold War.[115]

The Hungarian revolution had its idiosyncrasies but followed a similar model. Unlike Poland, Hungary had enjoyed the confidence of Western bankers in the mid-1980s and went on a credit binge but plunged into a debt crisis in 1987. Budapest had the highest debt per capita in the bloc and needed a hard currency trade surplus of $1 billion just to service the debt.[116] Already a member of the IMF, the regime approached it for help, and IMF officials demanded cuts to the trade deficit and consumer subsidies, price reform, and devaluations of the forint. Western officials had no interest in allowing Hungary to collapse. "If 'goulash communism' goes bankrupt, the old Stalinists would return— this could not be in our interest," Kohl commented to Shultz.[117] When Kádár dragged his feet, the IMF threatened to suspend negotiations in May 1988, providing the opportunity for the reformer Károly Grósz to assume power.

Grósz knew that the regime needed some level of popular support to implement the IMF's demands, and he invited various opposition groups for roundtable talks, which opened the floodgates for attacks on the regime. "Why aren't those incompetent leaders brought to account who squandered away $15 billion [Hungary's debt to the West]?" asked angry Hungarian miners in a confrontation with party leaders. "How come the socialist countries are getting poorer while nonaligned Austria and Finland have been getting richer? If the party and the government are so sure that they enjoy the confidence of the people, why don't we have free elections under international supervision?"[118]

Reformers mobilized the memory of the Hungarian Revolution of 1956 and launched an inquiry into the failed uprising, releasing a report that rehabilitated Imre Nagy and rewrote the events of 1956 as a heroic struggle against an oppressive political order and imperial hegemon. The reformers held a massive state funeral in June 1989 in which they reburied Nagy's remains, an event that two hundred thousand Hungarians attended. "In Hungary the processes are most probably unstoppable," Shevardnadze conceded.[119] In October 1989, the party rebranded itself the Socialist Party and the country was renamed the Republic of Hungary, eliminating the words "people's republic" that had identified Hungary as part of the socialist bloc.[120]

Gorbachev tried to influence events from the sidelines. He knew that Poland provided a crucial link to maintaining the Soviet position in East Germany. "If we cannot hold Poland, then we cannot hold the GDR either," Gorbachev had explained to the Politburo in July 1986. But with the Poles' crushing debt and the position of the PUWP slipping, he had neither the will nor the means to prop it up. "We grumble about the Poles' relationship with the IMF. But what should they do? The debt is $30 billion."[121] Gorbachev turned the Poles away when they knocked on Moscow's door for financial help, but he also encouraged the Poles to play hardball with Solidarity. He told Polish prime minister Mieczysław Rakowski that the PUWP should not concede the fundamental principles of socialism to the opposition and instead try to isolate those who were fighting to overthrow the system.[122]

Rather than intervene in the negotiations, Gorbachev tried to claim responsibility for the revolutions and pointed at them as proof that his new world order was becoming reality. He appreciated public statements from Western leaders that the Cold War had ended but challenged their assessments that the global balance had shifted against socialism.[123] Gorbachev appealed to the hearts and minds across Europe, constantly referring to his theme of the common European home. In July 1989, Gorbachev delivered a speech to the Parliament of Europe in Strasbourg in which he pitched his vision of bringing both halves of Europe together in a democratic and peaceful union.[124] He linked Western European integration and his stalled push for CMEA integration, which he privately admitted had failed, as part of the same process and declared that socialism was re-creating itself.

Socialism was not renewing, in fact. Financial pressures and popular unrest compelled political elites in the Soviet bloc to give up their power, even if contemporaries in the summer could still not see at that point how revolutionary the fall of 1989 would become. East Germany refused to consider IMF membership, but the financial dependence on West Germany de facto granted its rival similar leverage. After the *Milliardenkredite*, economic assistance bought West Germany increased cultural ties with its neighbor and relaxed travel restrictions. This process allowed East Germans to see even more clearly—whether on television, radio, print media, or in person—the stark difference between living standards in divided Germany. By 1988 several hundred thousand East Germans had filed applications for permanent emigration, setting the stage for a mass exodus that evoked memories of the 1950s and early 1960s. More sought protection in West German embassies in Prague and Budapest.[125] Having used its financial leverage cautiously, Bonn now acted decisively as it identified a window of opportunity. Kohl extended a credit of DM 1 billion to the bankrupt Hungarian government as a bribe to allow the East Germans to cross the border into neutral Austria, which Budapest did with Gorbachev's blessing. East Berlin howled but could do little to stop it.[126]

At this point, East Germany could stay solvent only with West German assistance. "Foreign debt is growing uncontrollably, but the leadership does not know what to do," the head of the SED International Department Günter Sieber reported to his Soviet counterpart Vadim Zagladin. Support for the regime waned within the SED rank-and-file. Party officials openly made "nasty" jokes about Honecker and other leaders as disillusionment festered. The SED inner circle "had genuine fear about the possible consequences of the evolving economic and political situation," Sieber relayed. "They feared the reappearance of the conditions of 1953 or something similar to the conditions in Poland." He could not answer how East Berlin planned to solve these problems. "That's the real tragedy," Sieber admitted; "at the moment there is simply no way out."[127]

As thousands of East Germans flocked to the open Hungarian border as a pathway to the West, many of those who remained behind took the streets in cities such as Leipzig and Dresden in early October 1989, braving the heavy-handed tactics of the riot police, to demand radical changes. Honecker contemplated using force to clear the protesters, but he equivocated. The Politburo replaced him with the reformer Krenz, who had a rude surprise when he learned the depth of East German economic failures. Schürer submitted a sweeping analysis at the end of the month that showed that if access to Western credits stopped, an austerity program would cause living standards to drop 25 to 30 percent, and this figure included the wishful assumption that East Germany could find foreign buyers for its products. East Germany had a debt-service ratio of 150 percent in relation to hard currency exports.[128] By the end of the month, East German debt totaled $26.5 billion.[129] "It was clear to me that the sovereignty of the GDR could only be maintained to a limited extent," Schürer remembered, because West Germany would make political demands in return for financial assistance.[130]

Moscow could not throw a lifeline. By this point, the Soviets could not even meet their bilateral trade obligations to East Berlin, let along scrounge enough hard currency to stabilize it.[131] "Without the help of the FRG, we will not keep it afloat anyway," Gorbachev conceded to the Politburo in early November 1989. With mounting pressure from below on the SED, "it might be better [for Krenz] to remove the Berlin Wall himself," Shevardnadze suggested. This was six days *before* East Germany dismantled it.[132]

The pressure on the East German regime continued to grow, and the ranks of protesters swelled to one million people. On November 9, SED press secretary Günter Schabowski made a faux pas for the ages when he, failing to complete his homework before meeting the international press, mistakenly announced at the podium the following evening that East Germans could travel abroad freely. Upon hearing the announcement, jubilant East Germans overwhelmed the border guards and poured into West Berlin. Schabowski's gaffe provided the proximate reason for the improvised fall of the Berlin Wall, but larger forces were already moving in this direction. Earlier that same day, Krenz and the SED leadership had agreed to give up the political monopoly and were already considering recognizing the New Forum as a legal opposition group and loosening restrictions on travel that would put the Berlin Wall implicitly on the trading block.[133] Events moved toward a negotiated end to the SED dictatorship.

The fall of the Berlin Wall catalyzed upheaval to the southeast, empowering protesters who could now believe that change was possible. Czechoslovakia had one of the highest standards of living within the CMEA, which said more about how dismal things had become for its neighbors than anything. Before World War II, the Czech regions and Moravia had a per capita GDP comparable to that of Belgium and higher than that of Austria. By the late 1980s, however, this statistic fell to about half of Austria's.[134] "The jalopy has run out of gas," *PlanEcon* noted.[135] While Czechoslovak debt was relatively low, particularly in comparison to Poland and East Germany, Prague quietly began exploratory discussions about rejoining the IMF and the World Bank, hoping to pave the way for secure access to foreign credits. It planned an ambitious economic reform program for 1990 that would suppress consumption by raising consumer prices, risking the same social unrest that challenged other regimes.[136]

Czechoslovak protesters did not give the regime the chance. Václav Havel, the founder of Charter 77, formed the opposition group Civic Forum and called for a general strike. The strike shut down the country, demonstrating the widespread opposition to the regime. For days protesters marched on Wenceslas Square, the same location where Warsaw Pact tanks had rolled in to squash the Prague Spring just two decades prior, chanting "Freedom" and "Now's the time." In the face of popular pressure, the Husák government resigned. At the end of December 1989, the legislature elected Havel—who had served as the director, playwright, stage manager, and leading actor of this "velvet revolution"—as president.[137]

While sheltered more from Western influence than most of the other CMEA states, Bulgaria also felt the strain of debt. By 1990, debt service alone claimed 75 percent of hard currency earnings—the highest ratio in the CMEA.[138] In desperation, Zhivkov launched a campaign against Bulgaria's ethnic Turkish minority (which represented more than 10 percent of the population) in the mid-1980s to distract the population from the country's escalating economic woes. They were a "fifth column against the Warsaw Pact," Zhivkov warned the skeptical Gorbachev.[139]

The transition toward a more market-based economy had begun in the late 1980s. "Here in this circle, we can say openly that the problem is thus: will socialism survive or not?" Zhivkov said to the Politburo in February 1988. "Interests and markets" would have to guide the economy, he admitted. "That is the cruel truth."[140] Zhivkov's Decree No. 56 in January 1989 outlined a radical economic restructuring along the lines of Gorbachev's perestroika, and Bulgaria announced at a June 1989 summit for the economic secretaries that it would adopt a "plan-market economy."[141] The haphazard blueprint marked one of the last straws for Bulgaria's political elite. The Politburo voted Zhivkov out of office the day after the fall of the Berlin Wall. Inspired by events to the north, tens of thousands of protesters swarmed central Sofia in mid-November 1989 and demanded free elections, which were held the following year.

Romania alone had launched a draconian austerity policy since the early 1980s to drive down its debt, eager to avoid giving Western creditors leverage over decisions in Bucharest. But rather than highlighting the array of options available to socialist policymakers as they grappled with how to respond to debt in the 1980s, the Romanian example provides a real-world counterfactual. Austerity ripened conditions for the overthrow of the regime. As a propaganda campaign informed Romanians that they lived in a "golden epoch," villages and many cities went pitch black at night to conserve energy. Empty shelves became a reality of everyday life. The regime used 40-watt light bulbs so that energy could be exported to the West for hard currency. To preserve petroleum, horse-drawn carts became the primary method of travel. The tone-deaf construction of Ceaușescu's ostentatious palace known as the "House of the People" clashed with the poverty among the general population, illustrating how out-of-touch the regime had become. On his visit to Bucharest in June 1987, Mikhail Gorbachev remembered "how frightened" the Romanian people seemed. Ceaușescu "tried to pass off [Romania] as a society of prosperity and democracy," but it "was nothing of the kind."[142] Austerity fanned the flames of economic and political frustrations simmering just under the surface, creating a combustible situation that resembled Russia in 1917. The question was when, not if, the explosion would occur in Romania.[143] Building on the momentum elsewhere in the bloc, Romanian protesters overran a pro-regime rally in late December 1989. Ceaușescu and his wife were executed by firing squad on Christmas Day.

The CMEA and Warsaw Pact still existed on paper, but the Soviet bloc as a socialist bloc dominated by Moscow had disappeared from the map. Gorbachev refused to believe that he had been beaten. He set out to convince the world that the Eastern European revolutions were his idea. At the Malta Summit in December 1989, he commented to Bush that the changes in Europe were "truly fundamental in nature." Once again, he made a false equivalence between the European Community and the CMEA. "And not only in Eastern Europe—in Western Europe, too." European integration accelerated, and Gorbachev commented that he "associated this movement with the idea of a common European home." He asserted that "people have no fear of choosing between one system and another. They are searching for their own unique possibility, one that will provide them with the best standard of living. When this search flows freely, then there is only one thing left to say: good luck."[144] The tactful Bush offered platitudes in response, knowing nothing could be gained from matching Gorbachev's posturing, which bore little relation to conditions on the ground. "Mikhail Gorbachev's new world order had been a slogan; George Bush's new world order was becoming a reality," James Graham Wilson summarizes.[145]

The unification of Germany demonstrated just how far the balance of power had shifted. When the Berlin Wall came down, Gorbachev tried to stall. As events overtook the superpowers and the East German masses rejected the SED, a growing number of Soviet policymakers understood that they had little leverage in the negotiations. The process "cannot be stopped," Ryzhkov conceded in January 1990. The Soviets could not "save the GDR. All barriers have already been torn down. The economy is breaking down. All state institutions have been dissolved."[146] The Soviets still had almost four hundred thousand Soviet troops stationed in East Germany, but Gorbachev knew that Moscow would lose any chance of Western financial assistance for the failing Soviet economy as well as completely undermine his attempt to remake the Soviet international image. The March 1990 East German elections demonstrated overwhelming support for unification, and both Bush and Kohl insisted on Germany remaining in NATO. "It is completely obvious that Germany will be in NATO," Chernyaev wrote Gorbachev in early May 1990. "We do not have any real leverage to prevent this."[147] Moscow received billions of dollars in credits from West Germany as well as a reformed NATO as carrots for accepting a unified Germany in NATO.[148] The settlement required delicate negotiations, but as James Davis and William Wohlforth contend, it is no surprise that the outcome aligned with the interests of the United States and West Germany, the most powerful countries involved.[149]

"Men make their own history, but they do not make it as they please," Karl Marx wrote in the Eighteenth Brumaire; "they do not make it under self-selected circumstances, but under circumstances existing already, given and transmitted from the past."[150] Gorbachev's failure to turn his vision of a new world order into reality provides a case in point. He made choices, but only within the severe constraints of the Soviet bloc's accumulated economic and political atrophy. He concluded arms agreements with the United States, became popular among Western policymakers and Eastern reformers, rethought relations with Eastern Europe, and withdrew from the Third World, but he could not escape the structural limits to turn his vision into reality. With most regimes already dependent on the West for survival and the Soviet Union unable to protect them, the Soviet bloc was already on life support when he entered office.

Conclusion

The end of the Cold War was a process that had its proximate roots in the 1970s. The global economic shocks of that decade presented the West and the Soviet bloc with a common set of challenges that struck at their cores. Their economic models sputtered as opportunities for extensive growth became exhausted and productivity gains diminished. The erosion of postwar conditions persuaded the industrial democracies to abandon the Bretton Woods system and the CMEA to revise the Bucharest formula. Industrial economies on both sides of the Iron Curtain had relied on inexpensive raw materials to drive growth but struggled to adapt to the upheaval in the commodities markets. Officials in Washington and Moscow struggled to hold their blocs together in an age of economic disruption.

This book has argued that the West's ability and East's inability to adapt to the global economic shocks of the 1970s played the crucial role in causing the end of the Cold War. While the cohesion of the core capitalist countries is often taken for granted, it was an essential part of the equation. The socialists declared not only that their ideological system aligned with the natural course of history but also that the inherent contradictions of capitalism would lead to a proletarian revolution in the West. The "palsied decrepitude of the capitalist world is the keystone of Communist philosophy," Kennan had argued in his July 1947 "X" article.[1] The socialists had watched hopefully as stagflation upended the industrial democracies, but contrary to Marxist-Leninist expectations, the postwar implosion of capitalism and the disintegration of the West did not occur.

This book has emphasized two factors to explain why the West did not collapse. First, democratic capitalism was adaptable. Noninflationary growth returned in the 1980s, giving the bloc a renewed source of legitimacy. The key was the unexpected interaction between the tight monetary policy of the Federal Reserve and the expansionary program of the Reagan administration. Volcker not only choked inflation at home and imparted a deflationary shock abroad, but high interest rates attracted the foreign capital necessary to fund Reagan's budget deficits and lubricate the economy. Aided by the decline of oil prices, the US consumer boom and strong dollar provided a stimulus to Western Europe, Japan, and the developing world. The recovery transformed the United States into a debtor nation with a large trade deficit while key US allies enjoyed large surpluses. The postwar imbalances had reversed but US hegemony remained, a structure that this book calls the inverted US welfare empire.

The reliance on foreign capital worked in the 1980s only because US policymakers had gradually aligned their interests with accelerating economic globalization during the previous decade. They made no purposeful choice to tear down the Bretton Woods system and replace it with a de facto dollar system in which capital flowed freely. They improvised in response to contingent events, and capital account liberalization came in steps.

Many scholars contend that the resurgence stemmed from a turn to neoliberalism, a broad ideology that describes the reduction of the state's footprint in the economy and society and the encouragement of freer markets.[2] Washington certainly encouraged deregulation, tax cuts, and privatization at home and abroad. But as Melvyn P. Leffler argues, the neoliberal argument overlooks the vital role that the government still played in ensuring that democratic capitalism worked effectively.[3] Governments utilized fiscal and monetary tools to provide social safety nets, moderate the business cycle, maintain monetary stability, and influence the value of their currencies. Often viewed as a neoliberal trailblazer, Reagan, for example, preached the mantra of small government, but US spending on social programs as a proportion of GDP increased from 12.9 percent to 13.2 percent during the 1980s.[4] The de facto dollar system afforded governments more flexibility to spend than under the Bretton Woods system or the gold standard because currencies now had no relationship to precious metals. Unlike during the Great Depression, governments in the post–Bretton Woods era provided social safety nets to cushion the blow of unemployment.

Second, Western officials and their constituents maintained their belief that their economic and security interests broadly accorded with the US vision of world order based on democratic capitalism and anchored by the US military umbrella. Even as stagflation sapped popular support for centrist parties, the Western European and Japanese people still chose leaders who thought their countries would be more prosperous and safer through cooperation with the United States. Unlike the Soviet counterpart, US hegemony did not prevent the allies from blazing their own paths, and various syntheses of democratic capitalism that conformed to local conditions coexisted across the bloc. For their part, US officials resisted protectionist and isolationist domestic pressure and did not deviate from their conviction that US national security depended on maintaining close relations with Western Europe and Japan. The lessons of the Great Depression loomed large, and leaders across the industrial democracies understood that allied cohesion required diplomacy and hard work. The institutionalization of the G7 summits after the mid-1970s symbolized the collective commitment to an open world economy and international cooperation, even if that forum hosted heated debates and disagreements. Meanwhile, the oppressive political conditions and economic want behind the Iron Curtain meant that Soviet socialism offered the Western public no attractive alternative to democratic capitalism.

The benefits of global capitalism's structural adjustment were not distributed equally in the West. The wealthy flourished as economic globalization surged, markets deregulated, taxes decreased, global financial markets expanded, and new fields in the information sector emerged. In contrast, labor unions had thrived in the postwar period, but their position deteriorated as the oil shocks made production more expensive, manufacturing jobs moved to the developing world, governments weakened labor protections, and the burden of monetary discipline fell hardest on them. The long-term decline of the working class became the price of a more efficient international division of labor and the maintenance of an open world economy.

US officials feared that protecting manufacturing jobs at home would lead to a breakdown of the free trade regime, hurt multinational corporations, and weaken US alliances. Instead, they focused on reorienting the US economy toward the information revolution and becoming more service oriented. US officials tried to cushion the blow to labor by maintaining social safety nets but generally accepted the increasing gap between the rich and the poor as a necessary cost. They disavowed responsibility by claiming that the growing inequality stemmed from market forces and unfair trading practices of other nations.

Officials in the Soviet bloc could not justify placing the burden of structural adjustment on the working class, however, because the socialist countries consisted of proletarian dictatorships that claimed to rule in the name of that very constituency. The ideological commitment to full employment and the rigidities of the command economy disincentivized reforms that entailed shedding jobs or falling short on production quotas. "Socialism's politically driven economy proved very good—too good—at putting up a rust belt," Stephen Kotkin explains in the case of the Soviet Union, "and, unlike a market economy, socialism proved very bad at taking its rust belt down."[5] In contrast to the ad hoc "creative destruction" in the West, the Soviet bloc maintained its increasingly anachronistic economic model that privileged heavy industry.

Soviet socialism lost the ideological battle with democratic capitalism well before the late 1980s, but that alone does not account for the collapse of the Soviet bloc. Cuba and North Korea demonstrate that there is nothing inevitable about the fall of impoverished and oppressive communist regimes. China and Vietnam have maintained their communist political monopolies while introducing market mechanisms into their economies, showing that Marxism-Leninism does not preclude a transition away from the command economy and the embrace of global markets.[6]

Two essential factors caused the collapse of the Soviet bloc. First, the accumulation of debt behind the Iron Curtain in the 1970s and 1980s distinguished Eastern Europe from other communist countries. The Soviet bloc could sustain itself as a relatively closed system because the regimes had the ability to crack down on their populations without fear of reprisal from the West, as the Hungarian Revolution and the Prague Spring demonstrated. The situation changed when the Eastern European regimes turned to a strategy of debt-led development during the late 1960s and early 1970s. Eastern Europe effectively cast its die. As the twin energy crises in the mid-1970s hit, the regimes continued to draw on Western credits to finance imports instead of limiting consumption. Western goods allowed the regimes to postpone a reckoning but did nothing to resolve the underlying problems. The Volcker shock reoriented global financial flows and precipitated a debt crisis behind the Iron Curtain, first erupting in Poland and then spreading to the other Eastern European countries. By this point, Soviet socialism not only lacked ideological appeal; it also depended on Western life support to exist.

The reliance on Western credits dripped with irony. As part of his sweeping denunciation of US foreign policy at the United Nations in September 1947, Soviet diplomat Andrei Vyshinsky had warned that countries accepting Marshall Plan assistance would be "giving up their inalienable rights to dispose of their own economic resources [and] to plan their own national economy as they see fit." The US offer constituted an imperialist plot to divide Europe into two camps, Vyshinsky declared, and "it is becoming more clear to everybody that . . . the Marshall Plan would mean the subjugation of European countries to economic and political control exercised by the United States of America, and direct interference on its part in the internal affairs of those countries."[7] No US conspiracy existed, and Western officials did not utilize their financial leverage as aggressively as they might have in the late 1970s and 1980s, but the broad outlines of Vyshinsky's fear that reliance on capitalist funds would provide the West with a tool to influence policies behind the Iron Curtain became reality a few decades later.

The Kremlin's willingness to cede its position in Eastern Europe after four decades of hegemony was the other essential ingredient in the bloc's collapse. As this book has shown, Soviet officials had started reevaluating the cost of their empire well before the Eastern European revolutions, with serious discontent building already in the 1970s. Moscow ceased serving as the bloc's guarantor by the early 1980s, and Western institutions and governments began to step into the vacuum. This process provided space for the Eastern European masses to overthrow the communist regimes and culminated in the 1989 revolutions. The Soviet bloc did not disintegrate in response to Gorbachev's reforms—it died a slow death.

The West had persisted, but it was not clear that the inverted US welfare empire framework could survive in the post–Cold War world. The twin budget and trade deficits in the 1980s heightened domestic calls for fiscal restraint and protectionism, and Reagan endeavored to reverse them in his second term. Reagan had limited success, but the William Clinton administration closed the budget deficit during the 1990s, even swinging the budget into surplus at the end of the decade. With the debt-to-GDP ratio decreasing, investors wondered whether the market for US Treasury bonds, which they viewed as a safe harbor, would dry up.[8]

The policies of the George W. Bush administration lessened those concerns. Echoing the supply-side arguments of the early Reagan years, the Bush administration assured the nation that it could simultaneously cut taxes and reduce the debt. "We can walk and chew gum," the incoming director of the Office of Management and Budget Mitchell E. Daniels Jr. told the Senate in his confirmation hearing in January 2001. Motivated by the September 11 attacks, Bush boosted defense spending to wage war against terrorism on top of his planned tax cuts. As the United States invaded and then became mired in Afghanistan and Iraq, defense spending rose as a percentage of GDP from 2.9 percent in 2001 to 4.6 percent in 2009. Mirroring the outcome in the 1980s, the US budget deficit exploded once more.[9] Sticking to the supply-side playbook, the Donald Trump administration claimed that the Tax Cuts and Jobs Act of 2017 would pay for itself, but the tax cuts only increased the budget deficit. Add in the massive fiscal responses to the 2008 financial crisis and the COVID-19 pandemic,

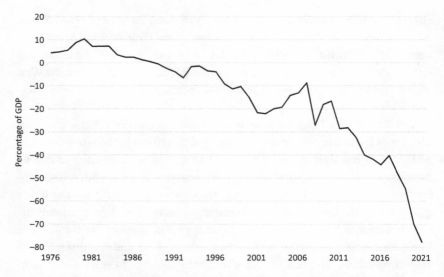

FIGURE C.1. US net international investment position as a percentage of GDP. Source: FRED, Federal Reserve Bank of St. Louis.

and US debt climbed north of $31 trillion by late 2022.[10] As a percentage of GDP, it jumped from 55 percent in 2001 to 120 percent in 2022.[11]

Foreign capital provided a safety valve that funded the budget deficits and kept interest rates lower than they would be otherwise. Rather than increase taxes, cut defense spending, or eliminate social programs to halt the slide—all of which would be politically unpopular—Democrats and Republicans have chosen to increase the national debt instead. The dollar retains its dominant place in global finance and international trade, which magnifies US power and allows Washington to borrow cheaply.[12]

Dollar hegemony has proven remarkably durable. The 2008 financial crisis appeared to be the moment when the world might turn away from the dollar. "Currencies of all countries, unite!" Russian journalists urged.[13] The unexpected result, however, was that the Great Recession reinforced the dollar's position. As Adam Tooze explains, banks around the world, particularly in Europe, became exposed to the financial crisis because they suffered from a dollar shortage. The Federal Reserve jumped into action, utilizing swap lines to make trillions of dollars available to foreign central banks within the US security umbrella, which then channeled the funds to distressed banks. The emergence of the Federal Reserve as the lender of last resort for the dollar-based financial system renewed investors' faith in the greenback amid the global turbulence, and the dollar emerged from the crisis with its position ironically solidified.[14]

The inverted US welfare empire endures to this day because it serves the economic and security interests of a variety of stakeholders, not just those of the United States. First, investors consider US Treasury debt among the very safest financial assets. Second, the US private sector is among the most dynamic and open in the world, and US political and legal institutions adeptly defend private property rights. Third, except for a brief reduction after the 2008 financial crisis, the US trade deficit has persistently increased, surpassing $1 trillion for the first time in 2021.[15] Manufactured products account for most of the deficits, and export-oriented economies around the world enjoy access to US consumers and their insatiable appetite for inexpensive products. "The sustained purchase of American debt was the price that Asian societies, above all," Charles S. Maier explains, "paid to acquire the manufacturing jobs American stockholders, if not American workers, wished to distribute abroad."[16] As of November 2022, foreigners own nearly $7.3 trillion of US public debt, with China and Japan holding for just over a quarter.[17] It is no coincidence that both countries have had large trade surpluses with the United States over recent decades. Finally, foreign investment helps directly and indirectly finance US defense spending, which surpasses that of the next nine countries combined.[18] The United States projects its power across the world and provides security benefits to those within the US-led system of alliances.

The integration of much of the former socialist world into the inverted US welfare empire in the post–Cold War period diluted its cohesion. "As new states entered the system, the old bargains and institutions that provided stability and governance were overrun," G. John Ikenberry writes. The inclusion of new countries in the network that neither share the West's values nor rely on the United States for security precipitated a "crisis of authority: new bargains, roles and responsibilities were now required."[19] While financial activity remains concentrated in the transatlantic community, the locus of US trade has shifted to East Asia, helping to create a great power challenger: China.

Few have benefited more from the US demand for imports than China. In the late 1970s and 1980s, Beijing adopted an export-oriented industrialization model while preserving the Chinese Communist Party's political monopoly. Hoping that economic prosperity would encourage Beijing to make democratic reforms and improve its record on human rights, US officials encouraged its deeper integration into global capitalism. Access to the US market helped transform China into the world's manufacturer, a position that the United States itself held not too long ago. In return, China became one of the largest holders of US debt and a provider of low-cost manufacturing exports, underwriting US military power, funding social safety nets, and providing US consumers with inexpensive goods. Economic interdependence has locked the two powers in a tight embrace.

Tensions have nevertheless grown between the United States and China because Beijing participates in the economic arrangement of the inverted US welfare empire but does not buy into the security logic. Through the 2008 financial crisis, Beijing generally was content to concentrate on economic development. Thereafter, Beijing has been much more aggressive countering the US vision of world order. Unlike Japan, which chose not to translate its economic might into geopolitical influence, China has built alternative institutions such as the Belt and Road Initiative and invested in its military to project power beyond its borders and challenge US hegemony.[20]

While China has a complicated relationship with the inverted US welfare empire, the Western attempt to integrate the Russian Federation into the system during the 1990s failed. Instead, the Russian president Vladimir Putin has responded violently to the encroachment of transatlantic institutions into post-Soviet space and has attempted to restore Russian hegemony in the so-called near abroad. A former KGB official stationed in Dresden at the time of the 1989 revolutions, he embraced a conspiratorial narrative about the end of the Cold War and the dissolution of the Soviet Union that echoes the stab-in-the-back myth (*Dolchstosslegende*), which became influential in Germany after World War I. German nationalists claimed that they had lost the war not because their military forces had been defeated but rather because civilian traitors on the home front betrayed the nation by negotiating a surrender. In the Russian iteration, the Soviet Union did not lose the Cold War on the battlefield. Instead, Gorbachev played the role of Matthias Erzberger, who had negotiated the armistice in November 1918, by naively abandoning Soviet hegemony in Eastern Europe and set in motion the collapse of the Soviet Union. In this telling, the chaos of the 1990s, the march of NATO and the European Union to Russia's doorstep, and the loss of Russia's imperial borderlands can be traced to Gorbachev's original sin of squandering Soviet power.

With his Weltanschauung rooted in Russian nationalism, Putin seeks to make Eurasia safe for authoritarianism and crony capitalism. No Russian welfare empire exists today, but the Kremlin utilizes some of the Soviet tactics to secure its geopolitical position, namely, the use of energy subsidies as a foreign policy tool. State-owned or -controlled companies such as Gazprom and Rosneft, known as "national champions," act in the Kremlin's interests, even when it clashes with their commercial interests. Russia provided energy subsidies to former Soviet republics such as Armenia, Moldova, and Ukraine in the post-Soviet period, but they have paid the largest geopolitical dividends in Belarus. Seeing the Belarusian president Alexander Lukashenko as a bulwark against color revolutions that have erupted across post-Soviet space, the Kremlin has provided discounted energy to Minsk to solidify Lukashenko's self-described position as Europe's "last dictator." Yet the subsidies come at a high political cost. "Lukashenko has ceded elements of Belarusian sovereignty to Russia in exchange for favorable energy prices," Angela Stent summarizes.[21] This became even clearer after popular protests erupted against the legitimacy of the Belarusian presidential election in August 2020. Under sanctions from the West, Belarus has gravitated further into the Russian sphere of influence, even serving as a staging ground for Russian forces during their invasion of Ukraine in February 2022.

While the failure to deter Putin's war of choice fed narratives about the West's decline, the robust response from the United States and its allies has displayed their unmatched hard and soft power. Reinvigorated with ideological purpose, the inverted US welfare empire roared to life. Financed through deficit spending, the Joseph Biden administration has provided massive financial and lethal assistance to Ukraine and has extended political support and shared intelligence. Weaponizing dollar hegemony and US technological prowess, Washington imposed financial sanctions and export controls against Russia. The European Union has implemented similar measures and extended aid to Ukraine, though the difference in scale has demonstrated just how dependent Europe, despite its economic strength, remains on the United States for its security.

With Chinese general secretary Xi Jinping declaring a strategic partnership with Russia, an authoritarian axis centered on Beijing and Moscow and supported by other states such as Iran and North Korea has emerged in opposition to the US-led system of alliances. Officials and analysts have reached back to the Cold War for a historical analogy to understand the present moment, but they should utilize it with caution. The battle between universalist ideologies made the Cold War unique. To be sure, China and Russia today promote a vision of world order that contrasts the West's, but their brands of authoritarianism are fundamentally rooted in nationalism, not internationalism. Furthermore, the economic interdependence between the United States and China makes the analogy specious.

This does not mean that scholars and policymakers have nothing to learn from the Cold War. It is instructive to return to George Kennan's "Long Telegram" of February 1946. Because the West was the stronger force, Soviet success "will really depend on [the] degree of cohesion, firmness and vigor which [the] Western world can muster," Kennan predicted. "World communism is like a malignant parasite which feeds only on diseased tissue," and

Washington needed to put forward "a much more positive and constructive picture of [the] sort of world we would like to see."[22] Just as was the case when Kennan authored his famous missive, the combined economic and military power of the industrial democracies still surpasses that of its rivals, and success will turn once more on the ability of the United States and its allies to lead by example.

The West's Cold War victory depended on the successful management of alliances and ability to make democratic capitalism work at home, and the United States today must manage its sprawling inverted welfare empire carefully. There are many challenges. In early 2023, a dangerous game of political chicken about raising the debt limit erupted in Congress. If the United States were to default on its debt, it would undermine Washington's ability to finance guns and butter based on debt. The promises of democratic capitalism also remain more aspirational than reality for many people. Nothing symbolized the feelings of many in middle America, often places that had endured deindustrialization, that the current system did not work for them more than Trump's election in November 2016. Similar anti-globalist movements have emerged in Europe and backed far-right leaders such as France's Marine Le Pen, Hungary's Viktor Orbán, and Italy's Giorgia Meloni. Investing in institutions at home and rejuvenating popular belief in democratic capitalism will enhance the US-led system of alliances as Washington and its partners prepare for the great power conflicts of the future. That is the lesson of the Cold War.

Notes

Abbreviations

AA	Auswärtiges Amt
AAPD	*Akten zur Auswärtigen Politik der Bundesrepublik Deutschland*
a.e.	arkhivna edinitsa
AMGF	Archive of the Mikhail Gorbachev Foundation
APP	American Presidency Project
AVP SSSR	Archiv vneshnei politiki Soiuza Sovetskikh Sotsialisticheskikh Respublik
BAB	Bundesarchiv Berlin-Lichterfelde
BAK	Bundesarchiv Koblenz
Bd.	Band
BIS	Bank for International Settlements
BK	Bundeskanzleramt
BKP	Bulgarska komunisticheska partiia
BMF	Bundesministerium der Finanzen
BMWi	Bundesministerium für Wirtschaft
CC	Central Committee
CIA	Central Intelligence Agency
CIAERR	CIA Electronic Reading Room
CWIHP	Cold War International History Project
DBSL	David Bishop Skillman Library
DDR	Deutsche Demokratische Republik
d.	delo
doc.	document
DPK	Durzhavna planova komisiia
ERP	*Economic Report of the President*
f.	fond
FCO	Foreign and Commonwealth Office
FRUS	*Foreign Relations of the United States*
GBPL	George H. W. Bush Presidential Library
GFPL	Gerald R. Ford Presidential Library
inv.nr.	inventaris nummer
IEMSS	Institut ekonomiki mirovoi sotsialisticheskoi sistemy
IMF	International Monetary Fund
JCPL	Jimmy Carter Presidential Library

MBZ   Ministerie van Buitenlandse Zaken
MF   Ministerie van Financiën
MTFDA   Margaret Thatcher Foundation Digital Archive
MVT   Ministerstvo vneshnei torgovli SSSR
NARA   National Archives and Records Administration
NL-HaNA   Nationaal Archief
NSAVRR   National Security Archive Virtual Reading Room
NSC   National Security Council
OA/ID   Oversize Attachment/Identification
OECD   Organisation for Economic Co-operation and Development
OMB   Office of Management and Budget
op.   opis'
PA-AA   Politisches Archiv des Auswärtigen Amts
PREM   Prime Minister's Office
PUS   Permanent Under Secretary
RG   Record Group
RGAE   Rossiiskii gosudarstvennyi arkhiv ekonomiki
RGANI   Rossiiskii gosudarstvennyi arkhiv noveshei istorii
RNPL   Richard Nixon Presidential Library
RRPL   Ronald Reagan Presidential Library
SAPMO   Stiftung Archiv der Parteien und Massenorganisationen der DDR
SecState   Secretary of State
SEV   Sovet ekonomicheskoi vzaimopomoshchi
SGML   Seeley G. Mudd Library
SML   Sterling Memorial Library
SPK   Staatliche Plankommission
T   Treasury
TNA   The National Archives (U.K.)
TsDA   Tsentralen durzhaven arhiv
TsK KPSS   Tsental'nyi komitet Kommunisticheskaia partiia Sovetskogo Soiuza
USIA   United States Information Agency
VM   Valuta Mark
vol.   volume
WHORM   White House Office of Records Management
ZA   Zwischenarchiv
ZBC   Zbigniew Brzezinski Collection
ZBM   Zbigniew Brzezinski Material
ZBSF   Zbigniew Brzezinski's Subject Files

Introduction

1. Diary entry for December 8, 1981, in Douglas Brinkley, ed., *The Reagan Diaries* (New York: HarperCollins, 2007), 53.

2. U.S. Bureau of the Census, *Foreign Trade Statistics*; U.S. Office of Management and Budget, Historical Tables, 1.1 and 7.2.

3. Oliver Wright to Geoffrey Howe, December 20, 1985, MTFDA, T 640/267.

4. In this book, "Eastern Europe" refers to Bulgaria, Czechoslovakia, East Germany, Hungary, Poland, and Romania.

5. This framework draws in inspiration from Daniel J. Sargent, "Pax Americana: Sketches for an Undiplomatic History," *Diplomatic History* 42, no. 3 (2018): 358.

6. Melvyn P. Leffler, *A Preponderance of Power: National Security, the Truman Administration, and the Cold War* (Stanford, CA: Stanford University Press, 1993); Melvyn P. Leffler, "National Security," in *Explaining the History of American Foreign Relations*, 3rd ed., ed. Frank Costigliola and Michael J. Hogan (New York: Cambridge University Press, 2016), 25–41; David Reynolds, *From Munich to Pearl Harbor: Roosevelt's America and the Origins of the Second World War* (Chicago: Ivan R. Dee, 2001); Odd Arne Westad, *The Cold War: A World History* (New York: Basic Books, 2017).

7. Leffler, *Preponderance of Power*. The US welfare empire framework counters elements of the Wisconsin School, which gained traction in the 1960s and 1970s but still frames some of the literature on the United States and the world. It disputes the revisionist claim that US foreign policy had only an exploitative and acquisitive logic. Among others, see Gabriel Kolko and Joyce Kolko, *The Limits of Power: The World and United States Foreign Policy* (New York: Harper & Row, 1972); Walter LaFeber, *America, Russia, and the Cold War, 1945–1971* (New York: Wiley, 1972); and William A. Williams, *The Tragedy of American Diplomacy* (Cleveland: World Publishing, 1959).

8. Charles S. Maier characterizes the United States during the postwar period as the "empire of production" in *Among Empires: American Ascendancy and Its Predecessors* (Cambridge, MA: Harvard University Press, 2007).

9. Although the question of whether Eastern Europe placed an economic burden on the Soviet Union preoccupied academics and analysts during the Cold War, scholars have generally neglected the issue since. The archival evidence presented here demonstrates that not only did Eastern Europe drain Soviet resources, but officials in Moscow grasped that reality. For a sample of the Cold War–era literature, see Valerie Bunce, "The Empire Strikes Back: The Evolution of the Eastern Bloc from a Soviet Asset to a Soviet Liability," *International Organization* 39, no. 1 (1985): 1–46; Paul Marer, "The Political Economy of Soviet Relations with Eastern Europe," in *Soviet Policy in Eastern Europe*, ed. Sarah Meiklejohn Terry (New Haven, CT: Yale University Press, 1984), 155–88; and Michael Marrese and Jan Vanous, *Soviet Subsidization of Trade with Eastern Europe: A Soviet Perspective* (Berkeley: Institute of International Studies, University of California, 1983). The essential starting point on the Council for Mutual Economic Assistance (CMEA) trade that draws on archival materials is Randall W. Stone, *Satellites and Commissars: Strategy and Conflict in the Politics of Soviet-Bloc Trade* (Princeton, NJ: Princeton University Press, 1996). On negotiations regarding energy, see William M. Reisinger, *Energy and the Soviet Bloc: Alliance Politics after Stalin* (Ithaca, NY: Cornell University Press, 1992).

10. Marrese and Vanous, *Soviet Subsidization of Trade*, 3; Institut ekonomiki mirovoi sotsialisticheskoi sistemy, *SSSR i sotsialisticheskaia ekonomicheskaia intergratsiia* (Moscow: Nauka, 1981), 151.

11. On transatlantic bargaining, see, among others, Jeffrey Glen Giauque, *Grand Designs and Visions of Unity: The Atlantic Powers and the Reorganization of Western Europe, 1955–1963* (Chapel Hill: University of North Carolina Press, 2002); William I. Hitchcock, *France Restored: Cold War Diplomacy and the Quest for Leadership in Europe, 1944–1954* (Chapel Hill: University of North Carolina Press, 1998).

12. Standing in for others, see Hope M. Harrison, *Driving the Soviets Up the Wall: Soviet-East German Relations, 1953–1961* (Princeton, NJ: Princeton University Press, 2003); Mary E. Sarotte, *Dealing with the Devil: East Germany, Détente, and Ostpolitik, 1969–1973* (Chapel Hill: University of North Carolina Press, 2001).

13. Among others, see Barry J. Eichengreen, *The European Economy since 1945: Coordinated Capitalism and Beyond* (Princeton, NJ: Princeton University Press, 2008); Scott O'Bryan, *The Growth Idea: Purpose and Prosperity in Postwar Japan* (Honolulu: University of Hawai'i Press, 2009); Matthias Schmelzer, *The Hegemony of Growth: The OECD and the Making of the Economic Growth Paradigm* (New York: Cambridge University Press, 2016); Tamás Vonyó, "War and Socialism: Why Eastern Europe Fell Behind between 1950 and 1989," *Economic History Review* 70, no. 1 (2017): 248–74. For the critics of growth, see Stephen Macekura, *The Mismeasure of Progress: Economic Growth and Its Critics* (Chicago: University of Chicago Press, 2020).

14. Angus Maddison, *The World Economy*, vol. 1, *A Millennial Perspective* (Paris: OECD, 2006), 265.

15. World Bank, World Development Indicators.

16. Charles S. Maier, "'Malaise': The Crisis of Capitalism in the 1970s," in *The Shock of the Global: The 1970s in Perspective*, ed. Niall Ferguson, Charles S. Maier, Erez Manela, and Daniel J. Sargent (Cambridge, MA: Belknap Press of Harvard University Press, 2011), 45. Maier has long contended that the crises of capitalism and socialism during the 1970s and 1980s were part of the same process. See particularly "The Collapse of Communism: Approaches for a Future History," *History Workshop Journal* 31, no. 1 (1991): 34–59.

17. World Bank, World Development Indicators.

18. Jeffry A. Frieden, *Global Capitalism: Its Fall and Rise in the Twentieth Century, and Its Stumbles in the Twenty-First* (New York: W. W. Norton, 2020), 397.

19. United Nations Conference on Trade and Development (UNCTAD), UNCTADstat.

20. Stanko Todorov, *Do vurkhovete na vlastta: Politicheski memoari* (Sofia: Khristo Botev, 1995), 130.

21. Leffler, *Preponderance of Power*.

22. World Bank, World Development Indicators.

23. Maddison, *World Economy*, 1:134.

24. Gennadii Zoteev, "The View from Gosplan: Growth to the Year 2000," in *The Destruction of the Soviet Economic System: An Insiders' History*, ed. Michael Ellman and Vladimir Kontorovich (New York: M. E. Sharpe, 1998), 87.

25. Gerhard Schürer, "Das reale Bild war eben katastrophal," in *Der Fall der Mauer: Die unbeabsichtigte Selbstauflösung des SED-Staates*, ed. Hans-Hermann Hertle (Opladen: Westdeutscher Verlag, 1996), 313.

26. On structural economic change in the late twentieth century, see, among others, Eric Helleiner, *States and the Reemergence of Global Finance: From Bretton Woods to the 1990s* (Ithaca, NY: Cornell University Press, 1994); Greta R. Krippner, *Capitalizing on Crisis: The Political Origins of the Rise of Finance* (Cambridge, MA: Harvard University Press, 2011); Daniel J. Sargent, *A Superpower Transformed: The Remaking of American Foreign Relations in the 1970s* (New York: Oxford University Press, 2015); Judith Stein, *Pivotal Decade: How the United States Traded Factories for Finance in the Seventies* (New Haven,

CT: Yale University Press, 2010; Susan Strange, *Casino Capitalism* (New York: Blackwell, 1986).

27. Archie Brown, *The Gorbachev Factor* (New York: Oxford University Press, 1996); Archie Brown, *The Human Factor: Gorbachev, Reagan, and Thatcher, and the End of the Cold War* (New York: Oxford University Press, 2020); Robert English, *Russia and the Idea of the West: Gorbachev, Intellectuals and the End of the Cold War* (New York: Columbia University Press, 2000); Melvyn P. Leffler, *For the Soul of Mankind: The United States, the Soviet Union, and the Cold War* (New York: Hill & Wang, 2007); Robert Service, *The End of the Cold War 1985–1991* (New York: PublicAffairs, 2015); William Taubman, *Gorbachev: His Life and Times* (New York: W. W. Norton, 2017); James Graham Wilson, *The Triumph of Improvisation: Gorbachev's Adaptability, Reagan's Engagement, and the End of the Cold War* (Ithaca, NY: Cornell University Press, 2014); Vladislav Zubok, *A Failed Empire: The Soviet Union in the Cold War from Stalin to Gorbachev* (Chapel Hill: University of North Carolina Press, 2009).

28. See Hal Brands, *Making the Unipolar Moment: U.S. Foreign Policy and the Rise of the Post–Cold War Order* (Ithaca, NY: Cornell University Press, 2016); William Inboden, *The Peacemaker: Ronald Reagan, the Cold War, and the World on the Brink* (New York: Dutton, 2022); Leffler, *For the Soul of Mankind*; Simon Miles, *Engaging the Evil Empire: Washington, Moscow, and the Beginning of the End of the Cold War* (Ithaca, NY: Cornell University Press, 2020); and Wilson, *Triumph of Improvisation*.

29. Matthew Evangelista, *Unarmed Forces: The Transnational Movement to End the Cold War* (Ithaca, NY: Cornell University Press, 1999); Stephanie Freeman, *Dreams for a Decade: Nuclear Abolitionism and the End of the Cold War* (Philadelphia: University of Pennsylvania Press, 2023); Timothy Garton Ash, *The Magic Lantern: The Revolution of '89 Witnessed in Warsaw, Budapest, Berlin and Prague* (New York: Random House, 1990); Michael Cotey Morgan, *The Final Act: The Helsinki Accords and the Transformation of the Cold War* (Princeton, NJ: Princeton University Press, 2017); Sarah B. Snyder, *Human Rights Activism and the End of the Cold War: A Transnational History of the Helsinki Network* (Cambridge: Cambridge University Press, 2011); Daniel C. Thomas, *The Helsinki Effect: International Norms, Human Rights, and the Demise of Communism* (Princeton, NJ: Princeton University Press, 2001).

30. Francis J. Gavin, *Gold, Dollars, and Power: The Politics of International Monetary Relations, 1958–1971* (Chapel Hill: University of North Carolina Press, 2004), 8.

31. See Giovanni Arrighi, "The World Economy and the Cold War, 1970–1990," in *The Cambridge History of the Cold War*, ed. Melvyn P. Leffler and Odd Arne Westad (New York: Cambridge University Press, 2010), 3:23–44; Fritz Bartel, *The Triumph of Broken Promises: The End of the Cold War and the Rise of Neoliberalism* (Cambridge, MA: Harvard University Press, 2022); Iván T. Berend, *Central and Eastern Europe 1944–1993: Detour from the Periphery to the Periphery* (New York: Cambridge University Press, 1996); Stephen G. Brooks and William C. Wohlforth, "Power, Globalization, and the End of the Cold War," *International Security* 25, no. 3 (2001): 5–53; Stephen Kotkin, "The Kiss of Debt: The East Bloc Goes Borrowing," in *Shock of the Global: The 1970s in Perspective*, ed. Niall Ferguson, Charles S. Maier, Erez Manela, and Daniel J. Sargent (Cambridge, MA: Belknap Press of Harvard University Press, 2011), 80–93; Stephen Kotkin with Jan Gross, *Uncivil Society: 1989 and the Implosion of the Communist Establishment* (New York: Modern Library, 2009); Maier, "Collapse of Communism"; Lorenz M.

Lüthi, *Cold Wars: Asia, the Middle East, Europe* (New York: Cambridge University Press, 2020); Charles S. Maier, *Dissolution: The Crisis of Communism and the End of East Germany* (Princeton, NJ: Princeton University Press, 1997); James Mark et al., *1989: A Global History of Eastern Europe* (New York: Cambridge University Press, 2019); Besnik Pula, *Globalization under and after Socialism: The Evolution of Transnational Capital in Central and Eastern Europe* (Stanford, CA: Stanford University Press, 2018); Westad, *Cold War*; and Philip Zelikow and Condoleezza Rice, *To Build a Better World: Choices to End the Cold War and Create a Global Commonwealth* (New York: Twelve, 2019).

32. See, for example, Mark Kramer, "The Demise of the Soviet Bloc," *Journal of Modern History* 83, no. 4 (2011): 788–854; Jacques Lévesque, *The Enigma of 1989: The USSR and the Liberation of Eastern Europe* (Berkeley: University of California Press, 1997); Zubok, *Failed Empire*. On the interaction between changes in the Soviet Union and Eastern Europe, see Renée De Nevers, *Comrades No More: The Seeds of Change in Eastern Europe* (Cambridge, MA: MIT Press, 2003). For excellent accounts of 1989 from below, see Ash, *Magic Lantern*; and Padraic Kenney, *Carnival of Revolution: Central Europe 1989* (Princeton, NJ: Princeton University Press, 2002).

33. This book aligns with those who have emphasized the deep material roots of the 1989 revolutions. Among others, see Bartel, *Triumph of Broken Promises*; Jeffrey Kopstein, *The Politics of Economic Decline in East Germany, 1945–1989* (Chapel Hill: University of North Carolina Press, 1997); Kotkin with Gross, *Uncivil Society*; Maier, "Collapse of Communism"; Mark et al., *1989*; and Matthew J. Ouimet, *The Rise and Fall of the Brezhnev Doctrine in Soviet Foreign Policy* (Chapel Hill: University of North Carolina Press, 2003). Svetlana Savranskaya highlights Gorbachev's ideals and priorities alongside the perceived economic burden and diminishing strategic value of Eastern Europe in "The Logic of 1989," in *Masterpieces of History: The Peaceful End of the Cold War in Europe, 1989*, ed. Svetlana Savranskaya, Thomas Blanton, and Vladislav Zubok (Budapest: Central European University Press, 2010), 1–47.

34. The collapse of the Soviet Union itself is beyond this book's scope. See Stephen Kotkin, *Armageddon Averted: The Soviet Collapse, 1970–2000* (New York: Oxford University Press, 2001); Serhii Plokhy, *The Last Empire: The Final Days of the Soviet Union* (New York: Basic Books, 2014); and Vladislav Zubok, *Collapse: The Fall of the Soviet Union* (New Haven, CT: Yale University Press, 2021).

35. Among others, see Mary E. Sarotte, *1989: The Struggle to Create Post–Cold War Europe* (Princeton, NJ: Princeton University Press, 2009); Kristina Spohr, *Post Wall, Post Square: How Bush, Gorbachev, Kohl, and Deng Shaped the World after 1989* (New Haven, CT: Yale University Press, 2019).

36. On the emergence of unipolarity as a process, see Brands, *Making the Unipolar Moment*.

1. American Power and the Collapse of the Bretton Woods System

1. Richard M. Nixon, "Address to the Nation Outlining a New Economic Policy: 'The Challenge of Peace,'" August 15, 1971, American Presidency Project (APP); ERP, 1972, 223.

2. Nixon.

3. Melvyn P. Leffler, *A Preponderance of Power: National Security, the Truman Administration, and the Cold War* (Stanford, CA: Stanford University Press, 1993).

4. C. Vann Woodward, "The Age of Reinterpretation," *American Historical Review* 66, no. 1 (1960): 2.

5. Franklin D. Roosevelt, "Fireside Chat," December 29, 1940, APP.

6. Leffler, *Preponderance of Power*.

7. Harry S. Truman, "Address on Foreign Economic Policy, Delivered at Baylor University," March 6, 1947, APP.

8. Leffler, *Preponderance of Power*.

9. Arthur M. Schlesinger Jr., *The Vital Center: The Politics of Freedom* (Boston: Houghton Mifflin, 1949), 226.

10. See Leffler, *Preponderance of Power*.

11. Timothy Andrews Sayle, *Enduring Alliance: A History of NATO and the Postwar Global Order* (Ithaca, NY: Cornell University Press, 2019), 5.

12. See Barry Eichengreen, *Golden Fetters: The Gold Standard and the Great Depression, 1919–1939* (New York: Oxford University Press, 1995).

13. Harold James, *International Monetary Cooperation since Bretton Woods* (New York: Oxford University Press, 1996), 27–57.

14. Judith Stein, *Pivotal Decade: How the United States Traded Factories for Finance in the Seventies* (New Haven, CT: Yale University Press, 2010), 7.

15. Peter G. Peterson, *The United States in the Changing World Economy*, vol. 1, *A Foreign Economic Perspective* (Washington, DC: U.S. Government Printing Office, 1971), 7.

16. United Nations Conference on Trade and Development (UNCTAD), UNCTAD-Stat, https://unctadstat.unctad.org.

17. *ERP*, 1972, 153, 296.

18. Melvyn P. Leffler, *For the Soul of Mankind: The United States, the Soviet Union, and the Cold War* (New York: Hill and Wang, 2007), 132.

19. See Michael Latham, *The Right Kind of Revolution: Modernization, Development, and U.S. Foreign Policy from the Cold War to the Present* (Ithaca, NY: Cornell University Press, 2011), 123–56.

20. Angus Maddison, *The World Economy*, vol. 1, *A Millennial Perspective* (Paris: OECD, 2006), 131, 139.

21. Peter Hall and David Soskice, eds., *Varieties of Capitalism: The Institutional Foundations of Comparative Advantage* (New York: Oxford University Press, 2001).

22. Maddison, *World Economy*, 1:135.

23. See Melvyn P. Leffler, "Victory: The 'State,' the 'West,' and the Cold War," in *International Relations since the End of the Cold War: New and Old Dimensions*, ed. Geir Lundestad (New York: Oxford University Press, 2013), 80–99.

24. Peterson, *United States in the Changing World Economy*, 2:6.

25. Francis J. Gavin, *Gold, Dollars, and Power: The Politics of International Monetary Relations, 1958–1971* (Chapel Hill: University of North Carolina Press, 2007), 1.

26. Gavin.

27. OMB Historical Tables, Tables 1.1 and 1.2, www.whitehouse.gov/omb/budget/historical-tables/.

28. *ERP*, 1978, 139.

29. "Inflation's Pain," *Wall Street Journal*, February 17, 1969.

30. Diane B. Kunz, *Butter and Guns: America's Cold War Economic Diplomacy* (New York: Free Press, 1997), 110.

31. BIS, *Annual Report*, 1973, 161.

32. British Embassy Paris (Reilly) to FCO, "United States Economic Measures," January 8, 1968, TNA, FCO 59/194.

33. See Gavin, *Gold, Dollars, and Power*, 180–85.

34. IMF, *Annual Report*, 1974, 5.

35. "Memorandum of Conversation," April 19, 1973, folder "UK Memcons (originals) January–April 1973 [2 of 2]," box 62, Henry A. Kissinger Office Files, RNPL.

36. Détente frames much of the scholarship on the history of US foreign policy during the 1970s. For an introduction to this vast literature, see Raymond L. Garthoff, *Détente and Confrontation: America-Soviet Relations from Nixon to Reagan* (Washington, DC: Brookings Institution, 1994); Jussi Hanhimäki, *The Flawed Architect: Henry Kissinger and American Foreign Policy* (New York: Oxford University Press, 2004); and Barbara Zanchetta, *The Transformation of American International Power in the 1970s* (New York: Cambridge University Press, 2013).

37. ERP, 1974, 350; Daniel J. Sargent, *A Superpower Transformed: The Remaking of American Foreign Relations in the 1970s* (New York: Oxford University Press, 2015), 102–12. On the U.S. economy during the Nixon years, consult Allen J. Matusow, *Nixon's Economy: Booms, Busts, Dollars, and Votes* (Lawrence: University of Kansas Press, 1998).

38. Richard M. Nixon, "Remarks to Midwestern News Media Executives Attending a Briefing on Domestic Policy in Kansas City, Missouri," July 6, 1971, APP.

39. Calculated from Susan B. Carter, Scott Sigmund Gartner, Michael R. Haines, Alan L. Olmstead, Richard Sutch, and Gavin Wright, eds., *Historical Statistics of the United States: Millennial Edition Online*, Tables Ee547 and Ee565/6 (New York: Cambridge University Press, 2006), https://hsus.cambridge.org/HSUSWeb/HSUSEntryServlet.

40. "Memorandum of Conversation," October 3, 1969, folder "FLWidman Chron.-Oct. 1969," box 3, F. Lisle Widman Files, RG 56, NARA.

41. Peterson, *United States in the Changing World Economy*, 2:21.

42. F. Lisle Widman to Paul Volcker and Petty, "Briefing for Meetings with Ambassador Armin Meyer," June 12, 1969, folder "FLWidman Chron.–June 1969," box 3, F. Lisle Widman Files, RG 56, NARA.

43. Memorandum from Peter G. Peterson to Richard Nixon, "Briefing on the U.S. in the Changing World Economy, Where Do We Go from Here, and Proposed Work Program of the Council," July 6, 1971, folder "Council of International Economic Policy 3 of 4," box 7, Records of Secretary George P. Shultz, RG 56, NARA.

44. FRUS, 1969–1976, vol. 19, part 2, doc. 87, 259–62.

45. On Nixon's approach to Western Europe, see Klaus Larres, *Uncertain Allies: Nixon, Kissinger, and the Threat of a United Europe* (New Haven, CT: Yale University Press, 2022); Luke A. Nichter, *Richard Nixon and Europe: The Reshaping of the Postwar Atlantic World* (New York: Cambridge University Press, 2015).

46. "Memorandum for the Record: The President's Meeting with Former High Government Officials and Military Officers on the Mansfield Amendment," May 24, 1971, folder "Mansfield Amendment [1971–1972][1 of 3]," box 824, NSC Files, RNPL.

47. Quoted in Michael Stewart, "Britain, Europe and the Alliance," *Foreign Affairs* 48, no. 4 (1970): 650.

48. Hugh T. A. Overton, "US/European Relations: Consultative Machinery," November 11, 1971, TNA, FCO 82/57.

49. Department of State, "NSSM 79 and 91: Enlargement of the European Community: Implications for the U.S. and Policy Options," attached to Martin Hillenbrand to Henry Kissinger, "Enlargement of the European Community, NSSM's 79 and 91," April 23, 1970, folder "NSSM-79 [1 of 2]," box H-164, NSC Institutional Files, RNPL.

50. "Statement by the Departments of Treasury, Commerce, Agriculture, and STR," April 22, 1970, folder "NSSM-79 [1 of 2]," box H-164, NSC Institutional Files, RNPL.

51. *FRUS, 1969–1976*, vol. 41, doc. 62, 269.

52. Sargent, *Superpower Transformed*, 58.

53. C. Fred Bergsten to Henry Kissinger, "The Absurdity of Possible Reductions in U.S. Forces Overseas for Balance of Payments Reasons," December 3, 1970, folder "Balance of Payments January 1969 to February 1972," box 309, NSC Files, RNPL.

54. John Darnton, "High Unemployment Is Giving Bristol, Conn., an Extra Inflationary Pinch," *New York Times*, August 6, 1970.

55. Richard J. Levine, "'Free Trade' Fight," *Wall Street Journal*, May 19, 1970.

56. C. Fred Bergsten, "Crisis in U.S. Trade Policy," *Foreign Affairs* 49, no. 4 (1971): 621.

57. Among others, see Thomas Borstelmann, *The 1970s: A New Global History from Civil Rights to Economic Inequality* (Princeton, NJ: Princeton University Press, 2012); Jeremi Suri, *Power and Protest: Global Revolution and the Rise of Détente* (Cambridge, MA: Harvard University Press, 2003).

58. "Extract Record of Conversation PM/Federal Chancellor at Schloss Gymnich on Thursday 1/3/1973," March 1, 1973, TNA, PREM 15/1540.

59. Sayle, *Enduring Alliance*, 172.

60. PUS to Cromer, "The US & Europe," no date, TNA, FCO 82/282.

61. F. Lisle Widman, "Memorandum for the Files," December 12, 1969, folder "FL-Widman Chron-December 69," box 3, F. Lisle Widman Files, RG 56, NARA.

62. A voluminous literature has accumulated on the collapse of the Bretton Woods system. For different approaches, see Fred L. Block, *The Origins of the International Economic Disorder: A Study of United States International Monetary Policy from World War II to the Present* (Berkeley: University of California Press, 1977); Kunz, *Butter and Guns*; and Sargent, *Superpower Transformed*. On the link between the Bretton Woods system and transatlantic security, see Gavin, *Gold, Dollars, and Power*. On West Germany's role, see Julian Germann, "State-led or Capital-driven? The Fall of Bretton Woods and the German Currency Float Reconsidered," *New Political Economy* 19, no. 5 (2014): 769–89; and William Glenn Gray, "Floating the System: Germany, the United States, and the Breakdown of Bretton Woods, 1969–1973," *Diplomatic History* 31, no. 2 (2007): 295–323.

63. Gavin, *Gold, Dollars, and Power*, 21.

64. Calculated from *Monthly Report of the Deutsche Bundesbank* 20, no. 11/12 (1968): 3 and 108.

65. Ian Kershaw, *The Global Age: Europe 1950–2017* (New York: Viking, 2018), 225–29.

66. "Record of a Meeting Held on 20 November 1968, between the Chancellor of the Exchequer, the Right Honourable Roy Jenkins, M.P., and the Federal German Minister of Economics, Dr. Karl Schiller," TNA, FCO 59/456.

67. William Glenn Gray, "'Number One in Europe': The Startling Emergence of the Deutsche Mark, 1968–1969," *Central European History* 39, no. 1 (2006): 68.

68. BIS, *Annual Report*, 1970, 4.

69. "Sondersitzung am 9. Mai 1969: Währungspolitische Lage," Die Kabinettsprotokolle der Bundesregierung online.

70. BIS, *Annual Report*, 1970, 4.

71. *Monthly Report of the Deutsche Bundesbank* 21, no. 11 (1969): 6.

72. Willem Drees Jr., "Gesprek met Belgen en Luxemburgers over monetaire unie in E.E.G.," April 7, 1970, NL-HaNA, 2.03.01, inv.nr. 8864.

73. William Nield, "Community Finance: Negotiating Objectives," December 2, 1970, TNA, PREM 15/62.

74. *Monthly Report of the Deutsche Bundesbank* 23, no. 5 (1971): 8; BIS, *Annual Report*, 1971, 23.

75. "Erklärung von Bundeswirtschaftsminister Professor Dr. Karl Schiller zu Beginn der Ratssitzung am 8. Mai 1971 in Brüssel," May 8, 1971, PA-AA, B 52, Bd. 585.

76. Karl Schiller, "Die Wirtschaftslage in der Bundesrepublik Deutschland im Frühjahr 1971, die weiteren Aussichten und wirtschaftspolitischen Schlussfolgerungen," May 5, 1971, BAK, B 102/84100.

77. "Notulen van de vergadering gehouden op zondag 9 mei 1971 in de vergaderzaal van het Kabinet van de Minister-President, aangevangen 's middags om 4 uur," May 9, 1971, NL- HaNA, 2.02.05.02, inv.nr. 1105.

78. Robert Solomon, *The International Monetary System, 1945–1981* (New York: Harper & Row, 1982), 169–70.

79. Geoffrey Bell, "Democratic Ginger for the American Economy," *The Times*, December 29, 1970.

80. Quoted in George C. Herring, *From Colony to Superpower: U.S. Foreign Relations since 1776* (New York: Oxford University Press, 2008), 782.

81. Peterson, *United States in the Changing World Economy*, 1:4–19.

82. *Action Now to Strengthen the U.S. Dollar: Report of the Subcommittee on International Exchange and Payments of the Joint Economic Committee Congress of the United States* (Washington, DC: U.S. Government Printing Office, 1971), 13.

83. BIS, *Annual Report*, 1972, 26.

84. A. M. Bailey to Robert Armstrong, January 13, 1972, TNA, PREM 15/838.

85. "Jobless Textile Workers Decry Plight in Alabama," *New York Times*, August 15, 1971.

86. Douglas Brinkley and Luke A. Nichter, eds., *The Nixon Tapes: 1971–1972* (Boston: Houghton Mifflin Harcourt, 2014), 237–40.

87. Paul A. Volcker to John B. Connally, August 13, 1971, folder "Econ. Game Plan Background Camp David 8/13–15, '71," box 7, Records of George P. Shultz, RG 56, NARA.

88. Diary entry for August 12, 1971, folder "Journal I-Green Notebook, January 20, 1969–August 12, 1971 (1)–(3)," Arthur F. Burns Handwritten Journals, GFPL.

89. Diary entry for August 22, 1971, folder "Journal II—Blue Notebook, August 22, 1971–July 25, 1974 (1)–(4)," Arthur F. Burns Handwritten Journals, GFPL.

90. Brinkley and Nichter, *Nixon Tapes*, 261.

91. "Telecon: The President/Mr. Kissinger," August 16, 1971, folder "1971 11–19 Aug (2 of 11) [2 of 2]," box 11, Henry A. Kissinger Telephone Conversation Transcripts (Telecons), RNPL.

92. "Telecon: Mr. Kissinger and John J. McCloy, 11-11-71; 7:30 P.M.," November 11, 1971, folder "9," box 184, Henry A. Kissinger Papers, Part III (MS 2004), SML.

93. Rowley Cromer to Alec Douglas-Home, November 2, 1971, TNA, PREM/1271.

94. Alec Douglas-Home to certain posts, "International Monetary Situation," August 17, 1971, TNA, FCO 59/650.

95. Paul A. Volcker with Christine Harper, *Keeping at It: The Quest for Sound Money and Good Government* (New York: PublicAffairs, 2018), 76.

96. Ton van de Graaf, "Conclusies van de bijzondere vergadering van de Raad voor Economische Aangelegenheden, gehouden op 16 augustus 1971 op het departement van Algemene Zaken, aangevangen te 14.00 uur," August 16, 1971, NL-HaNA, 2.03.01, inv.nr. 7684.

97. "Statement by Minister Professor Dr. Karl Schiller at the Group of Ten Conference, London, September 15 and 16, 1971," PA-AA, B 52, Bd. 634.

98. Quoted in Volcker with Harper, *Keeping at It*, 76.

99. Volcker with Harper, 76.

100. Diary entry for November 24, 1971, folder "Journal II—Blue Notebook, August 22, 1971–July 25, 1974 (1)-(4)," Arthur F. Burns Handwritten Journals, GFPL.

101. "Record of Restricted Sessions of Meetings of the Group of Ten and of E.E.C. Ministers in Rome on 30th November 1971 and 1st December 1971," December 2, 1971, TNA, PREM 15/812.

102. Solomon, *International Monetary System 1945–1981*, 205.

103. *ERP*, 1972, 143.

104. John B. Connally, *In History's Shadow: An American Odyssey* (New York: Hyperion, 1993), 247–48.

105. Volcker, *Keeping at It*, 79.

106. Brian Reading, "Back to Square One?," January 6, 1972, TNA, PREM 15/812.

107. "Oh No, Not EMU Again," *Economist*, February 12, 1972, 62.

108. Karl Schiller, "Internationale Wirtschafts- und Währungspolitik: Stand und nächste Aufgaben," May 2, 1972, BAK, B 102/84149.

109. Rowley Cromer to Edward Heath, June 27, 1972, TNA, PREM 15/1271.

110. *FRUS*, 1969–1976, vol. 40, doc. 370, 1043.

111. BMWi-W/VI A 3 (Pieske), "Deutsch-französisches Gespräch vom 20.6.1972 über Fragen der Reform des Währungssystems," June 21, 1972, BAK, B 102/84150.

112. William Glenn Gray, "'Learning to 'Recycle': Petrodollars and the West, 1973–1975," in *Oil Shock: The 1973 Crisis and Its Economic Legacy*, ed. Elisabetta Bini, Giuliano Garavini, and Federico Romero (London: I. B. Tauris, 2016), 177.

113. *FRUS*, 1969–1976, vol. 3, doc. 240, 649–50.

114. John M. Goshko, "Inflation Issue Perils Brandt Campaign," *Washington Post*, October 24, 1972.

115. World Bank, World Development Indicators.

116. BIS, *Annual Report*, 1973, 8–10.

117. Richard C. Longworth, "Common Market Nations Battling 'Cancerous' Inflation," *Boston Globe*, November 2, 1972.

118. *FRUS*, 1969–1976, vol. 3, doc. 239, 646–47.

119. *FRUS*, 1969–1976, vol. 1, doc. 121, 414–18.

120. Douglas Brinkley and Luke A. Nichter, eds., *The Nixon Tapes, 1973* (Boston: Houghton Mifflin Harcourt, 2015), 41.

121. James, *International Monetary Cooperation since Bretton Woods*, 241.

122. *AAPD*, 1973, Bd. 1, doc. 44, 218–19.

123. Gray, "Floating the System," 318.

124. *AAPD*, 1973, Bd. 1, doc. 46, 224.

125. *AAPD, 1973*, Bd. 1, doc. 50, 239–40.

126. British Embassy Bonn (Henderson) to FCO, March 2, 1973, TNA, FCO 59/854.

127. James, *International Monetary Cooperation since Bretton Woods*, 242–43.

128. Peter Marshall, "International Currency Crisis," March 14, 1973, TNA, FCO 59/856.

129. Quoted in Benjamin J. Cohen, "The Revolution in Atlantic Economic Relations: A Bargain Comes Unstuck," in *The United States and Western Europe: Political, Economic and Strategic Perspectives*, ed. Wolfram F. Hanrieder (Cambridge, MA: Winthrop, 1974), 129.

130. US Mission Berlin (Klein) 1584 to SecState, "Scheel-Kissinger Conversation," September 12, 1972, folder "POL 7 US/Kissinger 4/6/72," box 2693, Subject Numeric Files, 1970–73, Political & Defense, RG 59, NARA.

131. "Speech Delivered to the Associated Press Annual Luncheon in New York, on 23 April 1973, by Dr. Henry Kissinger, Special Adviser to the President of the United States," TNA, PREM 15/1541.

132. Defense Program Review Committee, Senior Review Group Meeting, May 25, 1973, folder "SRG Minutes (originals 1972–1973 [3 of 4]," box H-113, NSC Institutional Files, RNPL.

133. Hugh Overton, "US Policy towards Europe," May 21, 1973, TNA, FCO 82/284.

134. AA-204, "Was erwarten die Amerikaner von einer Atlantischen Erklärung anläßlich des Nixon-Besuches in Europa?," August 10, 1973, PA-AA, B 32 (ZA), Bd. 101383.

135. IMF, *Annual Report*, 1974, 2.

136. Rowley Cromer to Edward Heath, February 18, 1973, TNA, PREM 15/1458.

2. Eastern European Development and Soviet Subsidies

1. "Niederschrift über die Verhandlungen zwischen dem Vorsitzenden des Ministerrates der DDR, W. Stoph, und dem Vorsitzenden des Ministerrates der UdSSR, A.N. Kossygin, im Kreml am 20. August 1973," August 20, 1973, BAB, DE1/58507.

2. See László Borhi, *Hungary in the Cold War 1945–1956: Between the United States and the Soviet Union* (Budapest: Central European Press, 2004), 139–96; Norman Naimark, *The Russians in Germany: A History of the Soviet Zone of Occupation, 1945–1949* (Cambridge, MA: Belknap Press of Harvard University Press, 1995), 141–204.

3. "Record of Meeting at the Kremlin, Moscow, 9 October 1944, at 10 P.M.," October 9, 1944, History and Public Policy Program Digital Archive, Public Record Office, https://digitalarchive.wilsoncenter.org/document/123186.

4. "Telegram from Nikolai Novikov, Soviet Ambassador to the US, to the Soviet Leadership," September 27, 1946, History and Public Policy Program Digital Archive, AVP SSSR, f. 06. op. 8, p. 45, p. 759, published in Mezhdunarodnaia Zhizn' #11, 1990, pp. 148–54, translated for CWIHP by Gary Goldberg, https://digitalarchive.wilson center.org/document/110808.

5. On the evolution of Stalin's thinking about postwar Europe, see Norman Naimark, *Stalin and the Fate of Europe: The Postwar Struggle for Sovereignty* (Cambridge, MA: Belknap Press of Harvard University Press, 2019).

6. Melvyn P. Leffler, *For the Soul of Mankind: The United States, the Soviet Union, and the Cold War* (New York: Hill and Wang, 2007), 65–66.

7. Todor Zhivkov, *Memoari* (Sofia: Trud i pravo, 2006), 459.

8. Leffler, *For the Soul of Mankind*, 77–78.

9. Founding members of the CMEA included Albania (which stopped participating in the early 1960s amid the Sino-Soviet split), Bulgaria, Czechoslovakia, Hungary, Poland, Romania, and the Soviet Union. East Germany joined in 1950.

10. Leffler, *For the Soul of Mankind*, 90–91.

11. Ian Kershaw, *The Global Age: Europe 1950–2017* (New York: Viking, 2018), 113–17.

12. Georgi Chankov, "Informatsiia po rabotata na IV-ta sesiia na Suveta za ikonomicheska vzaimopomosht ot 26 i 27 mart 1954 godina," March 30, 1954, TsDA, f. 1B, op. 6, a.e. 2083.

13. "Notes of a Meeting between the CPSU CC Presidium and a HWP Political Committee Delegation in Moscow, June 13 and 16, 1953," in *The 1956 Hungarian Revolution: A History in Documents*, ed. Csaba Békés, Malcolm Byrne, and János M. Rainer (Budapest: Central European University Press, 2002), 22.

14. Randall W. Stone, *Satellites and Commissars: Strategy and Conflict in the Politics of Soviet-Bloc Trade* (Princeton, NJ: Princeton University Press, 1998), 30–33.

15. Tony Judt, *Postwar: A History of Europe since 1945* (New York: Penguin, 2005), 171.

16. See Kristy Ironside, *A Full-Value Ruble: The Promise of Prosperity in the Postwar Soviet Union* (Cambridge, MA: Harvard University Press, 2022).

17. Ivaylo Znepolski et al., *Bulgaria under Communism* (London: Routledge, 2019), 258.

18. "Razgovori mezhdu dr. Todor Zhivkov—purvi sekretar na TsK na BKP, i dr. Leonid Ilich Brezhnev—generalen sekretar na TsK na KPSS," September 22, 1966, TsDA, f. 1B, op. 34, a.e. 43.

19. Christopher Nehring, "Bulgaria as the Sixteenth Soviet Republic? Todor Zhivkov's Proposals to Join the USSR," *Journal of Cold War Studies* 24, no. 2 (2022): 29–45.

20. Georgy Shakhnazarov, *Tsena svobody: Reformatsiia Gorbacheva glazami ego pomoshchnika* (Moscow: Rossika, 1993), 97.

21. Quoted in Stone, *Satellites and Commissars*, 67.

22. The USSR did not grant all Eastern European requests for aid. Moscow rejected East Berlin's desperate pleas for hard currency in the 1950s, for example, instead yielding to First Secretary Walter Ulbricht's decision to build the Berlin Wall in August 1961

as the lesser evil. See Hope M. Harrison, *Driving the Soviets up the Wall: Soviet-East German Relations, 1953–1961* (Princeton, NJ: Princeton University Press, 2003).

23. Zhivkov, *Memoari*, 358.

24. Stone, *Satellites and Commissars*, 30–33.

25. Paul Marer, "The Political Economy of Soviet Relations with Eastern Europe," in *Soviet Policy in Eastern Europe*, ed. Sarah Meiklejohn Terry (New Haven, CT: Yale University Press, 1984), 165.

26. "Über die Prinzipien der Preisfestsetzung im Handel zwischen den sozialistischen Ländern," May 16, 1958, SAPMO, DY 30/3474.

27. IEMSS, *Statistika stran-chlenov SEV* (Moscow: Nauka, 1973), 234.

28. Alan Smith, *Russia and the World Economy: Problems of Integration* (London: Routledge, 1993), 45–48. One ruble equaled $1.50 in 1980 and $1.30 in 1983. See Marer, "Political Economy," 168.

29. On Soviet engagement with global capitalism, see particularly Oscar Sanchez-Sibony, *Red Globalization: The Political Economy of the Soviet Cold War from Stalin to Khrushchev* (New York: Cambridge University Press, 2014).

30. Stone, *Satellites and Commissars*, 33. On West German efforts to isolate East Germany, see William Glenn Gray, *Germany's Cold War: The Global Campaign to Isolate East Germany, 1949–1969* (Chapel Hill: University of North Carolina Press, 2003).

31. Odd Arne Westad, *Restless Empire: China and the World since 1750* (New York: Basic Books, 2012), 305.

32. See Odd Arne Westad, *The Global Cold War: Third World Interventions and the Making of Our Times* (New York: Cambridge University Press, 2007).

33. See Jeremy Friedman, *Shadow Cold War: The Sino-Soviet Competition for the Third World* (Chapel Hill: University of North Carolina Press, 2015).

34. Sara Lorenzini, *Global Development: A Cold War History* (Princeton, NJ: Princeton University Press, 2019), 81.

35. Westad, *Global Cold War*.

36. Lorenzini, *Global Development*, 82.

37. "Spravka o sostoianii i perspektivakh sovetsko-v"etnamskogo ekonomicheskogo sotrudnichestva na 1971–1975 gg.," n.d., RGANI, f. 5, op. 62, d. 481. Because of the uncertainties about North Vietnamese economic performance in wartime, Moscow limited its cooperation with Hanoi to annual rather than multiyear trade agreements.

38. Michael Marrese and Jan Vanous, *Soviet Subsidization of Trade with Eastern Europe: A Soviet Perspective* (Berkeley: Institute of International Studies, University of California, 1983), 3.

39. "The Kitchen Debate-Transcript," July 24, 1959, CIAERR.

40. Valerie Bunce, "The Empire Strikes Back: The Evolution of the Eastern Bloc from a Soviet Asset to a Soviet Liability," *International Organization* 35, no. 1 (1985): 13.

41. Barry J. Eichengreen, *The European Economy since 1945: Coordinated Capitalism and Beyond* (Princeton, NJ: Princeton University Press, 2008), 139–40.

42. Judt, *Postwar*, 171–72.

43. B. Zotov, "O razrabotke plana razvitiia narodnogo khoziaistva Chekoslovakii na 1971–1975 gg.," February 27, 1970, RGANI, f. 5, op. 62, d. 354.

44. "Informatsiia o besede zamestitelia predsedatelia Soveta Ministrov, predsedatelia Gosplana SSSR tov. N.K. Baibakov s predsedatelem VNR tov. Imre Padri," January 7, 1971, RGAE, f. 4372, op. 66, d. 4448.

45. See Eichengreen, *European Economy since 1945*, 142–45.

46. IEMSS, "O nekotorykh itogakh razvitiia evropeiskikh stran SEV v gody provedeniia khoziaistvennykh reform," July 3, 1970, RGANI, f. 5, op. 62, d. 473.

47. Political Department of the Polish United Worker's Party to fraternal socialist parties, December 1969, RGANI, f. 5, op. 62, d. 481.

48. Alexander Puzanov, "Zapis' besedy s pervym sekretarem TsK BKP, predsedatelem Soveta ministrov NRB tov. Todorom Zhivkovym," December 31, 1970, RGANI, f. 5, op. 63, d. 250.

49. B. Abramov, "O polozhenii na vnutrennem rynke ChSSR i o bor'be s infliatsiei," July 2, 1970, RGANI, f. 5, op. 62, d. 354.

50. IEMSS paper, "O nekotorykh itogakh razvitiia evropeiskikh stran SEV v gody provedeniia khoziaistvennykh reform," July 3, 1970, RGANI, f. 5, op. 62, d. 473.

51. Quoted in Stephen Kotkin with Jan Gross, *Uncivil Society: 1989 and the Implosion of the Communist Establishment* (New York: Modern Library, 2009), 47.

52. Gerhard Schürer, *Gewagt und Verloren: Eine deutsche Biografie* (Frankfurt an der Oder: Franfurter Oder Editionen, 1996), 75.

53. Hester Vaizey, *Born in the GDR: Living in the Shadow of the Wall* (New York: Oxford University Press, 2014), 48

54. Otdel gidov-perevodchikov, "Spravka o vyskazyvaniiakh nekotorykh turistov iz GDR, posetivshikh v poslednee vremia Sovetskii Soiuz," February 9, 1971, RGANI, f. 5, op. 63, d. 409.

55. Jeffrey Kopstein, *The Politics of Economic Decline in East Germany, 1945–1989* (Chapel Hill: University of North Carolina Press, 1997), 69.

56. SPK, "Persönliche Notizen über die Beratung der Parteigruppe des Ministerrates am 11.10.1971," October 12, 1971, BAB, DE 1/54544.

57. André Steiner, "The Decline of Soviet-Type Economies," in *The Cambridge History of Communism*, ed. Juliane Fürst, Silvio Pons, and Mark Selden, vol. 3, *Endgames? Late Communism in Global Perspective, 1968 to the Present* (New York: Cambridge University Press, 2017), 204.

58. Fyodor Titov, "Zapis' besedy o chlenov TsK VSRP, ministerom vneshnei torgovli VNR tov. Iozhefom Biro," December 20, 1969, RGANI, f. 5, op. 62, d. 390.

59. Oleg Bogomolov, "Ob itogakh i osnovnykh tendentsiiakh razvitiia ekonomicheskogo sotrudnichestva stran SEV posle XXIII spetsial'noi sessii soveta," RGANI, July 6, 1971, f. 5, op. d. 490.

60. Stepan Chervonenko to Vladimir M. Vinogradov, March 2, 1970, RGANI, f. 5, op. 62, d. 354.

61. Besnik Pula, *Globalization under and after Socialism: The Evolution of Transnational Capital in Central and Eastern Europe* (Stanford, CA: Stanford University Press, 2018), 103.

62. Suzanne F. Porter, *East-West Trade Financing: An Introductory Guide* (Washington, DC: U.S. Department of Commerce, 1976), 26.

63. David Holloway, *The Soviet Union and the Arms Race* (New Haven, CT: Yale University Press, 1983), 88.

64. See Gray, *Germany's Cold War*.

65. For an introduction to *Ostpolitik*, see Julia von Dannenberg, *The Foundations of Ostpolitik: The Making of the Moscow Treaty between West Germany and the USSR* (New York: Oxford University Press, 2009).

66. V. I. Kartsev and V. B. Iaroslav, "Potrebnosti evropeiskikh stran-chlenov SEV v nefti i vozmozhnosti ikh udovletvoreniia za schet importa iz razvitaiushchikhsia stran v period do 1990 g.," May 1975, RGANI, f. 5, op. 68, d. 1729; John P. Hardt, "Soviet Energy Policy in Eastern Europe," in Terry, *Soviet Foreign Policy in Eastern Europe*, 191.

67. V. I. Kartsev and V. B. Iaroslav, "Potrebnosti evropeiskikh stran-chlenov SEV v nefti i vozmozhnosti ikh udovletvoreniia za schet importa iz razvitaiushchikhsia stran v period do 1990 g.," May 1975, RGANI, f. 5, op. 68, d. 1729. The data showed that oil and natural gas constituted three-quarters of the energy consumption in Romania, but Bucharest relied on its own reserves.

68. PlanEcon, *Soviet and East European Energy Databank* (Washington, DC: PlanEcon, 1986), 2:S-2.

69. Alexander Puzanov, "Zapis' besedy s pervym sekretarem TsK BKP, predsedatelem Soveta ministrov NRB tov. Todorom Zhivkovym," December 31, 1970, RGANI, f. 5, op. 63, d. 250.

70. Oleg Bogomolov, "O nedostatochnoi obosnovannosti nekotorykh zadach ekonomicheskogo razvitiia Bolgarii," February 24, 1971, RGANI, f. 5, op. 63, d. 348.

71. IEMSS, *Vneshniaia torgovlia SSSR so stranami SEV* (Moscow: Nauka, 1986), 25.

72. Kopstein, *Politics of Economic Decline*, 73.

73. Quoted in Kopstein, 68–69.

74. Quoted in Kotkin with Gross, *Uncivil Society*, 48–49.

75. Kopstein, *Politics of Economic Decline*, 80–84.

76. Iu. Prokhorov and Kh. Toming, "Nekotorye aspekty otnosheniia VNR k sotsialisticheskoi ekonomicheskoi integratsii," March 31, 1970, RGANI, f. 5, op. 62, d. 390.

77. "Information zur Entwicklung des Außenhandels der RGW-Länder mit kapitalistischen Industrieländern im Zeitraum 1971–1974," n.d., SAPMO, DY 30/8935.

78. Paul A. Volcker to Henry A. Kissinger and Peter M. Flanigan, "Romanian Participation in the International Monetary Fund and World Bank," August 3, 1972, folder "Monetary Matters, Azores Dec 1971," Box 356, NSC Files, RNPL.

79. "Auswirkungen der Preisentwicklung von Rohstoffen und Materialien auf dem kapitalistischen Weltmarkt auf den Import der DDR," May 31, 1973, SAPMO, DY 30/J IV 2/2J/4717.

80. "Niederschrift über die Verhandlungen zwischen dem Vorsitzenden des Ministerrates der DDR, W. Stoph, und dem Vorsitzenden des Ministerrates der UdSSR, A.N. Kossygin, im Kreml am 20. August 1973," BAB, DE 1/58507.

81. Gerhard Schürer, "Gegenwärtiger Stand und Probleme der Ausarbeitung des Volkswirtschaftsplanes 1974," November 7, 1973, BAB, DE 1/58701. The VM was the GDR's foreign trade bookkeeping currency and equal to one West German Mark (DM). At the official rate, $1 equaled about VM 2.5.

82. "Zapis' besedy s predsedatelem vengerskogo revoliutsionnogo rabochekrest'ianskogo pravitel'stva, chlenom Politbiuro TsK VSRP tov. Enyo Fokom, s zam. predsedatelem pravitel'stva VNR tov. Matiashem Timarom i s chlenom Politbiuro TsK VSRP, zam. predsedatelem pravitel'stva tov. Laioshem Fekherom," March 17, 1970, RGANI, f. 5, op. 62, d. 390.

83. "Auswirkungen der Preisentwicklung von Rohstoffen und Materialien auf dem kapitalistischen Weltmarkt auf den Import der DDR," May 31, 1973, SAPMO, DY 30/J IV 2/2J/4717.

84. "Beratung der Parteigruppe MR zum VW-Plan 1972," October 11, 1971, BAB, DE 1/54544.

85. Komitee der Arbeiter-und-Bauern-Inspektion, "Information über die Kontrolle der Durchsetzung des Beschlusses des Ministerrates vom 28.7.1972 zur 'Analyse über die NSW-Importabhängigkeit,'" March 30, 1973, BAB, DC 14/137.

86. CIA Directorate of Intelligence, "Eastern Europe's Debt to the West: More Growth on the Installment Plan," December 1972, CIAERR.

87. Sava Dulbokov, Dimitar Popov, and Kiril Zarev to Stanko Todorov, "Sustoiani-eto na platezhniia balans na stranata i proekta na valutniia plan za perioda 1972–1975 godina," n.d., TsDA, f. 130, 23C, a.e. 1.

88. "Zapis' besedy predstavitelem Bolgarskogo narodnogo banka tov. K. Zarevym," June 14, 1970, RGANI, f. 5, op. 62, d. 337.

89. DPK to Todor Zhivkov, "Vnosa ot kapitalicheskite strani," April 30, 1971, TsDA, f. 130, op. 23C, a.e. 1.

90. "Zu bestehenden Disproportionen und deren Überwindung für Importabhängig-keit der DDR gegenüber kapitalistischen Ländern," n.d. (1971), SAPMO, DY 30/7148.

91. Heinz Klopfer, "Persönliche Niederschrift über eine Problemberatung beim Vor-sitzenden des Ministerrates am 26.3.1973," March 27, 1973, BAB, DE 1/58580.

92. Nikolai Sikachev, "O nekotorykh momentakh ekonomicheskogo razvitiia Ven-grii v 1971 godu," December 16, 1971, RGANI, f. 5, op. 63, d. 384.

93. "Handschriftliche Aufzeichnung von Werner Krolikowski vom 16. Januar 1990," in *Tatort Politbüro: Die Akte Honecker*, ed. Peter Przybylski (Berlin: Rowohlt, 1991), 323–34.

94. Kopstein, *Politics of Economic Decline*, 87.

95. IEMSS paper, "Ekonomicheskie voprosy mezhdunarodnoi sotsialisticheskoi in-tegratsii," July 30, 1970, RGANI, f. 5, op. 62, d. 473.

96. DeGolyer and MacNaughton, *Twenty-First Century Petroleum Statistics* (Dallas, TX, 2020), 3, 7; Arthur Jay Klinghoffer, *The Soviet Union & International Oil Politics* (New York: Columbia University Press, 1977), 40.

97. Thane Gustafson, *Crisis amid Plenty: The Politics of Soviet Energy under Brezhnev and Gorbachev* (Princeton, NJ: Princeton University Press, 1989), 73–77.

98. Gerhard Schürer, "Information über ein Gespräch mit Genossen Kossygin am 1.2.1973," February 2, 1973, BAB, DE 1/58701.

99. Quoted in "Siberia's 100-inch Pipelines," *Petroleum Press Service* 36, no. 10 (October 1969): 366.

100. Gerhard Schürer, "Information über die Beratungen in Moskau am 8. und 9.1972," December 11, 1972, BAB, DE 1/58701.

101. PlanEcon, *Soviet and East European Energy Databank*, 2:U-5.

102. Gerhard Schürer, "Information über die Beratungen zwischen Genossen Schürer und Genossen Baibakow über Grundfragen der Rohstofflieferungen der UdSSR in die DDR im Zeitraum 1976–1980 am 21.5.1973," May 22, 1973, BAB, DE 1/58507.

103. "Zapis' besedy: Predsedatelia Gosplana SSSR t. Baibakova N.K. s predsedatelem planovogo upravleniia VNR t. Padri I.," July 15, 1971, RGAE, f. 4372, op. 66, d. 4448.

104. Nicholas Henderson to R. H. Ellingworth, "B.P. Interest in Poland," April 9, 1970, TNA, FCO 67/405; Klinghoffer, *Soviet Union & International Oil Politics*, 189.

105. Bulgaria imported 20 percent from the nonsocialist world, Czechoslovakia 8.5 percent, East Germany 19 percent, Hungary 12 percent, and Poland 15 percent. Calculated from PlanEcon, *Soviet and East European Energy Databank*, 2:B-5, C-5, G-5, H-5, P-5.

106. Sabit A. Orudzhev to Alexei Kosygin, September 18, 1974, RGAE, f. 458, op. 1, d. 3728.

107. On the Soviet-Western European natural gas relationship, see Per Högselius, *Red Gas: Russia and the Origins of European Energy Dependence* (New York: Palgrave Macmillan, 2013).

108. PlanEcon, *Soviet and East European Energy Databank*, 2:C-6, P-6.

109. Konstantin Rusakov, "K voprosu o vypolnenii resheniia TsK KPSS i Soveta Ministrov SSSR otnositel'no podgotovki predlozhenii po sovershenstvovaniiu sistemy planirovaniia i rukovodstva vneshneekonomicheskoi deiatel'nost'iu," October 14, 1970, RGANI, f. 5, op. 62, d. 473.

110. Rusakov, "K voprosu o vypolnenii resheniia TsK KPSS i Soveta Ministrov SSSR otnositel'no podgotovki predlozhenii po sovershenstvovaniiu sistemy planirovaniia i rukovodstva vneshneekonomicheskoi deiatel'nost'iu," October 14, 1970, RGANI, f. 5, op. 62, d. 473.

111. N. M. Mitrofanova and V. M. Shastitko, "K voprosu sovershenstvovaniia tsenoobrazovaniia vo vzaimnoi torgovle stran SEV v usloviiakh sotsialisticheskoi ekonomicheskoi intergratsii," October 1974, RGANI, f. 5, op. 67, d. 626.

112. "K voprosu o prodovol'stvennoi probleme stran-chlenov SEV i nekotorykh merakh po stimulirovaniiu vzaimnogo eksporta sel'skokhoziaistvennykh tovarov," RGANI, f. 5, op. 63, d. 491.

113. See Elena Dragomir, "The Formation of the Soviet Bloc's Council for Mutual Economic Assistance: Romania's Involvement," *Journal of Cold War Studies* 14, no. 1 (2010): 34–47.

114. "Razgovori mezhdu dr. Todor Zhivkov—purvi sekretar na TsK na BKP, i dr. Leonid Ilich Brezhnev—generalen sekretar na TsK na KPSS," September 22, 1966, TsDA, f. 1B, op. 34, a.e. 43. On Brezhnev, see Susanne Schattenberg, *Brezhnev: The Making of a Statesman*, trans. John Heath (London: I. B. Tauris, 2022).

115. Alexander Puzanov, "Zapis' besedy s pervym sekretarem TsK BKP, predsedatelem Soveta ministrov NRB tov. Todorom Zhivkovym," December 31, 1970, RGANI, f. 5, op. 63, d. 250.

116. "Beseda na dr. Todor Zhivkov i dr. Leonid Brezhnev v pravitelstvenata preditsentsiia 'Voden,'" September 20, 1973, TsDA, f. 378B, op. 1, a.e. 693.

117. Suvi Kansikas, "Calculating the Burden of Empire: Soviet Oil, East-West Trade, and the End of the Socialist Bloc," in *Cold War Energy: A Transnational History of Soviet Oil and Gas*, ed. Jeronim Perović (Cham: Springer International Publishing, 2017), 354–57.

118. See David R. Stone, "CMEA's International Investment Bank and the Crisis of Developed Socialism," *Journal of Cold War Studies* 10, no. 3 (2008): 48–77.

119. Matthew J. Ouimet, *The Rise and Fall of the Brezhnev Doctrine in Soviet Foreign Policy* (Chapel Hill: University of North Carolina Press, 2003), 78.

120. M. Misnik, "Spravka o rezul'tatakh koordinatsii narodnokhoziaistvennykh pla-nov SSSR i stran-chlenov SEV na 1971–1975 gg.," February 19, 1971, RGANI, f. 5, op. 63, d. 490.

121. Kh. Toming, "Zapis' besedy s zaveduiushchim otdelom ekonomicheskoi poli-tiki TsK VSRP tov. Iozhefom Balintom," October 16, 1970, RGANI, f. 5, op. 62, d. 390.

122. "Einige Grundprobleme der Arbeitsteilung und der Entwicklung des gegen-seitigen Warenaustausches, die in der ersten Konsultation zur Koordinierung der Pläne im Zeitraum nach 1975 von der DDR-Seite gestellt wurden," n.d. (prepared for June 1972 CMEA meetings), BAB, DE 1/54796.

123. "Informatsiia o besede zamestitelia predsedatelia Soveta Ministrov, predsedate-lia Gosplana SSSR tov. N.K. Baibakov s predsedatelem VNR tov. Imre Padri," Janu-ary 7, 1971, RGAE, f. 4372, op. 66, d. 4448.

124. "Informatsiia o besede zamestitelia predsedatelia Soveta Ministrov, predsedate-lia Gosplana SSSR tov. N.K. Baibakov s predsedatelem VNR tov. Imre Padri."

125. Nauchno-issledovatel'skogo ekonomicheskogo instituta pri Gosplane SSSR, "Analiz tendentsii izmeneniia urovnei ekonomicheskogo razvitii a SSSR i evropeiskikh stran-chlenov Soveta Ekonomicheskoi Vzaimopomoshchi," n.d. (1971), RGANI, f. 5, op. 63, d. 490.

126. Nauchno-issledovatel'skogo ekonomicheskogo instituta pri Gosplane SSSR, "Analiz tendentsii izmeneniia urovnei ekonomicheskogo razvitii a SSSR i evropeiskikh stran-chlenov Soveta Ekonomicheskoi Vzaimopomoshchi."

127. Postscript, Diary of Anatoly S. Chernyaev, 1973, NSAVRR.

3. The West and the Oil Shock

1. Alec Douglas-Home to Edward Heath, "Copenhagen Summit: Kissinger's Pro-posal on Energy," December 13, 1973, TNA, PREM 15/2041.

2. *FRUS*, 1969–1976, vol. 37, doc. 9, 30–31.

3. This approach draws inspiration from the work of David S. Painter, who has long advocated that scholars pay closer attention to the link between oil and the Cold War. See, for example, "Oil and Geopolitics: The Oil Crises of the 1970s and the Cold War," *Historical Social Research* 39, no. 4 (2014): 186–208.

4. On the US "management" of economic interdependence during the mid-1970s, see Daniel J. Sargent, *A Superpower Transformed: The Remaking of American Foreign Re-lations in the 1970s* (New York: Oxford University Press, 2015), 165–97.

5. DeGolyer and MacNaughton, *Twentieth Century Petroleum Statistics: Historical Data (1918–1959)* (Dallas, TX), 3.

6. David S. Painter, "The Marshall Plan and Oil," *Cold War History* 9, no. 2 (2009): 160.

7. Painter, 161.

8. See Giuliano Garavini, *The Rise and Fall of OPEC in the Twentieth Century* (New York: Oxford University Press, 2019).

9. *BP Statistical Review of World Energy 2022*.

10. Daniel Yergin, *The Prize: The Epic Quest for Oil, Money, and Power*, 3rd ed. (New York: Free Press, 2009), 518–20.

11. Yergin, 523–36.

12. Cited in Duco Hellema, Cees Wiebes, and Toby Witte, *The Netherlands and the Oil Crisis: Business as Usual*, trans. Murray Pearson (Amsterdam: University of Amsterdam Press, 2004), 41.

13. Yergin, *Prize*, 523.

14. *BP Statistical Review of World Energy 2022*.

15. DeGolyer and MacNaughton, *Twenty-First Century Petroleum Statistics*, 20, 43.

16. Yergin, *Prize*, 596.

17. DeGolyer and MacNaughton, *Twenty-First Century Petroleum Statistics*, 29, 36–38.

18. DeGolyer and MacNaughton, 4.

19. See Christopher R. W. Dietrich, *Oil Revolution: Anticolonial Elites, Sovereign Rights, and the Economic Culture of Decolonization* (New York: Cambridge University Press, 2017).

20. See Yergin, *Prize*, 559–62.

21. "Brief for Anglo-US Oil Talks," October 28–29, 1971, TNA, FCO 67/609.

22. Giuliano Garavini, *The Rise and Fall of OPEC in the Twentieth Century* (New York: Oxford University Press, 2019), 203–9. The rise of oil prices was part of the larger inflation in the commodities markets during the early 1970s. The unraveling of the Bretton Woods system and the subsequent devaluation of the dollar added to the inflation in the trade of dollar-denominated goods.

23. *BP Statistical Review of World Energy 2022*.

24. James Akins, "The Oil Crisis: This Time the Wolf Is Here," *Foreign Affairs* 51, no. 3 (April 1973): 462–90.

25. *FRUS*, 1969–1976, vol. 36, doc. 230, 648.

26. Rowley Cromer to Thomas Brimelow, November 22, 1973, TNA, FCO 82/288.

27. Willis C. Armstrong to Henry Kissinger, October 13, 1973, "European Vulnerability to Arab Oil Embargo," folder "WSAG Meeting Middle East 10/14/73," box H-093, NSC Institutional Files, RNPL.

28. Yergin, *Prize*, 583–88.

29. Yergin, 595.

30. W.J.J.D. thoe Schwartzenberg to Max van der Stoel, "Verklaring betreffende de Iraakse oliepolitiek," November 14, 1973, NL-HaNA, 2.05.313, inv.nr. 14525.

31. Jan Lodal and Helmut Sonnenfeldt to Henry Kissinger, "Assistance for the Dutch," November 27, 1973, folder "Country Files-Europe: Netherlands Vol. II—1972 [1972–1974][1 of 3]," box 697, NSC Files, RNPL.

32. "Notulen van de vergadering gehouden op vrijdag 26 oktober 1973 in het Catshuis, aangevangen 's morgens om 10 uur en 's middags en 's avonds voortgezet," October 26, 1973, NL-HaNA, 2.02.05.02, inv.nr. 1237.

33. "Secretary's Staff Meeting," October 29, 1973, box 1, Transcripts of Secretary of State Henry Kissinger's Staff Meetings, 1973–77, RG 59, NARA.

34. Hans Lautenschlager, "Vermerk: Diplomatische Initiative der Neun in der Erdölfrage," November 12, 1973, PA-AA, B 71 (ZA), Bd. 113893.

35. MBZ (PLAN), "Neveneffekten [*sic*] van Amerikaanse oliehulp aan Nederland," December 5, 1973, NL-HaNA, 2.05.313, invr.nr. 14523.

36. DeGolyer and MacNaughton, *Twenty-First Century Petroleum Statistics*, 29, 36–37.

37. Hellema, Wiebes, and Witte, *Netherlands and the Oil Crisis*, 189; Ruud Lubbers, *Persoonlijke Herinneringen* (Amsterdam: Uitgeverij Balans, 2018), 133.

38. Yergin, *Prize*, 596; BIS, *Annual Report*, 1974, 4.

39. IMF, *Annual Report*, 1977, 3.

40. World Bank, World Development Indicators; Jeffry A. Frieden, *Global Capitalism: Its Fall and Rise in the Twentieth Century, and Its Stumbles in the Twenty-First* (New York: W. W. Norton, 2020), 366.

41. *ERP*, 1976, 141.

42. Meg Jacobs, *Panic at the Pump: The Energy Crisis and the Transformation of American Politics in the 1970s* (New York: Hill & Wang, 2016), 44–48.

43. Robert Kistler, "The Gas Line—A New Southland Life-Style," *Los Angeles Times*, March 2, 1974.

44. Jacobs, *Panic at the Pump*, 89–101.

45. John A. Love to Richard Nixon, "U.S. Domestic Response to Arab Oil Boycott," November 1, 1973, folder "WSAG Mtg. 11/2/73 Vietnam + Middle East [1 of 2]," box H-95, NSC Institutional Files, RNPL.

46. Cited in Salim Yaqub, *Imperfect Strangers: Americans, Arabs, and U.S.–Middle East Relations in the 1970s* (Ithaca, NY: Cornell University Press, 2016), 153.

47. F. Lisle Widman, "A Somber Look at International Economic Cooperation in 1974," December 28, 1973, folder "F. L. Widman-Chron-Dec. 1973," box 7, F. Lisle Widman Files, RG 56, NARA.

48. *FRUS*, 1969–1976, vol. 37, doc. 102, 362–63.

49. "Secretary's Staff Meeting," October 25, 1973, box 1, Transcripts of Secretary of State Henry Kissinger's Staff Meetings, 1973–77, RG 59, NARA.

50. Rowley Cromer to Alec Douglas Home, November 15, 1973, TNA, PREM 15/1767.

51. Rowley Cromer to Thomas Brimelow, "US, Europe and the Middle East," November 27, 1973, TNA, FCO 82/288.

52. U.S. Embassy Paris (Irwin) 28311 to SecState, "French Views on Consultation," November 1, 1973, folder "Country File Europe—France, Vol. XI, April–December 31, 1973," box 679, NSC Files, RNPL.

53. *FRUS*, 1969–1976, vol. 36, doc. 229, 642.

54. On transatlantic relations during the crisis, see, among others, Rüdiger Graf, *Oil and Sovereignty: Petroknowledge and Energy Policy in the United States and Western Europe in the 1970s* (New York: Berghahn Books, 2018); and Henning Türk, "Kooperation in der Krise? Die Ölkrise von 1973/74 und die multilaterale Zusammenarbeit der westlichen Industrieländer in der Energiepolitik," *Journal of European Integration History* 22, no. 1 (2016): 47–65.

55. *FRUS*, 1969–1976, vol. 38, part 1, doc. 24, 120–28.

56. "Memorandum of Conversation," February 27, 1973, folder "PET FR 1/1/70," box 1498, Subject Numeric Files, 1970–73 Economic, RG 59, NARA.

57. Detlev Rohwedder to Horst Grabert, "Gipfelkonferenz am 14./15. Dezember 1973," PA-AA, B 71 (ZA), Bd. 113893.

58. "Secretary's Staff Meeting, January 31, 1974," box 2, Transcripts of Secretary of State Henry Kissinger's Staff Meetings, 1973–77, RG 59, NARA.

59. *FRUS*, 1969–1976, vol. 36, doc. 269, 771.

60. Guiliano Garavini, *After Empires: European Integration, Decolonization, and the Challenge from the Global South 1957–1986*, trans. Richard R. Nybakken (New York: Oxford University Press, 2012), 184–85.

61. *FRUS*, 1969–1976, vol. 36, doc. 305, 860.

62. Willy Brandt to Richard Nixon, January 18, 1974, PA-AA, B 71 (ZA), Bd. 113893.

63. Michael D. Butler, "Political Implications of Issues Likely to Arise at the Washington Meeting on Energy," February 4, 1974, TNA, FCO 59/1155.

64. On French policymaking, see Aurélie Élisa Gfeller, *Building a European Identity: France, the United States, and the Oil Shock, 1973–1974* (New York: Berghahn Books, 2012).

65. "Opening Remarks of the Honorable Henry A. Kissinger, Secretary of State," February 11, 1974, PA-AA, B 71 (ZA), Bd. 113894.

66. J. L. Taylor to R. Arculus, "Follow-up to Washington Energy Conference," March 4, 1974, TNA, FCO 96/55.

67. *FRUS*, 1969–1976, vol. 36, doc. 321, 900.

68. "Question-and-Answer Session at the Executives' Club of Chicago," March 15, 1974, APP

69. *FRUS*, 1969–1976, vol. E-15, part 2, doc. 49, 207.

70. *FRUS*, 1969–1976, vol. E-15, part 2, doc. 50, 209–13.

71. "Declaration on the Establishment of a New International Economic Order," TNA, FCO 96/161.

72. See Adom Getachew, *Worldmaking after Empire: The Rise and Fall of Self-Determination* (Princeton, NJ: Princeton University Press, 2019), 142–75.

73. *FRUS*, 1969–1976, vol. 37, doc. 24, 95.

74. Walter J. Levy Consultants, "Implications of Exploding World Oil Costs," January 1974, TNA, FCO 59/1164.

75. IMF, *Annual Report*, 1977, 37.

76. *ERP*, 1978, 102.

77. *FRUS*, 1969–1976, vol. 36, doc. 360, 1024.

78. BK-IV/2 (Heick), "Maßnahmen gegen eventuelle wirtschaftliche und monetäre Repressionen durch die Araber," February 20, 1975, B 136/9302.

79. On petrodollar recycling, see William Glenn Gray, "'Learning to 'Recycle': Petrodollars and the West, 1973–1975," in *Oil Shock: The 1973 Crisis and Its Economic Legacy*, ed. Elisabetta Bini, Giuliano Garavini, and Federico Romero (London: I. B. Tauris, 2016), 172–97; David E. Spiro, *The Hidden Hand of American Hegemony: Petrodollar Recycling and International Markets* (Ithaca, NY: Cornell University Press, 1999); and David M. Wight, *Oil Money: Middle East Petrodollars and the Transformation of US Empire, 1967–1988* (Ithaca, NY: Cornell University Press, 2021).

80. Max van der Stoel to Joop den Uyl, "De Energieconferentie in Washington en het vervolg daarop," March 29, 1974, NL-HaNA, 2.05.213, inv.nr. 17519.

81. *FRUS*, 1969–1976, vol. 37, doc. 39, 132–33.

82. Hans Friderichs, "Indexierung der Ölpreise," May 20, 1975, BAK, B 136/9357.

83. *FRUS*, 1969–1976, vol. 31, doc. 216, 217.

84. "Attracting Petrodollars," *Wall Street Journal*, May 6, 1974.

85. AA-412, "Hauptprobleme der internationalen Währungslage," May 2, 1975, BAK, B 136/9302.

86. Odeh Aburdene, "1 Petrodollar=72 cents," *Euromoney* (May 1978): 36.

87. Gray, "'Learning to 'Recycle,'" 180.

88. "Memorandum of Conversation," December 5, 1974, folder "MTGS-5 Germany: Memcons 1972–1978," box 2, Briefing Memorandums on Switzerland, Japan and Germany, 1972–1980, Office of the Deputy Assistant Secretary for International Monetary Affairs, RG 56, NARA.

89. "The Oil Money," *New York Times*, July 20, 1974.

90. International Energy Affairs, "OPEC Objectives," April 4, 1975, folder "OPEC: FEA Study (1)," box 80, L. William Seidman Files, GFPL.

91. BIS, *Annual Report*, 1977, 103–5.

92. Mark Mazower, *Governing the World: The History of an Idea* (New York: Penguin, 2012), 347.

93. Ronald Nevans, "Foreign Banks in New York: The Great New Growth Centre," *Euromoney* (June 1977): 18–20.

94. Harold James, *International Monetary Cooperation since Bretton Woods* (New York: Oxford University Press, 1996), 257.

95. Samuel C. Gwynne, *Selling Money* (New York: Penguin, 1987), 44–52.

96. "Address by Herr Helmut Schmidt to the meeting at the Royal Institute of International Affairs, London, on 29, January 1974," TNA, PREM 15/2097.

97. BMF-VII A 4, "Zum Austritt Frankreichs aus der EG-Schlange," January 29, 1974, BAK, B 136/8056.

98. In 1975, France held $14.13 billion, and the United States owned $11.6 billion. IMF, International Financial Statistics.

99. *FRUS*, 1969–1976, vol. 31, doc. 63, 235.

100. The franc withdrew again in March 1976.

101. French Ministry of Finance and Economics paper, "Scheme of a Gradual Return to a System of Stable but Adjustable Par Values," n.d., BAK, B 136/9304.

102. N. P. Bayne to C. W. Fogarty, "Giscard's Proposal for a Monetary Conference," August 20, 1975, TNA, FCO 59/1365.

103. AA-412, "Giscards Idee einer internationalen Wirtschafts-und Währungskonferenz," July 11, 1975, PA-AA, B 202 (ZA), Bd. 105679.

104. Charles A. Cooper to William E. Simon, "Status of French Proposals for an Economic Summit," July 21, 1975, folder "F. L. Widman Chron July 1975," box 8, F. Lisle Widman Files, RG 56, NARA.

105. *FRUS*, 1969–1976, vol. 31, doc. 93, 304.

106. BMF-VII A 3, "Französischer Stufenplan für Rückkehr zu festen Wechselkursen," August 21, 1975, BAK, B 136/9304.

107. "Record of a Meeting at Chequers on Sunday 14 September," September 14, 1975, TNA, FCO 59/1366.

108. *FRUS*, 1969–1976, vol. 31, doc. 128, 458.

109. Hobart Rowen, "U.S. Is Big Winner at IMF Talks: Economic Impact U.S. Emerges as Winner at IMF Talks," *Washington Post*, January 18, 1976.

110. The Deutsche Mark was a distant second place at about 7 percent. IMF, *Annual Report*, 1983, 72.

111. Duccio Basosi, "Oil, Dollars, and US Power in the 1970s: Re-viewing the Connections," *Journal of Energy History* 3 (2020): 1–15. On the U.S.-Saudi relationship, see Victor McFarland, *Oil Powers: A History of the U.S.-Saudi Alliance* (New York: Columbia University Press, 2020).

112. BIS, *Annual Report*, 1976, 12.

113. BIS, *Annual Report*, 1977, 26.

114. World Bank, World Development Indicators. Inflation began to ease during the second half of 1974 because of the recession.

115. BIS, *Annual Report*, 1976, 22, 28–29; ERP, 1978, 15.

116. Working Party No. 4 of the Economic Policy Committee, "Recent Developments in Wages, Costs and Prices," May 15, 1975, OECD Archive, CPE/WP4(75)1.

117. World Bank, World Development Indicators.

118. World Bank.

119. *FRUS, 1969–1976*, vol. E-15, part 2, doc. 286, 881.

120. World Bank, World Development Indicators.

121. Angus Maddison, *The World Economy*, vol. 1, *A Millennial Perspective* (Paris: OECD, 2006), 134.

122. James, *International Monetary Cooperation*, 283.

123. James C. Abegglen and Thomas M. Hout, "Facing Up to the Trade Gap with Japan," *Foreign Affairs 57*, no. 1 (Fall 1978): 152.

124. Kaoru Sugihara, "East Asia, Middle East and the World Economy: Further Notes on the Oil Triangle," Afrasian Centre for Peace and Development Studies, Working Paper Series No. 9, 2006.

125. Quoted in Mark Mazower, *Dark Continent: Europe's Twentieth Century* (New York: Vintage, 1998), 323.

126. John Goshko, "Amazing Story of Europe's 'Lost Nation,'" *Boston Globe*, August 4, 1974.

127. Tony Judt, *Postwar: A History of Europe since 1945* (New York: Penguin, 2005), 457.

128. "Meeting with Joseph Luns Secretary General of NATO," February 24, 1975, folder "North Atlantic Treaty Organization (NATO), 1975 (2) WH," box 53, NSC Staff for Europe, Canada, and Ocean Affairs, National Security Adviser's Files, GFPL.

129. *FRUS, 1969–1976*, vol. E-15, part 2, doc. 233, 747; "Meeting with Joseph Luns Secretary General of NATO," February 24, 1975, folder "North Atlantic Treaty Organization (NATO), 1975 (2) WH," box 53, NSC Staff for Europe, Canada, and Ocean Affairs, National Security Adviser's Files, GFPL.

130. On Schmidt's approach to international economics, see Kristina Spohr, *The Global Chancellor: Helmut Schmidt and the Reshaping of the International Order* (New York: Oxford University Press, 2016).

131. "Record of a Meeting between the Prime Minister and the Federal German Chancellor at the Senat Guesthouse in Hamburg on Thursday 24 July 1975 at 4.15p.m.," TNA, PREM 16/427.

132. *FRUS, 1969–1976*, vol. 31, doc. 93, 308–11.

133. Winston Lord to Henry A. Kissinger, "International Disagreement on Economic and Monetary Issues," n.d. ("7/3/1975(?)" scribbled at top of page), folder "Briefing Memos, 1975, Folder 6," box 14, Records of Henry Kissinger, RG 59, NARA.

134. Edward Tomkins to James Callaghan, November 25, 1975, TNA, PREM 16/838.

135. BK-IV (Hiss), "Bewertung der Gespräche von Rambouillet," November 18, 1975, BAK, B 136/8482.

136. F. Lisle Widman to Gerald L. Parsky, "A Concern for Democracy in Western Europe," July 21, 1976, folder "FLWidman Chron Jul 1976," box 8, F. Lisle Widman Files, RG 56, NARA.

137. Policy Planning Staff, "Beyond Détente: East-West Relations in Europe After Helsinki," December 8, 1975, folder, "Dec. 1–15, 1975," box 359, Winston Lord Files, RG 59, NARA.

138. *FRUS*, 1969–1976, vol. E-15, part 2, doc. 77, 308–9.

139. Melvyn P. Leffler, *For the Soul of Mankind: The United States, the Soviet Union, and the Cold War* (New York: Hill and Wang, 2007), 59.

140. Edwin H. Yeo III, "The Current Situation in Italy," February 11, 1976, folder "F. L.Widman Chron Feb 1976," box 8, F. Lisle Widman Files, RG 56, NARA.

141. Henry A. Kissinger to Gerald R. Ford, "State Visit of French President Giscard d'Estaing," n.d., folder "Country File—France (1)," box 1, International Economic Affairs Staff: Files, National Security Adviser's Files, GFPL.

142. AA-212, "Teilnahme kommunistischer Parteien an europäischen Regierungen," June 22, 1976, BAK, B 136/17106.

143. Edwin H. Yeo III to William E. Simon, May 15, 1976, folder 37, drawer 25, series IIIB, William E. Simon Papers, DBSL.

144. See Edwin H. Yeo III to William E. Simon, May 14, 1976, folder 37, drawer 25, series IIIB, William E. Simon Papers, DBSL.

145. Sargent, *Superpower Transformed*, 195.

146. *FRUS*, 1969–1976, vol. 31, doc. 150, 585. On the G7 summits, see Emmanuel Mourlon-Druol and Federico Romero, eds., *International Summitry and Global Governance: The Rise of the G7 and the European Council, 1974–1991* (London: Routledge, 2014).

147. George Clark, "Mr. Callaghan's Grim Speech Wins Little Conference Applause," *The Times*, September 29, 1976.

148. On the British IMF crisis, see Kevin Hickson, *The IMF Crisis of 1976 and British Politics* (London: I. B. Tauris, 2005).

149. Seminar Transcript, June 16, 1976, box 10, Transcripts of Secretary of State Henry Kissinger's Staff Meetings, 1973–77, RG 59, NARA.

150. Quoted in AA-403 (Kruse), "Wirtschaftskrise und NATO," December 9, 1974, PA-AA, B 52, Bd. 117089.

151. *ERP*, 1978, 380.

152. Winston Lord, "Economic Health of the Industrial Democracies: A Larger View and Look Ahead," November 19, 1976, folder "Nov. 16–30, 1976," box 365, Winston Lord Files, RG 59, NARA.

4. Twin Oil Crises behind the Iron Curtain

1. DeGolyer and MacNaughton, *Twenty-First Century Petroleum Statistics*, 3, 7.

2. Anatoly Dobrynin, *In Confidence: Moscow's Ambassador to America's Six Cold War Presidents* (New York: Times Books, 1995), 408.

3. On the CSCE, see Michael Cotey Morgan, *The Final Act: The Helsinki Accords and the Transformation of the Cold War* (Princeton, NJ: Princeton University Press, 2017).

4. Vladislav Zubok, *A Failed Empire: The Soviet Union in the Cold War from Stalin to Gorbachev* (Chapel Hill: University of North Carolina Press, 2009), 247–54.

5. Paul Markowski, "Die gemeinsame Aussenpolitik der sozialistischen Staatengemeinschaft zur Durchsetzung der friedlichen Koexistenz zwischen Staaten unterschiedlicher Gesellschaftsordnung," April 26, 1973, SAPMO, DY 30/IV B 2/20/10.

6. Abteilung Internationale Verbindungen im ZK der SED, "Die Verwirklichung der Beschlüsse des VIII. Parteitages der SED auf internationalen Gebiet," December 17, 1975, SAPMO, DY 30/IV B 2/20/2.

7. Institut für Internationale Politik und Wirtschaft, "Zu einigen Entwicklungstendenzen der Wirtschaft in den kapitalistischen Hauptländern 1974," February 1974, SAPMO, DY 30/J IV 2/2J/5198.

8. Hermann Axen, "Die Aufgaben der Sozialistischen Einheitspartei Deutschlands und der Deutschen Demokratischen Republik nach dem 8. Plenum des Zentralkomitees," February 15, 1973, SAPMO, DY 30/IV B 2/20/10.

9. Nikolai Faddeev, "Doklad o dvadtsatipiatiletii Soveta Ekonomicheskoi Vzaimopomoshchi," March 21, 1974, RGANI, f. 5, op. 67, d. 608.

10. This included Romania, which would not import oil from the Soviet Union in significant quantities until the end of the 1970s and early 1980s. "Informatsiia o rabote biuro po nefti v 1973 g. i soobrazheniia dlia komiteta SEV po sotrudnichestvu v oblasti planovoi deiatel'nosti o konkretnikh vozmozhnostiakh sotrudnichestva stran-chlenov SEV, sviazannogo s priobreteniem nefti iz tretikh stran," April 1, 1974, TsDA, f. 130, op. 26C, a.e. 96.

11. Vladimir Bazovsky, "Zapis' besedy s chlenom Politbiuro TsK BKP, predsedatelem Soveta ministrov NRB tov. Stanko Todorov," December 25, 1973, RGANI, f. 5, op. 67, d. 489; and Vladimir Bazovsky, "Zapis' besedy s pervym sekretarem TsK BKP, predsedatelem Gossoveta NRB tov. Todorom Zhivkovym," December 26, 1973, RGANI, f. 5, op. 67, d. 488.

12. The proposed "confidential discount" decreased the price of oil departing Mediterranean ports from 96 rubles to 82 rubles per ton and leaving the Persian Gulf from 83.65 rubles to 66.92 rubles per ton. Soviet plans had budgeted 28 and 20 rubles per ton, respectively. See V. Novikov and M. Kuzmin to the Central Committee of the CPSU, January 14, 1974, RGANI, f. 3, op. 72, d. 597. On this point, see Lorenz M. Lüthi, "Drifting Apart: Soviet Energy and the Cohesion of the Communist Bloc in the 1970s and 1980s," in Cold War Energy: A Transnational History of Soviet Oil and Gas, ed. Jeronim Perović (Cham: Springer International Publishing, 2017), 371–99.

13. "Spravka o vozmozhnykh rezul'tatakh korrektirovki kontraktnykh tsen na neft' v torgovle SSSR so stranami SEV na 1976–1977 g.g. na baze mirovykh tsen za 1974–1975 gg.," May 17, 1974, RGANI, f. 5, op. 67, d. 617.

14. André Steiner, "'Common Sense Is Necessary': East German Reactions to the Oil Crises of the 1970s," Historical Social Research 39, no. 4 (2014): 233.

15. "Niederschrift über die Gespräche zwischen dem Ersten Sekretär des Zentralkomitees der SED, Erich Honecker, und dem Generalsekretär des Zentralkomitees der KPdSU, Leonid Iljitsch Breshnew, am 18. Juni 1974 in Moskau, Kreml," June 18, 1974, SAPMO, DY/30 IV 2/2.035/55.

16. Referenced in "Doklad za staniovishteto na NR Bulgariia po vuprosite, koito shte se razgladat na 69-oto zasedanie na Izpulnitelniia komitet na Suveta za ikonomicheska vzaimopomosht," October 4, 1974, TsDA, f. 1B, op. 35, a.e. 4991.

17. Gerhard Schürer, "Information über ein Gespräch zwischen Genossen Schürer und Genossen Baibakow am 9.12.1974 zu Preisfragen," BAB, DE 1/58589.

18. "Preise für den Import von Erdöl und Erdgas aus der UdSSR seit 1972 Gegenüberstellung dieser Preise zu den kapitalistischen Weltmarktpreisen und Ausweis des Vorteils für die DDR," n.d., BAB, DE 1/58747; and Soviet embassy in Budapest, "Informatsiia o rezul'tatakh vengero-sovetskikh peregovorov po voprosu ob izmenenii syr'evykh postavok i kontraktnykh tsen," February 24, 1975, RGANI, f. 5, op. 68, d. 1497.

19. Nikolai Baibakov, *The Cause of My Life*, trans. Vladimir Bisengaliev (Moscow: Progress, 1986), 182, 194.

20. Nikolai Baibakov, "O vneshneekonomicheskikh sviaziakh SSSR i GDR v 1974 godu," December 17, 1973, RGANI, f. 3, op. 72, d. 593.

21. Anatoly Komin, "Material k voprosy o sovershenstvovanii vneshnetorgovogo tsenoobrazovaniia," September 12, 1974, RGANI, f. 5, op. 67, d. 617.

22. Randall W. Stone, *Satellites and Commissars: Strategy and Conflict in the Politics of Soviet-Bloc Trade* (Princeton, NJ: Princeton University Press, 1998), 37.

23. Cited in IEMSS report, "Import mashin i oborudovaniia SSSR iz stran SEV i problemy ego razvitiia," June 10, 1975, RGANI, f. 5, op. 68, d. 1730.

24. Anatoly Komin, "Material k voprosy o sovershenstvovanii vneshnetorgovogo tsenoobrazovaniia," September 12, 1974, RGANI, f. 5, op. 67, d. 617.

25. "Plan podgotovki rabochimi gruppami predlozhenii sovetskoi storony k soveshchaniu na vysshem urovne po voprosam ekonomicheskogo sotrudnichestva," attached to Protocol No. 145, Zasedaniia Politbiuro TsK KPSS, August 1, 1974, RGANI, f. 3, op. 72, d. 625. The Politburo commissioned an interdepartmental group to study the issue. For the results, see Mefodi Sveshnikov, Vladimir Alkhimov, Viktor Dementsev, Yuri Ivanov, Nikolai Vorov, and Dmitry Kostyukhin to Mikhail Lesechko, Memorandum, September 30, 1974, RGANI, f. 5, op. 67, d. 634.

26. "Niederschrift über eine Zusammenkunft des Ministers für Außenhandel der DDR, Genossen Sölle, mit dem Minsiter für Außenhandel der UdSSR, Genossen Patolitschew, anläßlich der Übergabe des Aide-memoires zur Bildung der Vertragspreise im RGW 1976–1980 und 1975," October 3, 1974, BAB, DE 1/58588.

27. Treasury background paper, "Implications of the Growing External Debt of the Communist Countries," July 1976, folder "East-West Foreign Trade Board: Background Material, July 1976," box 56, L. William Seidman Files, GFPL.

28. Willi Stoph, "Information über die Beratung mit Genossen Kossygin am 10.12.1976 in Moskau," December 10, 1976, BAB, DE 1/58569.

29. Georgii Arbatov, *The System: An Insider's Life in Soviet Politics* (New York: Random House, 1992), 216–17.

30. Yegor Gaidar, *Collapse of an Empire: Lessons for Modern Russia*, trans. Antonina W. Bouis (Washington, DC: Brookings Institution Press, 2007), 98.

31. PlanEcon, *Soviet and East European Energy Databank* (Washington, DC: PlanEcon, 1986), 2:U-5.

32. CIA Directorate of Intelligence, *Soviet Energy Data Resource Handbook: A Reference Aid*, May 1990, CIAERR.

33. "Niederschrift über die Beratung zwischen Genossen Erich Honecker und Genossen Baibakow am 21.12.1974," December 21, 1974, BAB, DE 1/58586.

34. Vladimir Matskevich, "Informatsiia o peregovorakh ministerov vneshnei torgovli ChSSR i SSSR 3–4 sentiabria 1974 goda," September 30, 1974, RGANI, f. 5, op. 67, d. 501.

35. "Information über ein Gespräch mit dem Minister für Außenhandel der UdSSR, Genossen Patolitschew, am 11.11.1974," November 11, 1974, SAPMO, DY 30/J IV 2/2J/5517.

36. "Niederschrift über die Beratung zwischen Genossen Erich Honecker und Genossen Baibakow am 21.12.1974," December 21, 1974, BAB, DE 1/58586.

37. "Memorandum o besede zamestitelia ministra tov. Alkhimova V.S. s zamestitelem ministra vneshnei torgovli GDR tov. Fenske, sostoiavshiisia 29 oktiabria 1975 goda," October 29, 1975, RGAE, f. 413, op. 31, d. 7432.

38. Gerhard Schürer, "Information über ein Gespräch zwischen Genossen Schürer und Genossen Baibakow am 9.12.1974 zu Preisfragen," December 9, 1974, BAB, DE 1/58586.

39. Vladimir Matskevich, "Informatsiia o peregovorakh ministerov vneshnei torgovli ChSSR i SSSR 3–4 sentiabria 1974 goda," September 30, 1974, RGANI, f. 5, op. 67, d. 501.

40. Gerhard Schürer to Erich Honecker, December 14, 1973, BAB, DE 1/58701.

41. "Information über eine Konsultation mit dem Mitglied des Politbüros und Sekretär des ZK Genossen Hermann Axen, im ZK der im November 1974," SAPMO, DY 30/IV 2/2.2035/55.

42. "Suobrazheniia po razshiriavane na sutrudnichestvoto mezhdu NRB i SSSR i na mnogostranna osnova v oblastta na nefta i prirodniia gaz," August 26, 1974, TsDA, f. 130, op. 26C, a.e. 20.

43. On East Germany and the CMEA, see Ralf Ahrens, *Gegenseitige Wirtschaftshilfe? Die DDR im RGW—Strukturen und handelspolitische Strategien 1963-1976* (Köln: Böhlau Verlag, 2000).

44. Staatliche Plankommission, "Erste volkswirtschaftliche Einschätzung der für 1975 angekündigten Veränderung von RGW-Vertragspreisen im Handel mit der UdSSR," August 12, 1974, BAB, DE 1/58586.

45. No author, "Standpunkt der DDR zur Gestaltung der RGW-Preise 1976–1980," May 30, 1974, BAB, DE 1/58577.

46. Heinz Klopfer, "Persönliche Niederschrift über eine Beratung beim 1. Sekretär des Zentralkomitees der SED am 9.8.1974," August 9, 1974, BAB, DE 1/58586.

47. Klopfer, "Persönliche Niederschrift über eine Beratung beim 1. Sekretär des Zentralkomitees der SED am 9.8.1974."

48. "Information über ein Gespräch mit dem Minister für Außenhandel der UdSSR, Genossen Patolitschew, am 11.11.1974," November 11, 1974, SAPMO, DY 30/J IV 2/2J/5517.

49. "Niederschrift über die Beratung zwischen Genossen Erich Honecker und Genossen Baibakow am 21.12.1974," December 21, 1974, BAB, DE 1/58586.

50. N. Osipov and V. Sorokin, "Ob otnosheniia VNR k izmeneniiu tsen na mirovom sotsialisticheskom rynke," March 25, 1975, RGANI, f. 5, op. 68, d. 1496.

51. Nikolai Baibakov and Mikhail Lesechko, "O voprosakh sovetsko-vengerskogo ekonomicheskogo sotrudnichestva, zatronutykh chlenom Politbiuro, sekretarem TsK VSRP t. Nemetom K. na besadakh v TsKPSS," February 24, 1977, RGANI, f. 5, op. 69, d. 1786.

52. György Lázár to Nikolai Faddeev, "Predlozheniia-Vengerskoi Narodnoi Respubliki po dal'neishemu razvitiiu ekonomicheskogo sotrudnichestva stran-chlenov SEV," December 27, 1974, RGANI, f. 5, op. 68, d. 1673.

53. Charles Gati, *The Bloc that Failed: Soviet-East European Relations in Transition* (Bloomington: Indiana University Press, 1990), 119.

54. Quoted in Stone, *Satellites and Commissars*, 54–55.

55. Vladimir Bazovsky, "Zapis' besedy s pervym sekretarem TsK BKP, presdedatelem Gossoveta NRB tov. Todorom Zhivkovym," October 5, 1974, RGANI, f. 5, op. 67, d. 488.

56. "Protokol 'A' No. 466 na zasedanieto na Politbiuro na TsK na BKP ot 11.X.1974 g.," October 11, 1974, TsDA, f. 1B, op. 35, a.e. 4991.

57. "Plenum na Tsentralniia komitet na Bulgarskata komunisticheska partiia," November 26, 1974, TsDA, f. 1B, op. 58, a.e. 109.

58. "Stenograma ot razgovorite mezhdu drugaria Todor Zhivkov i drugaria Nikolae Chaushesku, sustoiali se v Durzhavniia suvet na Sotsialisticheska Republika Rumuniia," July 19, 1975, TsDA, f. 378B, op. 1, a.e. 696.

59. "Informatsiia za provedenata sreshta s drugaria Kosigin po otkritite vaprosi za sledvashtata petiletka," June 11, 1975, TsDA, f. 130, op. 27C, a.e. 8.

60. Todor Zhivkov to Leonid Brezhnev, n.d., TsDA, f. 378B, op. 1, a.e. 528.

61. Todor Zhivkov to Leonid Brezhnev, n.d., TsDA, f. 378B, op. 1, a.e. 528.

62. V. Pavlov, "Zapis' besedy s chlenom Politbiuro, sekretarem TsK VSRP tov. Karoem Nemetom," January 22, 1975, RGANI, f. 5, op. 68, d. 1506.

63. Marshall I. Goldman, *The Enigma of Soviet Petroleum: Half-full or Half-empty?* (London: Allen & Unwin, 1980), 103.

64. "Protokolen zapis na besedata na dr. Leonid Brezhnev s drugarite T. Zhivkov, E. Khoneker, E. Gerek, Ia. Kadar i G. Khusak v Budapeshta, na 18.III.1975 g.," March 18, 1975, TsDA, f. 378B, op. 1, a.e. 697.

65. Quoted in Stone, *Satellites and Commissars*, 53.

66. PlanEcon, *Soviet and East European Energy Databank*, 2:U-5.

67. "Niederschrift über die Verhandlungen zwischen dem Vorsitzenden des Ministerrates der DDR, Genossen Willi Stoph, und dem Vorsitzenden des Ministerrates der UdSSR, Genossen A.N. Kossygin, am 10.12.1976 in Moskau," December 13, 1976, SAPMO, DY 3023/1529.

68. Georgi Georgiev, Tsvetan Tsenkov, and Boris Boev to Ivan Iliev, "Dokladna zapiska: Rezultatite ot konsultatsiiata na spetsialisti na tsentralnite planovi organi na NRB i SSSR po svodnite vaprosi na ikonimicheskoto sutrudnichestvo prez 1976–1980 g.," July 13, 1973, TsDA, f. 130, op. 25C, a.e. 9.

69. Gerhard Schürer to Erich Honecker, April 27, 1973, BAB, DE 1/58578.

70. SEV: postoiannaia komissiia po neftianoi i gazovoi promyshlennosti, "Protokol sorokovogo pervogo zasedaniia," December 1974, RGAE, f. 302, op. 2, d. 1191.

71. Percentages calculated from statistics in "Ob"emy postavok iz SSSR v stranychleny SEV vazhneishikh vidov topliva i syr'ia v 1980 godu," included in Politburo Protocol No. 115, November 1973, RGANI, f. 3, op. 72, d. 586.

72. N. Kornienko, "Spravka ob orenburgskom gazokondensatnom mestorozhdenii i protekal magistral'nogo gazoprovoda Orenburg-zapadnaia granitsa SSSR," October 23, 1973, RGAE, f. 302, op. 2, d. 1063.

73. "Spravka za izpunenieto na protokola ot 21 avgust 1973 g. za pregovorite mezhdu predsedatelia na Ministerskiia suvet na NRB dr. Stanko Todorov i predsedatelia na Ministerskiia suvet na SSSR dr. A.N. Kosigin," January 1–2, 1974, TsDA, f. 130, op. 26C, a.e. 20.

74. Matthew J. Ouimet, *The Rise and Fall of the Brezhnev Doctrine in Soviet Foreign Policy* (Chapel Hill: University of North Carolina Press, 2003), 78.

75. "Ot Orenburga do zapadnoi granitsy," November 1, 1975, *Pravda*, 4.

76. Per Högselius, *Red Gas: Russia and the Origins of European Energy Dependence* (New York: Palgrave Macmillan, 2013), 172.

77. Ivan Iliev to Stanko Todorov, October 10, 1973, TsDA, f. 130, op. 25C, a.e. 10.

78. N. Osipov, "Zapis' besedy s zav. podotdelom Gosplana VNR t. D. Kovasnai," July 9, 1976, RGANI, f. 5, op. 69, d. 1787.

79. "Protokoll über die Abstimmung der endgültigen Höhe der Aufwendungen in frei konvertierbarer Währung für den Bau der Gasleitung 'Sojus,'" n.d. (included as an attachment to letter dated May 8, 1986), BAB, DN 10/1159. The figures correspond to the total credits that the participating countries received from the International Investment Bank in Moscow.

80. On East German concerns, see Wolfgang Rauchfluß and Harry Bernstein, "Zu ökonomischen Problemen bei der Realisierung der Erdgasleitung Orenburg-Westgrenze UdSSR und der damit verbundenen Erdgaslieferungen aus der UdSSR," May 4, 1977, SAPMO, DY 30/25763. For the prices between 1973 and 1984, see "Übersicht über die Preisentwicklung für Erdgas ab 1973," no date, BAB, DE 1/58747.

81. "Stenografische Niederschrift der Beratung des Vorsitzenden des Ministerrates der DDR, Genossen Willi Stoph, mit dem Vorsitzenden des Ministerrates der UdSSR, Genossen Alexej Kossygin, am Freitag, dem 8. Dezember 1978, in Moskau," BAB, DE 1/58666.

82. See Stone, Satellites and Commissars, 49–71.

83. FRUS, 1969–1976, vol. 31, doc. 125, 445.

84. "Stenografische Niederschrift der Beratung des Vorsitzenden des Ministerrates der DDR, Genossen Willi Stoph, mit dem Vorsitzenden des Ministerrates der UdSSR, Genossen Alexej Kossygin, am Freitag, dem 8. Dezember 1978, in Moskau," BAB, DE 1/58666.

85. Vladimir Matskevich, "O nekotorykh voprosakh ekonomicheskogo polozheniia ChSSR," November 3, 1975, RGANI, f. 5, op. 68, d. 1463.

86. André Steiner, "The Decline of Soviet-Type Economies," in The Cambridge History of Communism, ed. Juliane Fürst, Silvio Pons, and Mark Selden (New York: Cambridge University Press, 2017), 3:204–6.

87. "Informatsiia o besede zamestitelia predsedatelia Soveta ministrov, predsedatelia Gosplana SSSR tov. N.K. Baibakov s predsedatelem VNR tov. Imre Padri," January 7, 1971, RGAE, f. 4372, op. 66, d. 4448.

88. See Suvi Kansikas, Socialist Countries Face the European Community: Soviet-Bloc Controversies over East-West Trade (Frankfurt: Peter Lang, 2014).

89. "Stenograma ot razgovorite mezhdu drugaria Todor Zhivkov i drugaria Nikolae Chaushesku, sustoiali se v Durzhavniia suvet na Sotsialisticheska Republika Rumuniia," July 19, 1975, TsDA, f. 378B, op. 1, a.e. 696.

90. Morgan, Final Act, 160–61.

91. "Zapis' besedy: Ministra vneshnei torgovli tov. Patolicheva N.S. s ministrom ekonomiki FRG g-nom Kh. Friderikhs," March 30, 1976, RGAE, f. 413, op. 31, d. 8237.

92. Horst Kaminsky, "Zur gegenwärtigen Entwicklung der kapitalistischen Währungskrise," July 16, 1974, BAB, DN 10/463.

93. Lawrence J. Brainard, "The Outlook for East-West Trade Credit," Euromoney, July 1975: 27.

94. Richard Ensor and Francis Ghiles, "CMEA Debts May Be $45 Billion, but the Loans Have Kept Flowing," Euromoney (January 1977): 23.

95. Quek Peck Lim, "Comecon Debt: A Hectic Year of Borrowing," Euromoney (January 1978): 17.

96. *FRUS*, 1969–1976, vol. 31, doc. 149, 568.

97. *FRUS*, 1969–1976, vol. 31, doc. 149, 574.

98. *FRUS*, 1969–1976, vol. 31, doc. 149, 569–71.

99. Staatsbank (DDR), "Ergebnisse der durch die DABA mit NSW-Geschäftsbanken geführten Gespräche während der LHM 1976 (Zusammenfassung)," September 9, 1976, BAB, DN 10/447.

100. Deutsche Außenhandelsbank, "Vermerk," March 18, 1976, BAB, DN 10/447.

101. Deutsche Außenhandelsbank, "Bericht über die Dienstreise des Vizepräsidenten der Deutschen Außenhandelsbank, Genossen Dr. Polze, und des Leiters des Sektors Internationale Bankbeziehungen, Genossen Oehme, nach den USA in der Zeit vom 18.9. bis 4.10.1976," October 12, 1976, BAB, DC 20/17156.

102. Richard F. Janssen, "Soviet Bloc Borrowings from the West Surge, Amid Mystery and Fears," *Wall Street Journal*, February 22, 1977.

103. Yuri Balagurov, "Spravka ob ekonomicheskom i valiutno-finansovom polozhenii Vengerskoi narodnoi respubliki za 1975 god," August 3, 1976, RGANI, f. 5, op. 69, d. 1758. Balagurov used this term to describe Hungary.

104. Calculated from Angus Maddison, *World Economy*, vol. 1, *A Millennial Perspective* (Paris: OECD, 2006), 236.

105. Iu.S. Shiriaev, "Nekotorye voprosy ekonomicheskogo razvitiia ChSSR v usloviiakh rosta tsen na vneshnikh rynkakh," July 4, 1975, RGANI, f. 5, op. 68, d. 1463.

106. Günter Ehrensperger to Werner Krolikowski, "Material zu Fragen der Zahlungsbilanz im NSW," September 23, 1975, SAPMO, DY 30/25762.

107. "Redekonzeption Gen. Schürer, 2.6.77," June 2, 1977, BAB, DE 1/58632.

108. "Niederschrift über eine Beratung zum Entwurf des Fünfjahrplanes 1976–1980 unter Leitung des Generalsekretärs des ZK der SED, Genossen Erich Honecker, am 5.11.1976," November 5, 1976, BAB, DE 1/58633.

109. Ralf Ahrens, "Debt, Cooperation, and Collapse: East German Foreign Trade in the Honecker Years," in *The East German Economy, 1945–2010: Falling Behind or Catching Up?*, ed. Harmut Berghoff and Uta Andrea Balbier (Washington, DC: German Historical Institute; and New York: Cambridge University Press, 2013), 169.

110. M. Usmevich, "O nekotorykh aktual'nykh problemakh razvitiia ekonomiki VNR (spravka)," October 21, 1975, RGANI, f. 5, op. 68, d. 1491.

111. Stephen Kotkin, "The Kiss of Debt: The East Bloc Goes Borrowing," in *The Shock of the Global: The 1970s in Perspective*, ed. Niall Ferguson, Charles S. Maier, Erez Manela, and Daniel J. Sargent (Cambridge, MA: Harvard University Press, 2010), 89.

112. A. Godakov, "Memorandum o besedakh i.o. zamestitelia UTSAm tov. Mel'nikova A.V. s sotrudnikami pol'skikh vneshnetorgovykh organizatsii," August 7, 1974, RGAE, f. 413, op. 31, d. 6660.

113. Harold James, *International Monetary Cooperation since Bretton Woods* (New York: Oxford University Press, 1996), 564.

114. V. Svirin, "O nastroeniiakh v aktive v sviazi s gotoviashchimsia povysheniem tsen na prodovol'stvennye tovary," April 27, 1976, RGANI, f. 5, op. 69, d. 2336.

115. Kotkin, "Kiss of Debt," 85.

116. IMF, *International Financial Statistics: Yearbook*, 1981 (Washington, DC), 79.

117. "Zu Kaffee und Kakao (Beratung am 2.6.1977)," June 2, 1977, BAB, DE 1/58632.

118. André Steiner, *The Plans that Failed: An Economic History of the GDR*, trans. Ewald Osers (New York: Berghahn Books, 2010), 159. On the coffee crisis, see Anne Dietrich, "Kaffee in der DDR–'Ein Politikum ersten Ranges,'" in *Kaffeewelten: Historische Perspektiven auf eine Globale Ware im 20. Jahrhundert*, ed. Christiane Berth, Dorothee Wierling, and Volker Wünderich (Göttingen: V&R Unipress, 2015), 225–47.

119. "Zapis' besedy: Predsedatelia Gosplana SSSR tov. N.K. Baibakova s zamestitelem predsedatelia Soveta Ministrov NRB tov. A. Lukanovym," February 10, 1977, RGAE, f. 4372, op. 67, d. 819.

120. "Niederschrift über die Verhandlungen zwischen dem Vorsitzenden des Ministerrates der DDR, Genossen Willi Stoph, und dem Vorsitzenden des Ministerrates der UdSSR, Genossen A.N. Kossygin, am 10.12.1976 in Moskau," December 13, 1976, SAPMO, DY 3023/1529.

121. "Niederschrift über die Verhandlungen zwischen dem Vorsitzenden des Ministerrates der DDR, Genossen Willi Stoph, und dem Vorsitzenden des Ministerrates der UdSSR, Genossen A.N. Kossygin, am 10.12.1976 in Moskau."

5. The Travails of Jimmy Carter

1. *FRUS*, 1977–1980, vol. 3, doc. 73, 237–38.

2. W. Michael Blumenthal, *From Exile to Washington: A Memoir of Leadership in the Twentieth Century* (New York: Overlook, 2013), 295.

3. James T. Patterson, *Restless Giant: The United States from Watergate to Bush v. Gore* (New York: Oxford University Press, 2005), 111–12.

4. BIS, *Annual Report*, 1977, 31, 46.

5. W. Carl Biven, *Jimmy Carter's Economy: Economic Policy in an Age of Limits* (Chapel Hill: University of North Carolina Press, 2002), 61–74, 221–22.

6. Jimmy Carter, "Address to the Nation on Energy," April 18, 1977, APP.

7. Meg Jacobs, *Panic at the Pump: The Energy Crisis and the Transformation of American Politics in the 1970s* (New York: Hill & Wang, 2016), 173.

8. "Remarks of James R. Schlesinger before the Chamber of Commerce of the United States of America," June 24, 1977, folder "[Energy][2]," box 25, Charles L. Schultze's Subject Files, Records of the Council of Economic Advisers, JCPL.

9. Zbigniew Brzezinski to Jimmy Carter, "Weekly National Security Report #5," March 18, 1977, folder "Weekly Reports (to the President) 1–15 (2/77–6/77)," box 41, ZBSF, ZBC, JCPL.

10. Jimmy Carter, *White House Diary* (New York: Farrar, Straus and Giroux, 2010), 110.

11. DeGolyer and MacNaughton, *Twenty-First Century Petroleum Statistics* (Dallas, TX), 29, 43.

12. Zbigniew Brzezinski, Richard Gardner, and Henry Owen to Jimmy Carter, "Foreign Policy Priorities for the First Six Months," November 3, 1976, folder 19, box 9, Series II, Cyrus Vance Papers, MS 1664, SML. On world order politics, see Daniel J. Sargent, *A Superpower Transformed: The Remaking of American Foreign Relations in the 1970s* (New York: Oxford University Press, 2015), 229–60.

13. *FRUS*, 1977–1980, vol. 1, doc. 40, 170–76.

14. "European Council: Note of the First Session at 1520," March 25, 1977, TNA, PREM 16/1254.

15. IMF, *Annual Report*, 1978, 5.

16. *FRUS*, 1977–1980, vol. 1, doc. 49, 211–13.

17. *AAPD*, 1978, doc. 14, 82–83.

18. BMWi-V B 3, "Vermerk: Vorbereitung des Wirtschaftsgipfels III," March 14, 1977, BAK, B 136/11580.

19. C. Fred Bergsten to W. Michael Blumenthal, "The Vice President's Trip," February 2, 1977, folder "BP-4-1 Briefing Memos-WBlumenthal 1977," box 1, C. Fred Bergsten Records, RG 56, NARA.

20. Biven, *Jimmy Carter's Economy*, 102.

21. *FRUS*, 1977–1980, vol. 3, doc. 26, 79.

22. Zbigniew Brzezinski to Jimmy Carter, "Weekly National Security Report #4," March 11, 1977, folder "Weekly Reports (to the President) 1–15 (2/77–6/77)," box 41, ZBSF, ZBC, JCPL.

23. Zbigniew Brzezinski to Jimmy Carter, "Weekly National Security Report #16," June 10, 1977, folder "Weekly Reports (to the President) 16–30 (6/77–9/77)," box 41, ZBSF, ZBC, JCPL.

24. *FRUS*, 1977–1980, vol. 3, doc. 21, 59–60.

25. *FRUS*, doc. 27, 90.

26. *FRUS*, doc. 27, 85.

27. *FRUS*, doc. 35, 131.

28. *FRUS*, doc. 35, 131.

29. *FRUS*, doc. 44, 157–58.

30. C. Fred Bergsten to W. Michael Blumenthal, "Japanese Sub-Cabinet Meeting," August 31, 1977, folder "Meetings (MTG'S)," box 1, C. Fred Bergsten Records, RG 56, NARA.

31. Zbigniew Brzezinski to Jimmy Carter, "Trade Issues in our Relations with Japan," n.d. (likely November 1977), folder "Japan, 9–12/77," box 40, ZBM-Country Files (NSA 6), JCPL.

32. IMF, *International Financial Statistics: Yearbook 1991*, 387, 463.

33. IMF, 753–55.

34. BIS, *Annual Report*, 1978, 112.

35. Jimmy Carter, "United States Balance of Trade and Payments Statement Announcing Measures to Improve the U.S. Trade Position," December 21, 1977, APP.

36. BIS, *Annual Report*, 1978, 112.

37. *FRUS*, 1977–1980, vol. 3, doc. 98, 309–14.

38. BIS, *Annual Report*, 1978, 112.

39. *FRUS*, 1977–1980, vol. 3, doc. 108, 331.

40. *FRUS*, doc. 117, 348–49.

41. Gordon Richardson to James Callaghan, February 3, 1978, TNA, PREM 16/1604.

42. Anthony Solomon to W. Michael Blumenthal, "Draft: Memorandum for the President: Consequences of a Dollar Crisis," March 14, 1978, folder "TL Chron March–Apr. 1978," box 6, Chronological Files of Thomas Leddy, RG 56, NARA.

43. World Bank, World Development Indicators.

44. BMF-VII A 3, "Sitzung des Interim-Ausschusses und der Zehnergruppe am 29./30.4.1978 in Mexiko City," May 8, 1978, BAK, B 136/9307.

45. Sargent, *Superpower Transformed*, 245–47.

46. *FRUS*, 1977–1980, vol. 3, doc. 103, 325.

47. Hans Werner Lautenschlager, "Deutsch-amerikanische Divergenzen im Wirtschafts- und Währungsbereich," January 20, 1978, PA-AA, B 32 (ZA), Bd. 115944.

48. "Note for the Record: Prime Minister's Meeting with Chancellor Schmidt at the Bundeskanzlei, Bonn, on Sunday, 12 March 1978," TNA, PREM 16/1656.

49. BMWi-III D 1, "Weltwirtschaftsgipfel 1978; Energie," March 16, 1978, BAK, B 136/11583.

50. Klaus von Dohnanyi, "Gespräch mit Henry Owen, Beauftragter des amerikanischen Präsidenten für die Vorbereitung des Weltwirtschaftsgipfels, am 2. April 1978," April 3, 1978, BAK, B 136/11583.

51. Treasury brief, "Economic Summit, Bonn, 16–17 July 1978: Growth, Employment and Inflation," July 11, 1978, TNA, FCO 59/1550.

52. "Note for the Record: Prime Minister's Meeting with Chancellor Schmidt at Chequers on Sunday 23 April 1978 at 1945," TNA, PREM 16/1655.

53. Kristina Spohr, *The Global Chancellor: Helmut Schmidt & the Reshaping of the International Order* (New York: Oxford University Press, 2016), 28.

54. BK-42 (Heick), "Vermerk für die Kabinettsitzung am 19. Juli 1978," July 18, 1978, BAK, B 136/8487.

55. *ERP*, 1979, 142.

56. *FRUS*, 1977–1980, vol. 3, doc. 149, 477.

57. *AAPD*, 1978, doc. 32, 194.

58. Helmut Schmidt, *Men and Powers: A Political Retrospective*, trans. Ruth Hein (New York: Random House, 1989).

59. Carter, *White House Diary*, 337.

60. Zbigniew Brzezinski, *Power and Principle: Memoirs of the National Security Adviser, 1977–1981* (New York: Farrar, Straus and Giroux, 1985), 292.

61. MF, "Informatieve nota inzake huidige monetaire ontwikkelingen in de EEG t.b.v. de Europese Raad d.d. 7 en 8 april 1978 te Kopenhagen," NL-HaNA, 2.06.107, inv.nr. 2928.

62. Anton W. DePorte to Anthony Lake, "What Is Changing In Europe?," June 15, 1978, folder "TL 7/1–7/15/78," box 4, Records of Anthony Lake, RG 59, NARA; BIS, *Annual Report*, 1979, 47.

63. Emmanuel Mourlon-Druol, *A Europe Made of Money: The Emergence of the European Monetary System* (Ithaca, NY: Cornell University Press, 2012), 157.

64. K. R. Stowe, "Note for the Record: Proposals for a European Currency Reserve," April 11, 1978, TNA, PREM 16/1615.

65. BK-41 (Thiele), "Ihre Vermerke für den Bonner Wirtschaftsgipfel, bzw. den Carter-Besuch," July 11, 1978, BAK, B 136/11586.

66. Frits Kupers, "Europese Monetaire Samenwerking (EMS)," October 30, 1978, NL-HaNA, 2.06.107, inv.nr. 2929.

67. BMF-VII A 4, "Leitlinien zur Ausarbeitung des Europäischen Währungssystems," July 21, 1978, BAK, B 126/70439.

68. "Nota inzake het Europees Monetair Stelsel," October 5, 1978, NL-HaNA, 2.06.107, inv.nr. 2928.

69. M. J. Mitchell, "The Proposals for a European Monetary System, November 13, 1978, TNA, T 382/71.

70. A.C.S. Allan, "Lead in the Balloon," July 27, 1978, TNA, T 385/256.

71. Finance Council, "EMS-Monetary Aspects," November 20, 1978, TNA, T 382/71.

72. National Bank of Belgium, "Combination of the Parity Grid and the Indicator of Divergence: Implications of the 'Belgian Compromise,'" October 23, 1978, BAK, B 126/70441.

73. Michael Emerson, "The United Kingdom and the European Monetary System," June 1979, BAK, B 126/88637.

74. BMF, "Das Europäische Währungssystem," November 8, 1978, BAK, B 126 /70442.

75. American officials voiced their support for the EMS publicly but expressed concern privately. Solomon worried that the EMS would "revert to the approach of the Bretton Woods system" and put the United States "back in the strait jacket of the Bretton Woods system where other countries controlled the competitive position of American producers, and thus American jobs." Anthony M. Solomon to Henry Owen, "European Monetary Arrangements," n.d., folder "TL Chron July–August 1978," box 6, Thomas Leddy Files, RG 56, NARA.

76. BIS, *Annual Report*, 1979, 136.

77. *FRUS*, 1977–1980, vol. 3, doc. 155, 491–92.

78. Hobart Rowan, "The Dollar's Slide: What It Means," *Washington Post*, August 20, 1978.

79. Odeh Aburdene, "1 Petrodollar=72 cents," *Euromoney* (May 1978): 36.

80. F. Lisle Widman to Anthony Solomon, "Oil Prices and the Dollar," August 18, 1978, folder "Briefing for Appearance by Deputy Assistant Secretary Widman," box 5, Briefing Books, 1971–1980, Office of the Deputy Assistant Secretary for International Monetary Affairs, RG 56, NARA.

81. Iu.V. Balod, "Memorandum," August 31, 1978, RGAE, f. 413, op. 31, d. 9428.

82. *ERP*, 1978, 154.

83. "Charles Schultze Oral History," January 8–9, 1982, Jimmy Carter Oral History Project, Miller Center, University of Virginia.

84. Quoted in William L. Silber, *Volcker: The Triumph of Persistence* (New York: Bloomsbury, 2012), 139.

85. W. S. Ryrie to Ken Couzens, November 3, 1978, TNA, T 382/93.

86. *ERP*, 1979, 155.

87. Peter Jay to FCO, "U.S. Economic Policy," November 3, 1978, TNA, T 382/93.

88. *ERP*, 1979, 156.

89. Eric Helleiner, *States and the Reemergence of Global Finance: From Bretton Woods to the 1990s* (Ithaca, NY: Cornell University Press, 1994), 132.

90. Sargent, *Superpower Transformed*, 275–76.

91. "Minutes of the Cabinet Meeting," November 20, 1978, folder "Cabinet Meeting Minutes, '77–'78 [1]," box 8, Charles L. Schultze's Subject Files, Records of the Council of Economic Advisers, JCPL.

92. Robert J. Samuelson, "Future Mortgaged to Defend the Dollar," *Washington Post*, November 14, 1978.

93. Sargent, *Superpower Transformed*, 276–77.

94. Harold Lever, "Background to the Dollar Problem and the Remedy," November 17, 1978, TNA, T 382/93.

95. IMF, *Annual Report*, 1985, 54.

96. Otmar Emminger, "The Exchange Rate as an Instrument of Policy," December 7, 1978, TNA, T 382/93.

97. IMF, *Annual Report*, 1985, 54.

98. Peter Jay to FCO, "U.S. Economic Policy," November 3, 1978, TNA, T 382/93. He predicted that the dollar would surge "probably not later than next summer," so he got the timing wrong but not the substance.

99. David M. Wight, *Oil Money: Middle East Petrodollars and the Transformation of US Empire, 1967–1988* (Ithaca, NY: Cornell University Press, 2021), 183–90.

100. AA-405, "OPEC-Ölpreis," November 16, 1978, BAK, B 136/17947; Giuliano Garavini, *The Rise and Fall of OPEC in the Twentieth Century* (New York: Oxford University Press, 2019), 268–69.

101. *ERP*, 1980, 156.

102. Daniel Yergin, *The Prize: The Epic Quest for Oil, Money, and Power*, 3rd ed. (New York: Free Press, 2009), 660–62.

103. Department of Energy, "Reduction in Oil Supplies since the Iranian Revolution: Lessons for the West," December 29, 1980, TNA, FCO 8/3762.

104. Sargent, *Superpower Transformed*, 277–78.

105. CIA paper, no title, June 15, 1979, folder "Economic Summit Background Papers Book III, 6/28–29/79," box 23, ZBM-Trip Files (NSA 4), JCPL.

106. Calculated from *BP Statistical Review of World Energy 2022*.

107. Planning Staff (FCO), "The End of the Rainbow: Offshore Oil and British Foreign Policy," December 1974, TNA, FCO 49/509.

108. *BP Statistical Review of World Energy 2022*.

109. Jimmy Carter, "Energy Address to the Nation," April 5, 1979, APP.

110. *ERP*, 1980, 108.

111. DeGolyer and MacNaughton, *Twenty-First Century Petroleum Statistics*, 29.

112. Alan Richman, "Gas Lines Touch Off Arguments; Price Hits a Record in Manhattan," *New York Times*, May 26, 1979.

113. Fred Ferretti, "Pump's-Eye View of Gas-Hungry Drivers," *New York Times*, June 26, 1979.

114. Jacobs, *Panic at the Pump*, 207.

115. "Gas Lines Grow in US," *Boston Globe*, May 21, 1979.

116. "Brief Notes on the Friday Afternoon Energy Meeting," March 23, 1979, folder "Oil Pricing [2]," box 62, Charles L. Schultze's Subject Files, Records of the Council of Economic Advisers, JCPL.

117. "Letters to the Editor," *Washington Post*, June 25, 1979.

118. Karin Lissakers to Cyrus R. Vance, "Suggestions for an International Oil Policy," June 5, 1979, folder "TL 6/1–15/79," box 5, Records of Anthony Lake, 1977–1981, RG 59, NARA.

119. BMWi-V (Steeg), "Vermerk über das Gespräch zwischen BM Graf Lambsdorff und dem saudischen Finanzminister Abalkhail beim Mittagessen am 1.2.1979," February 1, 1979, BAK, B 102/281038.

120. "Note of a Discussion over Dinner at Chequers on Saturday, 16 June 1979," TNA, PREM 19/42.

121. *FRUS*, 1969–1976, vol. 37, doc. 200, 631.

122. Carter, *White House Diary*, 335–36.

123. Hobart Rowen and Edward Walsh, "Tokyo Summit Adopts Joint Oil Import Cuts," *Washington Post*, June 30, 1979.

124. BIS, *Annual Report*, 1980, 83.

125. Jimmy Carter, "Address to the Nation on Energy and National Goals," July 15, 1979, APP.

126. Carter.

127. Jacobs, *Panic at the Pump*, 231.

128. Quoted in Denis Healey, *The Time of My Life* (London: Michael Joseph, 1989), 436–37.

129. William J. Eaton, "Volcker Stands Tall in Economic Circles," *Los Angeles Times*, July 26, 1979.

130. Kai Bird, *The Outlier: The Unfinished Presidency of Jimmy Carter* (New York: Crown, 2021), 437–38.

131. Committee on Banking, Housing, and Urban Affairs, U.S. Senate, 96th Cong., 1st Sess., "Nomination of Paul A. Volcker," July 30, 1979 (Washington, DC: U.S. Government Printing Office, 1979), 5–6.

132. Paul A. Volcker to Jacob Javits, December 6, 1979, folder "Dec. 1979," box 9, Paul A. Volcker Papers, SGML.

133. Fritz Bartel, *The Triumph of Broken Promises: The End of the Cold War and the Rise of Neoliberalism* (Cambridge, MA: Harvard University Press, 2022), 70–72.

134. Greta R. Krippner, *Capitalizing on Crisis: The Political Origins of the Rise of Finance* (Cambridge, MA: Harvard University Press, 2011), 118.

135. *ERP*, 1982, 311.

136. Biven, *Jimmy Carter's Economy*, 8–9.

137. OMB Historical Tables, Tables 1.1 and 1.2, www.whitehouse.gov/omb/budget/historical-tables/.

138. Zbigniew Brzezinski to Jimmy Carter, "Weekly National Security Report #81," December 2, 1978, folder "Weekly Reports (to the President) 82–90 (12/78–3/79)," box 42, ZBSF, ZBC, JCPL.

139. Jimmy Carter, *Keeping Faith: Memoirs of a President* (New York: Bantam Books, 1982), 472–73.

140. *FRUS*, 1977–1980, vol. 1, doc. 138, 695.

141. Melvyn P. Leffler, *For the Soul of Mankind: The United States, the Soviet Union, and the Cold War* (New York: Hill and Wang, 2007), 335.

142. *ERP*, 1981, 157.

143. Victor McFarland, *Oil Powers: A History of the U.S.-Saudi Alliance* (New York: Columbia University Press, 2020), 227–31.

144. Department of Defense, *Annual Report: Fiscal Year 1981*, vii.

145. William E. Odom to Zbigniew Brzezinski, "East West-Relations: A Formula for U.S. Policy in 1981 and Beyond," September 3, 1980, folder "Weekly Reports (to the President) 136–150 (4/80–8/80)," box 42, ZBSF, ZBC, JCPL.

146. Department of Defense, *Annual Report: Fiscal Year 1981*, 3.

147. *FRUS*, 1969–1976, vol. 37, doc. 271, 852.

148. Patterson, *Restless Giant*, 148.

149. *ERP*, 1981, 37.

150. BIS, *Annual Report*, 1981, 28.

151. Caroline Atkinson, "Recession Hits Hard as Carter Seeks Remedies," *Washington Post*, August 31, 1980.

152. Carter, *White House Diary*, 468.

153. *ERP*, 1981, 7.

154. Adam Clymer, "Reagan and Carter Stand Nearly Even in Last Polls," *New York Times*, November 3, 1980.

155. *ERP*, 1981, 5.

156. BMF-VII A 3 (Saupe), "Konjunkturbericht für Januar 1981," January 13, 1980, BAK, B 126/119554.

157. Bird, *Outlier*, 439.

6. The Soviet Umbrella and the Volcker Shock

1. Andrzej Paczkowski and Malcom Byrne, eds., *From Solidarity to Martial Law: The Polish Crisis of 1980–1981* (Budapest: Central European University Press, 2007), 129–30.

2. Paczkowski and Byrne.

3. "The Next Poland?," *Euromoney* (August 1981): 7.

4. Sarah Martin, "The Secrets of the Polish Memorandum," *Euromoney* (August 1981): 14.

5. "Zapis' besedy: Zamestitelia predsedatelia Soveta ministrov SSSR, predsedatelia Gosplana SSSR Baibakova N.K. s poslom Iaponii v Moskve Tokichiro Yomoto," December 23, 1978, RGAE, f. 4372, op. 67, d. 1512.

6. "Summary of the President's Luncheon Meeting with Chancellor Helmut Schmidt of the Federal Republic of Germany," January 5, 1982, folder "Memorandums of Conversation—President Reagan (January 1982)," box 49, NSC Executive Secretariat Subject File, RRPL.

7. USIA paper, "Visit of FRG Chancellor Schmidt," February 28, 1980, folder "Germany, Chancellor Schmidt, 3/4–6/80: Briefing Book [II]," box 5, ZBM-VIP Visit Files (NSA 5), JCPL.

8. Vladislav Zubok, "Soviet Foreign Policy from Détente to Gorbachev, 1975–1985," in *The Cambridge History of the Cold War*, ed. Melvyn P. Leffler and Odd Arne Westad (New York: Cambridge University Press, 2010), 3:89.

9. "Informatsiia za streshtata v Krim na generalniia sekretar na TsK na BKP i predsedatel na Durzhavniia suvet na NRB Todor Zhivkov s generalniia sekretar na TsK na KPSS i predsedatel na Prezidiuma na Vurkhovniia suvet na SSSR Leonid Brezhnev," August 7, 1981, TsDA, f. 1B, op. 67, a.e. 405.

10. Melvyn P. Leffler, *For the Soul of Mankind: The United States, the Soviet Union, and the Cold War* (New York: Hill and Wang, 2007), 254.

11. See Odd Arne Westad, *The Global Cold War: Third World Interventions and the Making of Our Times* (New York: Cambridge University Press, 2007), 299–326.

12. Diary entry on November 1, 1980, Diary of Anatoly S. Chernyaev, 1980, NSAVRR.

13. See Artemy M. Kalinovsky, *A Long Goodbye: The Soviet Withdrawal from Afghanistan* (Cambridge, MA: Harvard University Press, 2011).

14. "Sreshta na drugite Leonid Ilich Brezhnev i Todor Zhivkov," August 7, 1980, TsDA, f. 1B, op. 66, a.e. 2507.

15. Jonathan Haslam, *Russia's Cold War: From the October Revolution to the Fall of the Wall* (New Haven, CT: Yale University Press, 2011), 313.

16. Quoted in David Holloway, *The Soviet Union and the Arms Race* (New Haven, CT: Yale University Press, 1983), 93–94.

17. Gerhard Schürer, "Information über ein Gespräch zwischen Genossen Tichonow und Genossen Schürer," March 21, 1979, BAB, DE 1/58658.

18. "Übersicht über die Preisentwicklung für Erdöl ab 1972," no date, BAB, DE 1/58747.

19. "Sreshta na drugite Leonid Ilich Brezhnev i Todor Zhivkov," August 7, 1980, TsDA, f. 1B, op. 66, a.e. 2507.

20. "Niederschrift über ein Gespräch mit dem Minister für Außenhandel der UdSSR, Genossen Patolitschew, am 6.6.1979," June 6, 1979, SAPMO, DY 30/IV 2/2 .2035/56.

21. "Informatsiia za streshtata v Krim na generalniia sekretar na TsK na BKP i predsedatel na Durzhavniia suvet na NRB Todor Zhivkov s generalniia sekretar na TsK na KPSS i predsedatel na Prezidiuma na Vurkhovniia suvet na SSSR Leonid Brezhnev," August 7, 1981, TsDA, f. 1B, op. 67, a.e. 405.

22. Paczkowski and Byrne, *From Solidarity to Martial Law*, 235.

23. A. G. Voronin to V. A. Peshkev, "Zadolzhennosti sotsialisticheskikh stran sovetskim bankam za granitsei," March 2, 1982, RGAE, f. 2324, op. 33, d. 403.

24. "Zapis' besedy: Predsedatelia Gosplana SSSR tov. N.K. Baibakova s zamestitelem predsedatelia Soveta ministrov NRB tov. A. Lukanovym," February 10, 1977, RGAE, f. 4372, op. 67, d. 819.

25. Todor Zhivkov to Leonid Brezhnev, April 12, 1978, TsDA, f. 1B, op. 66, a.e. 1176.

26. "Informatsiia za priiatelskata sreshta mezhdu drugarite Todor Zhivkov i Leonid Brezhnev, sustoiala se na 14 avgust 1978 god. v Krim," August 14, 1978, TsDA, f. 378B, op. 1, a.e. 742.

27. Znepolski et al., *Bulgaria under Communism* (London: Routledge, 2019), 270–71.

28. Diary entry on November 1, 1980, Diary of Anatoly S. Chernyaev, 1980, NSAVRR.

29. Martin Malia, *The Soviet Tragedy: A History of Socialism in Russia, 1917–1991* (New York: Free Press, 1994), 368.

30. Donald J. Raleigh, *Soviet Baby Boomers: An Oral History of Russia's Cold War Generation* (New York: Oxford University Press, 2012), 224–29.

31. Directorate of Intelligence, "Soviet Agriculture: Reviewing a Core Program," February 1983, CIAERR.

32. Yegor Gaidar, *Collapse of an Empire: Lessons for Modern Russia*, trans. Antonina W. Bouis (Washington, DC: Brookings Institution Press, 2007), 98.

33. Jimmy Carter, *White House Diary* (New York: Farrar, Straus and Giroux, 2010), 387–88.

34. Mikhail Gorbachev, *Memoirs* (New York: Bantam Books, 1997), 148.

35. Cited in Philip Hanson, *The Rise and Fall of the Soviet Economy: An Economic History of the Soviet Union from 1945* (London: Longman, 2003), 163.

36. Georgii Arbatov, *The System: An Insider's Life in Soviet Politics* (New York: Random House, 1992), 216.

37. Gaidar, *Collapse of an Empire*, 103.

38. Karl Grünheid, "Notizen über Ausführungen des Genossen Worow, Abteilungsleiter im Gosplan der UdSSR, zu Fragen der Entwicklung der Produktion und Lieferungen der UdSSR an Erdöl und Erdgas," August 1, 1977, SAPMO, DY 3023 / 1529.

39. "Sreshta na Politbiuro na TsK na BPK s drugaria Nikolai Tikhonov—chlen na Politbiuro na TsK na KPSS i predsedatel na Ministerskiia suvet na Suvetskiia suiuz," July 5, 1981, TsDA, f. 1B, op. 60, a.e. 281.

40. "Information über die Beratung mit Genossen Kossygin in Moskau am 8. Dezember," BAB, DE 1 / 58666.

41. Leffler, *For the Soul of Mankind*, 334.

42. "Zapis' besedy: Predsedatelia Gosplana SSSR tov. Baibakova N.K. s gossekratarem po ugliu i ugleprovodam narodnoi respubliki Mozambik t. A.M. Osmanom," November 11, 1980, RGAE, f. 4372, op. 67, d. 2810.

43. "Ausführungen des Genossen Erich Honecker auf der Beratung des Politbüros am 15.8.1978 zur Planerfüllung," BAB, DE 1 / 58647.

44. Günter Mittag, *Um jeden Preis: Im Spannungsfeld zweier Systeme* (Berlin: Das Neue Berlin, 2015), 79.

45. Horst Kaminsky, "Konzeption für Maßnahmen der Banken zur Beschaffung von Bankkrediten in konvertierbaren Devisen im Jahre 1981," December 10, 1980, BAB, DN 10 / 3067.

46. Werner Polze, "Information für Genossen Dr. Mittag," December 4, 1978, BAB, DN 10 / 447.

47. "Konzeption zum Abbau der Höhe der Verbindlichkeiten der DDR gegenüber dem nichtsozialistischen Wirtschaftsgebiet vom 27.6.1980," n.d., BAB, DE 1 / 58746, Bd. 1.

48. "Sreshta na Politbiuro na TsK na BKP s drugaria Nikolai Tikhonov—chlen na Politbiuro na TsK na KPSS i predsedatel na Ministerskiia suvet na Suvetskiua suiuz," July 5, 1981, TsDA, f. 1B, op. 60, a.e. 281.

49. Gosbank, "Spravka o sostoianii vneshnei zadolzhennosti Vengerskoi narodnoi respubliki," November 13, 1982, RGAE, f. 2324, op. 33, d. 441.

50. PlanEcon, *Soviet and East European Energy Databank* (Washington, DC: PlanEcon, 1986), 1:R-7.

51. Cornel Ban, "Sovereign Debt, Austerity, and Regime Change: The Case of Nicolae Ceausescu's Romania," *East European Politics and Societies* 26, no. 4 (2012): 758.

52. Matthew J. Ouimet, *The Rise and Fall of the Brezhnev Doctrine* (Chapel Hill: University of North Carolina Press, 2003), 111.

53. Timothy Garton Ash, *The Polish Revolution: Solidarity 1980–82* (London: Jonathan Cape, 1983), 16, 26.

54. Tony Judt, *Postwar: A History of Europe since 1945* (New York: Penguin, 2005), 582.

55. Editorial, "The Truth about Poland," *Euromoney* (March 1980): 5.

56. Ash, *Polish Revolution*, 18 and 29.

57. Gregory F. Domber, *Empowering Revolution: America, Poland, and the End of the Cold War* (Chapel Hill: University of North Carolina Press, 2014), 12.

58. Paczkowski and Byrne, *From Solidarity to Martial Law*, 62.

59. Ash, *Polish Revolution*, 71–73.

60. Todor Zhivkov to Politburo BKP, October 14, 1980, TsDA, f. 1B, op. 66, a.e. 2617.

61. Paczkowski and Byrne, *From Solidarity to Martial Law*, 243.

62. Paczkowski and Byrne, 125.

63. "Speech by Stanislaw Kania at Meeting of Party and State Leaders of the Warsaw Pact," December 5, 1980, History and Public Policy Program Digital Archive, ANIC, Central Committee of the Romanian Communist Party, chancellery, no. 5257, 9.12.1980. CWIHP Document Reader, vol. 2, "Romania and the Warsaw Pact, 1955–1989," http://digitalarchive.wilsoncenter.org/document/112068.

64. "Niederschrift über ein Gespräch des Genossen W. Jaruzelski mit Genossen G. Schürer am 26.2.1981," February 26, 1981, BAB, DE 1/58682.

65. On the delicate negotiations, see Fritz Bartel, "Fugitive Leverage: Commercial Banks, Sovereign Debt, and Cold War Crisis in Poland, 1980–1982," *Enterprise & Society* 18, no. 1 (2017): 72–107.

66. Ann Crittenden, "Polish Debt Enmeshes the West," *New York Times*, May 21, 1981.

67. Treasury paper, "Eastern European Indebtedness," December 17, 1981, TNA, FCO 28/4399.

68. Robert Armstrong to Margaret Thatcher, "Poland: Economic Assistance," December 9, 1980, TNA, PREM 19/559.

69. Martin, "Secrets of the Polish Memorandum," 9–15.

70. A. E. Montgomery, "The Polish Crisis: Western Policy Options," February 11, 1981, TNA, FCO 28/4517.

71. "Zapis' besedy: Zamestitelia predsedatelia pravleniia Gosbanka SSSR tov. Peshkeva V.A. s direktorom-konsul'tantom issledovatel'skogo tsentra Kongressa SShA Zh.P. Khardtom," December 8, 1980, RGAE, f. 2324, op. 32, d. 1421.

72. Paczkowski and Byrne, *From Solidarity to Martial Law*, 234–35.

73. Paczkowski and Byrne, 127.

74. Paczkowski and Byrne, 132–33.

75. Todor Zhivkov to Leonid Brezhnev, November 6, 1980, TsDA, f. 378B, op. 1, a.e. 259.

76. Leonid Brezhnev to Todor Zhivkov, August 27, 1981, TsDA, f. 1B, op. 67, a.e. 452A.

77. Gerhard Schürer, "Information über das Gespräch mit Genossen Baibakow," September 16, 1981, BAB, DE 1/58682.

78. PlanEcon, *Soviet and East European Energy Databank*, 2:U-5.

79. Gerhard Schürer, "Information über das Gespräch mit Genossen Baibakow," September 16, 1981, BAB, DE 1/58682.

80. Quoted in Jeffrey Kopstein, *The Politics of Economic Decline in East Germany, 1945–1989* (Chapel Hill: University of North Carolina Press, 1997), 93–94.

81. "Niederschrift über das Gespräch des Generalsekretärs des ZK der SED, Genossen Erich Honecker, mit dem Sekretär des ZK der KPdSU, Genossen Konstantin Viktorowitsch Russakow, am 21. Oktober 1981," October 21, 1981, SAPMO, DY 30/2379.

82. Paczkowski and Byrne, *From Solidarity to Martial Law*, 398.

83. Kiril Zarev, Khristo Khristov, and Georgi Pankov to Todor Zhivkov, September 25, 1981, TsDA, f. 1B, op. 67, a.e. 452A. I thank Andro Mathewson for his assistance translating this document. Bulgaria exported about 74,000 bpd to the West and imported 287,000 bpd from the Soviet Union in 1981. PlanEcon, *Soviet and East European Energy Databank*, 2:B-5.

84. "Informatsiia za streshtata v Krim na generalniia sekretar na TsK na BKP i predsedatel na Durzhavniia suvet na NRB Todor Zhivkov s generalniia sekretar na TsK na KPSS i predsedatel na Prezidiuma na Vurkhovniia suvet na SSSR Leonid Brezhnev," August 7, 1981, TsDA, f. 1B, op. 67, a.e. 405.

85. Quoted in Ouimet, *Rise and Fall*, 225.

86. Quoted in Domber, *Empowering Revolution*, 15.

87. Todor Zhivkov to Leonid Brezhnev, November 30, 1981, TsDA, f. 1B, op. 67, a.e. 667.

88. Archie Brown, *The Rise and Fall of Communism* (New York: Ecco, 2009), 433.

89. Ouimet, *Rise and Fall*, 189–90.

90. Shaknazarov, *Tsena svobody: Reformatsiia Gorbacheva glazami ego pomoshchnika* (Moscow: Rossika, 1993), 114–15.

91. Paczkowski and Byrne, *From Solidarity to Martial Law*, 398.

92. Paczkowski and Byrne, 453.

93. See Ouimet, *Rise and Fall*.

94. US estimate cited in Konrad Seitz, "Situation der polnischen Wirtschaft zum Zeitpunkt der Machtübernahme des Militärs," December 15, 1981, PA-AA, B 9 (ZA), Bd. 178494.

95. Paczkowski and Byrne, *From Solidarity to Martial Law*, 450.

96. Shakhnazarov, *Tsena svobody*, 115.

97. Quoted in Ouimet, *Rise and Fall*, 200.

98. "Zapis' besedy: Predsedatelia pravleniia Gosbanka SSSR tov. Alkhimova V.S. s predsedatelem pravleniia Gosbanka GDR tov. Kaminski," August 30, 1982, RGAE, f. 2324, op. 32, d. 2042.

99. David Shirreff, "Hungary and the Shadow of 1985," *Euromoney* (March 1982): 132. On the debt crisis, see Fritz Bartel, *The Triumph of Broken Promises: The End of the Cold War and the Rise of Neoliberalism* (Cambridge, MA: Harvard University Press, 2022), 155–65.

100. "Spravka ob usloviiakh predostavleniia kapitalisticheskimi stranami pogashe-niia vneshnei zadolzhennosti riadu razvivaiushchikhsia gosudarstv i sotsialisticheskikh stran," attached to letter from O.N. Kulikov to V. A. Pekshev, September 9, 1983, RGAE, f. 2324, op. 33, d. 443.

101. Horst Kaminsky to Willi Stoph, April 8, 1982, SAPMO, DY 30/25765.

102. Sekretariat des Ministerrates, "Niederschrift über die Beratung am 3.6.1982 im Ministerrat zu den staatlichen Aufgaben des Volkswirtschaftsplanes, des Staatshaush-altsplanes sowie zur Kreditbilanz 1983," n.d., SAPMO, DY 30/25765.

103. William P. Clark to Richard E. Lyng, January 22, 1982, folder "Poland—Debt Rescheduling (2)," Remote Archives Capture Program (RAC) box 3, Paula J. Dobrian-sky Files, RRPL.

104. AA-421 (Marx), "Ost-West-Wirtschaftsbeziehungen," March 25, 1982, BAK, B 136/17819.

105. Treasury paper, "Eastern European Indebtedness," December 17, 1981, TNA, FCO 28/4399.

106. BMF-VII A 3 (Knetschke), "Gespräch mit Mr. Whittome, Direktor für Europa im IWF, am 19.11.1981 im BMF," November 20, 1981, BAK, B 136/22789.

107. David Shirreff, "Romania Tries the Bankers' Nerves," *Euromoney* (November 1981): 15.

108. "Zapis' besedy: V.S. Alkhimov, predsedatel' pravleniia Gosbanka SSSR i Aleks Ross, vitse-prezident i glava predstavitel'stva 'Benkers trast ko.' v Frankfurte," January 14, 1982, RGAE, f. 2324, op. 32, d. 2043.

109. Padraic Fallon and David Shirreff, "The Betrayal of East Europe," *Euromoney* (September 1982): 22.

110. Mittag, *Um jeden Preis*, 82.

111. Iván T. Berend, *Central and Eastern Europe, 1944–1993: Detour from the Periphery to the Periphery* (New York: Cambridge University Press, 1996), 231.

112. "Niederschrift über die Ausführungen des Staatssekretärs Genossen Greß in der Beratung des Vorsitzenden des Ministerrates mit den Ministern über die Durchführung der Außenwirtschaftsaufgaben am 20. 5. 1981," SAPMO, DY 30/25765.

113. "Zapis' besedy mezhdu predsedatelem pravleniia Gosbanka SSSR tov. Alkhimovym V.S. i predsedatelem Bolgarskogo narodnogo banka tov. V. Kolarovym," July 12, 1984, RGAE, f. 2324, op. 32, d. 2674.

114. BIS, *Annual Report*, 1990, 47.

115. Heinz Klopfer, "Persönliche Niederschrift über die Beratung im Politbüro des ZK der SED am 16.2.1982," February 16, 1982, BAB, DE 1/58654.

116. Keith Crane, *The Soviet Economic Dilemma of Eastern Europe* (Santa Monica, CA: RAND, 1986), 38–39.

117. Tamás Vonyó, "War and Socialism: Why Eastern Europe Fell Behind between 1950 and 1989," *Economic History Review* 70, no. 1 (2017): 259.

118. Horst Kaminsky to Willi Stoph, April 8, 1982, SAPMO, DY 30/25765.

119. Gerhard Schmitz, "Information zu Meinungen sowjetischer Genossen über die Frage der Verschuldung sozialistischer Länder in konvertierbaren Devisen," March 3, 1982, SAPMO, DY 30/25765.

120. "Zapis' besedy: Predsedatelia pravleniia Gosbanka SSSR tov. Alkhimova V.S. s predsedatelem pravleniia Gosbanka GDR tov. Kaminski," August 30, 1982, RGAE, f. 2324, op. 32, d. 2042.

121. "Excerpt from 'Can the Soviets 'Stand Down' Militarily?," June 1982, folder "East/West Economics (OECD) (4/5–8/11/82)," box 29, NSC Executive Secretariat Subject File, RRPL.

122. Hanson, *Rise and Fall*, 169–72.

123. Nikolai Ryzhkov, *Desiat' let velikikh potriasenii* (Moscow: Assotsiatsiiia "Kniga. Prosveshchenie. Miloserdie," 1995), 50.

124. John Kifner, "Rumania's Enforced Austerity," *New York Times*, December 26, 1983.

125. Csaba Békés, *Hungary's Cold War: International Relations from the End of World War II to the Fall of the Soviet Union* (Chapel Hill: University of North Carolina Press, 2022), 273.

126. László Borhi, *Dealing with Dictators: The United States, Hungary, and East Central Europe, 1942–1989*, trans. Jason Vincz (Bloomington: Indiana University Press, 2016), 329.

127. János Kádár to Erich Honecker, November 23, 1981, SAPMO, DY 30/IV 2/2.036/124.

128. BIS, *Annual Report*, 1983, 164–65.

129. "Record of a Discussion between the Prime Minister and the Deputy Prime Minister of Hungary at 1100 Hours on Tuesday 8 March 1983 at 10 Downing Street," TNA, T 439/161.

130. British Embassy Warsaw (James) to FCO, "Poland: Economic Situation and Prospects," July 8, 1982, TNA, T 439/199.

131. "Zapis' besedy: N.K. Baibakova s poslom PNR v Moskve St. Kocholekom," April 14, 1984, RGAE, f. 4372, op. 67, d. 5528.

132. Randall W. Stone, *Satellites and Commissars: Strategy and Conflict in the Politics of Soviet-Bloc Trade* (Princeton, NJ: Princeton University Press, 1998), 109–11.

133. Paczkowski and Byrne, *From Solidarity to Martial Law*, 505.

134. Robert Service, *The End of the Cold War, 1985–1991* (New York: PublicAffairs, 2015), 71.

135. BMWi-VII (Wesselkock), "Sitzung der G5 am 11. Mai 1982 in Helsinki," May 14, 1982, BAK, B 136/22789.

136. "National Security Council Meeting Minutes," August 28, 1984, folder "NSC00109 28 Aug 1984 (2/2)," box 91303, NSC Executive Secretariat Meeting Files, RRPL.

137. See Maximilian Graf, "Before Strauß: The East German Struggle to Avoid Bankruptcy during the Debt Crisis Revisited," *International History Review* 42, no. 4 (2020): 737–54.

138. Alexander Schalck-Golodkowski, *Deutsche-deutsche Erinnerungen* (Hamburg: Rowohlt Verlag, 2000), 202.

139. "Handschriftliche Aufzeichnung von Werner Krolikowski vom 16. Januar 1990," in *Tatort Politbüro: Die Akte Honecker*, ed. Peter Przybylski (Berlin: Rowohlt, 1991), 327.

140. On the *Milliardenkredite*, see Stephan Kieninger, "Freer Movement in Return for Cash: Franz Josef Strauß, Alexander Schalck-Golodkowski, and the *Milliardenkredit* for the GDR, 1983–1984," in *New Perspectives on the End of the Cold War: Unexpected Transformations?*, ed. Bernhard Blumenau, Jussi M. Hanhimäki, Barbara Zanchetta (London: Routledge, 2018), 117–37.

141. Mittag, *Um jeden Preis*, 83, 86.

142. "Memorandum of Conversation," March 5, 1984, folder "Memorandum of Conversation-President Reagan (03/27/1984–04/04/1984)," box 52, NSC Executive Secretariat Subject File, RRPL.

143. Quoted in Directorate of Intelligence, "The East German Question Revisited," September 25, 1984, folder "Germany, Democratic Republic of (3)," RAC box 2, Paula J. Dobriansky Files, RRPL.

144. "Niederschrift über das Treffen zwischen Genossen Erich Honecker und Genossen Konstantin Ustinowitsch Tschernenko am 17. August 1984," August 17, 1984, SAPMO, DY 30/2380.

145. Henry S. Terrell, "Implications of a Default by Poland," December 4, 1981, folder "International Finance Memoranda, 1981," box 24, Paul A. Volcker Papers, SGML.

7. Managing the Inversion

1. "Statement by Paul A. Volcker, Chairman, Board of Governors of the Federal Reserve System before the Subcommittee on Domestic Monetary Policy of the Com-

mittee on Banking, Finance and Urban Affairs, House of Representatives," February 26, 1985, included as an attachment to H. G. Walsh to P. Wynn Owen, February 28, 1985, MTFDA, PREM 19/1654.

2. "Statement by Paul A. Volcker."

3. Alan Walters, "Dollars and Deficits: A Personal View of the United States Economy at Election Time," September 1984, MTFDA, PREM 19/1654.

4. Beth A. Fischer contends that a "Reagan reversal" occurred toward the end of his first term when Reagan shifted from a confrontational stance to one seeking negotiation with the Soviet Union. Beth A. Fischer, *The Reagan Reversal: Foreign Policy and the End of the Cold War* (Columbia: University of Missouri Press, 1997).

5. World Bank, World Development Indicators. Polls referenced in Martin Feldstein, "American Economic Policy in the 1980s: A Personal View," in *American Economic Policy in the 1980s*, ed. Martin Feldstein (Chicago: University of Chicago Press, 1994), 4.

6. Letter to Ronald Reagan, February 6, 1981, folder "BE004–02 (Inflation) (009000–029999)," WHORM Subject File, RRPL.

7. Ronald Reagan, "Inaugural Address," January 20, 1981, APP.

8. Lewis James, "Reagan's Economic Guru," *Euromoney* (August 1980): 31. The new administration became fertile ground for monetarism as well, though supply-side economics often came into conflict with it. While the former advocated steady monetary growth to moderate inflation, the latter advocated sharp tax cuts and an easy monetary policy to stimulate the economy.

9. Jonathan Levy, *Ages of American Capitalism: A History of the United States* (New York: Random House, 2021), 610.

10. "Prime Minister's Telephone Conversation with Chancellor Schmidt on Sunday 23 November 1980 at 1115 Hours," MTFDA, PREM 19/471.

11. OMB Historical Tables, Tables 1.1 and 1.2 www.whitehouse.gov/omb/budget/historical-tables/.

12. William Greider, "The Education of David Stockman," *Atlantic Monthly*, December 1981, 27–54.

13. Michael J. Boskin, *Reagan and the Economy: The Successes, Failures, and Unfinished Agenda* (San Francisco: Institute for Contemporary Studies Press, 1987), 176.

14. Judith Stein, *Pivotal Decade: How the United States Traded Factories for Finance in the Seventies* (New Haven, CT: Yale University Press, 2010), 268.

15. *ERP*, 1982, 83.

16. James Graham Wilson, *The Triumph of Improvisation: Gorbachev's Adaptability, Reagan's Engagement, and the End of the Cold War* (Ithaca, NY: Cornell University Press, 2014), 20.

17. Gallup poll attached to Richard S. Beal to William Clark, "Public Opinion on Defense Spending," March 8, 1983, NSC Executive Secretariat Subject File, box 20, RRPL.

18. Department of Defense, *Annual Report to Congress: Fiscal Year 1983*, February 8, 1982, I-4.

19. Colin Powell with Joseph E. Persico, *My American Journey* (New York: Random House, 1995), 258–59.

20. Hal Brands, *What Good Is Grand Strategy?: Power and Purpose in American Statecraft from Harry S. Truman to George W. Bush* (Ithaca, NY: Cornell University Press, 2014), 112.

21. Memorandum of Conversation, September 29, 1983, folder "United Kingdom-1983-(09/24/1983–10/10/1983)," RAC box 6, NSC European and Soviet Affairs Directorate Files, RRPL.

22. See Melvyn P. Leffler, "Ronald Reagan and the Cold War: What Mattered Most," *Texas National Security Review* 1, no. 3 (2018): 76–89.

23. "Campaign '80 Sampling: Reagan on Bush and Bush on Reagan," *Boston Globe*, July 18, 1980, 2.

24. Douglas Brinkley, ed., *The Reagan Diaries* (New York: HarperCollins, 2007), 109.

25. David Stockman, *The Triumph of Politics: Why the Reagan Revolution Failed* (New York: Harper & Row, 1986), 362.

26. Alexander L. Taylor III, "The Administration's Dr. Gloom," *Time*, November 7, 1983, 78.

27. Martin Feldstein, "Financing the Accumulating Debt," September 15, 1983, folder "Chron File: Memos [Including to the President] and Correspondence, September 1983," box OA9811, Martin Feldstein Files, RRPL.

28. Charles P. Alexander, "That Monster Deficit," *Time*, March 5, 1984, 61.

29. Alexander.

30. Brinkley, *Reagan Diaries*, 61.

31. Peter Field, "The Death of Reaganomics," *Euromoney* (September 1982): 96.

32. Richard Levine to William P. Clark, April 8, 1983, "Defense Budget-Senate Action," folder "Budget Deficit (3/16–5/27/83), box 20, NSC Executive Secretariat Subject File, RRPL.

33. Gallup poll attached to Beal to Clark, "Public Opinion on Defense Spending," March 8, 1983.

34. Edwin M. Truman to Paul Volcker, "Federal Reserve Targets," January 29, 1981, folder "International Finance Memoranda [2]," box 24, Paul Volcker Papers, SGML.

35. World Bank, World Development Indicators; *ERP*, 1986, 333.

36. BIS, *Annual Report*, 1985, 147.

37. *Historical Statistics of the United States: Millennial Edition*, Table Ee387.

38. Martin Feldstein to Ronald Reagan, "Japanese Trade and the Yen," January 17, 1983, folder "Chron File: Memos and Correspondence [Includes to the President], January 1983," box OA9811, Martin Feldstein Files, RRPL.

39. BMF-VII A 3 (Pieske), "Bericht über die Sitzung der G 7-Stellvertreter am 16. März 1983," March 21, 1983, BAK, B 136/22790.

40. Thomas Geoghegan, *Which Side Are You On? Trying to Be for Labor When It's Flat on Its Back* (New York: New Press, 2004), 85.

41. *ERP*, 1984, 121.

42. Nelson Lichtenstein, *State of the Union: A Century of American Labor* (Princeton, NJ: Princeton University Press, 2003), 213.

43. Robert A. Erlandson, "U.S. Chinese Irate After Killers Go Free," *Baltimore Sun*, November 14, 1983.

44. Paul Krugman to Martin Feldstein, "Is the Yen Undervalued?," September 30, 1982, folder "Memos to CEA Chairman from Paul Krugman (1 of 5)," box OA9810, Martin Feldstein Files, RRPL.

45. Feldstein to Reagan, "Japanese Trade and the Yen."

46. William E. Brock, "U.S. Trade Policy Toward Japan," December 7, 1984, CIAERR.

47. World Bank, World Development Indicators.

48. Taylor Waler, "Recession, Unemployment Lines Reach Once-Immune Sun Belt," *Baltimore Sun*, January 28, 1982.

49. William Greider, *Secrets of the Temple: How the Federal Reserve Runs the Country* (New York: Simon & Schuster, 1989), 454–55.

50. *ERP*, 1986, Table B-68.

51. Norman A. Bailey to William P. Clark, "The Course of the U.S. Economy," August 24, 1982, folder "International Financial: 04/20/1982–11/16/1982," RAC box 3, Roger W. Robinson Files, RRPL.

52. Sean Wilentz, *The Age of Reagan: A History 1974–2008* (New York: HarperCollins, 2008), 150.

53. *AAPD*, 1981, doc. 290, 1559.

54. World Bank, World Development Indicators.

55. *AAPD*, 1981, doc. 12, 68.

56. Alan Walters to Margaret Thatcher, "Feldstein's Parting Shots," July 9, 1984, MTFDA, PREM 19/1654.

57. Murray Weidenbaum, "OECD's Economic Policy Committee," June 9, 1981, folder "Ottawa Summit July 1981 (2 of 4)," RAC box 7, Norman A. Bailey Files, RRPL.

58. BMF-VII A 3 (Pieske), "Bericht über das Treffen zwischen Minister Matthöfer und Minister Regan am 15. Mai in Kronberg," May 15, 1981, BAK, B 126/88631.

59. BIS, *Annual Report*, 1984, 17.

60. BK-42 (Heick), "Vermerk über das Gespräch des Bundeskanzlers mit dem luxemburgischen Ministerpräsidenten Werner am 15. Juli 1980 während des Mittagsessens im Bundeskanzleramt," July 16, 1980, BAK, B 126/88640.

61. BIS, *Annual Report*, 1983, 98, 144–45.

62. Eric Helleiner, *States and the Reemergence of Global Finance: From Bretton Woods to the 1990s* (Ithaca, NY: Cornell University Press, 1994), 140–45.

63. "Record of a Conversation between the Prime Minister and the Chancellor of the Federal Republic in Bonn on Wednesday, 18 November at 1015 Hours," November 18, 1981, MTFDA, PREM 19/766.

64. On East-West relations during the early 1980s, see Simon Miles, *Engaging the Evil Empire: Washington, Moscow, and the Beginning of the End of the Cold War* (Ithaca, NY: Cornell University Press, 2020).

65. BMWi-III C 4 (Ritzmann), "Neues Erdgas-Röhren-Geschäft mit der UdSSR," February 27, 1981, BAK, B 102/27174.

66. AA-405, BMWi-III C 4, "Erdgasröhrengeschäft mit der Sowjetunion," May 26, 1982, BAK, B 136/17058.

67. *FRUS*, 1981–1988, vol. 3, doc. 145, 492–94.

68. BK-4 (Heick), "Ergebnisvermerk über das Ministergespräch beim Bundeskanzler vom 2. Juni 1982 zu den Ost-West-Kreditbeziehungen," June 2, 1982, BAK, B 136/17819.

69. Helmut Schmidt to Ronald Reagan, June 24, 1982, BAK, B 136/17057.

70. AA-421, "US-Sanktionsmaßnahmen betreffend das westeuropäische Erdgas-Röhrengeschäft mit der Sowjetunion," October 4, 1982, BAK, B 136/16921.

71. See, for example, A. J. Coles to Richard Mottram, "Soviet Pipeline," August 2, 1982, MTFDA, PREM 19/925.

72. Stephan Kieninger, *The Diplomacy of Détente: Cooperative Security Policies from Helmut Schmidt to George Shultz* (London: Routledge, 2018), 128–29.

73. *FRUS*, 1981–1988, vol. 3, doc. 246, 812–14.

74. "1 Million Protest Missiles in Europe," *The Sun*, October 23, 1983, A1.

75. "Missile Protests Dot Europe," *Atlanta Constitution*, October 30, 1983.

76. Susan Colbourn, *Euromissiles: The Nuclear Weapons That Nearly Destroyed NATO* (Ithaca, NY: Cornell University Press, 2022), 200.

77. Directorate of Intelligence, "Industrial Countries: The Youth Unemployment Problem," July 1982, CIAERR.

78. World Bank, World Development Indicators.

79. See Melvyn P. Leffler, "Victory: The 'State,' the 'West,' and the Cold War," in *International Relations since the End of the Cold War: New and Old Dimensions*, ed. Geir Lundestad (New York: Oxford University Press, 2013), 80–99.

80. OMB, Historical Tables, Table 14.5; and OECD.stat.

81. OMB, Historical Tables, Table 9.7.

82. See Michael Brenes, *For Might and Right: Cold War Defense Spending and the Remaking of American Democracy* (Amherst: University of Massachusetts Press, 2020), 200–35.

83. OMB, Historical Tables, Tables 1.1 and 1.2.

84. Greta R. Krippner, *Capitalizing on Crisis: The Political Origins of the Rise of Finance* (Cambridge, MA: Harvard University Press, 2011), 92–97; Jeffry A. Frieden, *Global Capitalism: Its Fall and Rise in the Twentieth Century, and Its Stumbles in the Twenty-First* (New York: W. W. Norton, 2020), 381.

85. *IMF International Financial Statistics Yearbook, 1990*, 733.

86. Leonard Silk, "Economic Scene," *New York Times*, September 14, 1984, D2.

87. Harold James, *International Monetary Cooperation since Bretton Woods* (New York: Oxford University Press, 1996), 419.

88. Padraic Fallon, Nigel Adam, and William Ollard, "The Great Deregulation Explosion," *Euromoney* (October 1984): 55–57.

89. James Sterngold, "A Nation Hooked on Foreign Funds," *New York Times*, November 18, 1984.

90. Robert Winder, "This Is the Answer—What's the Question?," *Euromoney* (February 1984): 18.

91. Helleiner, *States and the Reemergence*, 138–39, 148–49; Hobart Rowen, "U.S., Japan Set Major Yen Accord," *Washington Post*, May 30, 1984.

92. DeGolyer and MacNaughton, *Twenty-First Century Petroleum Statistics: Historical Data (1918–1959)* (Dallas, TX), 29 and 42.

93. *BP Statistical Review of World Energy 2022*.

94. Daniel Yergin, *The Prize: The Epic Quest for Oil, Money, and Power*, 3rd ed. (New York: Free Press, 2009), 700.

95. See Catherine R. Schenk, "The Oil Market and Global Finance in the 1980s," in *Counter-Shock: The Oil Counter-Revolution of the 1980s*, ed. Duccio Basosi, Giuliano Garavini, and Massimiliano Trentin (London: I. B. Tauris, 2018), 55–75.

96. William F. Martin to William P. Clark, "OPEC and the Oil Market Situation," March 16, 1983, folder "Oil and Gas Policy March–October 1983," box 7, Norman A. Bailey Files, RRPL.

97. Jane Seaberry, "Reagan Capitalizing on Economy," *Washington Post*, October 21, 1984.

98. World Bank, World Development Indicators.

99. BIS, *Annual Report*, 1985, 12.

100. "Statement by Paul A. Volcker, Chairman, Board of Governors of the Federal Reserve System before the Senate Foreign Relations Committee, United States Senate," February 27, 1985, MTFDA, PREM 19/1654.

101. World Bank, World Development Indicators.

102. Calculated from *Historical Statistics of the United States: Millennial Edition*, Tables Ee547 and Ee565/6.

103. Christopher Miller, *Chip War: The Fight for the World's Most Critical Technology* (New York: Scribner, 2022), 82.

104. Background paper for NSC meeting, "The U.S. Semiconductor Industry: A National Security Review," attached to Donald R. Fortier, "NSC Semiconductor Study," January 4, 1986, folder "National Security Council (1 of 4)," OA 17741, Beryl W. Sprinkel Files, RRPL; Miller, *Chip War*, 98–99.

105. Miller, *Chip War*, 87–88.

106. Helleiner, *States and the Reemergence*, 154.

107. Edwin A. Finn Jr., "In Japan We (Must) Trust," *Forbes*, September 21, 1987.

108. National Security Council Meeting Minutes, "NSSD-6: U.S. Japan Relations," October 13, 1982, folder "NSC 00063 10/13/1982," box 4, NSC Executive Secretariat Meeting Files, RRPL.

109. Frieden, *Global Capitalism*, 422–23. Although China cautiously reengaged global markets in the 1980s, its reintegration into global capitalism symbolized the failure of its previous autarkic model. See Ezra Vogel, *Deng Xiaoping and the Transformation of China* (Cambridge, MA: Belknap Press of Harvard University Press, 2011).

110. Henry R. Nau to William P. Clark, "Multiple Strategies for the Developing World," January 13, 1983, folder "East/West Economics (OECD) (12/23/82–2/28/83)," box 30, NSC Executive Secretariat Subject File, RRPL.

111. B-J 20 (Hogreve), "Beitrag zum Geschäftsbericht 1984," February 7, 1985, BAK, B 330/16292.

112. BIS, *Annual Report*, 1985, 18.

113. Angus Maddison, *The World Economy*, vol. 1, *A Millennial Perspective* (Paris: OECD, 2006), 134.

114. Maddison, 134.

115. CIA Directorate of Intelligence, "Western Europe: Caught in a Fiscal Squeeze," June 1983, CIAERR.

116. "Vermerk: Gespräch des Bundeskanzlers mit Präsident Reagan am Donnerstag, 7. Juni in London (Weltwirtschaftsgipfel)," June 14, 1984, BAK, B 136/30997.

117. On Mexico, see Ngaire Woods, *The Globalizers: The IMF, the World Bank, and Their Borrowers* (Ithaca, NY: Cornell University Press, 2006), 84–103.

118. U.S. embassy (Brasilia) 7712 to SecState, "Deterioration in Brazilian Foreign Borrowing," September 21, 1982, folder "International Debt Situation (9/9/82–9/23/82)," box 41, NSC Executive Secretariat Subject Files, RRPL.

119. Frieden, *Global Capitalism*, 375.

120. "Memorandum of Conversation," May 22, 1981, folder "Memorandums of Conversation—Vice President Bush (4/29/81–7/82)," box 47, NSC Executive Secretariat Subject File, RRPL.

121. NSDD 96, "U.S. Approach to the International Debt Problem," June 3, 1983, NSDD Digitized Reference Copies, RRPL.

122. See Woods, *Globalizers*, 141–78.

123. Paul Kennedy, *The Rise and Fall of the Great Powers: Economic Change and Military Conflict from 1500 to 2000* (New York: Vintage Books, 1987), 521–33. For another example, see David Calleo, *Beyond American Hegemony: The Future of the Western Alliance* (New York: Basic Books, 1987).

124. *Historical Statistics of the United States: Millennial Edition*, Ee387.

125. Clyde H. Farnswoth, "Battles Loom over Imports," *New York Times*, April 8, 1985.

126. BIS, *Annual Report*, 1988, 27–28.

127. BMF-VII A 1 (Berger), "Aktuelle währungspolitische Entwicklung," May 27, 1987, BAK, B 136/22794.

128. John S. Herrington to Ronald Reagan, March 16, 1987, folder "XVII (F) International Trade-Energy Security Study (1 of 2)," box 2, Stephen Danzansky Files (NSC), RRPL.

129. DeGolyer and MacNaughton, *Twenty-First Century Petroleum Statistics*, 5 and 29.

130. Beryl W. Sprinkel to Donald T. Regan, "Protectionism and the Great Depression," September 25, 1985, folder "Correspondence: Chief of Staff [Donald] Regan (1 of 9)," OA 17755, Beryl W. Sprinkel Files, RRPL.

131. Washington Embassy (Van Well) 309 to AA, "Washington-Aufenthalt BM Dr. Stoltenberg," January 18, 1985, BAK, B 136/30523.

132. Frieden, *Global Capitalism*, 384–85.

133. Hal Brands, *Making the Unipolar Moment: U.S. Foreign Policy and the Rise of the Post-Cold War Order* (Ithaca, NY: Cornell University Press, 2016), 192–93.

134. BIS, *Annual Report*, 1986, 149.

135. See C. Fred Bergsten and Russell A. Green, eds., *International Monetary Cooperation: Lessons from the Plaza Accord after Thirty Years* (Washington, DC: Peterson Institute for International Economics, 2016).

136. Wilentz, *Age of Reagan*, 205.

137. OMB, Historical Tables, Tables 1.1 and 1.2.

138. AA-211 (Anding), "Zusammentreffen des Herrn Bundeskanzlers mit den Ständigen Interparlamentarischen Delegationen des Europäischen Parlaments und des amerikanischen Kongresses am 13. Januar 1988," January 14, 1988, BAK, B 136/59726.

139. BIS, *Annual Report*, 1987, 29.

140. *ERP*, 1988, 114.

141. Finn Jr., "In Japan We (Must) Trust."

142. James Baker to Ronald Reagan (draft), September 16, 1987, folder 5, box 98, James A. Baker, III Papers, SGML.

143. Margaret Shapiro, "U.S. a Magnet for Foreign Investment," *Washington Post*, October 13, 1987.

144. *ERP*, 1989, 134.

145. James B. Stewart and Daniel Hertzberg, "Terrible Tuesday: How the U.S. Market Almost Disintegrated a Day after the Crash," *Wall Street Journal*, November 23, 1987.

146. Stewart and Hertzberg.

147. Bruce Bartlett to Gary Bauer, "International Cooperation," November 5, 1987, folder "FI003 (Bonds-Stocks-Investments)(61000-End)," WHORM Subject File, RRPL.

148. Karen DeYoung, "NATO Fears U.S. Cost Cutting," *Washington Post*, April 25, 1988.

149. DeYoung.

150. AA-212 (Kaestner), "Gespräch des Herrn Bundeskanzlers mit dem Vizepräsidenten der Vereinigten Staaten von Amerika, George Bush," October 5, 1987, BAK, B 136/59726.

151. Svetlana Savranskaya, Thomas Blanton, and Vladislav Zubok, eds., *Masterpieces of History: The Peaceful End of the Cold War in Europe, 1989* (Budapest: Central European University Press, 2010), 406.

152. "Europe: In Search of the High Ground," *Economist*, February 28, 1988.

153. Timothy Andrews Sayle, *Enduring Alliance: A History of NATO and the Postwar Global Order* (Ithaca, NY: Cornell University Press, 2019), 213.

154. Brent Scowcroft to George H. W. Bush, "Dealing with the Germans," August 7, 1989, folder "Germany, Federal Republic of—Correspondence [3]," OA/ID CF01413-015, Robert L. Hutchings Files, GBPL.

155. USIA Research Memorandum, "West Europeans Broadly Favor a Single German State but Not at the Cost of NATO," November 7, 1989, document number: 8908988, OA/ID 00689, NSC Numbered Files, GBPL.

156. Michael Alexander to Geoffrey Howe, June 22, 1989, MTFA, PREM 19/3101.

157. CIA National Intelligence Estimate, "Japan: Forces for Economic Change," April 1988, CIAERR.

8. The Collapse of the Soviet Welfare Empire

1. *Mikhail Gorbachev i germanskii vopros: Sbornik dokumentov 1986–1991* (Moscow: Ves' Mir, 2006), 235. English-language excerpts from the conversation can be found in *Masterpieces of History: The Peaceful End of the Cold War in Europe, 1989*, ed. Svetlana Savranskaya, Thomas Blanton, and Vladislav Zubok (Budapest: Central European University Press, 2010), 569–73.

2. Savranskaya, Blanton, and Zubok, *Masterpieces of History*, 572.

3. Quoted in Matthew J. Ouimet, *The Rise and Fall of the Brezhnev Doctrine in Soviet Foreign Policy* (Chapel Hill: University of North Carolina Press, 2003), 255.

4. Stephen G. Brooks and William C. Wohlforth, "Power, Globalization, and the End of the Cold War: Reevaluating a Landmark Case for Ideas," *International Security* 25, no. 3 (2001): 28.

5. Mikhail Gorbachev, *Memoirs* (New York: Bantam Books, 1997), 130.

6. *V Politbiuro TsK KPSS . . . : Po zapisiam Anatoliia Cherniaeva, Vadima Medvedeva, Georgiia Shakhnazarova 1985–1991* (Moscow: Al'pina biznes buks, 2006), 39.

7. "Zapis' besedy: Tov. N.K. Baibakova s chlenom Politbiuro TsK PORP, zamestitelem presdsedatelia Soveta ministrov PNR tov. Z. Messnerom," May 24, 1985, RGAE, f. 4372, op. 67, d. 6370.

8. Nikolai Baibakov, *Sorok let v pravitel'stve* (Moscow: Respublika, 1993), 5–8.

9. *V Politbiuro TsK KPSS*, 103.

10. "Session of the Politburo of the CC CPSU," April 4, 1985, NSAVRR.

11. Odd Arne Westad, *The Cold War: A World History* (New York: Basic Books, 2017), 535.

12. Georgi Atanasov to the BKP Politburo, "Informatsiia otnosno: Poseshtenieto v Suvetskiia suiuz," May 8, 1987, TsDA, f. 1B, op. 68, a.e. 2919.

13. "Belezhki ot sreshtata na generalniia sekretar na TsK na BKP Todor Zhivkov s generalniia sekretar na TsK na KPSS Mikhail Gorbachov," October 16, 1987, TsDA, f. 1B, op. 68, a.e. 3272.

14. Mikhail Gorbachev, *Perestroika: New Thinking for Our Country and the World* (New York: Harper & Row, 1988), 37.

15. See Serhii Plokhy, *Chernobyl: The History of a Nuclear Catastrophe* (New York: Basic Books, 2018).

16. *V Politbiuro TsK KPSS*, 56.

17. John Prados, *How the Cold War Ended: Debating and Doing History* (Washington, DC: Potomac Books, 2011), 107.

18. Quoted in Melvyn P. Leffler, *For the Soul of Mankind: The United States, the Soviet Union, and the Cold War* (New York: Hill and Wang, 2007), 375.

19. Savranskaya, Blanton, and Zubok, *Masterpieces of History*, 224.

20. An East German professor in the Institut für Internationale Politik und Wirtschaft der DDR, Heinz Kosin, used this language in a conversation with US embassy officials. U.S. Embassy East Berlin (Meehan) 3371 to SecState, "GDR Policies toward FRG, Poland, Gorbachev—An Insider's View," May 12, 1987, folder "GDR [German Democratic Republic]-Substance 1987 (1)," RAC box 1, Rudolph V. Perina Files, RRPL.

21. Charles Gati, *The Bloc that Failed: Soviet-East European Relations in Transition* (Bloomington: Indiana University Press, 1990), 126–27.

22. Keith Crane, *The Soviet Economic Dilemma of Eastern Europe* (Santa Monica, CA: RAND, 1986), vi, 3, and 9.

23. Savranskaya, Blanton, and Zubok, *Masterpieces of History*, 231.

24. *Otvechaia na vyzov vremeni: Vneshniaia politika perestroiki: Dokumental'nye svidetel'stva* (Moscow: Ves' Mir, 2010), 523.

25. *V Politbiuro TsK KPSS*, 103.

26. *V Politbiuro TsK KPSS*, 140–41.

27. Gerhard Schürer, "Information über ein Gespräch mit Genossen N. Baibakow am 14.06.1984," June 14, 1984, BAB, DE 1/58679.

28. "Zapis' besedy mezhdu predsedatelem Gosplana SSSR tov. Baibakovom N.K. i predsedatelem gosudarstvennoi planovoi komissii GDR tov. Shiurerom," September 19, 1985, RGAE, f. 4372, op. 67, d. 6370.

29. *Otvechaia na vyzov vremeni*, 534–35.

30. *Otvechaia na vyzov vremeni*, 518.

31. *V Politbiuro TsK KPSS*, 170.

32. Gati, *Bloc that Failed*, 105.

33. *V Politbiuro TsK KPSS*, 87.

34. James Graham Wilson, *The Triumph of Improvisation: Gorbachev's Adaptability, Reagan's Engagement, and the End of the Cold War* (Ithaca, NY: Cornell University Press, 2014), 101–3.

35. *FRUS, 1981–1988*, vol. 6, doc. 34, 127.

36. *V Politbiuro TsK KPSS*, 280.

37. Archie Brown, "The Gorbachev Revolution and the End of the Cold War," in *The Cambridge History of the Cold War*, ed. Melvyn P. Leffler and Odd Arne Westad (New York: Cambridge University Press, 2010), 3:248–49.

38. Christopher Miller, *The Struggle to Save the Soviet Economy: Mikhail Gorbachev and the Collapse of the USSR* (Chapel Hill: University of North Carolina Press, 2016), 132–33.

39. See Peter Schweitzer, *Victory: The Reagan Administration's Secretary Strategy that Hastened the Collapse of the Soviet Union* (New York: Atlantic Monthly Press, 1996).

40. See "Information über das Treffen des Genossen E. Honecker mit Genossen M.S. Gorbatschow am 20. April 1986 in Berlin," April 20, 1986, SAPMO, DY 30/2382.

41. See David S. Painter, "From Linkage to Economic Warfare: Energy, Soviet-American Relations, and the End of the Cold War," in *Cold War Energy: A Transnational History of Soviet Oil and Gas*, ed. Jeronim Perović (Cham: Springer International Publishing, 2017), 283–318.

42. *V Politbiuro TsK KPSS*, 66.

43. *V Politbiuro TsK KPSS*, 102.

44. *PlanEcon Report* 4, no. 28 (1988): 2–5.

45. *BP Statistical Review of World Energy 2022*.

46. Thane Gustafson, *Crisis amid Plenty: The Politics of Soviet Energy under Brezhnev and Gorbachev* (Princeton, NJ: Princeton University Press, 1989), 103–18.

47. "Zapis' besedy: Zamestitelia predsedatelia Soveta ministrov SSSR, predsedatelia Gosplana SSSR tov. N.K. Baibakova s ministrom promyshlennosti VNR tov. L. Kapoi," no date (1984), RGAE, f. 4372, op. 67, d. 5528.

48. Gustafson, *Crisis amid Plenty*.

49. PlanEcon, *Soviet and East European Energy Databank*, U-5.

50. "Zapis' besedy: Predsedatelia Gosplana SSSR t. N.K. Baibakova s predsedatelem Gosplana GDR t. G. Shyurerom," September 29, 1983, RGAE, f. 4372, op. 66, d. 4766.

51. *PlanEcon Report* 1, no. 2 (1985): 3, 10.

52. Olga Skorokhodova, "The Double Shock: The Soviet Energy Crisis and the Oil Price Collapse of 1986," in *Counter-Shock: The Oil Counter-Revolution of the 1980s*, ed. Duccio Basosi, Giuliano Garavini and Massimiliano Trentin (London: I. B. Tauris, 2018), 180–98.

53. *PlanEcon Report* 2, no. 25–26 (1986): 5.

54. *PlanEcon Report* 2, no. 27 (1986): 1.

55. Georgii Arbatov, *The System: An Insider's Life in Soviet Politics* (New York: Random House, 1992), 215–16.

56. Yegor Gaidar, *Collapse of an Empire: Lessons for Modern Russia*, trans. Antonina W. Bouis (Washington, DC: Brookings Institution Press, 2007), 123.

57. Gaidar, 97.

58. *V Politbiuro TsK KPSS*, 68.

59. Prados, *How the Cold War Ended*, 110.

60. Gaidar, *Collapse of an Empire*, 95.

61. *PlanEcon Report* 3, no. 16 (1987): 1. See Mark Kramer, "The Decline in Soviet Arms Transfers to the Third World, 1986–1991: Political, Economic, and Military Dimensions," in *The End of the Cold War and the Third World: New Perspectives on Regional*

Conflict, ed. Artemy M. Kalinovsky and Sergey Radchenko (London: Routledge, 2011), 46–100.

62. "Zapis' besedy: Predsedatelia pravleniia Gosbanka SSSR tov. Dementseva V.V. s predsedatelem Doiche banka, FRG F.V. Kristiansom," April 4, 1986, RGAE, f. 2324, op. 32, d. 3914.

63. *V Politbiuro TsK KPSS*, 242.

64. Gaidar, *Collapse of an Empire*, 128 and 151.

65. *V Politbiuro TsK KPSS*, 103.

66. Miller, *Struggle to Save the Soviet Economy*, 65.

67. Vadim Medvedev, *V komande Gorbacheva: Vzgliad iznutri* (Moscow: Bylina, 1994), 103.

68. See, for example, "Zapis' besedy: Predsedatlia pravleniia Gosbanka SSSR tov. Arkhimova V.S. s predsedatelem praveleniia Drezdner Banka G. Friderikhsom," Feburary 17, 1984, RGAE, f. 2324, op. 32, d. 2674.

69. "O valiutno-finansovom polozhenii sotsialisticheskikh stran," February 24, 1988, RGAE, f. 2324, op. 33, d. 696.

70. *V Politbiuro TsK KPSS*, 93.

71. West Germany and Japan were the two largest Western creditors to the Soviet bloc, lending just over 20 percent and 17 percent of the total. France came in third at 15 percent. US banks accounted for 21 percent of credits to Yugoslavia but less than 2 percent of loans to the seven European CMEA countries. See *PlanEcon Report* V, no. 31 (1989): 1–2.

72. Martin Ivanov, Tsvetlana Todorova, and Daniel Vachkov, *Istoriia na vunshniia durzhaven dulg na Bulgariia 1878–1990 g. v tri chasti* (Sofia: Bulgarska narodna banka, 2009), 213; Cited in Ralf Ahrens, "Debt, Cooperation, and Collapse: East German Foreign Trade in the Honecker Years," in *The East German Economy 1945–2010: Falling Behind or Catching Up?*, ed. Harmut Berghoff and Uta Balbier (Washington, DC: German Historical Institute; and New York: Cambridge University Press, 2013), 172.

73. "Stenografische Niederschrift der offiziellen Gespräche des Generalsekretärs des Zentralkomitees der Sozialistischen Einheitspartei Deutschlands und Vorsitzenden des Staatsrates der Deutschen Demokratischen Republik, Genossen Erich Honecker, mit dem Generalsekretär des Zentralkomitees der Bulgarischen Kommunistischen Partei und Vorsitzenden des Staatsrates der Volksrepublik Bulgarien, Genossen Todor Shiwkow, in Berlin," June 21, 1983, SAPMO, DY 30/2430.

74. "Pametna zapiska," June 15, 1983, TsDA, f. 1B, op. 67, a.e. 2249.

75. Stephen Kotkin, *Armageddon Averted: The Soviet Collapse, 1970–2000* (New York: Oxford University Press, 2001), 63–64.

76. Charles S. Maier, *Dissolution: The Crisis of Communism and the End of East Germany* (Princeton, NJ: Princeton University Press, 1997), 76.

77. "V Politbiuro na TsK BKP," April 19, 1987, TsDA, f. 1B, op. 68, a.e. 2837.

78. Vadim Medvedev, "Soveshchanie s rukovoditeliami nauchnykh uchrezhdenii po problematike sotsstran," November 25, 1987, AMGF, f. 4, op. 1.

79. "Belezhki ot sreshtata na generalniia sekretar na TsK na BKP Todor Zhivkov s generalniia sekretar na TsK na KPSS Mikhail Gorbachov," October 16, 1987, TsDA, f. 1B, op. 68, a.e. 3272.

80. *V Politbiuro TsK KPSS*, 54.

81. Todor Zhivkov to Mikhail Gorbachev, October 15, 1986, TsDA, f. 1B, op. 68, a.e. 2396.

82. Randall W. Stone, *Satellites and Commissars: Strategy and Conflict in the Politics of Soviet-Bloc Trade* (Princeton, NJ: Princeton University Press, 1998), 218.

83. Savranskaya, Blanton, and Zubok, *Masterpieces of History*, 321.

84. Quoted in Maier, *Dissolution*, 65.

85. Directorate of Intelligence, "Eastern Europe-USSR: Forging Economic Integration with 'Direct Links'—More Smoke than Fire," August 21, 1989, CIAERR.

86. "Zapis' besedy: General'nogo sekretaria TsK KPSS M.S. Gorbacheva s general'nym sekretarem TsK SEPG E. Khonekkerom," September 28, 1988, AMGF, f. 5, op. 1.

87. Savranskaya, Blanton, and Zubok, *Masterpieces of History*, 266.

88. Savranskaya, Blanton, and Zubok, 265.

89. Savranskaya, Blanton, and Zubok, 417.

90. *PlanEcon Report*, 5, no. 13–14 (1989): 1.

91. Quoted in Stone, *Satellites and Commissars*, 208.

92. "Pamiatnaia zapiska o konsul'tatsii spetsialistov Gosbanka SSSR i torgovogo sovetnika MVT GDR Giuntera Vidra," December 21, 1989, RGAE, f. 2324, op. 32, d. 3765.

93. Savranskaya, Blanton, and Zubok, *Masterpieces of History*, 267.

94. Savranskaya, Blanton, and Zubok, 266.

95. "Zapis' besedy: Predsedatelia Gosplana SSSR tov. Baibakov N.K. s chlenom Natsional'nogo rukovodstva sandinistskogo fronta natsional'nogo osvobozhdeniia, ministrom planirovaniia Nikaragua Genri Ruisom, sostaiavsheisia 12 maia 1982 g.," May 12, 1982, RGAE, f. 4372, op. 67., d. 4408.

96. Christopher Miller, "The Bureaucratic Bourgeoisie: How the Soviet Union Lost Faith in State-Led Economic Development," *History of Political Economy* 51 (2019): 231–52.

97. *V Politbiuro TsK KPSS*, 161.

98. Shakhazarov, *Tsena svobody*, 386.

99. Georgy Shakhnazarov, "Dokladnaia zapiska M.S. Gorbachevu o probleme otnoshenii s tret'im mirom," October 10, 1989, AMGF, f. 5, op. 1.

100. On the challenges of withdrawal, see Artemy M. Kalinovsky, *A Long Goodbye: The Soviet Withdrawal from Afghanistan* (Cambridge, MA: Harvard University Press, 2011).

101. Quoted in Leffler, *For the Soul of Mankind*, 407.

102. Robert Service, *The End of the Cold War, 1985–1991* (New York: PublicAffairs, 2015), 356–57.

103. *V Politbiuro TsK KPSS*, 426.

104. "Georgy Shakhnazarov's Preparatory Notes for Mikhail Gorbachev for the Meeting of the Politburo," October 6, 1988, History and Public Policy Program Digital Archive, published in G. Kh. Zhakhnazarov, *Tsena prozreniia* [*The Price of Enlightenment*], trans. Vladislav Zubok, http://digitalarchive.wilsoncenter.org/document/112474.

105. "Anatoli Cherniaev's Notes from the Politburo Session, 21 January 1989," *Cold War International History Project Bulletin* 12/13 (Fall/Winter 2001): 16.

106. Savranskaya, Blanton, and Zubok, *Masterpieces of History*, 353–64.

107. Savranskaya, Blanton, and Zubok, 365–81.

108. Savranskaya, Blanton, and Zubok, 365–81.

109. *V Politbiuro TsK KPSS*, 445–46.

110. Svetlana Savranskaya, "The Logic of 1989," in Savranskaya, Blanton, and Zubok, *Masterpieces of History*, 27.

111. William Taubman and Svetlana Savranskaya, "If a Wall Fell in Berlin and Moscow Hardly Noticed, Would It Still Make a Noise?," in *The Fall of the Berlin Wall: The Revolutionary Legacy of 1989*, ed. Jeffrey A. Engel (New York: Oxford University Press, 2009), 75.

112. Quoted in Taubman and Savranskaya, 70.

113. Directorate of Intelligence, "Poland: Limited Options in the Debt Dilemma," October 16, 1986, folder "Poland-Debt Rescheduling (7)," RAC box 3, Paula J. Dobriansky Files, RRPL.

114. Quoted in Fritz Bartel, *The Triumph of Broken Promises: The End of the Cold War and the Rise of Neoliberalism* (Cambridge, MA: Harvard University Press, 2022), 223.

115. Tony Judt, *Postwar: A History of Europe since 1945* (New York: Penguin, 2005), 605–8.

116. Stephen Kotkin with Jan Gross, *Uncivil Society: 1989 and the Implosion of the Communist Establishment* (New York: Modern Library, 2009), 64. On the Hungarian debt crisis, see Bartel, *Triumph of Broken Promises*, 233–58.

117. AA-212 (Kaestner), "Vermerk über das Gespräch des Herrn Bundeskanzlers mit dem Außenminister der Vereinigten Staaten von Amerika, George P. Shultz, am 15. Dezember 1987, von 11.05 bis 12.35 Uhr," December 16, 1987, BAK, B 136/59726.

118. Quoted in Charles Gati, "Eastern Europe on Its Own," *Foreign Affairs* 68, Special No. 1 (1988–1989): 110.

119. Savranskaya, Blanton, and Zubok, *Masterpieces of History*, 461.

120. William I. Hitchcock, *The Struggle for Europe: The Turbulent History of a Divided Continent, 1945 to the Present* (New York: Anchor, 2003), 360.

121. *V Politbiuro TsK KPSS*, 69.

122. Jonathan Haslam, *Russia's Cold War: From the October Revolution to the Fall of the Wall* (New Haven, CT: Yale University Press, 2011), 376.

123. Service, *End of the Cold War*, 403.

124. Savranskaya, Blanton, and Zubok, *Masterpieces of History*, 492–96.

125. James A. McAdams, *Germany Divided: From the Wall to Reunification* (Princeton, NJ: Princeton University Press, 1993), 171 and 185.

126. Savranskaya, Blanton, and Zubok, *Masterpieces of History*, 515–16.

127. Vadim Zagladin to Mikhail Gorbachev, June 6, 1988, AMGF, f. 3, op. 1.

128. "Analyse der ökonomischen Lage der DDR mit Schlußfolgerungen," Sitzung des Politbüros am 31. Oktober 1989, Protokoll Nr. 47/89, SAPMO, DY 30/J IV 2/2/2356.

129. Maier, *Dissolution*, 59.

130. Schürer, "Das reale Bild war eben katastrophal," in *Der Fall der Mauer: Die unbeabsichtigte Selbstauflösung des SED-Staates*, ed. Hans-Hermann Hertle (Opladen: Westdeutscher Verlag, 1996), 318–19.

131. Ahrens, "Debt, Cooperation, and Collapse," 172.

132. *V Politbiuro TsK KPSS*, 524.

133. Leffler, *For the Soul of Mankind*, 434. On the fall of the wall, see Mary E. Sarotte, *The Collapse: The Accidental Opening of the Berlin Wall* (New York: Basic Books, 2014).

134. *PlanEcon Report 5*, no. 38–39 (1989): 3.

135. *PlanEcon Report 4*, no. 6 (1988): 1.

136. Harold James, *International Monetary Cooperation since Bretton Woods* (New York: Oxford University Press, 1996), 573–74.

137. Timothy Garton Ash, *The Magic Lantern: The Revolution of '89 Witnessed in Warsaw, Budapest, Berlin and Prague* (New York: Random House, 1990), 79–80.

138. Iván T. Berend, *Central and Eastern Europe 1944–1993: Detour from the Periphery to the Periphery* (New York: Cambridge University Press, 1996), 231.

139. "Sreshta na Politbiuro na Tsentralniia komitet na Bulgarskata komunisticheska partiia s Mikhail Sergeevich Gorbachov–generalen sekretar na Tsentralniia komitet na Komunisticheskata partiia na Suvetskiia suiuz," October 24, 1985, TsDA, f. 1B, op. 60, a.e. 372.

140. "Suvmestno sasedanie na Politbiuro na TsK na BKP i Ministerskiia suvet s uchastieto na predsedatelite na stopanski asotsiatsii i purvite sekretari na oblastnite komiteti na BKP," February 9, 1988, TsDA, f. 1B, op. 68, a.e. 3373.

141. Maier, *Dissolution*, 69.

142. Gorbachev, *Memoirs*, 615.

143. Cornel Ban, "Sovereign Debt, Austerity, and Regime Change: The Case of Nicolae Ceausescu's Romania," *East European Politics and Societies* 26, no. 4 (2012): 760; Kotkin with Gross, *Uncivil Society*, 69; Judt, *Postwar*, 623–25; and John Connelly, *From Peoples into Nations: A History of Eastern Europe* (Princeton, NJ: Princeton University Press, 2020), 739.

144. Savranskaya, Blanton, and Zubok, *Masterpieces of History*, 644.

145. Wilson, *Triumph of Improvisation*, 171.

146. *V Politbiuro TsK KPSS*, 551–55.

147. *Mikhail Gorbachev i germanskii vopros*, 424–25.

148. See Mary E. Sarotte, *1989: The Struggle to Create Post–Cold War Europe* (Princeton, NJ: Princeton University Press, 2009), 150–94.

149. James W. Davis and William C. Wohlforth, "German Unification," in *Ending the Cold War: Interpretations, Causation, and the Study of International Relations*, ed. Richard K. Herrmann and Richard Ned Lebow (New York: Palgrave Macmillan, 2004), 151. Bartel also emphasizes the role of material factors in *Triumph of Broken Promises*, 292–329.

150. Karl Marx, "The Eighteenth Brumaire of Louis Bonaparte," https://www.marxists.org/archive/marx/works/1852/18th-brumaire/.

Conclusion

1. George F. Kennan ["X"], "The Sources of Soviet Conduct," *Foreign Affairs* 25, no. 4 (1947): 581.

2. A growing literature charts the emergence of neoliberalism in the late twentieth century. For diverse approaches, see Fritz Bartel, *The Triumph of Broken Promises:*

The End of the Cold War and the Rise of Neoliberalism (Cambridge, MA: Harvard University Press, 2022); Johanna Bockman, *Markets in the Name of Socialism: The Left-Wing Origins of Neoliberalism* (Stanford, CA: Stanford University Press, 2011); Julian Germann, *Unwitting Architect: German Primacy and the Origins of Neoliberalism* (Stanford, CA: Stanford University Press, 2021); Gary Gerstle, *The Rise and Fall of the Neoliberal Order: America and the World in the Free Market Era* (New York: Oxford University Press, 2022); David Harvey, *A Brief History of Neoliberalism* (New York: Oxford University Press, 2005); and Quinn Slobodian, *Globalists: The End of Empire and Birth of Neoliberalism* (Cambridge, MA: Harvard University Press, 2018).

3. Melvyn P. Leffler, "Victory: The 'State,' the 'West,' and the Cold War," in *International Relations since the End of the Cold War: New and Old Dimensions*, ed. Geir Lundestad (New York: Oxford University Press, 2013), 80–99.

4. OMB, Historical Tables, Table 14.5, www.whitehouse.gov/omb/budget/historical-tables/; and OECD.stat.

5. Stephen Kotkin, *Armageddon Averted: The Soviet Collapse, 1970–2000* (New York: Oxford University Press, 2001), 17.

6. Christopher Miller, *The Struggle to Save the Soviet Economy: Mikhail Gorbachev and the Collapse of the USSR* (Chapel Hill: University of North Carolina Press, 2016), 181.

7. "Text of Speech Delivered by A. Y. Vyshinsky at the General Assembly of the United Nations, September 18, 1947," September 18, 1947, History and Public Policy Program Digital Archive, For the Peace and Friendship of Nations, against the Instigators of a New War: Text of Speech Delivered by A. Y. Vyshinsky at the General Assembly of the United Nations, September 18, 1947 (Washington, DC: Embassy of the Union of Soviet Socialist Republics, 1947), https://digitalarchive.wilsoncenter.org/document/220070.

8. Barry Eichengreen et al., *In Defense of Public Debt* (New York: Oxford University Press, 2021), 165.

9. OMB, Historical Tables, Table 6.1.

10. Treasury.gov, FiscalData, https://ticdata.treasury.gov/resource-center/data-chart-center/tic/Documents/mfh.txt, accessed January 23, 2023.

11. Federal Reserve Economic Data (FRED), Federal Reserve Bank of St. Louis.

12. See particularly Carla Norrlöf, *America's Global Advantage: U.S. Hegemony and International Cooperation* (New York: Cambridge University Press, 2010).

13. Anna Kaledina and Tatiana Ternovskaia, "U SShA est' sposob spastis' ot krizisa," *Izvestiia*, December 4, 2008.

14. Adam Tooze, *Crashed: How a Decade of Financial Crises Changed the World* (New York: Viking, 2018), 202–19, 239–42.

15. U.S. Bureau of Economic Analysis, International Data.

16. Charles S. Maier, *Among Empires: American Ascendancy and Its Predecessors* (Cambridge, MA: Harvard University Press, 2007), 267.

17. The Treasury makes monthly data available at https://ticdata.treasury.gov/resource-center/data-chart-center/tic/Documents/mfh.txt, accessed January 22, 2023.

18. Peter G. Peterson Foundation, "U.S. Defense Spending Compared to Other Countries," May 11, 2022, https://www.pgpf.org/chart-archive/0053_defense-comparison.

19. G. John Ikenberry, *A World Safe for Democracy: Liberal Internationalism and the Crises of Global Order* (New Haven, CT: Yale University Press, 2020), 257. On the chal-

lenge of US bargaining in the post-Cold War era, see Michael Mastanduno, "System Maker and Privilege Taker: The United States and the International Political Economy," *World Politics* 61, no. 1 (2009): 121–54.

20. Among others, see Elizabeth Strange, *The Third Revolution: Xi Jinping and the New Chinese State* (New York: Oxford University Press, 2018).

21. Angela Stent, *Putin's World: Russia against the West and with the Rest* (New York: Twelve, 2019), 171.

22. *FRUS*, 1946, vol. 6, doc. 475, 696–709.

Bibliography

Archives

Bulgaria

Tsentralen durzhaven arkhiv, Sofia
    Fond 1B: Tsentralen komitet na Bulgarskata komunisticheska partiia
    Fond 130: Durzhavna planova komisiia
    Fond 378B: Todor Khristov Zhivkov

France

Organisation for Economic Co-operation and Development Library and Archives,
    Paris
    Working Party No. 4 of the Economic Policy Committee

Germany

Bundesarchiv, Berlin-Lichterfelde
    Deutsche Demokratische Republik mit sowjetischer Besatzungszone 1949–1990
        Außenhandelsbank
        Ministerium für Außenhandel und Innerdeutschen Handel
        Ministerrat der DDR
        Staatliche Plankommission
        Staatsbank der DDR
Bundesarchiv, Koblenz
    Bundesrepublik Deutschland mit westallierten Besatzungszonen
        B 102: Bundesministerium für Wirtschaft
        B 126: Bundesministerium der Finanzen
        B 136: Bundeskanzleramt
        B 330: Bundesbank
Politisches Archiv des Auswärtigen Amts, Berlin
    Auswärtiges Amt der Bundesrepublik Deutschland
        B 9: Planungsstab
        B 32: Länderreferate USA, Kanada
        B 52: Grundsatzfragen der Handelspolitik
        B 71: Internationale Energiepolitik
        B 202: Internationale Währungspolitik, Verkehrs-, Sozial- und Energiepolitik
          der EG

Stiftung Archiv der Parteien und Massenorganisationen der DDR (SAPMO),
Berlin-Lichterfelde
Sozialistische Einheitspartei Deutschlands (SED)
Abteilung Handel, Versorgung und Außenhandel
Abteilung Internationale Verbindungen
Abteilung Planung und Finanzen im ZK der SED

Netherlands

Nationaal Archief, The Hague
Kabinet van de Minister-President
Ministerie van Buitenlandse Zaken
Ministerie van Economische Zaken
Ministerie van Financiën
Ministerraad

Russia

Archive of the Mikhail Gorbachev Foundation, Moscow
Fond 3: Vadim Zagladin
Fond 4: Vadim Medvedev
Fond 5: Georgy Shakhnazarov
Rossiiskii gosudarstvennyi arkhiv ekonomiki, Moscow
Fond 302: Postoiannoe predstavitel'stvo SSSR pri Sovete ekonomicheskoi
vzaimopomoshchi
Fond 413: Ministerstvo vneshnei torgovli SSSR
Fond 458: Ministerstvo gazovoi promyshlennosti
Fond 2324: Gosbank
Fond 4372: Gosplan
Rossiiskii gosudarstvennyi arkhiv noveshei istorii, Moscow
Fond 3: Politbiuro TsK KPSS
Fond 5: Apparat TsK KPSS

United Kingdom

The National Archives, Kew
Foreign and Commonwealth Office
Prime Minister's Office
Treasury

United States

George H. W. Bush Presidential Library, College Station, TX
National Security Affairs
Gerald R. Ford Presidential Library, Ann Arbor, MI
Arthur Burns Papers
National Security Adviser's Files
National Security Council Institutional Files
L. William Seidman Files

Jimmy Carter Presidential Library, Atlanta, GA
    Council of Economic Advisers Files
    National Security Advisor Files
    Zbigniew Brzezinski Collection
National Archives and Records Administration II, College Park, MD
    RG 56: Records of the Department of the Treasury
    RG 59: Records of the Department of State
Richard M. Nixon Presidential Library, Yorba Linda, CA
    Henry A. Kissinger Office Files
    Henry A. Kissinger Telephone Conversation Transcripts
    NSC Files
    NSC Institutional Files
Ronald Reagan Presidential Library, Simi Valley, CA
    Beryl W. Sprinkel Files
    Martin Feldstein Files
    Norman A. Bailey Files
    NSC European and Soviet Affairs Directorate Files
    NSC Executive Secretariat Meeting File
    NSC Executive Secretariat Subject File
    Paula J. Dobriansky Files
    Roger W. Robinson Files
    Stephen Danzansky Files (NSC)
    WHORM Subject File
Seeley G. Mudd Manuscript Library, Princeton University, Princeton, NJ
    James A. Baker, III Papers
    Paul A. Volcker Papers
Special Collections & College Archives, Skillman Library, Lafayette College, Easton, PA
    William E. Simon Papers
Sterling Memorial Library, Yale University, New Haven, CT
    Cyrus R. Vance Papers
    Henry A. Kissinger Papers

Memoirs

Arbatov, Georgii. *The System: An Insider's Life in Soviet Politics.* New York: Random House, 1992.

Baibakov, Nikolai. *The Cause of My Life.* Translated by Vladimir Bisengaliev. Moscow: Progress, 1986.

——. *Sorok let v pravitel'stve.* Moscow: Respublika, 1993.

Blumenthal, W. Michael. *From Exile to Washington: A Memoir of Leadership in the Twentieth Century.* New York: Overlook, 2013.

Brzezinski, Zbigniew. *Power and Principle: Memoirs of the National Security Adviser, 1977–1981.* New York: Farrar, Straus and Giroux, 1985.

Carter, Jimmy. *Keeping Faith: Memoirs of a President.* New York: Bantam Books, 1982.

Connally, John B. *In History's Shadow: An American Odyssey.* New York: Hyperion, 1993.

Dobrynin, Anatoly. *In Confidence: Moscow's Ambassador to America's Six Cold War Presidents*. New York: Times Books, 1995.

Ford, Gerald R. *A Time to Heal: The Autobiography of Gerald R. Ford*. New York: Harper & Row, 1979.

Geoghegan, Thomas. *Which Side Are You On? Trying to Be for Labor When It's Flat on Its Back*. New York: New Press, 2004.

Gorbachev, Mikhail. *Memoirs*. New York: Bantam Books, 1997.

Gwynne, Samuel C. *Selling Money*. New York: Penguin, 1987.

Healey, Denis. *The Time of My Life*. London: Michael Joseph, 1989.

Lubbers, Ruud. *Persoonlijke Herinneringen*. Amsterdam: Uitgeverij Balans, 2018.

Medvedev, Vadim. *V komande Gorbacheva: Vzgliad iznutri*. Moscow: Bylina, 1994.

Mittag, Günter. *Um jeden Preis: Im Spannungsfeld zweier Systeme*. Berlin: Das Neue Berlin, 2015.

Powell, Colin, with Joseph E. Persico. *My American Journey*. New York: Random House, 1995.

Ryzhkov, Nikolai. *Desiat' let velikikh potriasenii*. Moscow: Assotsiatsiiia "Kniga. Prosveshchenie. Miloserdie," 1995.

Schalck-Golodkowski, Alexander. *Deutsche-deutsche Erinnerungen*. Hamburg: Rowohlt Verlag, 2000.

Schmidt, Helmut. *Men and Powers: A Political Retrospective*. Translated by Ruth Hein. New York: Random House, 1989.

Schürer, Gerhard. *Gewagt und Verloren: Eine deutsche Biografie*. Frankfurt an der Oder: Frankfurter Oder Editionen, 1996.

Shakhnazarov, Georgy. *Tsena svobody: Reformatsiia Gorbacheva glazami ego pomoshchnika*. Moscow: Rossika, 1993.

Stockman, David Alan. *The Triumph of Politics: Why the Reagan Revolution Failed*. New York: Harper & Row, 1986.

Todorov, Stanko. *Do vurkhovete na vlastta: Politicheski memoari*. Sofia: Khristo Botev, 1995.

Vaizey, Hester. *Born in the GDR: Living in the Shadow of the Wall*. New York: Oxford University Press, 2014.

Volcker, Paul A., with Christine Harper. *Keeping at It: The Quest for Sound Money and Good Government*. New York: PublicAffairs, 2018.

Zhivkov, Todor. *Memoari*. 2nd ed. Sofia: Trud i pravo, 2006.

Secondary Sources

Abegglen, James C., and Thomas M. Hout. "Facing Up to the Trade Gap with Japan." *Foreign Affairs* 57, no. 1 (Fall 1978): 146–68.

Ahrens, Ralf. "Debt, Cooperation, and Collapse: East German Foreign Trade in the Honecker Years." In *The East German Economy, 1945–2010: Falling Behind or Catching Up?*, edited by Harmut Berghoff and Uta Andrea Balbier, 161–76. Washington, DC: German Historical Institute; and New York: Cambridge University Press, 2013.

——. *Gegenseitige Wirtschaftshilfe? Die DDR im RGW—Strukturen und handelspolitische Strategien 1963-1976*. Köln: Böhlau Verlag, 2000.

Akins, James. "The Oil Crisis: This Time the Wolf Is Here." *Foreign Affairs* 51, no. 3 (April 1973): 462–90.

Arrighi, Giovanni. "The World Economy and the Cold War." In *Endings*, ed. Melvyn P. Leffler and Odd Arne Westad, 23–44. Vol. 3 of *The Cambridge History of the Cold War*. New York: Cambridge University Press, 2010.

Ash, Timothy Garton. *The Magic Lantern: The Revolution of '89 Witnessed in Warsaw, Budapest, Berlin and Prague*. New York: Random House, 1990.

———. *The Polish Revolution: Solidarity*. New Haven, CT: Yale University Press, 2002.

Ban, Cornel. "Sovereign Debt, Austerity, and Regime Change: The Case of Nicolae Ceausescu's Romania." *East European Politics and Societies* 26, no. 4 (2012): 743–76.

Bartel, Fritz. "Fugitive Leverage: Commercial Banks, Sovereign Debt, and Cold War Crisis in Poland, 1980–1982." *Enterprise & Society* 18, no. 1 (2017): 72–107.

———. *The Triumph of Broken Promises: The End of the Cold War and the Rise of Neoliberalism*. Cambridge, MA: Harvard University Press, 2022.

Basosi, Duccio. "Oil, Dollars, and US Power in the 1970s: Re-viewing the Connections." *Journal of Energy History* 3 (2020): 1–15.

Basosi, Duccio, Giuliano Garavini, and Massimiliano Trentin, eds. *Counter-Shock: The Oil Counter-Revolution of the 1980s*. London: I. B. Tauris, 2018.

Békés, Csaba. *Hungary's Cold War: International Relations from the End of World War II to the Fall of the Soviet Union*. Chapel Hill: University of North Carolina Press, 2022.

Berend, Iván T. *Central and Eastern Europe, 1944–1993: Detour from the Periphery to the Periphery*. New York: Cambridge University Press, 1996.

Bergsten, C. Fred. "Crisis in U.S. Trade Policy." *Foreign Affairs* 49, no. 4 (1971): 619–35.

Bergsten, C. Fred, and Russell A. Green, eds. *International Monetary Cooperation: Lessons from the Plaza Accord after Thirty Years*. Washington, DC: Peterson Institute for International Economics, 2016.

Bird, Kai. *The Outlier: The Unfinished Presidency of Jimmy Carter*. New York: Crown, 2021.

Biven, W. Carl. *Jimmy Carter's Economy: Economic Policy in an Age of Limits*. Chapel Hill: University of North Carolina Press, 2002.

Block, Fred L. *The Origins of the International Economic Disorder: A Study of United States International Monetary Policy from World War II to the Present*. Berkeley: University of California Press, 1977.

Bockman, Johanna. *Markets in the Name of Socialism: The Left-Wing Origins of Neoliberalism*. Stanford, CA: Stanford University Press, 2011.

Borhi, László. *Dealing with Dictators: The United States, Hungary, and East Central Europe, 1942–1989*. Translated by Jason Vincz. Bloomington: Indiana University Press, 2016.

———. *Hungary in the Cold War 1945–1956: Between the United States and the Soviet Union*. Budapest: Central European Press, 2004.

Borstelmann, Thomas. *The 1970s: A New Global History from Civil Rights to Economic Inequality*. Princeton, NJ: Princeton University Press, 2012.

Boskin, Michael J. *Reagan and the Economy: The Successes, Failures, and Unfinished Agenda*. San Francisco: Institute for Contemporary Studies Press, 1987.

Brands, Hal. *Making the Unipolar Moment: U.S. Foreign Policy and the Rise of the Post–Cold War Order*. Ithaca, NY: Cornell University Press, 2016.

——. *What Good Is Grand Strategy?: Power and Purpose in American Statecraft from Harry S. Truman to George W. Bush*. Ithaca, NY: Cornell University Press, 2014.

Brenes, Michael. *For Might and Right: Cold War Defense Spending and the Remaking of American Democracy*. Amherst: University of Massachusetts Press, 2020.

Brooks, Stephen G., and William C. Wohlforth, "Power, Globalization, and the End of the Cold War: Reevaluating a Landmark Case for Ideas." *International Security* 25, no. 3 (2001): 5–53.

Brown, Archie. *The Gorbachev Factor*. New York: Oxford University Press, 1996.

——. "The Gorbachev Revolution and the End of the Cold War." In *Endings*, ed. Melvyn P. Leffler and Odd Arne Westad, 244–66. Vol. 3 of *The Cambridge History of the Cold War*. New York: Cambridge University Press 2010.

——. *The Human Factor: Gorbachev, Reagan, and Thatcher, and the End of the Cold War*. New York: Oxford University Press, 2020.

——. *The Rise and Fall of Communism*. New York: Ecco, 2009.

Bunce, Valerie. "The Empire Strikes Back: The Evolution of the Eastern Bloc from a Soviet Asset to a Soviet Liability." *International Organization* 39, no. 1 (1985): 1–46.

Calleo, David. *Beyond American Hegemony: The Future of the Western Alliance*. New York: Basic Books, 1987.

Cohen, Benjamin J. "The Revolution in Atlantic Economic Relations: A Bargain Comes Unstuck." In *The United States and Western Europe: Political, Economic and Strategic Perspectives*, edited by Wolfram F. Hanrieder, 106–33. Cambridge, MA: Winthrop, 1974.

Colbourn, Susan. *Euromissiles: The Nuclear Weapons that Nearly Destroyed NATO*. Ithaca, NY: Cornell University Press, 2022.

Connelly, John. *From Peoples into Nations: A History of Eastern Europe*. Princeton, NJ: Princeton University Press, 2020.

Crane, Keith. *The Soviet Economic Dilemma of Eastern Europe*. Santa Monica, CA: RAND, 1986.

Davis, James W., and William C. Wohlforth. "German Unification." In *Ending the Cold War: Interpretations, Causation, and the Study of International Relations*, edited by Richard K. Herrmann and Richard Ned Lebow, 131–57. New York: Palgrave Macmillan, 2004.

De Nevers, Renée. *Comrades No More: The Seeds of Change in Eastern Europe*. Cambridge, MA: MIT Press, 2003.

Dietrich, Anne. "Kaffee in der DDR–'Ein Politikum der ersten Ranges.'" In *Kaffeewelten: Historische Perspektiven Auf Eine Globale Ware Im 20. Jahrhundert*, edited by Christiane Berth, Dorothee Wierling, and Volker Wünderich, 225–47. Göttingen: V&R Unipress, 2015.

Dietrich, Christopher R. W. *Oil Revolution: Anticolonial Elites, Sovereign Rights, and the Economic Culture of Decolonization*. New York: Cambridge University Press, 2017.

Domber, Gregory. *Empowering Revolution: America, Poland, and the End of the Cold War*. Chapel Hill: University of North Carolina Press, 2014.

Dragomir, Elena. "The Formation of the Soviet Bloc's Council for Mutual Economic Assistance: Romania's Involvement." *Journal of Cold War Studies* 14, no. 1 (2010): 34–47.

Eichengreen, Barry J. *The European Economy since 1945: Coordinated Capitalism and Beyond.* Princeton, NJ: Princeton University Press, 2008.

——. *Golden Fetters: The Gold Standard and the Great Depression, 1919–1939.* New York: Oxford University Press, 1995.

Eichengreen, Barry, Asmaa El-Ganainy, Rui Esteves, and Kris James Mitchener. *In Defense of Public Debt.* New York: Oxford University Press, 2021.

Ellman, Michael, and Vladimir Kontorovich, eds. *The Destruction of the Soviet Economic System: An Insiders' History.* New York: M. E. Sharpe, 1998.

English, Robert. *Russia and the Idea of the West: Gorbachev, Intellectuals and the End of the Cold War.* New York: Columbia University Press, 2000.

Evangelista, Matthew. *Unarmed Forces: The Transnational Movement to End the Cold War.* Ithaca, NY: Cornell University Press, 1999.

Feldstein, Martin, ed. *American Economic Policy in the 1980s.* Chicago: University of Chicago Press, 1994.

Fischer, Beth A. *The Reagan Reversal: Foreign Policy and the End of the Cold War.* Columbia: University of Missouri Press, 1997.

Franczak, Michael. *Global Inequality and American Foreign Policy in the 1970s.* Ithaca, NY: Cornell University Press, 2022.

Freeman, Stephanie. *Dreams for a Decade: Nuclear Abolitionism and the End of the Cold War.* Philadelphia: University of Pennsylvania Press, 2023.

Frieden, Jeffry A. *Global Capitalism: Its Fall and Rise in the Twentieth Century, and Its Stumbles in the Twenty-First.* New York: W. W. Norton, 2020.

Friedman, Jeremy. *Shadow Cold War: The Sino-Soviet Competition for the Third World.* Chapel Hill: University of North Carolina Press, 2015.

Gaddis, John Lewis. *Strategies of Containment: A Critical Appraisal of Postwar American National Security Policy.* 2nd ed. New York: Oxford University Press, 2005.

Gaidar, Yegor. *Collapse of an Empire: Lessons for Modern Russia.* Translated by Antonina W. Bouis. Washington, DC: Brookings Institution Press, 2007.

Garavini, Giuliano. *After Empires: European Integration, Decolonization, and the Challenge from the Global South 1957–1986.* Translated by Richard R. Nybakken. New York: Oxford University Press, 2012.

——. *The Rise and Fall of OPEC in the Twentieth Century.* New York: Oxford University Press, 2019.

Garthoff, Raymond L. *Détente and Confrontation: American-Soviet Relations from Nixon to Reagan.* Washington, DC: The Brookings Institution, 1994.

Gati, Charles. *The Bloc that Failed: Soviet-East European Relations in Transition.* Bloomington: Indiana University Press, 1990.

Gavin, Francis J. *Gold, Dollars, and Power: The Politics of International Monetary Relations, 1958–1971.* Chapel Hill: University of North Carolina Press, 2004.

Germann, Julian. "State-led or Capital-driven? The Fall of Bretton Woods and the German Currency Float Reconsidered." *New Political Economy* 19, no. 5 (2014): 769–89.

———. *Unwitting Architect: German Primacy and the Origins of Neoliberalism*. Stanford, CA: Stanford University Press, 2021.

Gerstle, Gary. *The Rise and Fall of the Neoliberal Order: America and the World in the Free Market Era*. New York: Oxford University Press, 2022.

Getachew, Adom. *Worldmaking after Empire: The Rise and Fall of Self-Determination*. Princeton, NJ: Princeton University Press, 2019.

Gfeller, Aurélie Élisa. *Building a European Identity: France, the United States, and the Oil Shock, 1973–1974*. New York: Berghahn Books, 2012.

Giauque, Jeffrey Glen. *Grand Designs and Visions of Unity: The Atlantic Powers and the Reorganization of Western Europe, 1955–1963*. Chapel Hill: University of North Carolina Press, 2002.

Goldman, Marshall I. *The Enigma of Soviet Petroleum: Half-full or Half-empty?* London: Allen & Unwin, 1980.

Gorbachev, Mikhail. *Perestroika: New Thinking for Our Country and the World*. New York: Harper & Row, 1988.

Graf, Maximilian. "Before Strauß: The East German Struggle to Avoid Bankruptcy during the Debt Crisis Revisited." *International History Review* 42, no. 4 (2020): 737–54.

Graf, Rüdiger. *Oil and Sovereignty: Petroknowledge and Energy Policy in the United States and Western Europe in the 1970s*. New York: Berghahn Books, 2018.

Gray, William Glenn. "Floating the System: Germany, the United States, and the Breakdown of Bretton Woods, 1969–1973." *Diplomatic History* 31, no. 2 (2007): 295–323.

———. *Germany's Cold War: The Global Campaign to Isolate East Germany, 1949–1969*. Chapel Hill: University of North Carolina Press, 2003.

———. "'Learning to 'Recycle': Petrodollars and the West, 1973–1975." In *Oil Shock: The 1973 Crisis and Its Economic Legacy*, edited by Elisabetta Bini, Giuliano Garavini, and Federico Romero, 172–97. London: I. B. Tauris, 2016.

———. "'Number One in Europe': The Startling Emergence of the Deutsche Mark, 1968–1969." *Central European History* 39, no. 1 (2006): 56–78.

Greider, William. *Secrets of the Temple: How the Federal Reserve Runs the Country*. New York: Simon & Schuster, 1989.

Gustafson, Thane. *The Bridge: Natural Gas in a Redivided Europe*. Cambridge, MA: Harvard University Press, 2020.

———. *Crisis amid Plenty: The Politics of Soviet Energy under Brezhnev and Gorbachev*. Princeton, NJ: Princeton University Press, 1989.

Hall, Peter, and David Soskice, eds. *Varieties of Capitalism: The Institutional Foundations of Comparative Advantage*. New York: Oxford University Press, 2001.

Hanhimäki, Jussi. *The Flawed Architect: Henry Kissinger and American Foreign Policy*. New York: Oxford University Press, 2004.

Hanson, Philip. *The Rise and Fall of the Soviet Economy: An Economic History of the USSR from 1945*. New York: Longman, 2003.

Hardt, John P. "Soviet Energy Policy in Eastern Europe." In *Soviet Policy in Eastern Europe*, edited by Sarah Meiklejohn Terry, 189–220. New Haven, CT: Yale University Press, 1984.

Harrison, Hope M. *Driving the Soviets Up the Wall: Soviet-East German Relations, 1953–1961*. Princeton, NJ: Princeton University Press, 2003.

Harvey, David. *A Brief History of Neoliberalism*. New York: Oxford University Press, 2005.

Haslam, Jonathan. *Russia's Cold War: From the October Revolution to the Fall of the Wall*. New Haven, CT: Yale University Press, 2011.

Helleiner, Eric. *States and the Reemergence of Global Finance: From Bretton Woods to the 1990s*. Ithaca, NY: Cornell University Press, 1994.

Hellema, Duco, Cees Wiebes, and Toby Witte. *The Netherlands and the Oil Crisis: Business as Usual*. Translated by Murray Pearson. Amsterdam: University of Amsterdam Press, 2004.

Herring, George C. *From Colony to Superpower: U.S. Foreign Relations since 1776*. New York: Oxford University Press, 2008.

Hickson, Kevin. *The IMF Crisis of 1976 and British Politics*. London: I. B. Tauris, 2005.

Hitchcock, William I. *France Restored: Cold War Diplomacy and the Quest for Leadership in Europe, 1944–1954*. Chapel Hill: University of North Carolina Press, 1998.

——. *The Struggle for Europe: The Turbulent History of a Divided Continent, 1945 to the Present*. New York: Anchor, 2003.

Högselius, Per. *Red Gas: Russia and the Origins of European Energy Dependence*. New York: Palgrave Macmillan, 2013.

Holloway, David. *The Soviet Union and the Arms Race*. New Haven, CT: Yale University Press, 1983.

Ikenberry, G. John. *A World Safe for Democracy: Liberal Internationalism and the Crises of Global Order*. New Haven, CT: Yale University Press, 2020.

Inboden, William. *The Peacemaker: Ronald Reagan, the Cold War, and the World on the Brink*. New York: Dutton, 2022.

Institut ekonomiki mirovoi sotsialisticheskoi sistemy (IEMSS). *SSSR i sotsialisticheskaia ekonomicheskaia intergratsiia*. Moscow: Nauka, 1981.

——. *Statistika stran-chlenov SEV*. Moscow: Nauka, 1973.

——. *Vneshniaia torgovlia SSSR so stranami SEV*. Moscow: Nauka, 1986.

Ironside, Kristy. *A Full-Value Ruble: The Promise of Prosperity in the Postwar Soviet Union*. Cambridge, MA: Harvard University Press, 2022.

Ivanov, Martin, Tsvetlana Todorova, and Daniel Vachkov. *Istoriia na vunshniia durzhaven dulg na Bulgariia 1878–1990 g. v tri chasti*. Sofia: Bulgarska narodna banka, 2009.

Jacobs, Meg. *Panic at the Pump: The Energy Crisis and the Transformation of American Politics in the 1970s*. New York: Hill & Wang, 2016.

James, Harold. *International Monetary Cooperation since Bretton Woods*. New York: Oxford University Press, 1996.

Judt, Tony. *Postwar: A History of Europe since 1945*. New York: Penguin, 2005.

Kalinovsky, Artemy M. *A Long Goodbye: The Soviet Withdrawal from Afghanistan*. Cambridge, MA: Harvard University Press, 2011.

Kansikas, Suvi. "Calculating the Burden of Empire: Soviet Oil, East-West Trade, and the End of the Socialist Bloc." In *Cold War Energy: A Transnational History of Soviet Oil and Gas*, edited by Jeronim Perović, 345–69. Cham: Springer International Publishing, 2017.

——. *Socialist Countries Face the European Community: Soviet-Bloc Controversies over East-West Trade*. Frankfurt: Peter Lang, 2014.

Kennan, George F. ["X"]. "The Sources of Soviet Conduct." *Foreign Affairs* 25, no. 4 (1947): 566–82.

Kennedy, Paul. *The Rise and Fall of the Great Powers: Economic Change and Military Conflict from 1500 to 2000*. New York: Vintage Books, 1987.

Kenney, Padraic. *Carnival of Revolution: Central Europe 1989*. Princeton, NJ: Princeton University Press, 2002.

Kershaw, Ian. *The Global Age: Europe 1950–2017*. New York: Viking, 2018.

Kieninger, Stephan. *The Diplomacy of Détente: Cooperative Security Policies from Helmut Schmidt to George Shultz*. London: Routledge, 2018.

——. "Freer Movement in Return for Cash: Franz Josef Strauß, Alexander Schalck-Golodkowski, and the *Milliardenkredit* for the GDR, 1983–1984." In *New Perspectives on the End of the Cold War: Unexpected Transformations?*, edited by Bernhard Blumenau, Jussi M. Hanhimäki, Barbara Zanchetta, 117–37. London: Routledge, 2018.

Klinghoffer, Arthur Jay. *The Soviet Union & International Oil Politics*. New York: Columbia University, 1977.

Kolko, Gabriel, and Joyce Kolko. *The Limits of Power: The World and United States Foreign Policy*. New York: Harper & Row, 1972.

Kopstein, Jeffrey. *The Politics of Economic Decline in East Germany, 1945–1989*. Chapel Hill: University of North Carolina Press, 1997.

Kotkin, Stephen. *Armageddon Averted: The Soviet Collapse, 1970–2000*. New York: Oxford University Press, 2001.

——. "The Kiss of Debt: The East Bloc Goes Borrowing." In *The Shock of the Global: The 1970s in Perspective*, edited by Niall Ferguson, Charles S. Maier, Erez Manela, and Daniel J. Sargent, 80–93. Cambridge, MA: Belknap Press of Harvard University Press, 2010.

Kotkin, Stephen, with Jan Gross. *Uncivil Society: 1989 and the Implosion of the Communist Establishment*. New York: Modern Library, 2009.

Kramer, Mark. "The Decline in Soviet Arms Transfers to the Third World, 1986–1991: Political, Economic, and Military Dimensions." In *The End of the Cold War and the Third World: New Perspectives on Regional Conflict*, edited by Artemy M. Kalinovsky and Sergey Radchenko, 46–100. London: Routledge, 2011.

——. "The Demise of the Soviet Bloc." *Journal of Modern History* 83, no. 4 (2011): 788–854.

Krippner, Greta R. *Capitalizing on Crisis: The Political Origins of the Rise of Finance*. Cambridge, MA: Harvard University Press, 2011.

Kunz, Diane B. *Butter and Guns: America's Cold War Economic Diplomacy*. New York: Free Press, 1997.

LaFeber, Walter. *America, Russia, and the Cold War, 1945–1971*. New York: Wiley, 1972.

Larres, Klaus. *Uncertain Allies: Nixon, Kissinger, and the Threat of a United Europe*. New Haven, CT: Yale University Press, 2022.

Latham, Michael E. *The Right Kind of Revolution: Modernization, Development, and U.S. Foreign Policy from the Cold War to the Present*. Ithaca, NY: Cornell University Press, 2011.

Leffler, Melvyn P. *For the Soul of Mankind: The United States, the Soviet Union, and the Cold War*. New York: Hill and Wang, 2007.

———. "National Security." In *Explaining the History of American Foreign Relations*, 3rd ed., edited by Frank Costigliola and Michael J. Hogan, 25–41. New York: Cambridge University Press, 2016.

———. *A Preponderance of Power: National Security, the Truman Administration, and the Cold War*. Stanford, CA: Stanford University Press, 1993.

———. "Ronald Reagan and the Cold War: What Mattered Most." *Texas National Security Review* 1, no. 3 (2018): 76–89.

———. "Victory: The 'State,' the 'West,' and the Cold War." In *International Relations since the End of the Cold War: New and Old Dimensions*, edited by Geir Lundestad, 80–99. New York: Oxford University Press, 2013.

Lévesque, Jacques. *The Enigma of 1989: The USSR and the Liberation of Eastern Europe*. Berkeley: University of California Press, 1997.

Levy, Jonathan. *Ages of American Capitalism: A History of the United States*. New York: Random House, 2021.

Lichtenstein, Nelson. *State of the Union: A Century of American Labor*. Princeton, NJ: Princeton University Press, 2003.

Lorenzini, Sara. *Global Development: A Cold War History*. Princeton, NJ: Princeton University Press, 2019.

Lüthi, Lorenz M. *Cold Wars: Asia, the Middle East, Europe*. New York: Cambridge University Press, 2020.

———. "Drifting Apart: Soviet Energy and the Cohesion of the Communist Bloc in the 1970s and 1980s." In *Cold War Energy: A Transnational History of Soviet Oil and Gas,* edited by Jeronim Perović, 371–99. Cham: Springer International Publishing, 2017.

Macekura, Stephen. *The Mismeasure of Progress: Economic Growth and Its Critics*. Chicago: University of Chicago Press, 2020.

Maier, Charles S. *Among Empires: American Ascendancy and Its Predecessors*. Cambridge, MA: Harvard University Press, 2007.

———. "The Collapse of Communism: Approaches for a Future History." *History Workshop Journal* 31, no. 1 (1991): 34–59.

———. *Dissolution: The Crisis of Communism and the End of East Germany*. Princeton, NJ: Princeton University Press, 1997.

———. "'Malaise': The Crisis of Capitalism in the 1970s." In *The Shock of the Global: The 1970s in Perspective*, edited by Niall Ferguson, Charles S. Maier, Erez Manela, and Daniel J. Sargent, 25–48. Cambridge, MA: Harvard University Press, 2010.

Malia, Martin. *The Soviet Tragedy: A History of Socialism in Russia, 1917–1991*. New York: Free Press, 1994.

Marer, Paul. "The Political Economy of Soviet Relations with Eastern Europe." In *Soviet Policy in Eastern Europe*, edited by Sarah Meiklejohn Terry, 155–88. New Haven, CT: Yale University Press, 1984.

Mark, James, Bogdan C. Iacob, Tobias Rupprecht, and Ljubica Spaskovska. *1989: A Global History of Eastern Europe*. New York: Cambridge University Press, 2019.

Marrese, Michael, and Jan Vanous, *Soviet Subsidization of Trade with Eastern Europe: A Soviet Perspective*. Berkeley: Institute of International Studies, University of California, 1983.

Mastanduno, Michael. "System Maker and Privilege Taker: The United States and the International Political Economy." *World Politics* 61, no. 1 (2009): 121–54.

Matusow, Allen J. *Nixon's Economy: Booms, Busts, Dollars, and Votes*. Lawrence: University of Kansas Press, 1998.

Mazower, Mark. *Dark Continent: Europe's Twentieth Century*. New York: Vintage, 1998.

——. *Governing the World: The History of an Idea*. New York: Penguin, 2012.

McAdams, A. James. *Germany Divided: From the Wall to Reunification*. Princeton, NJ: Princeton University Press, 1993.

McFarland, Victor. *Oil Powers: A History of the U.S.-Saudi Alliance*. New York: Columbia University Press, 2020.

Metcalf, Lee Kendall. *The Council of Mutual Economic Assistance: The Failure of Reform*. New York: Columbia University Press, 1997.

Miles, Simon. *Engaging the Evil Empire: Washington, Moscow, and the Beginning of the End of the Cold War*. Ithaca, NY: Cornell University Press, 2020.

Miller, Christopher. "The Bureaucratic Bourgeoisie: How the Soviet Union Lost Faith in State-Led Economic Development." *History of Political Economy* 51 (2019): 231–52.

——. *Chip War: The Fight for the World's Most Critical Technology*. New York: Scribner, 2022.

——. *The Struggle to Save the Soviet Economy: Mikhail Gorbachev and the Collapse of the USSR*. Chapel Hill: University of North Carolina Press, 2016.

Morgan, Michael Cotey. *The Final Act: The Helsinki Accords and the Transformation of the Cold War*. Princeton, NJ: Princeton University Press, 2017.

Mourlon-Druol, Emmanuel. *A Europe Made of Money: The Emergence of the European Monetary System*. Ithaca, NY: Cornell University Press, 2012.

Mourlon-Druol, Emmanuel, and Federico Romero, eds. *International Summitry and Global Governance: The Rise of the G7 and the European Council, 1974–1991*. London: Routledge, 2014.

Naimark, Norman M. *The Russians in Germany: A History of the Soviet Zone of Occupation, 1945–1949*. Cambridge, MA: Belknap Press of Harvard University Press, 1995.

——. *Stalin and the Fate of Europe: The Postwar Struggle for Sovereignty*. Cambridge, MA: Belknap Press of Harvard University Press, 2019.

Nehring, Christopher. "Bulgaria as the Sixteenth Soviet Republic? Todor Zhivkov's Proposals to Join the USSR." *Journal of Cold War Studies* 24, no. 2 (2022): 29–45.

Nichter, Luke A. *Richard Nixon and Europe: The Reshaping of the Postwar Atlantic World*. New York: Cambridge University Press, 2015.

Norrlöf, Carla. *America's Global Advantage: U.S. Hegemony and International Cooperation*. New York: Cambridge University Press, 2010.

O'Bryan, Scott. *The Growth Idea: Purpose and Prosperity in Postwar Japan*. Honolulu: University of Hawai'i Press, 2009.

O'Mara, Margaret. *The Code: Silicon Valley and the Remaking of America*. New York: Penguin Press, 2019.

Ouimet, Matthew J. *The Rise and Fall of the Brezhnev Doctrine in Soviet Foreign Policy*. Chapel Hill: University of North Carolina Press, 2003.

Painter, David S. "From Linkage to Economic Warfare: Energy, Soviet-American Relations, and the End of the Cold War." In *Cold War Energy: A Transnational History of Soviet Oil and Gas*, edited by Jeronim Perović, 283–318. Cham: Springer International Publishing, 2017.

——. "The Marshall Plan and Oil." *Cold War History* 9, no. 2 (2009): 159–75.

——. "Oil and Geopolitics: The Oil Crises of the 1970s and the Cold War." *Historical Social Research* 39, no. 4 (2014): 186–208.

Patterson, James T. *Restless Giant: The United States from Watergate to Bush v. Gore*. New York: Oxford University Press, 2005.

Perović, Jeronim, ed. *Cold War Energy: A Transnational History of Soviet Oil and Gas*. Cham: Springer International Publishing, 2017.

——. *Rohstoffmacht Russland: Eine Globale Energiegeschichte*. Vienna: Böhlau Verlag, 2022.

Peterson, Peter G. *The United States in the Changing World Economy*. 2 vols. Washington, DC: U.S. Government Printing Office, 1971.

Plokhy, Serhii. *Chernobyl: The History of a Nuclear Catastrophe*. New York: Basic Books, 2018.

——. *The Last Empire: The Final Days of the Soviet Union*. New York: Basic Books, 2014.

Porter, Suzanne F. *East-West Trade Financing: An Introductory Guide*. Washington, DC: U.S. Department of Commerce, 1976.

Prados, John. *How the Cold War Ended: Debating and Doing History*. Washington, DC: Potomac Books, 2011.

Pula, Besnik. *Globalization under and after Socialism: The Evolution of Transnational Capital in Central and Eastern Europe*. Stanford, CA: Stanford University Press, 2018.

Raleigh, Donald J. *Soviet Baby Boomers: An Oral History of Russia's Cold War Generation*. New York: Oxford University Press, 2012.

Reisinger, William M. *Energy and the Soviet Bloc: Alliance Politics after Stalin*. Ithaca, NY: Cornell University Press, 1992.

Reynolds, David. *From Munich to Pearl Harbor: Roosevelt's America and the Origins of the Second World War*. Chicago: Ivan R. Dee, 2001.

Romano, Angela, and Federico Romero, eds. *European Socialist Regimes' Fateful Engagement with the West: National Strategies in the Long 1970s*. Abingdon, UK: Routledge, 2021.

Sanchez-Sibony, Oscar. *Red Globalization: The Political Economy of the Soviet Cold War from Stalin to Khrushchev*. New York: Cambridge University Press, 2014.

Sargent, Daniel J. "Pax Americana: Sketches for an Undiplomatic History." *Diplomatic History* 42, no. 3 (2018): 357–76.

——. *A Superpower Transformed: The Remaking of American Foreign Relations in the 1970s*. New York: Oxford University Press, 2015.

Sarotte, Mary E. *1989: The Struggle to Create Post–Cold War Europe*. Princeton, NJ: Princeton University Press, 2009.

——. *The Collapse: The Accidental Opening of the Berlin Wall*. New York: Basic Books, 2014.

——. *Dealing with the Devil: East Germany, Détente, and Ostpolitik, 1969–1973*. Chapel Hill: North Carolina Press, 2001.

Savranskaya, Svetlana. "The Logic of 1989." In *Masterpieces of History: The Peaceful End of the Cold War in Europe, 1989*, edited by Svetlana Savranskaya, Thomas Blanton, and Vladislav Zubok, 1–47. Budapest: Central European University Press, 2010.

Savranskaya, Svetlana, Thomas Blanton, and Vladislav Zubok, eds. *Masterpieces of History: The Peaceful End of the Cold War in Europe, 1989*. Budapest: Central European University Press, 2010.

Sayle, Timothy Andrews. *Enduring Alliance: A History of NATO and the Postwar Global Order*. Ithaca, NY: Cornell University Press, 2019.

Schattenberg, Susanne. *Brezhnev: The Making of a Statesman*. Translated by John Heath. London: I. B. Tauris, 2022.

Schenk, Catherine R. "The Oil Market and Global Finance in the 1980s." In *Counter-Shock: The Oil Counter-Revolution of the 1980s*, edited by Duccio Basosi, Giuliano Garavini, and Massimiliano Trentin, 55–75. London: I. B. Tauris, 2018.

Schlesinger, Arthur M., Jr. *The Vital Center: The Politics of Freedom*. Boston: Houghton Mifflin, 1949.

Schmelzer, Matthias. *The Hegemony of Growth: The OECD and the Making of the Economic Growth Paradigm*. New York: Cambridge University Press, 2016.

Schweitzer, Peter. *Victory: The Reagan Administration's Secretary Strategy that Hastened the Collapse of the Soviet Union*. New York: Atlantic Monthly Press, 1996.

Service, Robert. *The End of the Cold War, 1985–1991*. New York: PublicAffairs, 2015.

Silber, William L. *Volcker: The Triumph of Persistence*. New York: Bloomsbury, 2012.

Skorokhodova, Olga. "The Double Shock: The Soviet Energy Crisis and the Oil Price Collapse of 1986." In *Counter-Shock: The Oil Counter-Revolution of the 1980s*, edited by Duccio Basosi, Giuliano Garavini, and Massimiliano Trentin, 180–98. London: I. B. Tauris, 2018.

Slobodian, Quinn. *Globalists: The End of Empire and Birth of Neoliberalism*. Cambridge, MA: Harvard University Press, 2018.

Smith, Alan. *Russia and the World Economy: Problems of Integration*. London: Routledge, 1993.

Snyder, Sarah B. *Human Rights Activism and the End of the Cold War: A Transnational History of the Helsinki Network*. Cambridge: Cambridge University Press, 2011.

Solomon, Robert. *The International Monetary System, 1945–1981*. New York: Harper & Row, 1982.

Spiro, David E. *The Hidden Hand of American Hegemony: Petrodollar Recycling and International Markets*. Ithaca, NY: Cornell University Press, 1999.

Spohr, Kristina. *The Global Chancellor: Helmut Schmidt and the Reshaping of the International Order*. New York: Oxford University Press, 2016.

———. *Post Wall, Post Square: How Bush, Gorbachev, Kohl, and Deng Shaped the World after 1989*. New Haven, CT: Yale University Press, 2019.

Stein, Judith. *Pivotal Decade: How the United States Traded Factories for Finance in the Seventies*. New Haven, CT: Yale University Press, 2010.

Steiner, André. "'Common Sense Is Necessary': East German Reactions to the Oil Crises of the 1970s." *Historical Social Research* 39, no. 4 (2014): 231–50.

———. "The Decline of Soviet-Type Economies." In *Endgames? Late Communism in Global Perspective, 1968 to the Present*, ed. Juliane Fürst, Silvio Pons, and Mark

Selden, 203–23. Vol. 3 of *The Cambridge History of Communism*. New York: Cambridge University Press, 2017.

———. *The Plans that Failed: An Economic History of the GDR*. Translated by Ewald Osers. New York: Berghahn Books, 2010.

Stent, Angela. *Putin's World: Russia against the West and with the Rest*. New York: Twelve, 2019.

Stewart, Michael. "Britain, Europe and the Alliance." *Foreign Affairs* 48, no. 4 (1970): 648–59.

Stone, David R. "CMEA's International Investment Bank and the Crisis of Developed Socialism." *Journal of Cold War Studies* 10, no. 3 (Summer 2008): 48–77.

Stone, Randall W. *Satellites and Commissars: Strategy and Conflict in the Politics of Soviet-Bloc Trade*. Princeton, NJ: Princeton University Press, 1998.

Strange, Elizabeth. *The Third Revolution: Xi Jinping and the New Chinese State*. New York: Oxford University Press, 2018.

Strange, Susan. *Casino Capitalism*. New York: Blackwell, 1986.

Sugihara, Kaoru. "East Asia, Middle East and the World Economy: Further Notes on the Oil Triangle." Afrasian Centre for Peace and Development Studies, Working Paper Series No. 9, 2006.

Suri, Jeremi. *Power and Protest: Global Revolution and the Rise of Détente*. Cambridge, MA: Harvard University Press, 2003.

Taubman, William. *Gorbachev: His Life and Times*. New York: W. W. Norton, 2017.

Taubman, William, and Svetlana Savranskaya. "If a Wall Fell in Berlin and Moscow Hardly Noticed, Would It Still Make a Noise?" In *The Fall of the Berlin Wall: The Revolutionary Legacy of 1989*, edited by Jeffrey A. Engel, 69–95. New York: Oxford University Press, 2009.

Terry, Sarah Meiklejohn, ed. *Soviet Policy in Eastern Europe*. New Haven, CT: Yale University Press, 1984.

Thomas, Daniel C. *The Helsinki Effect: International Norms, Human Rights, and the Demise of Communism*. Princeton, NJ: Princeton University Press, 2001.

Tooze, Adam. *Crashed: How a Decade of Financial Crises Changed the World*. New York: Viking, 2018.

Türk, Henning. "Kooperation in der Krise? Die Ölkrise von 1973/74 und die multilaterale Zusammenarbeit der westlichen Industrieländer in der Energiepolitik." *Journal of European Integration History* 22, no. 1 (2016): 47–65.

Woodward, C. Vann. "The Age of Reinterpretation." *American Historical Review* 66, no. 1 (1960): 1–19.

Vogel, Ezra. *Deng Xiaoping and the Transformation of China*. Cambridge, MA: Belknap Press of Harvard University Press, 2011.

von Dannenberg, Julia. *The Foundations of Ostpolitik: The Making of the Moscow Treaty between West Germany and the USSR*. New York: Oxford University Press, 2009.

Vonyó, Tamás. "War and Socialism: Why Eastern Europe Fell Behind between 1950 and 1989." *Economic History Review* 70, no. 1 (2017): 248–74.

Westad, Odd Arne. *The Cold War: A World History*. New York: Basic Books, 2017.

———. *The Global Cold War: Third World Interventions and the Making of Our Times*. New York: Cambridge University Press, 2007.

———. *Restless Empire: China and the World since 1750*. New York: Basic Books, 2012.

Wight, David M. *Oil Money: Middle East Petrodollars and the Transformation of US Empire, 1967–1988*. Ithaca, NY: Cornell University Press, 2021.

Wilentz, Sean. *The Age of Reagan: A History 1974–2008*. New York: HarperCollins, 2008.

Williams, William A. *The Tragedy of American Diplomacy*. Cleveland: World Publishing, 1959.

Wilson, James Graham. *The Triumph of Improvisation: Gorbachev's Adaptability, Reagan's Engagement, and the End of the Cold War*. Ithaca, NY: Cornell University Press, 2014.

Woods, Ngaire. *The Globalizers: The IMF, the World Bank, and Their Borrowers*. Ithaca, NY: Cornell University Press, 2006.

Yaqub, Salim. *Imperfect Strangers: Americans, Arabs, and U.S.–Middle East Relations in the 1970s*. Ithaca, NY: Cornell University Press, 2016.

Yergin, Daniel. *The Prize: The Epic Quest for Oil, Money, and Power*. 3rd ed. New York: Free Press, 2009.

Zanchetta, Barbara. *The Transformation of American International Power in the 1970s*. New York: Cambridge University Press, 2013.

Zelikow, Philip, and Condoleezza Rice. *To Build a Better World: Choices to End the Cold War and Create a Global Commonwealth*. New York: Twelve, 2019.

Znepolski, Ivaylo, Mihail Gruev, Momtchil Metodiev, Martin Ivanov, Daniel Vatchkov, Ivan Elenkov, and Plamen Doynov. *Bulgaria under Communism*. London: Routledge, 2019.

Zubok, Vladislav. *Collapse: The Fall of the Soviet Union*. New Haven, CT: Yale University Press, 2021.

——. *A Failed Empire: The Soviet Union in the Cold War from Stalin to Gorbachev*. Chapel Hill: University of North Carolina Press, 2009.

——. "Soviet Foreign Policy from Détente to Gorbachev, 1975–1985." In *Endings*, ed. Melvyn P. Leffler and Odd Arne Westad, 89–111. Vol. 3 of *The Cambridge History of the Cold War*. New York: Cambridge University Press, 2010.

Published Documents and Sources

Akten zur Auswärtigen Politik der Bundesrepublik Deutschland. Munich: Oldenbourg Wissenschaftsverlag, various years.

Bank for International Settlements. *Annual Report*. Basel, various years.

Békés, Csaba, Malcolm Byrne, and János M. Rainer, eds. *The 1956 Hungarian Revolution: A History in Documents*. Budapest: Central European University Press, 2002.

Brinkley, Douglas, ed. *The Reagan Diaries*. New York: HarperCollins, 2007.

Brinkley, Douglas, and Luke A. Nichter, eds. *The Nixon Tapes: 1971–1972*. Boston: Houghton Mifflin Harcourt, 2014.

——. *The Nixon Tapes, 1973*. Boston: Houghton Mifflin Harcourt, 2015.

Bundesbank. *Monthly Report of the Deutsche Bundesbank*. Frankfurt, multiple volumes.

Carter, Jimmy. *White House Diary*. New York: Farrar, Straus and Giroux, 2010.

DeGolyer and MacNaughton. *Twentieth Century Petroleum Statistics: Historical Data (1918–1959)*. Dallas, TX.

——. *Twenty-First Century Petroleum Statistics*. Dallas, TX, 2020.

Hertle, Hans-Hermann, ed. *Der Fall der Mauer: Die unbeabsichtigte Selbstauflösung des SED-Staates*. Opladen: Westdeutscher Verlag, 1996.

International Monetary Fund (IMF). *Annual Report*. Washington, DC, various years.
——. *International Financial Statistics Yearbook*. Washington, DC, various years.
Maddison, Angus. *The World Economy*. Vol. 1, *A Millennial Perspective*. Paris: OECD, 2006.
Mikhail Gorbachev i germanskii vopros: Sbornik dokumentov 1986–1991. Moscow: Ves'
    Mir, 2006.
Otvechaia na vyzov vremeni: Vneshniaia politika perestroiki: Dokumental'nye svidetel'stva.
    Moscow: Ves' Mir, 2010.
Paczkowski, Andrzej, and Malcom Byrne, eds. *From Solidarity to Martial Law: The
    Polish Crisis of 1980–1981*. Budapest: Central European University Press, 2007.
PlanEcon. *Soviet and East European Energy Databank*. Washington, DC: PlanEcon, 1986.
Przybylski, Peter, ed. *Tatort Politbüro: Die Akte Honecker*. Berlin: Rowohlt, 1991.
Savranskaya, Svetlana, Thomas Blanton, and Vladislav Zubok, eds. *Masterpieces of
    History: The Peaceful End of the Cold War in Europe, 1989*. Budapest: Central
    European University Press, 2010.
U.S. Department of Defense. *Annual Report*. Washington, DC, various years.
U.S. Department of State. *Foreign Relations of the United States*, various volumes.
    Washington, DC: Government Printing Office, various years.
*V Politbiuro TsK KPSS . . . : Po zapisiam Anatoliia Cherniaeva, Vadima Medvedeva,
    Georgiia Shakhnazarova 1985–1991*. Moscow: Al'pina biznes buks, 2006.
White House. *Economic Report of the President*. Washington, DC, various years.

Online Statistics

BP Statistical Review of World Energy 2022. https://www.bp.com/en/global
    /corporate/energy-economics/statistical-review-of-world-energy.html
Carter, Susan B., Scott Sigmund Gartner, Michael R. Haines, Alan L. Olmstead,
    Richard Sutch, and Gavin Wright, eds. *Historical Statistics of the United States:
    Millennial Edition Online*. New York: Cambridge University Press, 2006.
    https://hsus.cambridge.org/HSUSWeb/HSUSEntryServlet
Federal Reserve Economic Data (FRED). Federal Reserve of St. Louis. https://fred
    .stlouisfed.org
International Monetary Fund, *International Financial Statistics*. https://data.imf.org/
    ?sk=4C514D48-B6BA-49ED-8AB9-52B0C1A0179B
Organisation for Economic Co-operation and Development (OECD). OECDstat.
    https://stats.oecd.org
United Nations Conference on Trade and Development (UNCTAD). UNCTADstat.
    https://unctadstat.unctad.org
U.S. Bureau of the Census. *Foreign Trade Statistics*. https://www.census.gov/foreign
    -trade/data/index.html
U.S. Bureau of Economic Analysis. International Data. https://apps.bea.gov/iTable
    /?ReqID=62&step=1
U.S. Office of Management and Budget (OMB). Historical Tables. https://www
    .whitehouse.gov/omb/budget/historical-tables/
U.S. Treasury. Treasury International Capital System. https://home.treasury.gov
    /data/treasury-international-capital-tic-system
World Bank. World Development Indicators. https://data.worldbank.org

Digital Collections

The American Presidency Project. https://www.presidency.ucsb.edu
CIA Electronic Reading Room. https://www.cia.gov/readingroom/
Die Kabinettsprotokolle der Bundesregierung. www.bundesarchiv.de/cocoon/barch
    /0000/index.html
Margaret Thatcher Foundation Digital Archive. https://www.margaretthatcher.org
    /archive
National Security Archive Virtual Reading Room. https://nsarchive.gwu.edu/virtual
    -reading-room
Presidential Oral Histories. Miller Center of Public Affairs, University of Virginia.
    https://millercenter.org/the-presidency/presidential-oral-histories
Wilson Center Digital Archive. https://digitalarchive.wilsoncenter.org

Congressional Publications

*Action Now to Strengthen the U.S. Dollar: Report of the Subcommittee on International
    Exchange and Payments of the Joint Economic Committee Congress of the United
    States.* Washington, DC: U.S. Government Printing Office, 1971.
Committee on Banking, Housing, and Urban Affairs, U.S. Senate, 96th Congress,
    1st session, "Nomination of Paul A. Volcker," July 30, 1979. Washington, DC:
    U.S. Government Printing Office, 1979.

Periodicals

Atlanta Constitution
Atlantic Monthly
Baltimore Sun
Boston Globe
Cold War International History Bulletin
Economist
Euromoney
Forbes
Foreign Affairs
Izvestiia
Los Angeles Times
New York Times
Petroleum Press Service
PlanEcon Report
Pravda (Moscow)
Time
The Times
Wall Street Journal
Washington Post

INDEX

Printed in the USA
CPSIA information can be obtained
at www.ICGtesting.com
CBHW020810081024
15381CB00012B/25/J

9 781501 774119